RESEARCH IN MARITIME HISTORY
NO. 56

Evolution and Significance of the Powered Bulk Carrier

The Black Freighters

ROY FENTON

SERIES EDITOR

Professor Hugh MURPHY (University of Glasgow)

EDITORIAL BOARD

Professor Andrew D. LAMBERT (King's College, London)
Professor Jari OJALA (University of Jyväskylä, Finland)
Professor Raymond STOKES (Centre for Business History, University of Glasgow)
Professor Stig TENOLD (Norwegian School of Economics, Bergen)

INTERNATIONAL MARITIME HISTORY ASSOCIATION

President: Ingo HEIDBRINK (Old Dominion University, USA)
Vice President: Hanna HAGMARK (Åland Maritime Museum Trust,
Mariehamn, Finland)
Vice President: Apostolos DELIS (Institute for Mediterranean Studies, Crete, Greece)
Treasurer: Martin WILCOX (Blaydes Maritime Centre of the University of Hull, UK)
Secretary: Constantin ARDELEANUA (University of Galati / Institute for South-East
European History, Bucharest, Romania)

MAILING ADDRESS

Liverpool University Press
4 Cambridge Street
Liverpool L69 7ZU
United Kingdom

Recently Published Books in the Series

50: Torsten Feys, *The Battle for the Migrants: The Introduction of Steamshipping
on the North Atlantic and Its Impact on the European Exodus*
51: Anthony Slaven and Hugh Murphy (eds), *Crossing the Bar: An Oral History
of the British Shipbuilding, Ship Repairing and Marine Engine-Building Industries
in the Age of Decline, 1956–1990*
52: Olaf U. Janzen, *War and Trade in Eighteenth-Century Newfoundland*
53: Christopher W. Miller, *Planning and Profits: British Naval Armaments Manufacture
and the Military-Industrial Complex, 1918–1941*
54: Robb Robinson, *Fishermen, the Fishing Industry and the Great War at Sea:
A Forgotten History?*
55: David Morgan-Owen and Louis Halewood, *Economic Warfare and the Sea:
Grand Strategies for Maritime Powers, 1650–1945*

RESEARCH IN MARITIME HISTORY
NO. 56

Evolution and Significance of the Powered Bulk Carrier

The Black Freighters

ROY FENTON

First published 2023 by
Liverpool University Press
4 Cambridge Street
Liverpool
L69 7ZU

This paperback edition published 2025

Copyright ©2025 Roy Fenton

Roy Fenton has asserted the right to be identified as the author of this work in accordance with the Copyright, Designs and Patents Act 1988.

All rights reserved. No part of this book may be reproduced, stored in a retrieval system, or transmitted, in any form or by any means, electronic, mechanical, photocopying, recording, or otherwise, without the prior written permission of the publisher.

British Library Cataloguing-in-Publication data
A British Library CIP record is available

ISBN 978-1-80207-859-6 (hardback)
ISBN 978-1-83624-584-1 (paperback)

Typeset by Carnegie Book Production, Lancaster

Contents

List of Illustrations — vii

List of Tables — xi

Acknowledgements — xiii

Preface — xv

1 Introduction: What is bulk shipping? — 1

2 First steps: The screw collier — 11

3 Refining the steam bulk carrier — 37

4 Maximisation: Screw collier into ocean-going tramp — 63

5 Miniaturisation: The birth of the steam coaster — 87

6 Steam bulk carrying dominant — 111

7 Steam tramp to motor tramp — 135

8 Steam coaster to motor coaster — 161

9 Tramp ship into bulk carrier — 199

10 The shipping industries and powered bulk carrying — 217

11 The consequences of the bulk carrier for industry and society — 227

12 Black freighters: Lines of development — 235

Select Bibliography — 239

General Index — 249

Ship Index — 260

Illustrations

1 The steam collier *James Joicey* of 1863 was built by Palmer Brothers of Jarrow for a consortium of coal industry investors, including her namesake colliery owner and coal merchant William Cory. Fitting a triple-expansion engine in 1885 prolonged her life and after 48 years in the coal trade she was broken up in 1911. *Author's collection* 27

2 Built at Belfast in 1879, the typical small steam coaster *Galgorm Castle* would have been considerably rebuilt during her 47 years of life in the coastal trade, during which she had been salved and rebuilt after sinking in the Menai Straits in 1891. Seen towards the end of her life when owned in Birkenhead, the closed wheelhouse belies her age. *Ships in Focus* 45

3 At 226 feet, *Medway* of 1879 was at the larger end of the size range for screw colliers. She was built at Sunderland for Lambert Brothers, who moved into deep sea tramps after selling their colliers to Cory in 1896. She retained her two-cylinder compound engine throughout her life, which ended in a Boulogne shipbreaking yard in 1910. *Author's collection* 72

4 *Sybil* shows an early stage in the evolution of the steam tramp, retaining the raised quarterdeck of the screw collier, but enlarged to 266 feet, comparatively large for the year 1879. Compare her profile with the smaller *Medway*, completed in the same year. Built with a two-cylinder compound engine, *Sybil*'s machinery was replaced with a triple-expansion engine in 1893, extending her life considerably. Whilst under the Swedish flag as *Goosebridge*, she was captured and sunk by a U-boat on New Year's Day 1917. *Author's collection* 80

5 *Edith* represents the smallest steam coasters: she was just 100 feet in length. Built by prolific west coast Scottish yard, Scott and Sons of Bowling for Merseyside owners in 1900, she survived to be fitted with an oil engine by Danish owners in 1947 and was not deleted from *Lloyd's Register* until the 1970s. *Ships in Focus* 92

6 The 142-foot *Ashfield* of 1914 is an example of the most numerous design of long raised quarterdeck steam coasters. She was built by the Lytham Shipbuilding and Engineering Co. Ltd for the Zillah Shipping and Carrying Co. Ltd of Liverpool, remaining with this owner until broken up in 1954. *Ships in Focus* — 94

7 The large, engines-aft collier *J.R. Hinde* of 1864 sails from Hull well loaded. The Cory family were the biggest shareholders in the ship when new, and she was in their ownership when broken up at Boulogne in 1910. *Ships in Focus* — 96

8 Large colliers like *Hurstwood* of 1906 tended to have their engines amidships with a long raised quarterdeck stretching to the stern. Built by S.P. Austin and Son Ltd, Sunderland for William Cory, she was torpedoed by a German submarine north-east of Whitby in February 1917. *World Ship Society Ltd* — 100

9 The steam tramp *Runswick* was built at Sunderland for Headlam and Sons of Whitby in 1930, by when the well-deck type was all but obsolete. Her flag of convenience buyers in 1955 did not agree, and she steamed on until 1971. *Ships in Focus* — 113

10 The photograph of the Greek *Adelfotis* shows the unusual shape of a turret steamer's hull. She was built in 1908 as *Penrose* for R.B. Chellew of Truro, and was sold in 1927, the photograph being taken soon after her sale. Note the name of her port of registry, Andros, being painted on her stern. *Author's collection* — 119

11 The Swedish-flag *Yngaren* of 1921 was the outcome of development work by Sunderland shipbuilder William Doxford and Sons Ltd to produce a reliable oil engine for ocean-going ships. *Yngaren* was torpedoed and sunk in an Atlantic convoy on 12 January 1942. *Ships in Focus* — 139

12 Owen and Watkin Williams' ill-judged venture into new technology began with *Margretian* in 1923, an early British motor tramp. After being twice re-engined, she lasted until the 1960s, long outlasting her unfortunate owners. *Author's collection* — 143

13 The Doxford 'Economy' type motor tramp *Fernmoor* was built in 1934 for W. Runciman and Co. Ltd of Newcastle She was wrecked in the Philippines in February 1954. *Ships in Focus* — 151

14 *Eucadia* was one of the last generation of British motor tramps, built for Walter Runciman and Company as *Linkmoor* in 1961, but seen here in November 1974 masquerading as a cargo liner for the associated Anchor Line. She came from the yard of Hawthorn,

Leslie (Ship Builders) Ltd with a licence-built Doxford engine. Note the antiquated split superstructure. Sold to Sri Lankan owners in 1981, she was broken up in 1983. *Author*   152

15 Although Austin and Pickersgill's SD14s were designed to replace ageing tramps, a number like the *Arrino* were built for liner companies, in her case the Australind Steam Shipping Co. Ltd. However, she was soon sold and passed through four other ownerships before being broken up at Alang, India in 1998. *Author's collection*   155

16 *Innisshannon* was one of two motor vessels of the Coasting Motor Shipping Co. Ltd with a wheelhouse right forward but was rebuilt to move it aft. She was one of the longer-lived of the company's ships, wrecked in the Red Sea in 1953. *Author's collection*   166

17 Everard's *Ability* of 1928 was a development of earlier motor ships, one of the first of a recognisably British design with her raised forecastle and poop. Just 115 feet in length when built at Great Yarmouth, she was lengthened to 137 feet in 1939. She was lost when mined in the North Sea during November 1940. *Ships in Focus*   172

18 The *Antilope* of 1939 exemplifies the single-masted Dutch coaster, with derricks offset to allow the mast to be folded. Note that she has accommodation for a captain/owner's family ahead of the wheelhouse, and that she has a modern, cruiser stern. She was heavily damaged during a collision with another Dutch coaster in August 1971 and was subsequently sold for scrap. *World Ship Society Ltd*   183

19 Displaying the angular lines which facilitated prefabrication, the Empire F type yet gave good service to various owners post-war. *Lynn Trader* was built in 1944 as *Empire Fairplay* and eventually passed to Egyptian owners. Her fate is unknown. *Ships in Focus*   188

20 Typical of post-war, raised quarterdeck coasters with bridge aft, the modest sized Irish-owned *River Avoca* was built at Goole in 1948 as *Stevonia*. She had lost her derricks by the time she was photographed in September 1975. She was broken up 1980. *Author*   189

21 *Century* was a larger, oil-engined version of the *Ashfield*, built at Goole in 1956, and somewhat longer at 204 feet. Note her wooden wheelhouse. Her made-up name was bestowed because she was wrongly believed to be the hundredth ship owned by F.T. Everard and Sons Ltd. Photographed in September 1975, she was sold later that year. *Author*   197

22 *Holstentor* is a typical, gearless and sheerless motor coaster,
    built in Spain, owned in Germany, but registered under a flag of
    convenience in Antigua and Barbuda. Her single hatch with its
    mechanical cover extends almost the full width of her deck. With a
    length of 285 feet, and a deadweight of 3,432, she is of a similar size
    to the average steam tramp of 1890. Photographed in April 2013, she
    is now under the Latvian ownership as *Salar. Author*   198

23 Although not built specifically to suit the needs of the British Iron
    and Steel Corporation, *Weser Ore* was nevertheless on charter to
    them when seen leaving Birkenhead Docks in October 1975. She
    had been alongside the gantries in Bidston Dock so that her cargo
    could be unloaded and railed to the steel works at Queensferry,
    North Wales. Built in 1959 at Hamburg and owned in Liberia, she
    was converted to an offshore mining vessel in 1977, as which she
    survived until 1993. *Author*   204

24 An early British steam bulk carrier, France, Fenwick's *Rookwood* of
    1952 owes its design to builders J. Readhead and Sons Ltd of South
    Shields, who built similar ships for other British owners. She was
    sold to Bulgaria in 1961 and survived until 1974. *Author's collection*   205

25 A modern black freighter: the bulk carrier *CMB Virginie* is
    anchored off Gibraltar waiting for bunkers in October 2011. She is
    described as 'large, handy size'. Built at Zhenjiang, China in 2011
    for the Belgian company Bocimar, she is still in existence in 2022
    as *Racoon*, Greek-owned and Panama-flagged. *Author*   211

26 *Stolt Vista* was built in 1955 at Malmo for Trafik A/B Grängesberg-
    Oxelösund as the combination ore-oil carrier *Vistasvagge*. When
    this photograph was taken in May 1974 she was probably carrying
    chemicals. She was broken up in 1979. *Author*   214

Tables

1.1 Numbers of British steam ships operated by liner and tramp
companies in 1892   5

1.2 Numbers of ocean-going vessels in British ownership by presumed
employment in 1926 and 1955   6

2.1 Chronological list of known screw colliers built to 1859   17

2.2 Tonnages of coal carried to London by sea and rail, 1844–1868   20

3.1 Effect of increasing boiler pressure in reducing heat losses   41

3.2 Boiler pressures of typical British east coast colliers in the late 1870s   44

3.3 Boiler pressures of typical steam coasters in the late 1870s   44

4.1 Names, dates and fates of vessels owned by the General Iron Screw
Collier Co. Ltd   67

4.2. Names, dates and fates of vessels owned by the London Steam
Navigation Co. Ltd and its successors   68

4.3. Steam tramp owners originally involved in collier trades   70

4.4 Characteristics of colliers and tramps built around 1860   74

4.5 Characteristics of colliers built 1860–1890   76

4.6 Characteristics of tramps built in the 1860s and in years 1870, 1880
and 1890   77

4.7 Major builders of screw colliers, 1860s–1890   81

4.8 Major builders of steam tramps, 1860s–1890   82

5.1 West coast bulk-carrying steamers, 1849–1869   89

5.2 Numbers of bulk carriers in service on the east and west coasts of
the United Kingdom, 1860–1910   89

5.3 Net tonnages of steam coasters and screw colliers in service, 1860–1910 90

5.4   Characteristics of steam coasters below 130 feet in length — 91

5.5   Characteristics of steam coasters 130 to 160 feet in length — 93

5.6   Characteristics of steam coasters over 160 feet in length — 95

5.7   Characteristics of screw colliers with engines aft — 97

5.8   Characteristics of screw colliers with engines amidships — 99

5.9   Known builders of bulk-carrying steamers up to 1870 — 102

5.10 Steam coasters built 1870–1880 by region of build — 107

6.1   Tonnage of British steam and sailing ships, 1870–1890 — 111

6.2   Characteristics of steam tramps built from 1890 to 1956 — 114

6.3   Single-deck cargo ships built during the First World War — 123

6.4   'League table' of world tramp steamer building in 1914 — 129

6.5   'League table' of world tramp steamer building in 1939 — 130

6.6   Comparison of British and overseas-built steam tramps completed in 1939 — 132

7.1   Candidate ocean-going tramp ships, 1910–1924 — 140

7.2   Numbers of ocean-going motor ships built, 1910–1924 — 144

7.3   Comparison of steam and motor tramps built in 1930 — 145

7.4   Characteristics of motor tramps built 1924–1970 — 146

8.1   Types ordered by the Coasting Motor Shipping Co. Ltd — 165

8.2   Chronological list of early British motor coasters, 1911–1929 — 167

8.3   Chronological list of early British motor coasters, 1930–1939 — 175

8.4   Single-deck coasters completed on Government account, 1940–1945 — 186

9.1   Comparison of motor tramps and bulk carriers built in 1960 — 207

9.2   Characteristics of bulk carriers built 1960–2020 — 208

Acknowledgements

Although not wishing to belittle the contribution of those in academia, my first acknowledgement is to my wife Heather, who has provided support during my research and writing, and has not demurred at (indeed, often made the sandwiches for) my repeated absences in libraries and on research expeditions.

The late Professor John Armstrong of Thames Valley University was a natural choice as supervisor of my PhD thesis, with his deep interest in coastal shipping. Not only wise about the literature, he also gave invaluable guidance in the ways of those who award degrees. His interest, support and friendship plus gentle nudging about progress contributed to completing my thesis. My external supervisor, Professor Sarah Palmer of Greenwich Maritime Institute, complemented John's close-in support with very useful offshore coverage.

For the present work, I am indebted to Professor Hugh Murphy, whose enthusiasm for *Research in Maritime History* steered me towards contributing to this series, and who gave willing help at each stage during the writing of this book. I would also like to thank for their companionship and stimulus my fellow enthusiasts for tramp ships and coasters, who are mostly members of the World Ship Society.

The librarians and archivist to whom I owe thanks are too numerous to list, but I would especially thank Barbara Jones of Lloyd's Register Foundation for her interest, help and friendship over many years in which I haunted the hallowed halls of Fenchurch Street.

For their help, professionalism and patience, I am also grateful to those responsible for producing this book, including but not limited to Series Editor Professor Hugh Murphy, Alison Welsby of Liverpool University Press and Sarah Davidson and colleagues of Carnegie Book Production.

Preface

Compared with the image that 'ocean liner' evokes, the bland terms 'tramp' and 'bulk carrier' are hardly romantic, and the former has indeed been used pejoratively. Yet these ships – workhorses of the seas – have been an essential part of the shipping industry for 175 years and continue to be vital to the world's economy. As instruments of globalisation, they are quite as important as the container ship, which can boast barely a half-century of existence.

Although 'freighter' is rather a vague term in maritime history, all the ships in this book definitely carried freight. Very many of them – especially the steamers – were painted as black as the coal they often carried. Since first hearing the Berthold Brecht/Kurt Weill song 'Pirate Jenny' from 'A Threepenny Opera', the phrase 'the black freighter' has haunted me, and I have borrowed and pluralised it to give a portmanteau term for the ships I am discussing.

This volume had its germination with my doctoral thesis, which set out to answer the question, 'Why was the British east coast coal trade so quickly taken over by iron-hulled steamships in the 1850s, while the hardly less important trade on the west coast remained with wooden sailing vessels for another 25 years?'[1] Researching this meant delving into the origins of both the screw collier of the British east coast and the smaller steam coaster of the west coast, and considering the differences in the trades and ports they served. This took me into the development of steam engines and boilers, the construction of iron and later steel hulls, and the search for a way of cheaply, rapidly and conveniently ballasting a ship. Completion of this work led me to consider whether the principal characteristics of the screw collier were applied to larger steam tramps, operating well beyond the British coast. My conclusion was that there was a strong likelihood of this and, while it cannot be 'proved', the idea has not been challenged. I provide supporting evidence for the claim in this volume.

For a hundred years, the tramp ship multiplied and evolved, the only major development being the gradual replacement of steam machinery by oil engines. Although sleeker, larger and somewhat more economical, those built in the 1960s were not fundamentally different in concept from the pioneering ocean tramps of

---

[1]   R.S. Fenton, 'Transition in the UK Coastal Bulk Trades: 1840 to 1914', PhD thesis, Thames Valley University, 2005.

the 1860s. The term 'tramp' fell out of use in the 1960s, 'bulk carrier' being the preferred and less offensive term for the ships which took on their work. Again, size increased and machinery improved, but the bulk carrier was by no means revolutionary. It is argued that, like its predecessor the tramp, it embraced all the principles established by the iron screw colliers of the 1850s: large holds and hatches, economical machinery and a capacity to carry water as ballast.

Steam and the screw propeller took a long time to displace sail in bulk trades. The first successful, although still relatively crude, examples appeared only some four decades after the *Comet* had demonstrated the feasibility of offshore navigation under steam. In contrast, steam carriage of passengers, mail, perishable cargoes and other merchandise was very quickly established, especially in the short-sea and coastal trades. Steam vessels were expensive to build and operate, but passengers and shippers of perishable and high-value goods would willingly pay premiums for fast, dependable and scheduled steam services, rather than cheap but unpredictable and often uncomfortable passages in sailing ships.

Introducing steam to the bulk trades was a much more difficult undertaking. There was usually no urgency to deliver cargoes such as coal, ore, stone or timber, which were of relatively low value and did not deteriorate during a prolonged voyage, so they continued to be carried cheaply in sailing vessels. To offset the far greater capital and running costs of the steam bulk carrier, it could offer only that, largely independent of weather and tide, it would carry significantly more cargo in a given period than a sailing vessel. To fulfil its potential, multiple obstacles had to be overcome in terms of construction and operation.

I make no apology for concentrating, for at least half the period under review, on the contribution made by British naval architects, shipbuilders and owners. Between them they pioneered and developed the screw collier, the steam coaster and the ocean-going steam tramp, and until the First World War Britons owned most of these ships and built the majority. Even beyond this period, and despite a long-term decline, British shipping and shipbuilding continued to be major forces up until the end of the twentieth century. This is reflected in the literature on the subject, with a substantial number of authors using British statistics and case studies. During the bulk carrier era, roughly from 1960 onwards, ownership became more international as well as more opaque, with the flag a ship flies having less and less relationship to its ownership, its financiers and especially the national origins of its crew. Uncovering the identity of an owner of a modern ship is often an exercise in detective work.

In offering the present volume I believe it to be the first detailed account for non-specialists of the design, shipbuilding and engineering work which over 175 years went into developing powered bulk-carrying vessels. The chapters of this book dealing with steam colliers, steam coasters and steam technology draw heavily on my doctoral thesis. The methods used in that study have been extended to the development of the ocean-going tramps and bulk carriers and carried forward to the present day. These involved compilation of constructional data on individual ships from register books and other sources to provide comparisons over time. This has allowed the plotting of growth in size together with changes in ballast capacity, engine type and power, hull structure and equipment. This data grounds the discussions of the reasons for these changes, which follow the results of the surveys.

To those who look askance at lumping ocean tramps and coasters together, I would stress that the majority of the latter were designed for bulk carrying and therefore shared the characteristics of their larger brethren. The term 'coaster' is notoriously difficult to define, as ships could and did readily switch from coastal to ocean-going trades. I have regarded a coaster as a small ship trading generally between ports on the same land mass or making relatively short-sea crossings.

Discussion of the design and construction of powered dry bulk carriers is more than sufficient to fill one volume, and I have left it to other authors to consider the many facets of financing these ships and organising their employment. However, this book does consider the implications of the bulk carrier for shipping and other industries which they served, and the wider economic consequences of their large-scale adoption, including their contribution to industrialisation, urbanisation, globalisation and their environmental effects.

Some conventions have been adopted in this book. Although figures for tonnage – whether gross, net or deadweight – are regularly quoted as an indication of size, these figures are confusing, subject to change over time and do little to help indicate which ports a ship can use. Gross and net tonnages are measures of volume, not weight, with the net figure representing the space theoretically available to carry cargo. Both figures can vary according to the skills of a shipbuilder or surveyor in minimising them, as net tonnage is often the basis of fees for using harbours and canals. In contrast, deadweight does mean weight: that of the cargo, fuel and stores the ship can carry when it is floating down to its marks. However, until relatively recently, register books did not quote deadweights and they are not readily available for many of the ships surveyed in this work. Waine, in his seminal work on steam coasters, made use of length as an invariable indicator of which waterways and ports a vessel could use, and the current author has followed suit, but with the addition of figures for beam and depth.

Although individual ownership of ships is a field to which this author has devoted many words, it is covered here in general terms only, usually by nationality rather than owning company. However, no excuse is offered for the concentration on British ownership in the chapters on steam and motor tramps: not only is written material on these readily accessible but, at least until the advent of the bulk carrier, British tramps predominated.

CHAPTER ONE

Introduction: What is bulk shipping?

I

Freight transport by sea can be broadly divided into two major categories: liner and bulk shipping. Differentiating these trades requires consideration of the routes and regularity of sailings, the commodities carried, the shoreside organisation required and the types of vessels involved.

A liner service, so called because of the conceit that the operator has a 'line' of ships linking terminal ports, has been defined by Fayle as 'a fleet of ships, under common ownership or management, which provide a fixed service, at regular intervals, between named ports, and offer themselves as common carriers of any goods or passengers requiring shipment between those ports and ready for transit by their sailing dates'.[1] A vessel in the liner trade will typically carry a number of packets of different commodities, in varying quantities. These commodities are not necessarily loaded to the vessel's capacity: maintaining a schedule is usually judged more important than maximising the cargo carried on a particular voyage. The liner operator sees his best opportunity for profit in providing a reliable service to shippers on a long-term basis. To do this a considerable shoreside organisation is required, represented at each port regularly served. In addition to those administering the ships and crews, personnel are required to canvass shippers, to accept cargo and to supervise its loading and discharge, and to expedite onward delivery. Although containerisation over the last half-century has brought enormous changes to the liner trade, including the extinction of the conventional cargo and passenger liners, the principles of providing a reliable, scheduled service capable of moving a wide variety of cargoes endure.

No definition of bulk trades parallel to that of Fayle has been found.[2] The major characteristic common to all bulk trades is that only one type of commodity is usually carried on a given voyage, and it is rare for this to involve more than

---

[1] C.E. Fayle, *A Short History of the World's Shipping Industry* (London, 1933), 373.

[2] Although not attempting a definition, Sturmey lists some of the characteristics of bulk shipping discussed here. S.G. Sturmey, *British Shipping and World Competition* (London, 1962), 211–12.

two ports. The ship may equally be spot chartered for a single voyage or have a longer-term, even lifetime contract to carry one commodity between two ports. Loading and discharge are the responsibility of the shipper or charterer. Bulk cargoes are relatively low-value raw materials or manufactured items which can be handled on a large scale. Normally, for at least one leg of the voyage, these are loaded to the carrying capacity of the vessel, either in terms of weight or of stowage space above or below decks. Smaller loads may be accepted if that is all that is available, or where there are constraints on loading or discharge, such as draft restrictions in a port, canal or channel. Although any shipowner relishes the opportunity to carry a cargo in both directions, and so avoid the expense of a ballast voyage, this is generally possible only in the liner trade.[3] For the bulk carrier, such opportunities for carrying back cargoes are limited and, when they are available, they tend to depress freight rates.[4] The bulk carrier operator requires only a relatively lean headquarters operation, with staff involved principally in fixing cargoes, handling finance, managing crews and supervising new buildings and repairs. Almost invariably, administrative matters in distant loading and discharge ports are handled by agents or shippers.

II

The different characteristics of the tramp and liner trades strongly influence the type of ship required for each. The steam and diesel cargo liners which served this trade for at least a century were designed to carry a wide range of relatively high-value manufactured goods and food stuffs including livestock and perishables. They were mainly multi-deck vessels, with the facility to separate different types of cargo, and in certain trades had a capacity for refrigerated produce or deep tanks for liquids. Cargo gear was extensive in order to facilitate rapid loading and discharge at ports lacking sufficient shoreside equipment. Capacity for water ballast was usually modest, as the designer usually assumed that on most voyages the ship would carry at least some cargo. Most cargo liners had some accommodation for passengers, although relatively few carried more than the 12 which regulations permitted to travel without a medical doctor on board. Perhaps surprisingly, some container ships still carry a few passengers. Cargo liners were often relatively high powered in order to maintain a schedule in the face of delays which were beyond the control of the management or crew.

---

[3] For a century, the cargo liner generally sailed outward from western Europe or North America with manufactured goods, returning with foodstuffs and other raw materials. Recently, the rise of manufacturing in the Far East has partly reversed this flow of trade.

[4] A staple of the European tramp trade in the nineteenth century and beyond was the shipment of coal from Europe to the Mediterranean, Black Sea or South American ports, with grain as a return cargo. This trade declined in importance after the First World War in concert with the reduction in British coal mining.

Container shipping, with its emphasis on speed of delivery, has put a premium on high speed,[5] while construction of container terminals has eliminated much of the need for cargo gear.[6]

The ideal bulk carrier has only one deck with large holds, free of obstructions, and equally generous hatch dimensions to facilitate loading and discharge. Widespread reliance on shoreside equipment has meant cargo gear has often been dispensed with, and even when fitted has not been as lavish as in the cargo liner. Engines are usually of modest power, but reliability and economy are essential. A facility to carry water ballast is vital, as up to half the bulk carrier's time at sea will be spent on voyages without cargo. Provision to accommodate passengers has been extremely rare, which is not to say they were never carried. The transition from the steam and diesel freighters, commonly described as 'tramps', to the bulk carrier, which gathered pace in the 1960s, has not fundamentally altered these design principles, although – as in other areas of shipping – increase in size of vessels has produced significant economies.

The word 'ideal' in the above paragraph should be stressed, as in practice by no means all bulk-carrying ships have been single-deckers. In the 1930s, traditional tramp ship operators grasped the opportunity to build ships which could work in the bulk trades but could also be chartered to liner companies needing additional tonnage at short notice. These were usually multi-decked ships, often benefiting from arcane rules which meant significant space below a weather deck did not count towards measurement of tonnage on which harbour and canal dues were calculated. The largest groups of standardised ships ever built were those constructed in the United States, Canada and the United Kingdom during the Second World War, especially the US 'Liberty' type.[7] In almost all of these, the holds were divided longitudinally by a second or 'tween

---

[5]   Containerisation also increased the security of cargoes and expedited transfer to and from the land transport which delivered the container to the ship and carried it to the end user. Major changes which containerisation has brought about in the shipping industry include the contraction in the number of companies and consortia operating container ships. The number of ports with facilities to handle the ships has also been reduced, as a few major hubs are served by the largest ships, with feeder vessels serving many hitherto important ports handling lesser volumes of traffic.

[6]   Some smaller container vessels do have electric cranes for use when not alongside a specialist terminal. They are generally sited to one side of the deck so as maximise space for a deck cargo and not to interfere with the working of shoreside gear.

[7]   The design of the 'Liberty' type was derived from that of British tramp steamers. Its immediate precursor was the 'Ocean' type, a British design of which 60 were ordered from US yards in late 1940. In turn, the 'Ocean' design was based on that of the *Dorington Court*, completed by J.L. Thompson's shipyard on the River Wear in 1939. She was an example of a 'tween deck ship built for a tramp owner who was anxious to have the opportunity of chartering it to a liner company. The major alterations in turning the 'Ocean' into the 'Liberty' were the consolidation of the split superstructure into one unit and adapting the boilers which supplied steam to the triple-expansion engines for burning

deck. Sold in huge numbers post-war, the majority of these ships entered the tramp trades, despite the incumbrance of the intermediate deck when it came to taking on or discharging a bulk cargo.[8] Although the wartime ships had mostly been scrapped by the end of the 1960s, further 'Liberty replacement ships' with a 'tween deck were built, such as the British SD14 or Japanese 'Freedom' types, mostly marketed to and bought by tramp ship operators.[9] In addition, when liner companies decided their multi-decked cargo liners were becoming obsolete, they were often sold to work for a few years longer in the tramp trades.

An important distinction within bulk carrying is between ships carrying dry cargoes and those handling liquids in bulk. Liquid cargoes originally comprised crude petroleum, but this category has expanded greatly to include liquefied petroleum gas and natural gas, refined products of oil, industrial chemicals, edible oils, wines and even fruit juices. As the design, construction, operation and trades of dry and liquid bulk carriers are significantly different, this work will concentrate entirely on dry bulk carriers.

Dry cargoes carried in bulk have altered in character and tonnages over the 170 years of this survey. Such cargoes were initially dominated by coal, metallic ores, stone, grain, fertilisers and timber. Although recently coal has massively declined in significance, the other categories remain important, especially grain and ores, and have been joined by scrap iron, wood pulp, a wide range of industrial chemicals, china clay, other foodstuffs including sugar and soya meal, and steel and other metals as billets or partly manufactured items such as plates, tubes and girders.[10] These commodities may seem mundane, but their importance to the world's economy is immense, and their carriage is a highly significant aspect of world shipping.

Inevitably, there are sectors of dry cargo shipping which do not fit neatly into either the liner or bulk-carrying categories, but like the latter they involve one type of cargo, with a ship which may be spot chartered for one voyage or for a series. Carriage of fruit has usually involved fast, often relatively small vessels, whose routes and trades are determined mainly by growing seasons. Development of specialised vessels to carry cargoes, once largely the preserve of cargo liners,

---

oil rather than coal. See M. Cooper, *The Ocean Class of the Second World War* (Barnsley, 2022).

[8]   Elphick estimates that about 950 of the 'Liberty' type traded commercially post-war, about one-third of the total of some 2,700 built. Some of the remainder worked for the US armed forces, but the majority were laid up in reserve. US owners were the largest initial purchasers, followed by Britain, Greece, Italy, France, the Netherlands, Norway and China. Inevitably, these ships changed hands and flags, with an estimated 800 eventually passing through Greek ownership (although not necessarily flying the Greek flag). P. Elphick, *Liberty: The Ships That Won the War* (London, 2001), 402–3.

[9]   J. Lingwood, *SD14: The Full Story* (Preston, 2004).

[10]   See, for instance, B.N. Metaxas, *The Economics of Tramp Shipping* (London, 1971), 34 (table 4), although this figure is now 50 years out of date.

including livestock and motor vehicles, has been hastened by containerisation. Specialised heavy-lift ships have carried indivisible cargoes since the 1920s, and from the 1930s cargo liners began grasping some of this trade. The demise of the cargo liner has accelerated developments of specialised heavy-lift ships, some with spectacular abilities, for instance to carry an entire ship. Charters are usually for single trips between two ports, very like bulk shipping.

III

Estimation of the number of ships engaged in the tramp trades cannot rely on statistics of world trade, which simply record the weights of cargoes carried. Although many bulk cargoes – e.g., coal, ores and grain – would be carried in tramps, cargo liners would handle some of these cargoes when other commodities were not available. Neither can the basic entries for ships in shipping registers allow liners and tramps to be distinguished. For this study, an attempt has been made to quantify the numbers of ships available for the tramp and liner trades by counting those operated by British companies in both aspect of shipping. The validity of this method rests on the tendency of owners to specialise in either the tramp or the liner trades, with their ships and the organisations designed to suit their choice. The year 1892 was taken as being near to the peak of British tonnage and having a source readily available to the author.[11] Results are shown in Table 1.1.

Table 1.1 Numbers of British steam ships operated by liner and tramp companies in 1892

	Liner trades		Tramp trades		Combined trades
	Number	**% of total**	**Number**	**% of total**	
Ships	2,017	46.0%	2,366	54.0%	4,383
Operators	258	28.3%	653	71.7%	911
Ships per operator	7.8	–	3.6	–	4.8

It is likely that the small preponderance of tramps in terms of numbers apparent in Table 1.1 would turn into a modest deficit if tonnages were calculated, as ships in the liner trade tended to be larger, especially those carrying passengers. Nevertheless, the figures indicate the importance of tramp shipping, both to the

---

[11] *Lloyd's Confidential Index* for 1892. This lists by owner all British ships over 100 tons in service, giving in most cases details of recent voyages (although not cargoes).

British merchant marine and, given the international dominance of Britain, to world trade. The world total of steam tonnage in 1890 was 2,293,000 tons, with the British Empire accounting for 62 per cent of this. British dominance in terms of shipbuilding was similar; in 1914, British yards accounted for 59 per cent of the world's output of tonnage.[12]

Compiling the figures in Table 1.1 has also revealed the much larger number of companies, individuals and partnerships running tramps compared with those operating liner services in 1892. A total of 658 operators of tramps were identified with an average of just 3.6 ships each, compared with 258 in the liner trade with 7.8 ships per fleet. Not only were the liner fleets larger, in several cases they completely dwarfed the tramp fleets. British India had 100 ships, Peninsular and Oriental (P&O) 57, while Ocean Steam, Lamport and Holt and General Steam had 48 each. In contrast, the only tramp fleets to exceed 20 ships were those of Ropner with 34, the Pyman family with 31, Morel Brothers with 30, Gordon with 26 and John Cory with 23. A relatively small fleet, plus a domicile in a coal-exporting port in South Wales or the north-east of England, is an excellent indicator of a tramp fleet.

Extending the study into the twentieth century indicates that the number of tramps and cargo liners over 1,000 tons gross in the British fleet declined both in absolute numbers and as a percentage of the British fleet (Table 1.2).[13]

Table 1.2 Numbers of ocean-going vessels in British ownership by presumed employment in 1926 and 1955

	1926	1955
Liners	1,771 (58%)	848 (62%)
Tramps	1,281 (42%)	516 (38%)
Total dry cargo	3,052	1,364

The figures above for the numbers of tramp ships and their fluctuations over time are in line with those quoted by Thomas over roughly ten-year periods from 1910 to 1949, although this author does not state his criteria for defining a tramp nor his sources.[14]

---

[12]   S. Pollard and P. Robertson, *The British Shipbuilding Industry, 1870–1914* (Cambridge, MA, 1979), 45.

[13]   For 1876 and 1899, the 'Shipowners List', in *Lloyd's Register* provided this data, and for 1926 and 1955 *Lloyd's Confidential Index* was used, having the advantage of separate volumes for British and Foreign tonnage.

[14]   P.N. Thomas, *British Ocean Tramps*, vol. 1, *Builders and Cargoes* (Wolverhampton, 1992); vol. 2, *Owners and Their Ships* (Albrighton, 1992).

Few other comparisons have been found of the relative importance of bulk and liner shipping. Kaukiainen presents a graph which compares the total gross tonnage of bulk carriers with those of 'general carriers' between 1970 and 2000. This shows the former consistently leading by about 10 per cent, but the meaning of 'general carriers' is unclear.[15]

Some caveats are necessary concerning the above figures. Companies engaged in bulk shipping have been only too willing to charter a ship to a liner company which was temporarily short of tonnage. Indeed, to ensure the ready availability of temporary tonnage, several large British liner companies acquired whole fleets of tramps, including P&O with the Hain Steamship Co. Ltd and Clan Line with King Line. A further complication has been the tendency of companies established as successful tramp operators to move into liner shipping when they saw opportunities, offenders including the Cardiff-based Reardon Smith and the Glasgow and London-based Bank Line.

Under flags other than Britain, the differences in importance of the two trades varied widely. In Germany, two large liner companies, HAPAG and Norddeutscher Lloyd, owned a high proportion of the country's total tonnage. In contrast, of Greece's large fleet, almost 100 per cent have been involved in the bulk carrying of dry and liquid cargoes. With its relatively small industrial and agricultural sectors, Norway occupies an intermediate position, with much of its large fleet tramping, but also operating liners mainly in cross trades.[16]

IV

The literature concerning the bulk trades is patchy and is particularly poor on evolution of the ship's design. Some of the more prominent British tramp shipping companies have had histories written.[17] However, the involvement of the

---

[15] Y. Kaukiainen, 'Growth, Diversification and Globalization: Main Trends in International Shipping since 1850', in L.R. Fischer and E. Lange, *International Merchant Shipping in the Nineteenth and Twentieth Centuries: The Comparative Dimension* (St. John's, Newfoundland, 2008), 17.

[16] S. Tenold, 'Norwegian Shipping in the Twentieth Century', in Fischer and Lange, *International Merchant Shipping in the Nineteenth and Twentieth Centuries*.

[17] The most detailed and accessible include the following: H.S. Appleyard, *Bank Line, 1885–1985* (Kendal, 1985); D. Jenkins, *Graig: One Hundred Years in Shipping* (Preston, 2019); M. Cooper, *J. and C. Harrison: The History of a Family Shipping Venture* (Preston, 2012); J. Orbell, *From Cape to Cape: The History of Lyle Shipping* (Edinburgh, 1978); P.M. Heaton, *The Reardon Smith Line: The History of a South Wales Shipping Venture* (Newport, 1984); D. Jenkins, *From Ship's Cook to Baronet: Sir William Reardon Smith's Life in Shipping, 1856–1935* (Cardiff, 2011); I. Dear, *The Ropner Story* (London, 1986); A.S. Mallett, *Idyll of the Kings: The History of King Line, 1889–1978* (Kendal, 1980); K.J. O'Donoghue and H.S. Appleyard, *Hain of St Ives* (Kendall, 1986).

founders and managers of the companies in the writing and publication of certain of these volumes may distort objectivity. These, together with a host of shorter books and articles, usually include a detailed list of the dimensions, builders and careers of the ships owned. These should not be lightly dismissed, as knowledge of the type, size, age and fates of ships owned is fundamental to understanding the company's importance, its trade and not least its success or failure.

Although its scope extends well beyond bulk shipping, Sturmey's *British Shipping and World Competition* has much detail on the economics of bulk shipping, inevitably concentrating on the British fleet. Metaxas, *The Economics of Tramp Shipping*, is an important source, although not discussing the design and construction of tramp ships. Despite its promising title, *The Deep Sea Tramp* is heavily anecdotal.[18]

Brief, but to the point, is Robin Craig's *The Ship: Steam Tramps and Cargo Liners, 1850–1950*,[19] which does address constructional and engineering issues of both types of ship in the limited space allowed in the National Maritime Museum's series entitled simply *The Ship*. The tenth and last book in the series, *The Revolution in Merchant Shipping*, by E.C.B. Corlett, has a chapter entitled 'Oil Tankers and Bulk Carriers', which seriously disappoints, devoting almost all its text to oil/bulk/ore ships, which the author admits represent just one-fifth of bulk carrier tonnage.[20] Nick Tollerton's *Bulk Carriers* is more thorough and accessible and has been much referenced in this work.[21]

The first of Thomas's two-volume *British Ocean Tramps* has some brief histories of shipbuilders who built tramps, useful chapters on tramp ship cargoes and ship broking, and perhaps the most ambitious attempt made up to then to discuss the design evolution of the tramp, although missing the potential connection with the screw collier. The second volume covers a large number of owners of tramp ships, although the accounts tend to give start and end dates, important casualties and sample voyages, with virtually nothing on finance and management strategies.[22]

Charles Waine's books have long been invaluable sources of reference on coastal ships, and the present author has been privileged to assist him with a third edition of *Steam Coasters and Short Sea Traders*.[23] Waine's ultimate work, *British Motor Coasters*, more or less completes his oeuvre.[24] Its value is in the intimate details it provides on design and operation of these vessels, particularly

---

[18]   A.G. Course, *The Deep Sea Tramp* (London, 1960).

[19]   R. Craig, *The Ship: Steam Tramps and Cargo Liners, 1850–1950* (London, 1980).

[20]   E.C.B. Corlett, *The Ship: The Revolution in Merchant Shipping, 1950–1980* (London, 1981).

[21]   N. Tolerton, *Bulk Carriers: The Ocean Cinderellas* (Christchurch, NZ, 2005).

[22]   Thomas, *British Ocean Tramps*, vols 1 and 2.

[23]   C.V. Waine and R.S. Fenton, *Steam Coasters and Short Sea Traders*, 3rd ed. (Albrighton, 1994).

[24]   C.V. Waine, *British Motor Coasters* (Lydney, 2018).

post-Second World War, mostly drawn from interviews with crews or the staff of the owners, and has been invaluable for compiling this work.

Individual papers in academic and technical journals figure considerably in the bibliography of this book, but few give as useful an overview as Craig's 1978 paper, which discusses the origins of the steam tramp and its spread beyond the coastal coal trade.[25] In view of the arguments to be put forward in a later chapter of the current work on the origin of the deep-sea tramp, it is interesting that Craig makes no distinction other than in size between early screw colliers and the steam tramps which quickly followed them.

---

[25] R. Craig, 'Aspects of Tramp Shipping and Ownership', in K. Matthews and G. Panting (eds), *Ships and Shipbuilding in the North Atlantic Region* (St. John's, Newfoundland, 1978), 222. This is reprinted as the first chapter in Craig's contribution to the Research in Maritime History series, R. Craig, *British Tramp Shipping, 1750–1914* (St. John's, Newfoundland, 2003).

CHAPTER TWO

First steps: The screw collier

I

Authors discussing the early development of the steamship concur that it took place almost exclusively within the coastal trade.[1] Improvement of the steamer up to the mid-nineteenth century in the liner trades has been well covered, and this chapter concentrates on the introduction of steam to the bulk trades, a Cinderella subject in comparison.[2]

The steam engine was used successfully for water transport before it was employed to propel land vehicles. In Kennedy's attempt to record all British steamships, his first record – albeit a very sketchy one – dates from 1704, and he lists ten further examples from the eighteenth century.[3] He is at one with other authors in admitting the *Comet* of 1812 as the first practical steamer in the United Kingdom.[4] However, he is in no doubt that the vessel credited with having the first iron hull, the *Aaron Manby* of 1822, is an impostor, and awards this distinction to Symington's *Experiment* of 1788.

---

[1] See, for example, J. Kennedy, *The History of Steam Navigation* (Liverpool, 1904). This book is notable for the attention it gives to coastal companies, albeit mainly those in the liner trades, and devotes chapters to these as well as to the far grander ocean liner companies.

[2] B. Greenhill (ed.), *The Advent of Steam: The Merchant Steamship before 1900* (London, 1993). Part of a series promoted as 'the first detailed and comprehensive account' of the ship, this book exemplifies both the scholarship that has gone into the historiography of the early steamship and the neglect of the later development of steam in the bulk trades. Greenhill's early chapter on the paddle steamer gives coastal shipping its due, but subsequent chapters on the screw and triple-expansion machinery ignore the bulk trades completely in favour of passenger and cargo liners, masterfully mistaking the grandiose for the important.

[3] N.W. Kennedy, *Records of Early British Steamships* (Liverpool, 1933).

[4] For instance, R. Hope, *A New History of British Shipping* (London, 1990), 266–7; J. Kennedy, *History of Steam Navigation*, 34; S. Palmer, 'Experience, Experiment and Economics: Factors in the Construction of Early Merchant Steamships', in K. Matthews and G. Panting (eds), *Ships and Shipbuilding in the North Atlantic Region* (St. John's, Newfoundland, 1978), 233.

The years immediately following the success of the *Comet* saw further pioneering voyages along coasts and across exposed waters which established the viability of the steamship.[5] Between 1819 and 1825, a number of regular steamer services were established on estuarial, coastal and short-sea routes, one of the most distinguished providers of these being the General Steam Navigation Company formed in 1824.[6] However, despite technical progress on the Clyde and the Thames, the marine steam engine remained an extremely inefficient prime mover and it was only on short routes and with coal readily available that steamers could operate successfully. These services catered for passengers, who would pay a high price for the dependability and speed of a steam packet, and also for small quantities of high-value goods such as mails, and for perishable cargoes such as livestock. As a result, even by the 1850s, steamships represented only a small proportion of the total British merchant fleet. Palmer notes that, of 1,218 vessels on the British register in 1852, only 247 (20 per cent) were steamers.[7] However, this may underestimate the importance of steam to the coastal trade, as even by 1830, steamships represented 10 per cent of the entries by tonnage in the coastal trade.[8]

The inherent drawbacks of the early steamer meant the continued preponderance of sailing ships in the bulk cargo trades in the mid-nineteenth century. The disadvantages of the steamer included its high cost of construction and the space which needed to be dedicated to the engines, boilers and bunkers.[9] Added to these were the cost of the coal and the wages of firemen and engineers who were needed in addition to the hands required to navigate the vessel and handle the sails (contemporary illustrations and models show that pioneer steamers carried a full suit of sails). Use of paddle wheels for propulsion did not favour cargo-carrying, as the engines had to be placed amidships and high up in the part of the hull most useful for cargo.[10] In addition, paddle propulsion was not suited to the variations in draft consequent upon the need to sail in both loaded and unloaded conditions. These factors meant that low-value bulk commodities – and in particular coal, stone and ore, but also grain and timber – continued to be carried by sailing ships.

The potential benefit of using a steamer in the bulk trades was that it was faster on average than a sailing vessel and – most important – it was almost independent of wind and tide so that it could make more passages in a given period and hence carry more cargo than a sailing ship. Given favourable

---

⁵   Hope, *New History of British Shipping*, 266–7.

⁶   Hope, *New History of British Shipping*, 266–7; Kennedy, *History of Steam Navigation*, 34; Palmer, 'Experience, Experiment and Economics', 236; K.T. Rowland, *Steam at Sea: A History of Steam Navigation* (Newton Abbot, 1970), 59.

⁷   Palmer, 'Experience, Experiment and Economics', 233.

⁸   J. Armstrong, and P.S. Bagwell, 'Coastal Shipping', in D.H. Aldcroft and M.J. Freeman (eds), *Transport in the Industrial Revolution* (Manchester, 1983), 145–6.

⁹   Hope, *New History of British Shipping*, 267.

¹⁰   J.G. Bruce, 'The Contribution of Cross-Channel and Coastal Vessels to Developments in Marine Practice', *Journal of Transport History*, 4, no. 2 (1959), 65–80.

circumstances, the additional earnings would be sufficient to offset the steamer's higher capital, crew and fuel costs and provide a profit.

II

The 1840s saw a number of well-documented attempts to exploit the advantages of the steamer for bulk cargoes, including efforts to build a screw collier. For various technical and commercial reasons, few of these vessels were a lasting success.

First and best-documented of these attempts is the *Bedlington*, completed on the Tyne in September 1842.[11] Quite apart from an iron hull and a steam engine (which was of the side-lever type, used in paddle steamers), she embodied three major innovations: water ballast tanks, twin screws and three lines of rails laid in her hold to accommodate coal-laden railway wagons. Her purpose was to carry coal from the Bedlington Colliery's jetty on the River Blyth to South Shields on the Tyne, where it was transhipped to sailing colliers to be conveyed to markets in the south. Although she achieved this purpose for four years, repairs needed were both expensive and so frequent that she must have been out of service for long periods. It seems that in 1846 the owners decided not to return the *Bedlington* to service after one of the more damaging of several strandings in the River Blyth. She did not see further service in the coal trade.

Next in order of documented attempts at screw collier construction is the *Q.E.D.* built at Walker-on-Tyne in 1844.[12] Compared to *Bedlington*, she was more typical of later colliers, having holds into which coal was tipped conventionally. Notably, she was fitted with what sounds like a double bottom for water ballast, although details are very sparse.[13] However, her steam engines were of only 20 horsepower, scarcely sufficient to drive her at 5 knots (like other early colliers, she carried a full set of sails), and the engine was probably fitted mainly to pump out the water ballast. Indeed, it was reported as being 'adequate to discharge her water ballast when she arrived in harbour'; not a great testimony to its power. In contrast, the engines of *Bedlington* were rated at 60 horsepower.[14] The engine of *Q.E.D.* was either inadequate or unreliable, as in January 1846 – only 14 months

---

[11]   S.B. Martin and N. McCord, 'The Steamship Bedlington, 1841–54', *Maritime History*, 1, no. 1 (1971), 46–72. Registration documents in The National Archives, Kew (TNA), class BT 107 give a date for issuing *Bedlington*'s builder's certificate as 22 September 1842, although Martin and McCord indicate she was completed in 1841.

[12]   J.A. Macrae and C.V. Waine, *The Steam Collier Fleets* (Albrighton, 1990), 12.

[13]   *Illustrated London News*, 28 September 1844, reproduced in Macrae and Waine, *Steam Collier Fleets*, 9.

[14]   Nominal horsepower figures quoted on registration documents for early steamers need to be treated with caution as they were arrived at from applying a mathematical formula rather than by measurement, as was later done with indicator diagrams and brakes. This leads to some anomalies: replacement engines, although usually both more

after she had been built – she was re-registered after her machinery had been removed by her owner and builder.[15]

The *Experiment* of 1845 had a wooden hull and is said to have been a collier, the first built on the Wear, but she was lost by fire within a few years.[16] The *Conside* of 1847 was evidently conceived as a collier,[17] but was placed into regular liner trades between Leith and Hamburg immediately on completion.[18] She was lost in 1852.

The name of the Clyde-built *Collier* of 1849 leaves no doubt about her intended trade, but again commercial pressures led her to be employed on regular general cargo routes. She was completed in January 1849 but was not registered until 29 April 1850.[19] The 15-month delay suggests difficulty in finding a buyer, and her initial owner, an associate of the London, Brighton and South Coast Railway Company, placed her into a regular service on the English Channel, sailing twice weekly between Shoreham and Jersey.[20] *Collier* survived until 1914, in the latter part of her long life undoubtedly carrying the cargo for which she had been named.

The small, South Wales-built *Augusta* of 1849 appears to be the only one of these early steam bulk carriers to have been an immediate and lasting success in her intended trade of carrying ore for ironmaster Henry W. Schneider.[21] Research by the present author has found no evidence that the *Augusta* had any capacity for water ballast when new.[22] However, after east coast screw colliers had established the usefulness of water ballast tanks, other steamers built for the iron ore trade, *Arthur Gordon* and *Iron Age* of 1854, had them fitted.[23]

Generally accepted as the most successful early screw collier was the *John Bowes* of 1852, built by the Palmer Brothers' newly set up Jarrow yard.[24]

---

powerful and much more efficient, are often rated at the same, or even lower, horsepower than the machinery they replaced.

[15]   R. Craig, 'Aspects of Tramp Shipping and Ownership', in Matthews and Panting, *Ships and Shipbuilding in the North Atlantic Region*, 214.

[16]   R. Craig, *The Ship: Steam Tramps and Cargo Liners, 1850–1950* (London, 1980), 5.

[17]   Macrae and Waine, *Steam Collier Fleets*, 12.

[18]   TNA, closed register, class BT 98/1354.

[19]   TNA, crew agreement, class BT 98/2233.

[20]   TNA, crew agreement, class BT 98/2233.

[21]   Craig, 'Aspects of Tramp Shipping and Ownership', 210. *Augusta* would most likely work mainly between Workington and Cardiff with iron ore, carrying steam coal northwards, at least as far as Liverpool. An extensive rebuild and lengthening in 1855 may well have seen ballast tanks added. She survived until stranded in 1886. TNA, London customs register, CUST 130/51.

[22]   R.S. Fenton, 'Transition in the UK Coastal Bulk Trades: 1840 to 1914', PhD thesis, Thames Valley University, 2005, 76–99.

[23]   E.E. Allen, 'On the Comparative Cost of Transit by Steam and Sailing Colliers, and on the Different Methods of Ballasting', *Proceedings of the Institute of Civil Engineers*, 14 (1854–5), 353.

[24]   Craig, *The Ship*, 7.

Launched on 30 June 1852, *John Bowes* set out from the north-east on her first voyage on 27 July, unloaded 500 tons of coal in the Thames (where she was pictured by the *Illustrated London News*) and returned to the Tyne on 3 August. It was claimed that in one week the *John Bowes* had done the work which would normally take two collier brigs a month.[25]

Early bulk-carrying steamers adopted a number of relatively recent innovations, notably the iron hull, the screw propeller and developments which made the steam engine more economical. A further significant feature of the *John Bowes* was a single hatch, 60 feet in length, which allowed the coal to be teemed very easily into all parts of the hold, greatly reducing the need for trimming.[26] The long, unobstructed hatch facilitated loading and discharge.[27]

However, the development which was probably of most significance in ensuring the commercial success of the early screw colliers was an arrangement for carrying water ballast.[28] Ballast, originally in the form of sand or shingle, was essential when making a passage without cargo, as it increased stability in a seaway, ensured the screw remained underwater, and helped trim the vessel on an even keel. Using water saved the time and cost of queuing for and loading shingle or chalk for the unladen return voyage and of unloading this ballast on arrival at the coal port. A number of methods for carrying water ballast were tried, including barrels in the hold and canvas bags, but ultimately the most successful were McIntyre tanks fitted between the bottom of the hull and the floor of the hold, with transverse and longitudinal partitions (the former the frames of the ship) to prevent surging.[29] The tanks were filled and emptied by pumps working off the main engine. There is some uncertainty as to which was the first vessel fitted with McIntyre tanks, and – despite its claims as the pioneering vessel – it was certainly not the *John Bowes*, although such tanks were later fitted to this collier. Several authors believe that she originally relied on traditional chalk ballast, and that she later carried barrels of water as ballast.[30] It has also been stated that she was initially fitted with collapsible canvas bags to hold water ballast,[31] a system devised by a Dr White of Newcastle and fitted to 50 vessels by 1855, according to Allen.[32]

---

[25]   This figure is widely quoted and probably originates with Charles Palmer. See, for instance, Macrae and Waine, *Steam Collier Fleets*, 13; Craig, 'Aspects of Tramp Shipping and Ownership', 209–30 and also F.C. Bowen (writing as 'FCB'), 'Ships That Made History 5, the *John Bowes*', *Shipbuilding and Shipping Record* (30 September 1937), 421–2.

[26]   Macrae and Waine, *Steam Collier Fleets*, 13.

[27]   Craig, 'Aspects of Tramp Shipping and Ownership', 222.

[28]   Craig, *The Ship*, 5; Macrae and Waine, *Steam Collier Fleets*, 12.

[29]   Craig, *The Ship*, 7; C.V. Waine and R.S. Fenton, *Steam Coasters and Short Sea Traders*, 3rd ed. (Albrighton, 1994), 49. No details have been found of the builders of *Q.E.D.*, *Experiment*, *Resolute* or *Vedra*.

[30]   Macrae and Waine, *Steam Collier Fleets*, 12.

[31]   Craig, *The Ship*, 7.

[32]   Allen, 'Comparative Cost of Transit', 318–73.

In the discussion following Allen's paper, however, Charles Palmer himself explained that at least four methods had been tried in *John Bowes*: ceilings of iron, ceilings of timber, large tanks in the sides and bag ballast, all of which were rejected.[33] For subsequent vessels, Palmer adopted large flat iron tanks, running from one end of the hold to the other. These floor tanks had been invented by John McIntyre, who had previously worked on the Clyde and was engaged by Charles Palmer on 10 May 1852,[34] just six weeks before the *John Bowes* was launched. Craig cites the *Samuel Laing* of 1854, Palmer's yard number 12, as the first vessel fitted with McIntyre tanks.[35]

Following the *John Bowes*, expansion of the east coast steam collier fleet was rapid. Table 2.1. lists ships of this type known to have been built in the 1840s and 1850s.[36] A total of 43 of these had been completed and entered service by February 1855. However, there were dissenting voices. In the discussion to Allen's paper, Ralph Jackson – who had interests in both the port facilities and shipping at West Hartlepool – referred to his Liverpool-built *Hunwick* of 1852. Jackson claimed that after a trial of four years (an exaggeration, as she was only 27 months old when Allen's paper was discussed) he had found it so unprofitable to run her in the coal trade that he switched her to carrying general cargo to Hamburg.[37] Jackson believed that Allen had underestimated the costs of steam ships and the work that sailing vessels could do, and his experience of both steam and sailing colliers convinced him the latter was more profitable. Neither was the General Iron Screw Collier Co. Ltd totally convinced by its decision to operate colliers: after building at least ten vessels in 18 months during 1854 and 1855,[38] it was looking to sell its fleet in 1858.[39] Nevertheless, the steam collier became a permanent feature of the coal trade: around 50 were registered in Newcastle alone in the early 1870s, at least half of which were loading coal on the Tyne for London and the south coast.[40] In 1863, 25 per cent of the coal arriving by sea in London ('sea-coal') was carried by screw collier, and by 1873 almost 100 per cent is said to have arrived this way.[41] The average coal cargo delivered to London per ship also grew, from 536 tons in 1875, 709 tons in 1880, 790 tons in 1890 to 1,133 tons in 1900.[42]

---

[33]   Allen, 'Comparative Cost of Transit', 365.

[34]   Charles Palmer's Letter Book, Newcastle Libraries.

[35]   Craig, *The Ship*, 7.

[36]   Data for this table comes primarily from Parliamentary papers, Returns of Registered Steam Vessels of UK, 1851–9 (see bibliography). TNA, closed register, class BT 108, plus Macrae and Waine, *Steam Collier Fleets*, and yard lists compiled and held by the World Ship Society.

[37]   Allen, 'Comparative Cost of Transit', 356.

[38]   Macrae and Waine, *Steam Collier Fleets*, 15.

[39]   Craig, 'Aspects of Tramp Shipping and Ownership', 215.

[40]   Macrae and Waine, *Steam Collier Fleets*, 12.

[41]   R. Smith, *Sea-coal for London: History of the Coal Factors in the London Market* (London, 1961), 276.

[42]   Smith *Sea-coal for London*, 324.

Table 2.1 Chronological list of known screw colliers built to 1859

Name	Registration	Builder
Bedlington	1 October 1842	Marshall, Newcastle
Q.E.D.	1844	Newcastle
Experiment	1845	South Shields
Conside	4 February 1847	Marshall, Newcastle
John Bowes	24 July 1852	Palmer, Tyne
Haggerston	30 August 1852	Vernon, Mersey
Hunwick	23 November 1852	Vernon, Mersey
Lady Berriedale	15 January 1853	Scott Russell, Thames
William Hutt	8 March 1853	Palmer, Tyne
Lady Alice Lambton	5 April 1853	Marshall, Newcastle
Countess of Strathmore	11 May 1853	Palmer, Tyne
Rajah	18 June 1853	Mare, Thames
Northumberland	25 June 1853	Palmer, Tyne
Eagle	19 July 1853	Scott Russell, Thames
Sir John Easthope	26 July 1853	Palmer, Tyne
Chanticleer	18 August 1853	Denny, Dumbarton
Durham	30 August 1853	Palmer, Tyne
Caroline	7 October 1853	Scott Russell, Thames
Tyne	14 November 1853	Palmer, Tyne
Falcon	14 December 1853	Scott Russell, Thames
Hawk	8 February 1854	Scott Russell, Thames
Marley Hill	9 February 1854	Palmer, Tyne
Ross D. Mangles	18 May 1854	Palmer, Tyne
Nicholas Wood	3 June 1854	Palmer, Tyne
Union	16 June 1854	Lungley, Thames
Black Prince	28 August 1854	Vernon, Mersey
Great Northern	31 August 1854	Laing, Sunderland
Briton	26 September 1854	Samuda, Thames
Firefly	30 September 1854	Vernon, Mersey
Saxon	10 October 1854	Samuda, Thames
Pioneer	13 November 1854	Scott Russell, Thames
Norman	24 November 1854	Lungley, Thames
Hetton	28 November 1854	Mitchell, Newcastle

Name	Registration	Builder
Imperial	6 December 1854	Scott Russell, Thames
Earl of Durham	13 December 1854	Mitchell, Newcastle
Cochrane	19 December 1854	Palmer, Tyne
Black Boy	28 December 1854	Palmer, Tyne
Whitley Park	29 December 1854	Palmer, Tyne
Samuel Laing	2 January 1855	Palmer, Tyne
Black Sea	4 January 1855	Palmer, Tyne
Chester	17 January 1855	Cramm, Chester
Killingworth	17 January 1855	Mitchell, Newcastle
New Pelton	26 January 1855	Scott Russell, Thames
Normanby	5 March 1855	Palmer, Tyne
Dane	16 March 1855	Lungley, Thames
Wearmouth	17 March 1855	Laing, Sunderland
Countess of Durham	19 April 1855	Rich, Duck, Stockton
Derwent	24 April 1855	Cramm, Chester
Black Diamond	11 June 1855	Laing, Sunderland
George Hawkins	30 August 1855	Palmer, Tyne
Earsdon	10 September 1855	Palmer, Tyne
Vedra	18 September 1855	Sunderland
Rechid	4 October 1855	Richardson, Stockton
Sardinian	20 October 1855	Palmer, Tyne
Hutton Chaytor	24 October 1855	Palmer, Tyne
Carbon	8 November 1855	Clayton, Liverpool
Berwick	8 November 1855	Scott, Greenock
General Codrington	5 January 1856	Palmer, Tyne
Vulture	10 January 1856	Laing, Sunderland
Florence Nightingale	21 January 1856	Richardson, Stockton
Tyne	7 February 1856	Palmer, Tyne
Marmora	14 February 1856	Palmer, Tyne
Eupatoria	3 April 1856	Mitchell, Newcastle
William France	6 May 1856	Simons, Renfrew
Viscount Lambton	14 May 1856	Richardson, Duck, Stockton
Resolute	11 April 1857	Whiteinch
Seaton	16 May 1857	Palmer, Tyne

Name	Registration	Builder
Lyon	16 May 1857	Mitchell, Newcastle
William Cory	27 July 1857	Mitchell, Newcastle
Londonderry	14 August 1857	Pile, Hartlepool
Hercules	22 August 1857	Laing, Sunderland
Rouen	10 September 1857	Palmer, Tyne
Contest	2 November 1857	Simons, Renfrew
Lambton	5 December 1857	Mitchell, Newcastle
James Dixon	13 September 1859	Palmer, Tyne

III

There were no technological breakthroughs that presaged the explosion of interest in screw colliers in the early 1850s: developments such as the practical use of water ballast were made during the refinement of this type of craft. However, there were commercial factors in play. In an 1863 paper, the shipbuilder Charles Palmer asserted that the impetus for developing the iron collier came from railway competition to the sailing collier, claiming that, by 1850, rail carriage of coal began seriously to affect sale of north-country coal in London.[43] He added that coalfields closer to the capital such as those in the Midlands and Yorkshire were threatening the business of the coal owners in Durham and Northumberland who were largely reliant on delivering coal to the Thames by collier brigs.

A series of figures for coal arriving into the port of London was compiled and published by J.R. Scott in 1869.[44] Table 2.2 shows that rail was very far from eclipsing sea carriage in 1850, although in that year rail deliveries showed a spectacular leap, increasing fivefold. This is the first year in which Scott cites the Great Northern Railway as a significant coal hauler, and it is likely that this company was now bringing in coal from the Yorkshire and Derbyshire fields. Table 2.2 demonstrates the very strong growth of rail-borne coal in the 1850s and 1860s, finally eclipsing sea transport in 1867. It is noteworthy, however, that sea transport, although losing market share strongly, shows only a slight overall decline in tonnage.

Rail carriage of coal had certainly grown spectacularly in the years immediately prior to the first steam collier being completed in 1852. However,

---

[43]   C.M. Palmer, 'On the Construction of Iron Ships and the Progress of Iron Shipbuilding on the Tyne, Wear and Tees', *Report of the British Association for the Advancement of Science for 1863*, 694–701.

[44]   J.R. Scott, *An Epitome of the Progress of the Trade in Coal to London since 1755* (London, 1869).

**Table 2.2 Tonnages of coal carried to London by sea and rail,
1844–1868**

Year	By sea	By rail
1844	2,491,910	–
1845	3,403,320	8377
1846	2,935,755	11,698
1847	3,280,420	19,336
1848	3,418,340	37,888
1849	3,339,146	19,639
1850	3,553,304	55,095
1851	3,236,542	247,908
1852	3,330,428	377,907
1853	3,373,256	629,712
1854	3,399,561	945,056
1855	3,016,868	1,137,835
1856	3,119,884	1,246,299
1857	3,133,459	1,206,775
1858	3,266,446	1,190,521
1859	3,299,170	1,191,169
1860	3,573,377	1,477,545
1861	3,567,607	1,642,502
1862	3,442,402	1,513,296
1863	3,335,174	1,775,487
1864	3,116,703	2,342,440
1865	3,161,683	2,733,056
1866	3,033,193	2,969,896
1867	3,016,416	3,295,652
1868	2,981,230	2,979,933

Source: J.R. Scott, *An Epitome of the Progress of the Trade in
Coal to London since 1755* (London, 1869).

in 1852 the tonnage of coal brought to London by rail was equivalent to a mere
7 per cent of that brought by sea. Sea-borne tonnage had shown a decline in
1851, but it is not true to aver that, as Palmer did, rail transport was 'seriously
damaging' the collier business in the early 1850s. It could well be that the

singularly high annual growth rate in 1851 had rattled the north-east coast coal owners, but if so they were showing very unusual foresight: it was not until 1867, 16 years later, that rail eclipsed sea transport in the London market. In addition, the coal owners must have been aware that the overall market was growing at such a rate that rail was unlikely to be able to convey all the coal needed: total tonnage reaching London almost doubled in the years from 1851 and 1867. Palmer was writing in 1863, when railways were indeed threatening to overtake sea transport in tonnage carried, and it is likely this had clouded his memories of the situation ten years earlier. The screw collier undoubtedly helped the north-east coast coal owners maintain their sales tonnages, and in 1868 to reverse the losses to rail, but it is barely credible that the quarter of a million tons of coal 'lost' to rail in 1851 would by itself have stimulated several shipyards, and a considerable number of investors, to go to the trouble of developing the screw collier. It may have been a factor but is unlikely to have been the only one. London gas companies, major consumers of coal from the Tyne and Wear, showed very little interest in contracting railways to supply coal, despite being very concerned about ensuring regular deliveries (see below).

IV

A likely reason for the sudden interest in the screw collier is the growing demands of the London gas industry for coal from the north-east. The gas industry had begun to demand large, but above all regular and uninterrupted, deliveries of coal to enable it to maintain its supplies of gas to its customers, and therefore would be expected to be eager users of screw colliers. Interruptions in generation of gas would threaten not only their business, but also the lives of customers and employees, by allowing potentially explosive mixtures of gas and air to accumulate in its pipes. It needs to be asked how important were the gas companies to the growth of the screw collier fleet, and would the screw collier have developed when it did without the London gas industry?

In his history of the Gas Light and Coke Company, Everard mentions that in 1853 Ford and Jackson of the General Iron Screw Collier Co. Ltd offered the colliers *Caroline* and *Hawk* to the Gas Light and Coke Company on a minimum of one-year's charter at a 'low rate per ton' but with high demurrage charged for detention longer than three days.[45] Smith repeated this in his history of the Coal Factors Society,[46] and so did the present author in his work on the screw colliers owned by the gas and electricity industries.[47]

---

[45]   S. Everard, *The History of the Gas Light and Coke Company, 1812–1949* (London, 1949), 194.

[46]   Smith, *Sea-coal for London*, 287.

[47]   D.R. Chesterton and R.S. Fenton, *Gas and Electricity Colliers* (Kendal, 1984), 40.

However, there are a number of problems with Everard's statement. First, neither Ford and Jackson nor the *Caroline* and *Hawk* had any connection with the General Iron Screw Collier Co. Ltd.[48] Ford and Jackson were amongst the owners of *Caroline*, but not *Hawk*, although both had been built by John Scott Russell at Millwall. *Hawk* was not completed until early in 1854, and Ford and Jackson – with their association with Scott Russell – were offering her to the gas company before she was completed. According to Everard, only the *Caroline* was taken up initially, for a one-year charter, with the *Hawk* being chartered a year later for a period of three years. Everard has the *Carbon* of 1855 'soon' chartered, along with a collier from the General Iron Screw Collier Co. Ltd and one owned by Stobart of Wearmouth Colliery. These colliers discharged their coal in Victoria Dock.

Everard continues that the Imperial Gas Light Company (a rival which amalgamated with Gas Light and Coke in 1872) took steam colliers 'one year later' (i.e., 1855 or 1856), with two vessels of the General Iron Screw Collier Co. Ltd, *Nicholas Wood* (1854), *Ross D. Mangles* (1854) plus the *New Pelton* (1854). Further, Everard maintains that the Imperial Company took half shares in *Black Diamond* and *Wearmouth*. It is significant that there were disruptions to coal supplies when several of these colliers were 'released' by the gas companies on requisition by the Government to take stores to the Black Sea during the Crimean War.

Everard notes that by 1863 the practice of the Gas Light and Coke company was to buy coal from the collieries in bulk on long-term contracts for large amounts, such as 100,000 tons. He says that 'When orders were placed on that scale, coal-owners found it economically worthwhile to build steam colliers for the express purpose of making deliveries to a single buyer'. In their volume on the steam collier, Macrae and Waine also make reference to gas companies, noting that 'their business would have been of particular interest to a steam collier owner'.[49] Middlemiss, in a superficial review of east coast collier ownership, says that ships of the General Iron Screw Collier Co. Ltd were chartered long-term to gas companies to carry prompt and regular supplies of coal to the Thames, but does not provide a source.[50] Further evidence for the close ties between London gas companies and screw collier interests comes from registration details of these ships and, especially, from minutes of the gas companies for the 1850s, which thanks to nationalisation of the gas industry in 1948 have survived well. Indeed, these documents are the only contemporary records that have been found which refer to the use of screw colliers, no documentation for this period being known to have survived for any owner of screw colliers. These connections repay consideration in detail.

---

[48]   Among the initial subscribers were coal merchant William Cory, coal owner Matthew Hutton Chaytor and shipbuilder Charles Mark Palmer. TNA, closed register, class BT 31/172519.

[49]   Macrae and Waine, *Steam Collier Fleets*, 14.

[50]   N.L. Middlemiss, *Black Diamond Fleets* (Gateshead, 2000), 11.

Terms of their founding charters initially precluded the gas companies from owning ships, and although the Gas Light and Coke Company obtained such powers in 1872, chartering colliers remained the norm until the beginning of the twentieth century.[51]

However, officials of the gas companies did own shares in several screw colliers. The registers of *Wearmouth* and *Black Diamond* of 1855 confirm Everard's statement (see above) that the Commercial Gas Company had an indirect interest in both,[52] and the minutes of its Court confirm that the company's Governor, Sir James Duke, was nominated as shareholder, although the money came from the gas company.[53] Shares in the *James Joicey, Ellen Sinclair*[54] of 1863 and the *Trevethick*[55] of 1866 were held by officials of the Gas Light and Coke Company, including John Orwell Phillips and Frederick John Evans. Macrae and Waine name William Prinstep of the London Gas Company and Thomas Miers of the Commercial Gas Company as directors of the General Iron Screw Collier Co. Ltd.[56] There may be names of other gas officials in the lists of shareowners of colliers, but they tend to hide their identity by describing themselves on registration documents simply as 'gentleman'.

There are other connections between gas companies and steam colliers, superficial but unlikely to be coincidental. The *Haggerston* of 1852 was named after the district in which the Independent Gas Light and Coke Company had a gasworks (in 1852 the works was not, as Macrae and Waine have it, owned by the Gas Light and Coke Company; amalgamation with the Independent Company did not happen until 1876).[57] The *Imperial* of 1854 was named to flatter the Imperial Gas Company for whose charter it was built, while *Sir James Duke* of 1861 took its name from the Governor of this gas company.[58] Stephenson Clarke's *C.S. Butler* of 1865 was named after the Chairman of the Commercial Gas Company.

Gas Light and Coke Company

The minutes of gas companies vary in the detail they give. In laconic style, the minutes of the meetings of the Court of the Gas Light and Coke Company

---

[51]   Chesterton and Fenton, *Gas and Electricity Colliers*, 50.

[52]   TNA, London customs registers, CUST 130/50.

[53]   London Metropolitan Archives, IMP/GLC/20.

[54]   Both TNA, London customs registers, CUST 130/56. Details of ownership of screw colliers referred to in this chapter are also from the London, Newcastle-upon-Tyne and Sunderland customs registers, held in Tyne and Wear Archives and TNA.

[55]   Customs registers for Newcastle-upon-Tyne, held in Tyne and Wear Archives, Newcastle-upon-Tyne.

[56]   Macrae and Waine, *Steam Collier Fleets*, 15.

[57]   The London Metropolitan Archives catalogue has brief histories of the Gas Light and Coke Company and the companies they took over.

[58]   London Metropolitan Archives, IMP/GLC/20.

simply record that approaches from owners of screw colliers were made and either approved or rejected. The first mention of a screw collier is in May 1853 when shipbuilder John Scott Russell approached the company to propose that it consider using such a vessel.[59] He offered a freight rate of 7s.6d. per ton of coal, whereas the company was currently paying around 9s. with sailing colliers. This approach provoked much discussion amongst members of the Court over the next few months. In the interim, Scott Russell's associates Ford and Jackson saw gas company officials, including the Secretary of the General Iron Screw Colliery Co. Ltd. Charles Palmer was approached by the gas company about building a screw collier, the Coal Turn Act was scrutinised and James Dixon and Frederick Harris – coal factors and major suppliers to the Gas Light and Coke Company – were summoned to give their expert opinion. Dixon and Harris were in favour of iron screw colliers, especially when the Coal Turn Act did not interfere to prevent their despatch. Eventually, in late September 1853,[60] Scott Russell's *Caroline* was chartered for one year at 8s.6d. per ton – the freight rate discussed had steadily floated upwards since May when the gas company felt it should not exceed 6s.9d. (typical rates for sailing colliers, reported in the minute books at this time, are around 11s.3d. per ton). The *Caroline's* owners undertook to load at any of the coal drops of collieries under contract to the gas company. However, it was insisted by the *Caroline's* owners that only three days were allowed for discharging before demurrage at the rate of £35 per day became payable. The gas company's loading agent in the north-east was told to put *Caroline* on the loading list for South Peareth coals and was ordered 'to afford *Caroline* every despatch in loading', to load her with any coal available to avoid delays and to take a steam tug if necessary. The progress of the *Caroline* was followed minutely as she sailed from Greenhithe on 22 October 1853 for Shields, and then proceeded to Sunderland where she loaded 499 tons of coal supplied from three collieries and returned to the Thames on 11 November (a typical sailing collier loaded about 350 tons, according to figures in contemporary minutes). Subsequent minutes recorded the Court's concerns about meeting the onerous conditions of loading and unloading *Caroline*. In December 1853, there was a warning that she might have to lie for two weeks before loading. Early in 1854, Harris and Dixon were awarded additional money for the extra expense of discharging *Caroline*.

Minutes for 1854 and 1855 recorded that *Caroline* continued to load in Sunderland.[61] In May 1854, William Bell, proprietor of the Wearmouth Colliery, obtained a contract to supply 40,000 tons of coal on the understanding that 'the

---

[59]   This and subsequent discussions are in London Metropolitan Archives, B/GLCC/23/1.

[60]   The delay may not be due simply to the slow pace of machinations at the gas company. *Caroline* was not completed until the first week in October 1853 according to her registration documents. TNA, London customs registers, CUST 130/48.

[61]   London Metropolitan Archives, B/GLCC/24/1 (minutes) and B/GLCC/24/2 (index to the minutes).

screw steamer is loaded within 48 hours'; this evidently referred to *Caroline*, although it would have been impossible for her to carry 40,000 tons coal in a year. Satisfaction with *Caroline* was evident, as Ford and Jackson's offer of a further collier built by Scott Russell, the *Hawk*, was accepted, and she obtained a three-year charter at 7s.9d. per ton, with demurrage payable after two days when loading and three when discharging. *Hawk*, which had been completed in February 1854, began her Gas Light and Coke charter in October. In February 1854, the gas company began negotiations to extend *Caroline*'s charter on a three-year basis like that of *Hawk*. It is not apparent why these two colliers are favoured, and in particular why the gas company was prepared to wait for *Hawk* to complete other work,[62] as further screw colliers were available to them. In May and again in June, the Scott Russell-built *Eagle* was offered to them for 12 months at 8s. per ton without demurrage but made only two voyages: her dimensions were practically identical to those of *Hawk*. In May, Harris and Dixon offered to deliver coal by screw collier for 12 months, but a decision on this was deferred. Perhaps most surprisingly, Alfred Holt – later to found the Ocean Steamship Co. Ltd – was approached in June 1854 and asked for terms to charter for two to three years his screw collier which was almost complete. Nothing further was recorded in the minutes about this approach.[63]

In February 1855, the War Office requested the gas company to provide two screw colliers as store carriers for the Crimean War; *Caroline* being released for this work almost immediately and *Hawk* following in March. The gas company received compensation from the colliers' owners of £200 and £300 per month respectively for the loss of these steamers, sums presumably taken into account when the rate at which the vessels were chartered to the government was fixed. Loyalty to *Caroline* and *Hawk* continued, however, and throughout 1856 the gas company was continually pressing Ford and Jackson to return them, although the latter were clearly at the mercy of the War Office who were reluctant to send them home. Even offers to charter the *Earsdon* on the same conditions as *Caroline* and the *Vulture* in lieu of the *Hawk* were declined by the gas company. Just one voyage by a screw collier, the *Carbon*, was recorded in the minutes for 1856.

---

[62]   *Hawk*'s crew agreements for 1854 show that she was initially employed between the Tyne and Lowestoft. Her co-owner was J.V. Gooch, locomotive superintendent of the Eastern Counties Railway, and his interest in colliers (which extended financially to the Scott Russell-built *Falcon* and *Eagle*) was in moving coal from the north-east to Lowestoft, where the railway company had coke ovens to supply the needs of its locomotives. Information on Gooch kindly provided by J. Swieskowski, historian of the maritime activities of the ECR and its successor, the Great Eastern Railway.

[63]   Holt's vessel was the iron steamer *Cleator*, built at Liverpool in 1854 for Alfred and his brother Philip but largely financed by the Ainsworth family of Cleator. The vessel is said to have been built to carry coal or ore. M. Falkus, *The Blue Funnel Legend* (London, 1990), 94; D. Haws, *Merchant Fleets 6: Blue Funnel Line* (Torquay, 1984), 39.

The next minute book made fewer specific references to screw colliers, but all vessels chartered were recorded in the minutes and appeared in the index.[64] During the period of 26 months from May 1856 to July 1858 there were 326 separate charters of vessels by the Gas Light and Coke Company, some individual ships being chartered many times. Screw colliers were chartered on 80 occasions, this representing nine individual vessels with three predominating: *Caroline* (27 charters), *Hawk* (21) and *Vulture* (17). Thus, 20 per cent of the total number of charters were of screw colliers. The total coal carried by screw collier was greater than this suggests, however. According to Allen,[65] a screw collier could carry twice as much as a typical sailing collier on each voyage, although figures from contemporary gas company minutes suggest larger sailing colliers were being chartered, perhaps with 70 per cent of the capacity of a screw collier. Again according to Allen, a screw collier could make some 30 voyages each year compared with the 10 made by a sailing collier. Thus, on one voyage, a screw collier would carry about 30 per cent more coal than a sailing collier, meaning that about one-third of the gas company's coal was arriving by steamer. Charter rates for screw colliers were within the range 7s.9d. to 8s.6d. per ton, compared with 11s.3d. to 11s.6d. for sail.

Minutes for the period July 1858 to August 1860 recorded a number of offers of screw colliers, and on one occasion the Secretary was actually asked to 'get a screw collier', presumably to investigate having one built for the company, but nothing further was heard of this.[66] From the minutes it seems that only five screw colliers were definitely running for the company in the period, and only *Hawk*, *Black Diamond* (still owned in part by James Duke of a rival gas company) and possibly *Vedra* appeared to be in anything like full-time employment; the other screw colliers, *New Pelton* and *Great Northern*, were mentioned just once. However, it is clear that screw colliers not directly chartered by the gas company were also delivering coal to its works: during 1862 the company's Court was asked to accept 'the suspension of one of the Lambton steamers for a fortnight'. By now the owner of the Lambton collieries had six screw colliers of his own.[67] One of these, *Lady Alice Lambton*, was carrying coal for the gas company when lost in collision with another screw collier in September 1862.[68]

By 1863, freight rates for screw colliers between 5s. and 5s.10½d. per ton were being quoted. These rates may be exceptionally low: the screw collier in question, *James Joicey*, was a relatively large vessel of 200 feet, and its owners

---

[64]   London Metropolitan Archives, B/GLCC/25/1 (minutes) and B/GLCC/25/2 (index to the minutes).

[65]   Allen, 'Comparative Cost of Transit', 318–73.

[66]   London Metropolitan Archives, B/GLCC/26/1 (minutes) and B/GLCC/26/2 (index to the minutes).

[67]   Middlemiss, *Black Diamond Fleets*, 65–72.

[68]   London Metropolitan Archives, B/GLCC/28/1 (minutes) and B/GLCC/28/2 (index to the minutes).

1: The steam collier *James Joicey* of 1863 was built by Palmer Brothers of Jarrow for a consortium of coal industry investors, including her namesake colliery owner and coal merchant William Cory. Fitting a triple-expansion engine in 1885 prolonged her life and after 48 years in the coal trade she was broken up in 1911. *Author's collection*

included the coal owner James Joicey as well as three members of the Court of the gas company. The charter proposal was part of an offer to supply 30,000 to 50,000 tons of coal from Joicey's New Pelton colliery, and a low freight rate may have been quoted to secure this business. In July 1864, the Court expressed some anxiety about high freight rates and the effect they were having on costs, and they endeavoured to renew charters of screw colliers for periods of up to three years. *Ellen Sinclair*, in which once again gas company governors held shares, was taken up for three years but no rate was quoted in the minutes. Rates do not seem to have advanced very far, however: when an extra steamer was thought necessary in September 1865, *Magna Charta* was chartered at 5s.6d. per ton.[69]

It is clear from the minutes that the Gas Light and Coke Company was not relying completely on screw colliers, and until at least 1867 sailing vessels were carrying probably half its requirements. The company had its own sailing collier, the *Despatch*, and there were references in 1865 and 1866 to losses amongst the sailing colliers on charter. Sailing vessels were vulnerable to the 'tempestuous weather', which in December 1865 led to the non-availability of coal, and in

---

[69]   London Metropolitan Archives, B/GLCC/29/1 (minutes) and B/GLCC/29/2 (index to the minutes).

consequence of which another steamer was chartered. Only in February 1867 was discussed 'a scheme for delivery by steam ship of the estimated quantity of coal consumed by the company in the present year'. This was approved by the Court, but the minute book ends in April 1867, and in the next volume there is no mention whatsoever of ships or shipping.[70] These topics may well have been referred to another committee, but if so its minutes appear not to have survived. The Court's minutes from April 1867 were largely concerned with the company's scheme to build an enormous new gasworks at Beckton to the east of London on a riverside site to provide relatively deep-water berths for screw colliers.[71] The rationale for Beckton included the plan to make greater use of screw colliers, and the Gas Light and Coke Company applied to Parliament for powers to operate such vessels in 1872, although these powers were not exercised until 1911.[72]

Imperial Gas Light and Coke Company
With works at Fulham, Bow and Limehouse, the Imperial Gas Light and Coke Company was second to the Gas Light and Coke Company in size. Its minutes are unusually useful in recording brief discussions of why decisions concerning colliers were made.

During the autumn of 1853, the company was taking its suppliers Jonassohn and Elliott to task for failing to meet their contracted obligations.[73] The suppliers were expected to make up the difference in cost of buying coal on the open market, their defence being that they could not get ships at an economical freight rate. There followed one of only two suggestions found in gas company minutes of supplying coal by rail. This was tried, but the Great Northern Railway fell out with Jonassohn and Elliott as early as November 1853 and defaulted on its contract in January 1854. Meanwhile, the gas company negotiated with the General Iron Screw Collier Co. Ltd for two 600-ton screw colliers at 6s.6d. per ton for three years, to be loaded in two days and unloaded in three or face demurrage of £10 per day. A contract was signed in December 1853, and the Thornley Colliery near Hartlepool was told to meet the loading conditions. The screw colliers for this contract, *Ross D. Mangles* and *Nicholas Wood*, were delivered in May and June 1854. The nervousness of the gas companies at accepting these conditions on loading and discharging times was evident from the Imperial board asking what would happen if, for instance, two screw colliers arrived at Hartlepool to load on the same day.

In April 1854, negotiations began with William Stobart who was associated with William Bell's Wearmouth Colliery and were concluded in May with an agreement that he supply coal by 600-ton steam collier for three years at a rate

---

[70]   London Metropolitan Archives, B/GLCC/30/1 (minutes) and B/GLCC/30/2 (index to the minutes).

[71]   Everard, *History of the Gas Light and Coke Company*, 194.

[72]   Chesterton and Fenton, *Gas and Electricity Colliers*, 40.

[73]   London Metropolitan Archives, B/IMPGLC/20, minutes 8/1853-7/1855, B/IMPGLC/21 minutes 7/1855-7/1857 and B/IMPGLC/30, index to minute books, 1855–74.

of 15s.3d. per ton to include both the cost of coal and carriage. Stobart did not have colliers available, but ordered two from Laing of Sunderland, with a major shareholder in both being James Duke, Governor of the Imperial Gas Company. *Wearmouth* was delivered in March 1855 and *Black Diamond* in June, but both were immediately taken up by the War Office to convey stores to the Crimean War.

Notwithstanding four screw colliers being delivered or on order to meet its needs, the Imperial board was unhappy in July 1854. Sailing vessels could not be procured at rates of under 9s. per ton for one year, and owners would not charter for a shorter period. Because screw colliers were not to be had, John Scott Russell was contracted to deliver 50,000 tons of New Pelton coal per year in two new screw colliers at a rate of 7s.9d. per ton. These were delivered in June 1855 as *Imperial* and *New Pelton*, again being immediately taken up for government service, the Imperial Company receiving compensatory payments from the screw colliers' owners. The 50,000 tons per year envisaged in this contract was very ambitious (reflecting Scott Russell's character: he was the only shipbuilder willing to take on Brunel's *Great Eastern*); given that the two colliers could lift 600 tons per voyage, each would need to make 42 voyages annually. Crew agreements for Scott Russell's *Caroline* show that she could achieve barely 30 voyages between the Tyne or Wear and London in a 12-month period.[74] A further risk was achieving the rate of discharge required under the contract, and initially the Imperial Company's lighterage contractor, a Mr Tomlin, decided he could not meet the conditions required. He later reconsidered but asked for more money.

At the meeting of shareholders of the Imperial Company in April 1855, the directors were boastful of their foresight. They were apprehensive about the increasing price of coal (it had risen some 30 per cent since 1852). 'However, arrangements for iron screw colliers have left them little to apprehend, and thus the permanent prosperity of the company is assured'. This was pride coming before a fall, as War Office service was soon to deprive them of four of their six screw colliers, and it was expected that *Nicholas Wood* and *Ross D. Mangles* would soon have to be given up as well.[75] Nevertheless, the Imperial Company was more advanced than the Gas Light and Coke Company in grasping the savings and greater regularity of supply resulting from the screw collier.

Commercial Gas Light and Coke Company

The Commercial Gas Light and Coke Company supplied the East End of London, much of its gas coal being unloaded in the Regents Canal Dock.[76] In 1853, it required about 50,000 tons of coal annually, and in May approached the Regents Canal Company to see what 'dispatch they will give to screw colliers unloading'.

---

[74]   TNA, crew agreements, class BT 98/4867.
[75]   This did not happen, according to the screw colliers' crew agreements for 1855. TNA, crew agreements, classes BT 98/3875 and BT 98/3881.
[76]   London Metropolitan Archives, B/CGC/3, minutes 11/1851 to 3/1855.

When the canal company declined to give any guarantee, the gas company looked at building its own wharf at Ratcliff. Over the next two years the gas company experienced problems with coal supplies, with John Bowes and Partners, part owners of the eponymous *John Bowes*, failing to meet their contracted deliveries, and having to pay compensation to the gas company. However, the gas company was still unable to decide whether to charter screw colliers. The General Iron Screw Collier Co. Ltd, Stephenson Clarke and Alfred Prior individually made offers, but – in spite of assurances from lightermen that arrangements had been made to despatch steamers – the gas company quibbled about conditions, asked others to tender and by mid-1855 had still not undertaken to unload the coal within the period required by those offering ships.

London Gas Light and Coke Company
The London Gas Light and Coke Company had works at Vauxhall, consuming at least 350 tons per week during the winter months of the early 1850s. Its minutes from May 1850 to October 1855 recorded that the winters of 1851/2 and 1852/3 saw difficulties with coal supplies, with one of the Cory family and Charles Palmer attending separate meetings to plead that extraordinary circumstances had made it impossible to keep up a uniform supply. The board believing that 'one or two steam colliers would lessen the price for coal', the secretary was asked in July 1853 to approach the General Iron Screw Collier Co. Ltd to see if 6s. per ton was an acceptable charter rate. Evidently it was, but it fell to Charles Palmer to charter two of the General Iron Screw steamers on behalf of John Bowes and Partners, taking the *Durham* from new in August 1853 and the *Jarrow* on completion in November 1853. The 6s. per ton was well below the 8s.6d. per ton which *Caroline* was getting from the Gas Light and Coke Company in September 1853. No doubt Palmer – who was a subscriber to the General Iron Screw Collier Co. Ltd – was willing to accept this rate to secure long-term contracts for another of his business interests, the collieries of John Bowes and Partners. The *Durham* and *Jarrow* had more than enough capacity, at about 600 tons each, to supply the 350 tons per week which the London Gas Light and Coke Company required, and crew agreements indicate the *Jarrow*, at least, was fully employed in the east coast coal trade for only five months of the year.[77] The London Gas Light and Coke Company may well have been the first gas company to rely completely on steam colliers, and if so deserve credit for their pioneering and far-sighted business acumen.

Equitable Gas Light Company
Minutes of the Equitable Gas Light Company from September 1852 to July 1858 indicate that this company's works at Pimlico consumed about 30,000 tons of coal annually.[78] During the winter of 1853/4, concerns were expressed

---

[77]   TNA, closed register, class BT 98/3868.
[78]   London Metropolitan Archives, B/EGLC/8, minutes 9/1852–7/1858.

about problems with coal deliveries, but discussions with Stephenson Clarke and with the General Iron Screw Collier Co. Ltd were inconclusive. After placing applications for tenders in various London and regional newspapers, it accepted an offer from the Glasgow steamship owners Mories, Munro and Nicol to charter their *Progress* for 10 months from November 1854 at 7s.9d. per ton for the first 30 voyages to Sunderland, and 7s. per ton for any voyages achieved thereafter. William Bell of the Wearmouth Colliery agreed to load the *Progress* within two days. The owners of the *Progress* considerably undercut the only other bidder, E. Allen of Price and Company of London, who quoted 9s. per ton.[79] The General Iron Screw Collier Co. Ltd were asked to accept 8s. per ton but declined. Mories, Munro and Nicol were inexperienced, or more likely *Progress* was unsuitable for the coal trade (she probably had no arrangements for water ballast, which would greatly increase her turnround times) as dissatisfaction at her performance was expressed at a gas company board meeting in May 1855. No further reference to screw colliers was made until March 1858, but this makes it apparent that the colliery owners, and not the gas company, were providing screw colliers. An interesting aside is that in July 1858 Samuel Plimsoll, of the eponymous line, was offering to supply the company railway coal at 14s.9d. per ton, but the offer was declined.

South Metropolitan Gas Light and Coke Company
The South Metropolitan Gas Light and Coke Company occupied a site alongside the Grand Surrey Canal at Rotherhithe and required 20,000 to 25,000 tons of coal per year in the 1850s.[80] The company's coal had to be unloaded from colliers and lightered to its works on the canal. Minutes for the period 1850 to 1857 have little to say on coal, and its supply and delivery were left in the hands of a Mr Harrison, who is presumably a contractor. In March 1854, the board thought it 'expedient to charter a steamer' and approached Duncan Dunbar, an established shipowner but not one known to be involved in the east coast coal trade. An offer was made to charter one of his vessels at 7s.6d. per ton, the gas company undertaking to discharge it at 100 tons per day. Dunbar replied that he would have to build a suitable steamer, and to make it pay must discharge it at 300 tons per day. In July 1854, the General Iron Screw Collier Co. Ltd graciously made it known to the gas company that they were ready to receive tenders for their vessels on condition they loaded in two days and discharged in three after which £10 per day demurrage would be charged.[81] The South Metropolitan declined,

---

[79]   This is almost certainly the E.E. Allen who that year submitted a detailed paper to the Civil Engineers on screw collier design and economics. Allen, 'Comparative Cost of Transit', 318–73.

[80]   London Metropolitan Archives, SMet/III/4/1 and 4/2.

[81]   This rate of demurrage is considerably lower than the £35 per day which Scott Russell and his associates were quoting the Gas Light and Coke Company for *Caroline* in September 1853. The gas companies' minutes repeatedly suggest that the rate of

being unable to meet such 'stringent conditions'. It was not until 1880, after absorption of the rival Phoenix Gaslight and Coke Company, that the South Metropolitan began to build a new gasworks at East Greenwich with a riverside jetty that could be used by screw colliers.[82]

From the above details, it is apparent the newly developed screw collier was embraced by the London gas companies to varying degrees in the 1850s, so how important were they overall to the gas industry? The Imperial Gas Light and Coke Company quickly arranged for all its coal requirements to be delivered by steam, as did the smaller London Gas Light and Coke Company. The biggest company, the Gas Light and Coke, was more cautious and only met about 50 per cent of its coal requirements with steam, satisfying the rest with sailing vessels. The Equitable Gas Light Company made the mistake of going for the cheap option and hired a steamer which was unsuitable. Of other companies whose records survive, the Commercial Gas Light and Coke Company dithered and was still relying on sailing colliers up to 1857; the South Metropolitan Gas Company was constrained by the narrowness both of its directors' minds and of the canal entrance which gave access to its works and rejected colliers; and the Wandsworth and Putney Gas Company was too small and remote to contemplate using screw colliers.

For those companies that did turn towards steam, major incentives were avoiding a repeat of the disruptions of coal supplies experienced during the winters of the early 1850s and the need to counter the steep rises in coal and freight costs in the middle of this decade.

Conclusions from the above must be drawn with caution, as the minutes scanned are those which have survived: no minutes are extant for a significant minority of London gas companies.[83] From the available evidence, it is tentatively estimated that half the London gas industry's total requirements for coal came by screw collier by the late 1850s once those screw colliers requisitioned to serve as Crimean war transports had returned home. Thus, the screw collier quickly became an important instrument of the London gas industry, helping to assure regular coal deliveries and offering economies on transportation, which represented approximately half the cost of the industry's major raw material. However, it should be noted that the screw collier was not to be so important to the gas companies that they invested to any great extent

---

demurrage was a stumbling block and was holding back acceptance of screw colliers. Presumably Palmer has trimmed his demands for demurrage accordingly, especially to the conservative South Metropolitan Company.

[82]   Chesterton and Fenton, *Gas and Electricity Colliers*, 26.

[83]   Other London gas companies known to have been in existence in the 1850s are the Brentford Gas Company, the City of London Gas Light and Coke Company, the Great Central Gas Consumers Company, the Independent Gas Light and Coke Company, the Phoenix Gas Light and Coke Company, Ratcliffe Gas Company, Victoria Docks Gas Company and the Western Gas Light Company.

in them until 1902.[84] The particular problem which the screw collier presented, and limited its even greater acceptance, was that of loading and discharging it with sufficient despatch to meet the strict conditions of demurrage, particularly when much coal was lightered from the river to gas works by contractors not under the company's direct control. The solution was mechanical handling equipment, and it was installed quite rapidly. Evidence given in 1857 to a Parliamentary select committee on a proposed Coal Whippers' Act was that at least ten machines were then operating on the Thames, each capable of unloading 200 to 300 tons per day.[85] Indeed, even better discharge rates could be achieved; in Victoria Dock, which opened in 1855 and was equipped with hydraulic cranes, screw colliers carrying 700 to 800 tons were regularly unloaded in as little as 12 hours.[86]

How important was the screw collier to the coal industry? In the 1850s and 1860s, the screw collier was built more often to support the coal trade than to earn profits. The gas company minutes shed important light on this. In 1852 and 1853, the gas companies were very concerned about the failure of coal suppliers to meet their contracted deliveries, a problem caused or greatly compounded by the vulnerability of the sailing collier to weather conditions, and the inability to predict when deliveries would be made. The coal suppliers, including coal factors and coal owners, were penalised financially for any poor performance, the gas companies insisting the coal interests paid the difference in cost of buying coal on the open market to make up any shortfall in what they delivered. The screw collier offered much greater certainty of delivery, and – by owning their own screw colliers – the coal suppliers could win contracts to supply and deliver coal stretching over two to three years. There is some evidence that freight rates offered for screw colliers such as the *James Joicey*, which were part-owned by coal owners and coal factors, tended to be lower than those of independently owned vessels such as *Caroline*. Thus coal owners appeared to be willing to tolerate minimal or even negative profits on their steamers to ensure long-term coal sales. The screw collier was therefore an important tool of the coal industry.

V

Would the screw collier have been born in early 1850s, and rapidly multiplied, without the gas industry? Owners of screw colliers or their agents were offering the vessels to gas companies well before they were completed, and several screw colliers were built in response to definite contracts, for example at least

---

⁸⁴ The first gas company to own steam colliers was the Commercial Gas Company, in 1902. Chesterton and Fenton, *Gas and Electricity Colliers*, 14.

⁸⁵ Parliamentary Papers, Select Committee Report on Coal Whippers' Act, 1857, xii.

⁸⁶ Smith, *Sea-coal for London*, 290.

four of the six vessels used by the Imperial Gas Light and Coke Company. However, there is no evidence that the gas companies – whose minutes reveal their commercial temerity – were willing to adopt the screw collier until they had firm evidence of its efficiency. The pioneer builders such as Palmer and Scott Russell therefore had to finance and construct screw colliers such as the *John Bowes* and *Lady Berriedale* to prove the concept before the gas companies showed any interest. As a partner in the major coal supplier John Bowes and Partners, Palmer no doubt believed that a successful screw collier would appeal to the gas companies. Shipbuilder Scott Russell, meanwhile, was interested in finding a potentially lucrative technical solution to the problem of carrying bulk cargoes by steamer. Without the market provided by the gas industry in the 1850s, the development of the screw collier may well have been delayed, although it was entrepreneurs such as Palmer, Scott Russell and their backers who made the concept a reality.

By the close of 1855, a total of 60 screw colliers had been delivered, although a few had been lost and several had been diverted to other trades. Thus, screw colliers known to be in regular employment with gas companies accounted for about 25 per cent of those available, with perhaps another 10 per cent in irregular use, so no more than 30 per cent of the fleet was working for the gas companies. Analysis of voyages made during the 1850s estimated that screw colliers were working in the east coast coal trade for only 60 per cent of their time.[87] So, of the screw colliers actually employed on the coast at any one time, about half would be employed by the gas industry. This is a significant percentage, of course, but clearly the remaining screw collier capacity was employed elsewhere, bringing coal for other industries, for government establishments such as Woolwich Arsenal, local authorities, steamship bunkers, railway locomotives and for the large domestic market.[88]

From indications in the minutes quoted above, the gas companies referred to were taking around 350,000 tons of coal in the mid-1850s.[89] To this may to be added an estimated 100,000 for other gas companies. In 1855, about 3,500,000 tons of coal arrived on the Thames from the north-east.[90] Thus, the entire London gas industry consumed only around 13 per cent of the coal arriving in the capital from the Tyne, Wear and Tees.[91] Indeed, a single coal merchant, William Cory,

---

[87]   Analysis based on crew agreements for this period. TNA, company registration papers, class BT 98.

[88]   C. Capper, *The Port and Trade of London* (London, 1862).

[89]   Estimates are Gas Light and Coke Company 120,000; Imperial 100,000; Equitable 30,000; Commercial 50,000; SMGC 25,000; London 20,000.

[90]   Scott, *Epitome of the Progress of the Trade in Coal*.

[91]   The gas industry as a whole in the UK was using only about 6 per cent of total coal production, according to R. Pope, *Atlas of British Social and Economic History since c.1700* (London, 1989), 83. Pope's figures refer to 1869, but the percentage is likely to have been no larger in the 1850s.

claimed that in 1862 he was handling 1,000,000 tons of coal annually, implying that much of this came by steam collier.[92]

It is concluded that the London gas industry was a major user of screw colliers, and one whose use of such vessels was far out of proportion to its consumption of the total shipments of coal arriving in the city. The emergence of these vessels was stimulated and their growth considerably accelerated by the industry, but the screw collier was not totally dependent on gas companies. Without these, the screw collier would probably have been delayed and certainly built in smaller numbers, but it would still have been developed.

Further, albeit circumstantial, evidence for the London gas industries' importance comes from the situation on the west coast of the United Kingdom, discussed in a subsequent chapter. Here, despite there being a healthy trade in seaborne coal, there were no waterside gas works of comparable size, and no apparent demand for steamers to carry coal for at least 20 years.

---

[92] Parliamentary Papers, Report of the Select Committee on Thames Conservancy, 1863, Q.4687–954, 3102, 2127–31; Q.2959.

Chapter Three

Refining the steam bulk carrier

I

Many early steam colliers were operated by those in the coal industry, who accepted modest returns on their investment in order to support other aspects of their activity. This suggests that early steam colliers were not efficient enough to attract those who made a living purely from shipowning.[1] Hence, steamers did not immediately spread from coal into other bulk trades.

It is proposed that technology advanced sufficiently between 1850 and the 1880s to make buying and operating steam bulk carriers an economic proposition for those whose living came from shipowning. Further, these developments made it possible on the one hand to build bulk-carrying steamers which could operate profitably in trades where there were long distances between coaling ports, and on the other to compete with small sailing ships in coastal bulk trades, often involving small cargoes and smaller ports. This chapter examines these technological advances, looking first in general terms at the changes in industry and technology during the period, and then more specifically at improvements in the efficiency and proficiency of marine engineering and in shipbuilding.

II

The years after 1850 saw great changes in British industry, especially manufacturing. In 1850, the great majority of Britain's industrial workers were skilled craftsmen, while in 1914 mechanisation and factory organisation had led to the decline of craft skills.[2] In shipbuilding, the skills of shipwrights working in wood almost became extinct, but with the change to iron other skills grew

---

[1]   A case in point was the General Iron Screw Collier Co. Ltd, set up in 1852 as one of the first limited liability joint stock companies to own ships and discussed in more detail in a subsequent chapter. It was aimed at the coastal coal trade, but during its rather precarious existence turned a profit largely by deploying its colliers in more distant trades.

[2]   D.J. Starkey, 'Industrial Background to the Development of the Steamship', in B. Greenhill (ed.), *The Advent of Steam: The Merchant Steamship before 1900* (London, 1993), 129.

in importance, such as boiler making, plating and riveting. However, there was some dilution of the craft content of the shipbuilding labour force. For instance, each plater in a yard building iron ships required at least two unskilled helpers to assist in putting plates into position (including a 'holder-up'), and in the typically unmechanised yards of the period an army of labourers were employed in tasks such as carrying plates to the point where they were to be erected.[3]

Starkey notes that limitations of technique and supply which had afflicted early development of the steam ship were successfully addressed during the third quarter of the nineteenth century.[4] A notable example was the production of iron plates for shipbuilding and boiler making, the inconsistent quality and high price of which constrained the development of the iron steamship until the 1860s. Harley echoes Starkey's point: 'At any given time techniques in use appear to have been pushing against constraints provided by existing knowledge and skill'.[5] This is exemplified by the search for greater efficiency in marine boilers, where improvements were achieved through better design and manufacturing techniques and in the understanding of physics.

Harley attributes the improvements in marine engineering in the period to an interaction between developing knowledge in thermodynamics and metallurgy and increasing skills and sophistication in metal working.[6] For example, the work of Professor Macquorn Rankine[7] in the early 1850s gave a clearer understanding of the thermodynamics of the steam engine and how higher pressures would provide greater efficiency.[8] To put this into practice, however, there had to be advances in the techniques of manufacturing iron plates and fabricating them into boilers capable of withstanding high pressures.

---

[3] B. Newman, *Plate and Section Working Machinery in British Shipbuilding, 1850–1945* (Glasgow, 1993); B. Newman, *Materials Handling in British Shipbuilding, 1850–1945* (Glasgow, 1996).

[4] Starkey, 'Industrial Background', 133.

[5] C.K. Harley, 'Shipbuilding and Shipping in the Late 19th Century: A Study of Technological Change, Its Nature, Diffusion and Impact', PhD thesis, Harvard University, 1972, 220.

[6] Harley, 'Shipbuilding and Shipping in the Late 19th Century'. This is a particularly interesting source as the US author is concerned largely with British shipbuilding, which was leading the world in the adoption of metal hulls and steam machinery. He concentrates on the gains in efficiency of steamships brought about by increasing boiler pressures but pays less attention to factors which improved hull construction, such as developments in shipyard machinery and techniques. Harley also discusses gains in efficiency of steamships primarily on ocean routes in C.K. Harley, 'The Shift from Sailing Ships to Steamships, 1850–1890: A Study in Technological Change and Its Diffusion', in D.N. McCloskey, *Essays on a Mature Economy: Britain after 1840* (Princeton, NJ, 1971).

[7] Rankine was Regius Professor of Civil Engineering and Mechanics at the University of Glasgow from 1855 to 1872.

[8] Harley, 'Shipbuilding and Shipping in the Late 19th Century', 220.

The period from 1850 also saw progress in the 'professionalisation' of engineering. The inaugural meeting of the Institution of Engineers and Shipbuilders in Scotland was held in May 1857,[9] and John Scott Russell – a notable builder of steam colliers – was instrumental in founding the Institution of Naval Architects in London during 1860.[10] Local and national institutions like these were important for encouraging and spreading knowledge of technological developments, and inculcating methods of scientific thought amongst their membership which would result in improved design, materials and working techniques. They were not without opposition, however. Palmer cites a number of examples of practical shipbuilders being opposed to applying scientific principles, and notes that builders of merchant ships largely ignored the Institution of Naval Architects.[11]

Developments in engine and boiler technology were made steadily rather than in major leaps forward. They proceeded in parallel with improvements in design, materials and construction methods, and indeed were critically inter-related. For instance, higher boiler pressures needed not just stronger plates, but better methods of joining the plates together. In turn, higher boiler pressures required advances in engine design such as compounding in order to deliver their full benefit. This account will discuss each of the improvements more or less in chronological order, examining how they affected performance and when and if they were applied to the steam bulk carrier, and then summarise how, together, they came to increase its efficiency.

III

The most critical improvement was to boilers. There were three objectives: increasing operating pressure; improving thermal efficiency (transfer of heat from the combustion of fuel to the water); and improving safety by minimising the risk of boiler explosions (which went hand in hand with the first objective).

In a marine engine, steam is a medium for conveying the energy released from the combustion of fuel to a point where it can do useful work, that is, move a piston in a cylinder, which in turn rotates the shaft turning a paddle or propeller. Major energy losses are inherent in this process, including the heat lost in exhaust gases; the heat required to turn the boiler water into steam (latent

---

9   P. Gifford, in the introduction to Institution of Engineers and Shipbuilders in Scotland, *Mirror of History: A Millennium Commemorative Volume* (Glasgow, 2000), 11–14.

10   G.T. Emmerson, *John Scott Russell: A Great Victorian Engineer and Naval Architect* (London, 1977).

11   S. Palmer, 'Experience, Experiment and Economics: Factors in the Construction of Early Merchant Steamships', in K. Matthews and G. Panting (eds), *Ships and Shipbuilding in the North Atlantic Region* (St. John's, Newfoundland, 1978), 238.

heat of evaporation); and losses of heat by radiation and conduction through the walls of the furnace, the boiler cladding, the pipe work connecting boiler to cylinder, the cylinder walls; and losses in the condenser. These losses mean that the overall efficiency of the steam engine was lamentably low, and in the 1880s an anonymous technical author (probably on the staff of the 'Shipping World') claimed that only 5 per cent of the energy from burning coal could be translated into propulsive power.[12] Improvements in boiler and engine design could reduce the conduction and radiation losses, but not the loss of heat through the need to evaporate water.

Latent heat of evaporation is the energy required to turn liquid water at a given temperature into steam at the same temperature. On a molecular level, it involves putting in energy to break the bonds which hold the water molecules in a liquid form. When steam condenses to liquid water, the process is reversed, so that energy is given up by the steam. However, in a marine steam engine condensation is achieved by cooling the exhaust steam with sea water. The latent heat of evaporation is not regained in such a condensing process but is wasted in that it merely warms the surrounding sea.

For purposes of conveying energy, the useful property of steam (and, indeed, any gas) is that it is highly compressible. The more the steam is compressed, the greater the energy stored in it, and hence its expansive power. The more energy which can be stored in the steam, the smaller in proportion will be the loss of latent heat during its generation. Efforts to improve the efficiency of the steam engine therefore concentrated on increasing the pressure at which steam was generated and used.

The 'Shipping World' author gives a worked example, shown in Table 3.1.[13] His units of degrees are not ideal, as heat is conventionally expressed as calories or joules. His expression 'sensible heat' is presumed to mean the amount of heat available for raising the temperature of the steam and therefore theoretically available for turning into propulsive power. Despite increases in boiler pressure, the dead loss of energy resulting from the latent heat remained a factor limiting the efficiency of the steam engine throughout its long life.[14]

The first boilers which were installed in water craft, for instance in the *Charlotte Dundas* of 1801, were primitive. They were merely cylinders containing water placed on a brick base, which was arranged so that a series of passageways – the flues – conducted the gases under and around the boiler

---

[12]   L.E. Bertin and L.S. Robertson, *Marine Boilers: Their Construction and Maintenance* (London, 1898).

[13]   Bertin and Robertson, *Marine Boilers*.

[14]   Bertin and Robertson, *Marine Boilers*. The author considered the theoretical maximum pressure for a boiler to be 350 p.s.i., at which pressure the temperature of steam would be 430°, close to that at which boiler iron would melt. This pressure figure was later greatly increased (especially in water tube boilers) because the steel which was slowly becoming available in 1880s could withstand much higher temperatures.

Table 3.1 Effect of increasing boiler pressure in reducing heat losses

Boiler pressure	Latent heat	Sensible heat	Proportion sensible heat/total heat
60 p.s.i.	900°	307°	25%
300 p.s.i.	820°	420°	33%

shell before entering the chimney.[15] Mere 'kettles', Griffiths calls these boilers. Boiler manufacturers developed a variety of designs, but what was regarded as best practice in the 1830s had a system of flues which were rectangular in cross section and which conducted hot gases from furnace to funnel along a pathway designed to ensure the maximum heating surface.[16] The flues were usually large enough for a person to crawl through in order to clean them and effect minor repairs. The boiler was of a box shape, which made it relatively easy to fit stays between the sides to withstand the higher steam pressure. The boilers of the 1838 *Great Western*, regarded by Griffiths as the best of their type, had a working pressure of just 5 lb per square inch (p.s.i.).

During the 1840s, boiler makers began to move from flues to fire tubes, these being narrower than flues, much more numerous and usually circular in cross section. Fire tubes improved the efficiency of heat transfer by increasing the area of contact between the hot gases and water.[17] In addition, the tubes gave the boiler greater longitudinal strength, supplementing the stays. Tubular boilers were more compact, and so took up less space in the ship's hull.

The standard tubular boiler of the 1840s and 1850s had a bank of tubes which conducted the hot gases from a combustion chamber at the back of the furnace through the water space to a smokebox placed above the fire door on the front of the boiler.[18] This was referred to as a return-tube type of boiler, because the gases were returned from the back of the boiler to the front.

A drawing reputed to be of the early collier *Lady Berriedale* of 1852 shows her to be fitted with a box-type, return-tube boiler, typical of practice at the time.[19]

---

[15]   D. Griffiths, *Steam at Sea: Two Centuries of Steam-powered Ships* (London, 1997), 58.

[16]   Griffiths, *Steam at Sea*, 58–9. This type of boiler was installed in Brunel's first ship and the one which was commercially successful, the *Great Western*.

[17]   Fire tubes could be too efficient. Bertin and Robertson, *Marine Boilers* describes boilers in which the number and diameter of fire tubes was such that the temperature of the exhaust emerging from the funnel was too low to provide a good draught for the fire. Eventually, this problem was overcome by the use of forced rather than natural draught, but in coastal vessels this was not adopted until the 1920s.

[18]   Griffiths, *Steam at Sea*, 63.

[19]   The drawing from S.J. Russell, *The Modern System of Naval Architecture* (London, 1865) is reproduced in J.A. Macrae and C.V. Waine, *The Steam Collier Fleets* (Albrighton,

This boiler, and those of two other screw colliers completed on the Thames in 1852, *Eagle* and *Caroline*, had a working pressure of just 12 p.s.i., according to notes made by their builder, John Scott Russell.[20] The 1856-built collier *Florence Nightingale* still had a boiler working at 12 p.s.i., even though considerably higher pressures were being used in boilers being installed in other ships built by Scott Russell. For instance, his paddle steamer *Dieppe* of 1854 had a working boiler pressure of 20 p.s.i., the *El Ray James II* (probably also of 1854) worked its boilers at 22 p.s.i. The *Great Eastern* was built at Scott Russell's yard, and Brunel accepted Scott Russell's design for the ship's paddle engines. Agreed in 1854, this was designed for a working pressure of 25 p.s.i.[21]

Early colliers were clearly not fitted with the most technically advanced boilers. However, boilers needed periodic replacement, as at this time they seldom lasted more than five years, and this need for renewal meant shipowners could retro-fit their vessels with new and improved boilers, confident of an improvement in efficiency. The boiler was therefore often more up to date than the engine and hull.

Of particular relevance to the development of the steam collier and coaster was the introduction of the cylindrical Scotch boiler by James Howden, which dates from about 1862.[22] These incorporated a furnace in which coal was burnt on a grate consisting of a number of fire bars. Below this was a pit in which the ash collected. At the opposite end from the door by which the furnace was stoked was a combustion chamber, partially separated from the furnace by a firebrick arch. This chamber turned the combustion gases through 180 degrees back into a large number of fire tubes which were surrounded by the boiler water. As this part of the boiler was above the combustion chamber, the water was heated not only by conduction from the gases passing through the fire tubes, but also by direct convection and radiation from the fire. After passing through the fire tubes, the gases were collected in a flue which exhausted them through the ship's funnel. The cylindrical drum of a Scotch boiler gave the necessary strength to

---

1990), 14. The dimensions given are close to those of the *Lady Berriedale*, built by Scott Russell in 1852, and Macrae and Waine believe it to depict her. However, it is reasonable to question whether the drawing shows *Lady Berriedale* as built. Scott Russell's book was published over ten years after the completion of the collier, and the drawing – in which the ship is not named – may represent an idealised collier, incorporating improvements made over the decade since *Lady Berriedale* had been built. Scott Russell's notebooks give many details of the dimensions of the boilers fitted to his colliers, but it is not possible to deduce their type from these details.

[20]   Scott Russell's notebooks are held in the Science Museum Library, London. This data is from notebook 2, Science Museum MS 516/2.

[21]   D. Griffiths, A. Lambert and F. Walker, *Brunel's Ships* (London, 1999), 148.

[22]   C.V. Waine and R.S. Fenton, *Steam Coasters and Short Sea Traders*, 3rd ed. (Albrighton, 1994), 38–9; D. Griffiths, 'Triple Expansion and the First Shipping Revolution', in Greenhill, *Advent of Steam*, 106–26.

withstand higher pressures, while the tube plates at each end of the boiler were supported by some of the fire tubes themselves, which acted as stays.

A typical Scotch boiler had a heating surface of 925 square feet, compared with the 1,125 square feet of the boilers fitted to *Lady Berriedale*, *Eagle* and *Caroline*.[23] A considerably greater pressure was achieved with a reduction in heating surface. The more compact boiler also represented a significant saving in space, increasing cargo capacity.

The development of higher boiler pressures in Great Britain was held back by the 1854 Merchant Shipping Act, which made steamships liable to inspection by the Board of Trade.[24] The inspectors erred on the side of caution, demanding that boilers were hydraulically tested to twice their working pressure, and regarded 25 p.s.i. as the safe maximum working pressure for use at sea, a figure which was well exceeded by steam engines on land. This was recognised by Alfred Holt, who, although coming from a merchant and shipowning background, had served an apprenticeship in locomotive engineering, probably the cutting edge of mechanical engineering at the time. When he entered shipowning Holt began to experiment with a compound engine using steam at 60 p.s.i., which was installed in his *Cleator* in 1864.[25] The boiler appears to be closely related to the Scotch boiler.[26] A development of the *Cleator*'s boiler, also working at 60 p.s.i., was used in Holt's trio of steamers (although fitted with sails), built by Scott of Greenock. Beginning with *Agamemnon*, which entered service in 1865, these ships inaugurated the Ocean Steamship Company, better although unofficially known as the Blue Funnel Line.[27] Alfred Holt's engine reduced coal consumption to 2.2 lb per indicated horsepower per hour (lb/horsepower/hour): half that of Brunel's *Great Britain* of 20 years earlier.[28]

One of the limiting factors in the ability of a Scotch boiler to withstand high pressures was the strength of its furnace. There was little scope for fitting stays, as was done in the water space, because the rivets would be weakened by the heat. The solution was the corrugated furnace, patented by Samson Fox in 1877, and quickly adopted, so that by the 1880s most boilers were built to Fox's patent or similar designs.[29] As with corrugated iron plates, the folds gave additional longitudinal strength.

---

[23] Scott Russell's notebook 4, Science Museum MS 516/4.

[24] A. Jarvis, 'Alfred Holt and the Compound Engine', in Greenhill, *Advent of Steam*, 158.

[25] Jarvis, 'Alfred Holt and the Compound Engine', 157.

[26] Jarvis, 'Alfred Holt and the Compound Engine', 158 includes a drawing of a 'later Holt-type boiler', which is described as being like two *Cleator* boilers back-to-back. They appear identical to Scotch boilers.

[27] Anon., *Two Hundred and Fifty Years of Shipbuilding by the Scotts at Greenock* (Glasgow, 1961), 43. *Agamemnon*, *Ajax* and *Achilles* had gross tonnages of 2,347 tons.

[28] E.C.B. Corlett, 'The Screw Propeller and Merchant Shipping, 1840–1865', in Greenhill, *Advent of Steam*, 99.

[29] Griffiths, *Steam at Sea*, 69.

Table 3.2 Boiler pressures of typical British east coast colliers in the late 1870s

Name	Built/reboilered	Boiler pressure
Berrington	1865/1876	75 p.s.i.
Biddick	1864/1878	65 p.s.i.
Blue Cross	1869/1877	70 p.s.i.
Contest	1880	75 p.s.i.
Erasmus Wilson	1876	70 p.s.i.
Fenella	1870/1878	77 p.s.i.
Gracie	1879	80 p.s.i.
Laffitte	1877	70 p.s.i.
Nerissa	1877	80 p.s.i.
Shoreham	1872/1879	80 p.s.i.

Source: *Lloyd's Register*, 1880–1.

Table 3.3 Boiler pressures of typical steam coasters in the late 1870s

Name	Built/re-boilered	Boiler pressure
Agate	1878	70 p.s.i.
Amethyst	1870/1880	60 p.s.i.
Ardclinis	1870/1880	70 p.s.i.
Captain McClure	1876	65 p.s.i.
Eglinton	1877	70 p.s.i.
Elagh Castle	1879	70 p.s.i.
Emerald	1879	70 p.s.i.
Galgorm Castle	1879	70 p.s.i.
Saxon	1879	70 p.s.i.
Tolfaen	1877	70 p.s.i.

Source: *Lloyd's Register*, 1880–1.

2: Built at Belfast in 1879, the typical small steam coaster *Galgorm Castle* would have been considerably rebuilt during her 47 years of life in the coastal trade, during which she had been salved and rebuilt after sinking in the Menai Straits in 1891. Seen towards the end of her life when owned in Birkenhead, the closed wheelhouse belies her age. *Ships in Focus*

By 1875, a pressure of 75 p.s.i. was considered the safe maximum for a marine boiler.[30] But pressures continued to rise, and Stephenson Clarke's collier *Gracie*, completed in 1879, had a boiler pressure of 80 p.s.i.[31] The description published in a contemporary technical journal suggests this pressure was unusually high. In the mid-1870s, *Lloyd's Register* began publishing boiler pressures as part of the technical information given for each ship it listed. Table 3.2 lists the pressures for ten randomly selected colliers, either built or re-boilered in the late 1870s, and shows that by then pressures of 70 p.s.i. to 80 p.s.i. were usual. Table 3.3 repeats the exercise for bulk-carrying coasters, in which boiler pressures were slightly lower, in the range 60 p.s.i. to 70 p.s.i. Colliers and their steam coaster relatives of this era were therefore keeping up with contemporary marine engineering practice in terms of high boiler pressures.

Attempts to dramatically increase boiler pressure saw water tube boilers being designed in which the hot combustion gases passed around tubes containing

[30] D. Griffiths, 'Marine Engineering Development in the Nineteenth Century', in Greenhill, *Advent of Steam*, 171.

[31] *Marine Engineer* (June/July 1883), quoted in Macrae and Waine, *Steam Collier Fleets*, 51.

water – the reverse of the traditional, fire tube boiler. Such boilers working at pressures as high as 150 p.s.i. were tried in 1874, albeit unsuccessfully, to provide steam for the pioneering triple-expansion engines in the *Propontis*.[32] Leakage and corrosion of tubes ensured that such boilers remained experimental, and it was many years before water tube boilers became a viable proposition for merchant ships,[33] and none is known to have been fitted in colliers or other steam bulk carriers built until the 1950s.

Conventional fire tube boilers working at 120 p.s.i. were successfully used in the 1874-built *Sexta*. An anonymous 'Shipping World' author, writing in the late 1880s, discusses double-ended, cylindrical, tubular boilers – Scotch boilers with furnaces at both ends – working at 150 p.s.i. as if they were normal contemporary practice.[34]

Increases in boiler pressures also required improvements in methods of constructing boilers. The introduction of hydraulic riveting made boilers stronger and presumably quicker to build. The major constructional change was the introduction of steel, which became more readily available and cheaper with developments in the open-hearth furnace method of smelting iron in the 1870s. It is claimed that by the mid-1880s most boilers were constructed of steel.[35] Steel was stronger, weight for weight, than iron, and withstood higher steam temperatures, which in turn permitted higher working pressures.

By the late 1880s, the development of boiler design for small merchant ships was almost complete. A steel Scotch boiler with corrugated furnaces and working at a pressure of 150 p.s.i. was now (and remained) the usual equipment of the steam collier or coaster.[36] With some improvements in detail, and further modest increases in working pressure, the Scotch boiler proved remarkably long-lived, and saw out the life of the steam coaster and collier. Thus, in the three decades from the introduction of screw colliers, their boiler pressures had risen from 12 p.s.i. to 150 p.s.i.[37] The last steam colliers built for the east coast coal trade in the 1950s had boilers working at 220 p.s.i.[38]

Boiler development was characterised not just by increases in pressure and consequent greater economy. The improved boilers also represented 'a very large diminution of weight and space required for a given pressure'.[39] The decreasing size of boilers improved carrying capacity and reduced weight. Installing a smaller boiler meant that with no increase in hull size more space could be

---

[32] Griffiths, 'Triple Expansion and the First Shipping Revolution', 107.

[33] Griffiths, *Steam at Sea*, 70.

[34] Bertin and Robertson, *Marine Boilers*. This view is endorsed by Griffiths, *Steam at Sea*, 70.

[35] Harley, 'Shipbuilding and Shipping in the Late 19th Century', chap. 7.

[36] Griffiths, *Steam at Sea*, 70.

[37] Bertin and Robertson, *Marine Boilers*.

[38] Waine and Fenton, *Steam Coasters*, 120.

[39] Bertin and Robertson, *Marine Boilers*.

devoted to a paying cargo. It also meant that a given quantity of cargo could be carried in a smaller and perhaps shallower hull – which was less expensive to build and maintain – and could use a wider range of smaller ports, harbours and waterways – a very important consideration in the coasting trade.

IV

As with boilers, improvements in the efficiency of engines came through a number of developments in the design of machinery and ancillary equipment and was made at a steady rather than a spectacular pace.

The earliest marine engines drove paddle wheels and were designed to turn at a relatively slow speed to suit the rotation of the paddle wheel. For efficiency, the screw had to be driven at a higher speed, at least 60 r.p.m. compared with 20 r.p.m. for a paddle steamer.[40] Various methods of achieving an increase in shaft speed were tried, including gearing on the *Archimedes* of 1840 and chain drive on Brunel's *Great Britain*, completed in 1843.[41] Gearing was simpler to construct, and was technically successful, but introduced the extra expense of gears (which were difficult to cut and wore out alarmingly quickly), which were also noisy (Brunel's reason for specifying chain drive) and reduced efficiency through frictional losses.[42] Direct-drive engines were therefore desirable.

At the time of the earliest screw steamers in the 1840s, the typical machinery was an oscillating engine which had the piston rod attached directly to the crankshaft, with the cylinders oscillating from side to side. This obviated the need for complex valve gear, for the admission and exhaust ports were covered and uncovered as the cylinders oscillated. However, the increase in rotational speed required to directly drive a screw meant that the vibration associated with oscillating cylinders became unacceptable.

Several different designs of engines were tried, including beam engines, which had a massive beam mounted above the vertical cylinder from which the drive was taken to a gear wheel connected to the screw shaft.[43] Horizontal screw engines, with the cylinders placed across the ship, were built for the *Great Eastern* in 1854 and some warships,[44] but were only feasible in ships of considerable breadth. None of these was a mainstream development, however, and it was the inverted direct-acting engine which became almost universally employed in coastal and indeed most other cargo-carrying screw steamers.

The inverted engine may have been produced as early as 1846 by Caird and Company of Greenock for the coastal steamer *Northman*, but details

---

[40] Waine and Fenton, *Steam Coasters*, 34.

[41] Griffiths, *Steam at Sea*, 34.

[42] Griffiths, *Steam at Sea*, 37.

[43] Griffiths, *Steam at Sea*, 36.

[44] Griffiths, *Steam at Sea*, 37–8.

are sparse,[45] and this engine was not produced in quantity until the 1850s. 'Inverted' referred to the placing of the cylinders above rather than below the crankshaft, as had been the norm in paddle steamer engines. The cylinders (usually two) were attached vertically and in line astern on a heavy casting known as the bedplate which also supported the bearings for the crankshaft. Piston rods from each cylinder passed through the lower cylinder cover and were attached to a crosshead, from which a connecting rod transmitted the power to turn the crankshaft. Unlike the oscillating engine, some form of valve gear was necessary, this usually being placed between the two cylinders. The advantages of the inverted (or, as it was sometimes known, vertical) engine were compactness plus a simple, robust design that was relatively easy to build, maintain and to develop. Indeed, the basic layout of this engine was largely maintained throughout the long lifetime of the bulk cargo-carrying steamship.

The early screw colliers did not have the most technically advanced machinery. They arrived before the inverted engine had become established, and early examples were fitted with a variety of machinery types. *John Bowes* was built with a two-cylinder engine driving a single shaft; this arrangement lasting until 1864 when this pioneering collier was fitted with an inverted engine.[46] *Haggerston* is described as having a two-cylinder direct-acting engine, but no further details are known.[47] *Lady Berriedale*, the third successful screw collier, completed in 1852, had a two-cylinder oscillating engine,[48] and the later products of Scott Russell's yard – *Eagle, Caroline, Falcon* and *Hawk* – probably had similar machinery. Details of engine types for other colliers from the 1850s are unknown, as such information was not routinely recorded in registration documents until the 1860s, and even later in *Lloyd's Register*.[49] Details found

---

45   Griffiths, *Steam at Sea*, 39. Thomson on the Clyde is credited with popularising this type of engine.

46   Macrae and Waine, *Steam Collier Fleets*, 13. No source is given for this data, and the surviving author (Waine) is not aware of its origin.

47   Macrae and Waine, *Steam Collier Fleets*, 14, quoting from a government report on the state of the merchant marine.

48   A drawing of a 'water ballast steamer', reproduced as Plate 4 in E.E. Allen, 'On the Comparative Cost of Transit by Steam and Sailing Colliers, and on the Different Methods of Ballasting', *Proceedings of the Institute of Civil Engineers* 14 (1854–5), following page 348, is thought by Waine to illustrate *Lady Berriedale*, and clearly shows her oscillating engine. The notebooks of Scott Russell, builder of the *Lady Berriedale*, are rich in costs, dimensions and other details of his ships, but give no clue to the engine design.

49   Very few if any early colliers were classed by Lloyd's Register of Shipping, whose surveyors were initially very distrusting of iron ships. This meant that the ship's engine details only appeared in the Society's *Register Book* from the 1880s, when competition from Bureau Veritas encouraged Lloyd's Register of Shipping to list in their *Register Book* all ships over a certain modest tonnage, whether classed by them or not. Even then, for non-classed ships, engine details can be sparse, Lloyd's Register of Shipping not having detailed records of these ships.

for the colliers built in the 1860s invariably show they had two-cylinder inverted engines.[50]

Most marine steam engines were fitted with a condenser to turn the steam exhausted from the cylinders back to water. The condenser improved efficiency, as the lower the final temperature of the exhaust steam, the more energy is extracted from it as power for the engine. With early condensers a jet of sea water was played on the steam while a pump created a modest vacuum in the condenser. The condensed water was collected in a hot well and returned to the boiler. As this process was repeated, salt from the sea water accumulated in the boiler, its build-up on the plates reducing the transmission of heat to the boiler water. It became the practice to periodically 'blow down' the boiler, opening a valve in the bottom to run off the saline solution, but this was wasteful of heat.[51] The salt in the boiler water also contributed to corrosion, with hydrochloric acid forming at temperatures achieved with a boiler working at a pressure as low as 15 p.s.i.[52] Corrosion was intensified by the breakdown of the fatty acids used in contemporary lubricants. The life of a boiler working with a jet condenser was therefore only four or five years. The problems of corrosion and the need to blow down the boiler periodically militated against adoption of high boiler pressures.

The surface condenser patented by Samuel Hall in 1834 offered a solution to these problems, although it was many years before materials and construction methods improved sufficiently for the design to be universally adopted.[53] The surface condenser allowed the boiler water and the sea water which cooled it to be kept rigorously apart, the latter being pumped through a nest of brass tubes while steam was admitted to space around the tubes and condensed on their cold surfaces.[54] Thus, boilers could use entirely fresh water, with only a small quantity needing to be carried to offset losses due to steam leaks or to the safety valves blowing off. Contamination with lubricating oil and its breakdown products still occurred, and indeed the problem actually increased: with the boiler water no longer needing to be blown off and topped up, meaning that the contaminants built up. Early enthusiasm for surface condensers soon evaporated, and they had fallen out of use by the time the first steam colliers were built. It was not until the 1860s and 1870s that the problems with surface condensers were overcome, by filtering the water to remove oil before returning it to the boiler, by use of lubricants that did not breakdown so readily, and by the availability of chemicals to treat boiler water. Hence, it was not until 30 years after Hall patented his surface condenser that his invention began to deliver the benefits it promised.

---

[50]   The National Archives, Kew (TNA), registration documents, classes BT 108, BT 110 and CUST 130. Macrae and Waine, *Steam Collier Fleets*, 18, 20 include drawings of colliers from the 1860s, which clearly show this type of engine.

[51]   Waine and Fenton, *Steam Coasters*, 35.

[52]   Harley, 'Shipbuilding and Shipping in the Late 19th Century', 224.

[53]   Griffiths, *Steam at Sea*, 13.

[54]   Waine and Fenton, *Steam Coasters*, 35–6.

V

One of the reasons for the longevity of the inverted engine design was its suitability for adaptation to compounding.[55] Indeed, some engines were physically adapted to compound working, as registration documents and register books refer to the engines of certain early colliers being 'compounded', rather than the vessels being re-engined. The compound engine used the expansive power of steam in two stages, to move first the piston in the high- and then in the low-pressure cylinder. Patented in 1853 by the engineers Charles Randolph and John Elder,[56] compounding was first used in the steam coaster *Brandon*, in 1854.[57]

Compounding was a necessary step in employing higher steam pressures. A high degree of expansion was theoretically possible in a single-cylinder simple engine, but in practice the heat losses were severe.[58] Maximising the efficiency of a steam engine required the difference between the temperatures of steam generated in the boiler and of the condenser to be as great as possible.[59] However, large temperature differences led to equally large losses of heat when the steam entered the cylinder. The compound engine reduced these losses by expanding the steam in stages. Steam from the boiler first entered the high-pressure cylinder and expanded to a certain pressure and temperature, pushing out the piston. Valves then admitted this steam without significant change of pressure or temperature to the second, low-pressure (and larger) cylinder where it expanded further until it reached the temperature of the condenser. The individual cylinders in a compound engine worked at a narrower range of temperatures and pressures than the single cylinder in a simple engine using steam at the same pressure, thereby reducing heat losses.

In the *Brandon* boiler pressure was around 30 p.s.i., and coal consumption about 3¼ lb/horsepower/hour, compared with 4 to 4½ lb/horsepower/hour in her most economical predecessor. Compounding achieved a reduction in fuel consumption of some 30 per cent to 40 per cent,[60] with an approximately 20 per cent increase in first cost of the engine.[61] It has been suggested that the wider introduction of compounding was encouraged by the 'coal famine' of the 1870s, which saw the price of Welsh steam coal double between 1871 and 1873.[62] However, this famine was a temporary phenomenon, and by 1876 the price of coal had fallen to its 1871 level and then continued to drop. Introduction of compounding was one of the major factors which allowed working pressures to increase steadily, from

---

[55] Griffiths, *Steam at Sea*, 40.

[56] Starkey, 'Industrial Background', 133.

[57] R. Craig, *The Ship: Steam Tramps and Cargo Liners, 1850–1950* (London, 1980), 11.

[58] Corlett, 'The Screw Propeller', 98.

[59] J.K. Roberts, *Heat and Thermodynamics*, cited by Harley, 'Shipbuilding and Shipping in the Late 19th Century'.

[60] Craig, *The Ship*, 11.

[61] Harley, 'Shipbuilding and Shipping in the Late 19th Century', 229.

[62] Harley, 'Shipbuilding and Shipping in the Late 19th Century', chap. 7.

an initial 30 p.s.i. to 40 p.s.i. in the 1860s after the general adoption of the surface condenser, to 60 p.s.i. by 1866 and 70 p.s.i. by the mid-1870s.[63]

The first record found of a compound engine being fitted in a newly built steam collier is in 1870, when several were completed with this type of machinery,[64] and thereafter most new buildings had compound engines. The same year conversions and replacements of older machinery began. The first record found is of the *Upton*'s simple inverted engines, which were no more than five years old, being altered (or replaced, it is not clear which) in 1870.[65] By early in the 1880s, almost all of the older colliers had received compound engines. One of the last was the pioneering *John Bowes*, the compound engines fitted in 1883 being her third and final set of machinery.[66]

With further increases in boiler pressure, the logical development was to move from the two-stage expansion of the compound engine to the triple-expansion engine, which had high-, intermediate- and low-pressure cylinders. Again, the design of the inverted engine proved very adaptable, being simply a matter of adding a third cylinder in line with the others. The first triple-expansion engine was designed as a matter of necessity to make best use of steam at the then high pressure of 150 p.s.i., specified by the owner of the steamer *Propontis* being built by Elders on the Clyde in 1874.[67] Although the water-tube boilers in *Propontis* proved disastrous, Elder's engine designer, A.C. Kirk, realised that similar high pressures could be developed in the much more reliable Scotch boilers. He persuaded other shipowners of the economies of triple expansion (when working, *Propontis* gave coal consumption figures of 1.3 lb/horsepower/hour), and the first successful application was in the *Aberdeen* of 1881. As with superheating, the economies produced by triple-expansion engines were not immediately realised in the coastal trade, this type of machinery not being generally adopted for ocean-going bulk carriers until the 1890s, and never succeeding in replacing the compact two-cylinder compound in smaller coastal steamers.[68] The logical progression, the quadruple-expansion engine, was developed by another Clyde engineer, Walter Brock of Denny Brothers, but was only worthwhile for relatively large vessels, and few examples have been found amongst steam bulk carriers.

Superheating or steam drying, to raise its temperature well above the boiling point of water, has the potential to improve efficiency in the same way as increasing boiler pressure. Superheated steam has greater expansive power and a lesser tendency to condense to water in the cylinders. Apparatus for steam drying had been devised as early as 1827, but superheating was not generally applied

---

63   Craig, *The Ship*, 11.

64   An early example was Doxford's *Amy*. TNA, London customs registers, CUST 130.

65   Data from contemporary *Lloyd's Registers*.

66   Data from contemporary *Lloyd's Registers*.

67   Griffiths, 'Triple Expansion and the First Shipping Revolution'; Griffiths, *Steam at Sea*, 8.

68   Waine and Fenton, *Steam Coasters and Short Sea Traders*, 35.

until the 1860s.[69] A saving of about 20 per cent could be obtained by raising the temperature of steam at 20 p.s.i. by 100°F.[70] However, when boiler pressures reached about 60 p.s.i., problems were encountered, as the high steam temperatures of around 400°F decomposed the animal and vegetable fat lubricants then available. Without effective lubrication, wear of cylinders, pistons and valves became excessive, and were not compensated for by fuel savings. Experiments with superheating were abandoned until about 1900 when better mineral-oil based lubricants had been developed. Even then, only the engines of large vessels were fitted; superheating did not spread to steam coasters until the 1920s.

VI

Throughout the period under review improvements in engine efficiency were achieved through developments in technology and metal working skills. Closer tolerances gave tighter joints, and with better cylinder packing steam losses were reduced.[71] Improved bearings, superior lubricants, better balancing of moving parts – all reduced frictional losses. Developments in materials technology and methods of construction, and better understanding of stresses allowed weight to be reduced, especially that of moving parts. An example was the lengthening of the rod which connected piston and crankshaft, encouraged by the availability of better and cheaper iron.[72] Lengthening this rod meant the piston could be positioned further from the crankshaft. This in turn allowed a longer piston stroke, so that the cylinder could be longer and narrower and yet give the same swept volume – such cylinders being cheaper to fabricate.

Two independent assessments are in broad agreement that spectacular improvements in efficiency were achieved over the three decades following the introduction of the first steam bulk carriers in 1852. The anonymous 'Shipping World' author reckoned that Scotch boilers of 150 p.s.i. typical of the 1880s gave a fourfold reduction in coal consumption compared with boilers from the 1850s, from 6 lb/horsepower/hour to 1.5 lb/horsepower/hour.[73] Harley, in an assessment as part of his study of changes in shipbuilding technology, estimates the improvements from 1855 to 1890 as 5 lb/horsepower/hour to 1.7 lb/horsepower/ hour, a threefold gain in efficiency (see Graph 1).[74]

---

[69]   Griffiths, *Steam at Sea*, 63–4.

[70]   Griffiths, *Steam at Sea*, 63–4.

[71]   Harley, 'Shipbuilding and Shipping in the Late 19th Century', 223.

[72]   A.E. Seaton, 'Progress in Marine Engineering in the Mercantile Marine', *Transactions of the Institute of Naval Architects*, 33 (1892), 74–80.

[73]   Bertin and Robertson, *Marine Boilers*.

[74]   Harley, 'Shipbuilding and Shipping in the Late 19th Century', 218 (Fig. 7.1). The graph is based on Harley's reading of papers by F.J. Bramwell, W.P. Marshall and A. Blechynden in *Proceedings of the Institution of Mechanical Engineer*.

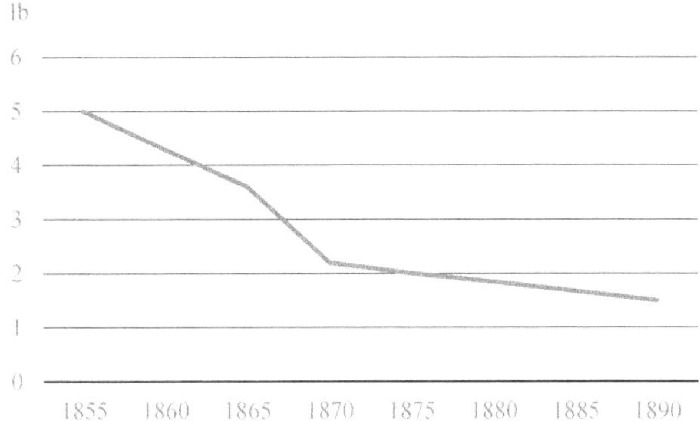

Graph 1: Coal consumption of marine steam engines per indicated horsepower per hour, 1855–1890

Although the 'Shipping World' author cites boiler improvement as the reason for the gains, it is impossible to separate the economies achieved through higher pressure boilers and those gained through building more efficient engines. The two were complementary, and the three- to four-fold measures of improved fuel efficiency were an achievement of both boiler and engine designers. Less well documented than gains in economy, but also relevant to a shipowner, improvements in engine and boiler design and construction improved reliability, increasing the time a ship was working for its living.

VII

Developments from 1850 in the materials, skills and technology used in the construction of hulls in iron and later steel helped deliver a more efficient, economical and reliable ship to the owner. Use of iron in shipbuilding grew fast, eclipsing wood in terms of the tonnage launched from British yards around 1863.[75] By 1871, 90 British yards building in iron were employing almost 50,000 men.[76]

Production of iron grew massively during the middle years of the nineteenth century, from 1.24 million tons in 1839 to 6.4 million tons in 1875.[77] Contributing factors included the increase in sizes of furnaces and new methods of iron production, such as the introduction of the regenerative hot blast furnace in 1860.

---

[75]   Starkey, 'Industrial Background', 134; Pope gives the date as 1862. R. Pope, *Atlas of British Social and Economic History since c.1700* (London, 1989), 49.

[76]   Pope, *Atlas*, 51.

[77]   Pope, *Atlas* 46.

Importantly for the shipbuilder, quality improved through better process control, and the cost of iron fell. Harley quotes prices for iron taken from trade journals of the period, and from the records of Clyde shipbuilders Denny Brothers of Dumbarton and Alexander Stephen of Linthouse, and finds an overall fall from £10 per ton in 1855 to a low of £5 per ton in 1886 (about the time steel generally replaced iron), after which there was a short-lived rise (his series ends in 1890).[78] Allowing for other factors (the other major input determining price was shipbuilding wages, which rose by about 50 per cent overall during this period), Harley considers the decline in iron prices to have reduced shipbuilding costs by about 20 per cent.

Steel became a major competitor to iron in the 1860s with the development of the Bessemer converter and the open hearth furnace,[79] but it was some years before it could compete on price with iron for shipbuilding. The replacement of iron by steel for hull and boiler building then occurred over a relatively short period, at least by comparison with the speed other improvements such as mechanisation were adopted by the shipbuilding industry. For example, Denny of Dumbarton began building in steel in 1878 and by 1883 had completely abandoned iron. In the industry as a whole, over 90 per cent of ships were still built of iron in 1881 but growth in steel shipbuilding was then so strong that it overtook iron in 1884–5.[80] There are suggestions that the change was not geographically even: yards on the Clyde adopting steel earlier than their rivals on the Tyne and Wear because there were steel plate manufacturers in the west of Scotland but not in the north-east of England.[81]

Steel was stronger, weight for weight, than iron, and its adoption meant that 15 per cent less metal was required in the average hull.[82] This did not immediately give a proportionate cost reduction, as steel began to be adopted as soon as its price per ton dropped to within 15 per cent of iron, but as steel prices continued to fall economies were achieved. The move to constructing hulls from steel became an important factor in achieving economies in steamers during the latter part of the nineteenth century.

VIII

Iron shipbuilding was highly labour intensive, and there was considerable scope for improving its efficiency through mechanisation. The three areas where such efficiencies could be realised were in moving plates and frames about the yard

---

[78]   Harley, 'Shipbuilding and Shipping in the Late 19th Century', 89 (fig. 5.2).

[79]   Pope, *Atlas*, 46–7.

[80]   Harley, 'Shipbuilding and Shipping in the Late 19th Century', chap. 2.

[81]   *Engineering* (1 September 1882), cited by S. Pollard and P. Robertson, *The British Shipbuilding Industry, 1870–1914* (Cambridge, MA, 1979), 259.

[82]   Harley, 'Shipbuilding and Shipping in the Late 19th Century', chap. 2.

and into position on the growing hull, in cutting and forming the ironwork and especially the hull plates, and in riveting the iron work. There is, however, little evidence that major economies were actually achieved, certainly in the period from 1850 to 1880.

Newman looked at materials handling in shipyards from 1850 and concluded that there was no dramatic progress in shipyard handling of materials to 1900.[83] Much of the work remained manual, with horses being used to move the heavier materials around the yard[84] and pole derricks of limited capacity being used to hoist iron work for hull construction.

Newman cites two reasons for the reluctance of shipbuilders to invest in handling machinery, one physical and the other financial. Shipyards needed to extend their berths as the size of ships increased, and in many areas such as in Glasgow and along the Tyne and Wear there was simply no room to expand the boundaries of the yard. Hence, there was often limited space between berths in which to add craneage. Vertical pole derricks of limited lifting capacity, and often hand-powered, were the only pieces of machinery which could be added without taking space from adjacent berths. The second and probably more significant factor was the shipbuilders' strong awareness of the extreme cyclical nature of the industry. They were reluctant to invest heavily in capital equipment which during a downturn in orders would be under-employed. Manual and casualised labour, in contrast, was flexible: it could simply be hired and dismissed as the order book grew or contracted. Indeed, its supply could be attuned to demand almost on a day to day basis. Pollard and Robertson contrast this situation with that in overseas yards of the period, which were often better equipped. They conclude that such yards often rued their investment during periods of depression, and do not believe that low investment was a debilitating factor in British yards, with their ready supply of skilled and unskilled labour.[85]

The introduction of steel plate in the 1880s did accelerate the adoption of handling machinery in the latter part of our period. Unlike iron plate manufacturing, production of steel imposed virtually no limits on the size of plates. Shipbuilders who were anxious to reduce the number of joints needed between plates willingly embraced larger plates. The weight of an iron plate 10 × 3 feet in 1850 was 0.5 ton; by 1905, the typical steel plate was 36 × 7 feet and weighed

---

[83] Newman, *Materials Handling.*

[84] But not the very heaviest loads. Newman quotes an example of two particularly large boilers being moved to a fitting-out berth through a major Clydeside yard. There were problems obtaining enough horses, and concerns about controlling them, so a team of 600 men was used to haul the vehicles carrying each boiler, an operation that took two hours for each. It is an almost biblical image, but this was a major yard at the height of Clydeside's reputation as the world's leading shipbuilding region. Newman, *Materials Handling.*

[85] Pollard and Robertson, *British Shipbuilding Industry*, chap. 6 and particularly 129.

5 tons.[86] The price for reduction in riveting was investment in machinery to lift and carry the bigger steel plates.

The situation with plate and other iron working machinery has also been reviewed by Newman,[87] whose view is that there were continuous, but relatively small, adaptations and improvements throughout the period from 1850 to 1914. Again, this was most marked after about 1880 and the advent of steel. Prior to this the only machinery available had been steam driven, and its usefulness was limited by the need to provide separate boilers or steam lines for each individual item of equipment about the yard. The development of hydraulic, pneumatic and particularly electrical machinery overcame these problems, as water pipes, air lines or electrical cable could be run to any part of the yard. This equipment was slowly but steadily adopted from about 1880, although British shipbuilders still remained reluctant to commit themselves to heavy capital expenditure.

The availability of hydraulic and pneumatic power also allowed gradual mechanisation of riveting, one of the most labour-intensive jobs in the shipyard: a large ocean-going steamer needed almost one million rivets and two million drilled or punched rivet holes.[88] There was some opposition from the strongly unionised shipyard workers, who feared their piece-work rates and craft status would be affected by pneumatic or hydraulic powered riveting. However, this was tempered by the realisation that the machinery reduced the severe physical demands of the job and meant career riveters could continue to work beyond middle age.[89] Welding as a means of joining plates was eventually to replace riveting altogether, but in British yards before 1939 it was not used for hull construction, although it was employed in repair work.

The modest mechanisation of shipbuilding did eventually have its effect on productivity. Figures for productivity changes in British yards are calculated and cited by Pollard and Robertson for the period from the mid-1880s to 1914, and these show a gain of about 50 per cent over these years.[90] The sluggish adoption of mechanisation makes it likely that productivity gains were more modest from 1850 to 1880, if indeed there were any such gains.

The evidence base for improvements in efficiency is relatively small, and those calculating them have been mostly concerned with the bigger yards, which in the main were constructing large, ocean-going ships. Were the same efficiencies achieved in the yards constructing colliers and coastal bulk carriers?

---

86   Newman, *Materials Handling*.

87   Newman, *Plate and Section Working Machinery*.

88   Newman, *Plate and Section Working Machinery*, 122–3.

89   Pollard and Robertson, *British Shipbuilding Industry*, 122.

90   Pollard and Robertson, *British Shipbuilding Industry*, 186–94. The authors calculate their own figures, based on data relating to the Denny and Connell yards on the Clyde, and also cite a price index compiled by Feinstein. There are divergences in the figures, but the overall increases are very close to 50 per cent for both series.

No information has been found on efficiency changes in the west coast yards building steam coasters. However, it must be remembered that the yards building coastal vessels were not necessarily small: Charles Palmer, for instance, was not only a major builder of early colliers but was also amongst the largest and most forward-looking of shipbuilders, even investing in his own steel works as early as the 1850s.[91] The smaller yards had to compete for orders with the likes of Palmer, which gave them every incentive to stay competitive by matching the admittedly modest productivity gains of the flagship yards.

IX

Lloyd's Register of Shipping, the major British classification society, was extremely cautious in its rules covering the use of iron for shipbuilding.[92] However, the scientific approach to building in iron pioneered by men such as Scott Russell, Brunel, Fairbairn, Rankine and Napier was eventually instrumental in persuading Lloyd's Register of Shipping to revise its rules. Nevertheless, major change did not come until 1870 when surveyor Bernard Waymouth (later Secretary to Lloyd's Register of Shipping) was largely responsible for rewriting the rules for iron ships.[93] The new rules recognised that the stresses on a hull at sea required it to be strongest towards the centre of the hull, and therefore to require proportionally thicker iron work (the scantlings) at this point, while the extremities were subject to less stress and could be built more lightly. The overall result was to reduce the weight of iron work in a hull by 20 per cent. The corresponding reduction in price was so significant that construction of some ships was actually held back in anticipation of the new rules coming into effect, and the changes in rules undoubtedly helped fuel the boom in iron shipbuilding of the early 1870s.

The changes were an important factor in reducing the price of iron bulk carriers, probably more significant than improvements in yard efficiency and certainly more dramatic in their effect of stimulating demand for ships.

Developments in constructing iron steam ships would be expected to be reflected in reduced prices, encouraging owners to move from wooden sailing ships to iron steamers. Two estimates of the prices of iron steam ships over the period are available. Maywald appears to have looked at hull prices, as he includes in his calculations figures for iron-hulled sailing ships, which he quite reasonably

---

[91]   Pollard and Robertson, *British Shipbuilding Industry*, 29.

[92]   Frustration with this caution was a factor in underwriters based in Liverpool, publishing their own register annually from 1862: *Liverpool Underwriters' Registry for Iron Vessels*.

[93]   J. Coates and B. Waymouth, 'The Change from Wood to Steel Ships', *Transactions of the Newcomen Society*, 71 (1999–2000), 257–68.

argues have costs similar to iron-hulled steamers.[94] Harley constructed his own series of prices, based on quotations and actual contracts prepared by the Clyde shipbuilder Alexander Stephen and Company.[95] The two series show considerable divergence, but remarkably similar overall trends for the period from 1855 to 1890, with a 30 per cent reduction in ship prices.

The price charged to the customer depended not only costs of materials and labour, but also on demand. A boom in iron ship construction, with a steep rise in prices from about 1870 to 1875, was apparent from both sets of figures. From the mid-1850s to the late 1860s, there was no clear trend in iron ship prices. After the boom had blown itself out in the mid-1870s, there was a steady and maintained downward trend in price.

The figures used by Harley for Stephen's shipyard reflect the output of a company building a wide variety of types and sizes of ship, which Walker describes as 'custom requested vessels of unimpeachable quality ... [although] not in the forefront of technical development'.[96] Although Stephen built some smaller ships, these were relatively sophisticated coastal liners which were higher powered and better equipped than the typical bulk carrier.

Company registration documents give an indication of average prices by year for new coastal bulk carriers of a range of sizes built at various yards.[97] Over a 20-year period, the price of coastal bulk carriers declined by 33 per cent, from an average of £24 to £16 per ton. The fall between 1880 and 1890 is similar to that which Harley records. Average costs per ton for small steamers are much greater than for the ships in the two series cited by Harley, the latter finding £12 per gross ton in 1890 while that year the coastal bulk carrier cost £19 per gross ton. The small ship required most of the equipment of the large ship: engines, boilers, auxiliaries, steering gear, anchors, pumps and windlasses. The equipment for a large ship will be bigger, stronger and more powerful, but its cost will not increase in proportion. For instance, machinery with twice the power will not

---

[94]   K. Maywald, 'The Construction Costs and the Value of the British Merchant Fleet, 1850–1938', *Scottish Journal of Political Economy*, 3 (February 1956).

[95]   Harley, 'Shipbuilding and Shipping in the Late 19th Century', 129.

[96]   F.M. Walker, *Song of the Clyde: A History of Clyde Shipbuilding* (Cambridge, 1984), 179.

[97]   These figures were sourced from the files for single-ship and other registered companies contained in TNA, company registration papers, class BT 31. In a number of instances, the memorandum of association of a company gives the price at which the ship is to be acquired from the promoter of the company and if the ship is new this will be close to its building price. The nominal capital for a single-ship company is usually found to be just a little more than the cost of acquiring its ship and so where no purchase price is available this has been taken as indicative of the ship's price. In some years, data is available for up to four ships, but in several cases no ships built that year have been found. The data is confined to the period during which it was possible readily to register a limited liability company, so no data before 1880 is included.

cost twice as much to build: a major component of the cost will be labour, which, while greater, will not be proportionately so. As the capacity of a ship increases as the cube of one of its linear dimensions, doubling its capacity will not involve doubling the number of frames and plates needed. The observation that a small steam ship is relatively much more expensive to build than a large one helps explain why steam was adopted more slowly in trades where only smaller vessels were viable, as in many coastal bulk trades

Factors affecting the cost of a steamship included the price of the metal from which hull and machinery was fabricated, labour costs, the degree of mechanisation employed and hence the productivity of the shipyard, and design considerations – especially the rules governing the size and strength of metalwork. In all but wage costs, changes in these factors were in favour of more economically constructed ships in the period from 1850, although the gains to the 1870s were modest, with most improvement being realised thereafter, with changes to Lloyd's Register of Shipping's rules, the adoption of steel and the cautious but steady adoption of mechanisation in shipyards.

A bulk-carrying steamer built in the 1880s may have cost only a little less than one of equivalent size built 30 years earlier, but owners were getting much more ship for their money, especially in the engine room. The machinery and boilers of the 1880s were far more sophisticated pieces of equipment, capable of delivering at least the same power for up to only a quarter of the fuel required in the 1850s and offering a reduction in the numbers of crew needed to tend the machinery. Not only were the 1880s ships more economical, but they were also more efficient. Their hulls were lighter and stronger and, with more compact machinery and smaller bunkers, could carry more cargo on a shallower draft.

Knauerhase has compiled productivity figures for German ships between 1871 and 1887, based on manning levels per net ton of ship.[98] Although he looked at the whole trade of Germany, his figures which show that productivity of steam ships increased by 37 per cent provide support for the 1870s and 1880s being a period of improvement in efficiency.

Paradoxically, the improvements in boiler, machinery and hull design and construction discussed above made it possible to build both larger and smaller bulk-carrying steamers which were competitive with sailing ships. Expanding the steam collier to twice its capacity to fit it for more distant trades did not double its price, as the same components were required and just needed to be somewhat bigger or stronger. Developing a coastal steam bulk carrier was trickier, and took longer, because all the components had to be present but smaller to capture trade from the sailing ship by carrying relatively small consignments between ports where draft considerations and the needs of small shippers constrained the size of the ship. However, the gains in shipyard

---

[98]   R. Knauerhase, 'The Compound Steam Engine and Productivity Changes in the German Merchant Fleet, 1871–1887' *Journal of Economic History*, 27 (1968), 395–6.

productivity and use of steel did mean that the coastal bulk carrier of 1900 cost less than an equivalent built in 1880.

X

In the 30 years following the introduction of the steam collier in 1852, there were notable advances in marine engineering and shipbuilding. Most significant were the developments in design and construction of higher-pressure boilers and compound and later triple-expansion engines, which achieved a massive reduction in coal consumption. There were three direct results of this. First, the cost of fuel required was reduced. Second, the number of firemen and engineers needed decreased, probably not in direct proportion to the saving in fuel, but certainly enough to give meaningful economies in wages. Third, the space needed for coal bunkers was reduced, allowing more space and weight to be devoted to carrying a paying cargo.

The gains made by fitting better boilers and engines are well illustrated by the impressive extensions to the lives of old steam colliers obtained by updating their machinery. One of the most notable cases was *John Bowes*, the first successful screw collier, and small by standards of even a few years later. In 1883, a set of compound engines was installed in her hull that was already over 30 years old and these extended her working life for another 50 years. Even then, at the height of a depression, she was not taken out of service because she was uneconomic but foundered in a storm.[99]

In a parallel development to the use of higher steam pressures, the trend to smaller and more compact engines and boilers also allowed cargo space to be increased, or – a development particularly welcome in coastal steamers trading to small ports and up shallow waterways – the reduced weight of engines, boilers and bunkers allowed a shallower draft. The gains in overall economy and efficiency were, then, even greater than the impressive savings in coal consumption.

Improvements in efficiency through developments in hull building were more modest but became more important as steam bulk carriers were enlarged. Better and cheaper iron and later steel, the adoption of rules recognising the true strength of these materials, slow gains in the productivity of shipyards; all these meant that in the 1880s a much more efficient, probably safer and certainly more capacious bulk carrier could be built at a price no higher than that ruling 30 years earlier.

By 1880, relatively large colliers operating on the east coast would be much more economical than their predecessors of the 1850s. This is apparent from their ability to counter the competition from railways, and to wrest back trade

---

[99]   *Lloyd's Register*, various years.

lost since 1850. In the 1870s, steam colliers carried about 38 per cent of all coal coming in to London, but by 1898 this had reached 52 per cent. Tonnages of coal shipped coastwise on the east coast almost doubled from 3 million in 1870 to 5.8 million in 1892.[100]

Particularly germane to the subject of this volume, the massive gains in efficiency of steam engines from 1850 to 1880 and the improvements in hull capacity could be expected to make economically viable both the larger steamers working on longer routes and smaller coastal steamers trading to minor ports.

---

[100]   J. Armstrong, 'Climax and Climacteric: The British Coastal Trade, 1870–1930', in D.J. Starkey and A.G. Jamieson (eds), *Exploiting the Sea: Aspects of Britain's Maritime Economy since 1870* (Exeter, 1998), 39.

CHAPTER FOUR

Maximisation: Screw collier into ocean-going tramp

I

Once the screw collier had been accepted in the British east coast coal trade, it would have become clear that such vessels were useful in longer distance trades, for instance the export of coal to the Baltic and Scandinavia. Further extensions, to the Mediterranean and Black Sea trades were also feasible. As iron steamers sharing the characteristics of screw colliers, especially water ballast capacity and large hatches and holds, grew in size and improved technologically, they became the ocean-going tramp steamers. This progression has not been well documented, but neither has there been a challenge to the suggestion made by the present author that the ubiquitous deep-sea tramp was a development of the screw collier.[1] This chapter draws together various strands of evidence which support the theory that the screw collier was instrumental in producing the ocean-going steam tramp.

The first strand is evidence that early colliers were quite capable of making relatively distant voyages. It is then considered if the yards which had built screw colliers and the individuals who had owned them exploited their facilities, experience and skills by constructing and operating larger steamers. Lastly, the characteristics and dimensions of colliers and tramps are compared over a time period from 1860 to 1890 and conclusions drawn as to their similarities and differences, and how the two types developed.

Surveys made for this chapter allow the charting of the development of the ocean-going steam tramp from its inception in the 1860s to 1890.

II

The British government was not slow to recognise the usefulness of screw colliers beyond coastal and short-sea trades and chartered a number of them as transports to support the fighting in the Crimea between 1853 and 1856. This encouraged

---

[1] R.S. Fenton, 'The Introduction of Steam to UK Coastal Bulk Trades: A Technological and Commercial Assessment', *International Journal of Maritime History*, 20, no. 2 (2008), 175–200.

owners to send their colliers on longer voyages, and there is ample evidence of these from crew lists.[2] Their cargoes were not recorded in these documents, but the ports visited suggest these colliers made 'tramp' voyages with coal to the Baltic, to the bay ports of France, to the Mediterranean and the Black Sea. Return cargoes possibly comprised grain from the Black Sea or Baltic, timber (especially pit-wood) from the Baltic, iron ore from Spain or perhaps marble or even fruit from Italy.[3] Some examples follow.

Black Diamond	April 1860: sailed for Danzig and Memel.
Black Prince	August 1856: sailed from London to Montreal.
Carbon	November 1858: sailed from Shields for ports in the Greek Islands, Black Sea, Danube, Sea of Azof. March 1859: sailed from London for Cadiz, Malaga and Corunna.
Caroline	1859: made four voyages to the Baltic via Antwerp, and one voyage to the Black Sea.
Chanticleer	1858: sailed Newcastle to Hamburg, spent March to November in the Baltic trade. 1860: all voyages to the Baltic, usually from London.
Chester	October 1858 to November 1859: at least five voyages from London to the Mediterranean, often via Cardiff or Newport. One foreign voyage to unknown destination, and two to Danzig, again from London with a call at Newport.
Earsdon	1859: three voyages to the Mediterranean, at least one with coal; one voyage London to Cronstadt via Cardiff.
Jarrow	1858: five Mediterranean voyages.
Marley Hill	September 1858: Newport to Riga, Cronstadt, Memel and Copenhagen.
Nicholas Wood	1859: voyages to the Baltic and Mediterranean.
Sardinian	September 1856: sailed Sunderland for Hamburg.
Sir John Easthope	1857: made 13 voyages from Cardiff to Dieppe. 1859: two voyages Newport to the Baltic, one voyage Cardiff to France.
Vedra	1858: three voyages from Sunderland to the Baltic.
William Hutt	1858: two Baltic voyages from Cardiff and from London via Cardiff and Newport to Riga and Cronstadt; one voyage Sunderland to Bremerhaven.

---

[2] Crew agreements for the 1850s are in The National Archives, Kew (TNA), company registration papers, class BT 98.

[3] Fruit seems a likely return cargo for a collier calling at three Italian ports before returning to the United Kingdom.

From the sample of crew agreements examined it is estimated that for no less than 40 per cent of their time in the late 1850s the screw colliers were working outside the purely coastal collier trade. Although not quoting names, Craig cites coal cargoes loaded in steamers at Sunderland in June 1862 comprising 700 tons for Shanghai and 900 tons for Alexandria.[4]

Macrae has used records kept by the harbour master of Northumberland Dock at North Shields to study ships loading there between August 1869 and November 1873.[5] He found that about half of the cargo steamers registered at Newcastle at that time loaded coal in this dock, mostly for London or the south coast ports. The ships were mostly between 190 and 225 feet in length. Ownership was complex, with the 64th shares predominantly registered to coal owners, coal fitters, coal merchants and shipbuilders. There were numerous examples of ships loading coal for overseas ports. Although the value of his findings is reduced because there is no comparative data for sailings to domestic ports, they illustrate that modest-sized colliers were regularly working outside the east coast trade. Examples cited include:

– *Black Swan* of 1864 loaded coal for Hamburg on 23 August 1869.
– *Tyne* of 1863 loaded coal for Hamburg and sailed on 4 September 1869.
– *Joseph Straker* of 1863 loaded some 906 tons of coal and sailed to Hamburg on 5 September 1869.
– *Lindisfarne* of 1870 sailed for Hamburg on 12 March 1872.

Fenham of 1868 appears to have been built for the Baltic and Mediterranean trades but is also recorded as loading for London on 7 January 1873. With a marked seasonality in the demand for coal, it was not unusual to see vessels diverted from more distant trades to carry coal to London in the winter.

III

Registration papers and annual reports of several shipping companies set up in the 1860s provide further evidence that their subscribers wanted to extend the use of early screw colliers into longer distance trades.

The General Iron Screw Collier Co. Ltd was one of the first limited liability joint stock companies to own ships, and the first set up to operate screw colliers. It was provisionally registered on 19 March 1852, but the registration process was not completed until 14 September 1852.[6] The company's stated aim was first to

---

[4]   R. Craig, 'Aspects of Tramp Shipping and Ownership', in K. Matthews and G. Panting (eds), *Ships and Shipbuilding in the North Atlantic Region* (St. John's, Newfoundland, 1978), 212.
[5]   J.A. Macrae and C.V. Waine, *The Steam Collier Fleets* (Albrighton, 1990), 25–9.
[6]   TNA, company registration papers, class BT 31/172/519.

build, purchase and own iron steam vessels equipped with screw propellors for the transfer of coals and other merchandise from port to port.

Initial subscribers were a mix of 'gentlemen' and businessmen, the latter including the coal merchant William Cory, coal owner Matthew Chaytor, and Charles Mark Palmer, who described himself as a coal owner but was already a shipbuilder. According to Macrae and Waine, two of the directors were associated with London gas companies: William Prinsep of the London Gas Company and Thomas Miers of the Commercial Gas Company.[7] Between 1853 and 1872, the company took delivery of 23 screw colliers, the majority built by Palmer at Jarrow, a choice of yard clearly influenced by Palmer's association with the company (see Table 4.1).[8] It is interesting to speculate whether the pioneering *John Bowes*, which was registered in July 1852, was intended for ownership by the General Iron Screw Collier Co. Ltd, a plan thwarted by the delay from March and September of that year in completing registration of the company.

Amongst the company's registration papers in the National Archives, some annual reports and other documents have survived. Receipts from freights are recorded only for 1854, when £33,135 was earned from 'outward freights for colliers' and a massive £64,913 'from transports'. The latter figure reflects the Government charter of a number of the company's colliers to take material for the Crimean War to Constantinople and the Black Sea. A dividend of £34,837 was paid in December 1854. The only other dividend reported in surviving returns filed with the Registrar of Companies is £15,126 in 1856. It is clear that the east coast coal trade was insufficiently profitable to provide what its investors considered were adequate returns, and this led to much friction at annual general meetings. According to *Mitchell's Steam-Shipping Journal* in 1859, 'It is said that the fleet of the Iron Screw Collier Co. which has recently been sold [*sic*], will be withdrawn from the Italian trade and once more employed in the coal trade'.[9] The company's reported problems included the massive repair bills for what were novel vessels, the lack of adequate provision for deterioration, and its inability to replace the losses of no fewer than 16 of its ships. However, the company does illustrate the willingness of directors and investors to place early screw colliers in more distant trades, and the apparent ability of these steamers to operate satisfactorily albeit as yet insufficiently profitably. Its shipowning came to an end only in March 1881 with the sale of *Hutton Chaytor*, one of only seven of its ships not to have been wrecked, foundered or posted missing.

The problems of the General Iron Screw Collier Co. Ltd do not seem to have inhibited Charles Palmer and others in the coal trade from investing in steam

---

[7]   Macrae and Waine, *Steam Collier Fleets*, 15.

[8]   TNA, London customs registers, CUST 130.

[9]   *Mitchell's Steam-Shipping Journal* (9 December 1859). The reported sale quickly fell through.

**Table 4.1 Names, dates and fates of vessels owned by
the General Iron Screw Collier Co. Ltd**

Name	Completed	Fate/Disposal
William Hutt	March 1853	lost November 1864
Countess of Strathmore	May 1853	lost July 1853
Northumberland	June 1853	sold 1864
Sir John Easthope	July 1853	missing 1863
Durham	August 1853	lost November 1857
Jarrow	November 1853	lost October 1867
Marley Hill	February 1854	sold 1863
Ross D. Mangles	May 1854	lost 1866
Nicholas Wood	June 1854	missing 1861
Black Prince	August 1854	sank off Lisbon 1860
Firefly	September 1854	wrecked Cape St Vincent 1867
Derwent	April 1855	wrecked on South Uist 1865
Hutton Chaytor	June 1855	sold 1881
Eupatoria	March 1856	wrecked Flamboro' August 1857
Brunette	December 1861	sold 1871
Blonde	December 1863	sold foreign 1872
May Queen	June 1864	sank in collision 1878
Lady Derby	October 1865	wrecked 1877
Cromwell	May 1865	missing 1878
Fairfax	June 1865	wrecked 1881
J.E. McConnell	December 1867	sold 1880
Dromedary	December 1869	foundered 1873
H.P. Stephenson	June 1872	sold 1881

bulk carriers and companies to operate them. The London Steam Navigation Co. Ltd was registered in March 1864 with a massive nominal capital of £250,000 in 2,500 £100 shares.[10] Its Memorandum of Association included as its first aim the acquisition of screw or other steam vessels to carry passengers and goods in all parts of Great Britain and Ireland as well as foreign. Amongst the 53 individual shareholders about 40 per cent were actively involved in the coal trade, especially

---

[10]   TNA, company registration papers, class BT 31/916/1069c.

Table 4.2 Names, dates and fates of vessels owned by the London Steam Navigation Co. Ltd and its successors

Name	Built	Fate/disposal
Italia	1860	sold 1886 to Italy
Minerva	1861	sold 1883 to Dublin for general cargo trade
Europa	1862	sold 1883 for general cargo trade
Justitia	1862	sold 1885 to Venezuela
Aurora	1863	sold 1886 to Italy
Latona	1863	sunk in collision 1876
Adria	1864	sold 1885 to Fenwicks and others for coal trade
Medora	1864	sold 1885 to Fenwicks and others
Venetia	1864	sunk in collision 1884
Miranda	1865	sold 1885 to Fenwicks and others for coal trade
Sabrina	1865	sold 1885 to Fenwicks and others for coal trade
Statira	1865	sold 1885 for general cargo trade
Camilla	1866	sold 1885 to Fenwicks and others for coal trade
Palmyra	1866	sold 1885 to Fenwicks and others for coal trade
Oriana	1867	wrecked 1877
Roxana	1868	sold 1885 to Fenwicks and others for coal trade

coal factors and coal owners, including John Fenwick, members of the Lambert and Straker families, plus the Hills of London and Southampton. Its registered address was the London Coal Exchange.

The company was voluntarily wound up in November 1866 and its assets transferred to a new company, the London Steamship Co. Ltd.[11] The successor company hung on until 1883, but then suffered the same fate, giving way to the London Steam Shipping Co. Ltd.[12] On both occasions the previous company's shares were purchased by the new undertaking for substantially less than their nominal value, and the price of further share issues was successively reduced. Shares in the original company had now been effectively devalued by 60 per cent. The London Steam Shipping Co. Ltd was voluntarily wound up in May 1885, just over two years after its formation. A total of 16 ships were bought or ordered by these companies between 1865 and 1868, Palmer again winning

---

[11]   TNA, company registration papers, class BT 31/1305/3344.
[12]   TNA, company registration papers, class BT 31/3143/18154.

the orders (Table 4.2).[13] Smallest was *Europa*, which had been built in 1862, of 207 feet in length, and the largest *Miranda*, built in 1865 of 211 feet. On winding up of the final company, the London Steam Shipping Co. Ltd, seven of its remaining ships passed to collier owner John Fenwick and associates, the five others going into general cargo trades for owners in Dublin, London, Italy and Venezuela.

Only two of the 16 ships were lost during their service with the companies. Neither of these was replaced, however, and after the *Roxana* was completed in 1868, no further ships were acquired. The three successive 'London' companies lasted for 21 years, outliving the General Iron Screw Collier Co. Ltd, and their combined longevity can be counted as an achievement of sorts. However, the companies appear not to have passed the test of any successful commercial enterprise, in that they failed to generate (or perhaps retain) sufficient profits to replace their major assets, the steam colliers; no further examples being acquired after 1868 despite two losses. That lack of earnings was more the problem than, say, disagreement amongst its shareholders is suggested by the 1883 reformation. Neither were the assets worn out: most of the colliers which the company owned had useful lives after the 1885 liquidation.

Although the travails of the General Iron Screw Collier Co. Ltd and the London Steam Navigation Co. Ltd and its two successors might cast doubts on the success of larger screw colliers in longer distance trades, the failures seem to lie in the optimism of their founders and subscribers, greatly overestimating potential earnings and disregarding such fundamental problems as depreciation, replacement and maintenance costs. The ships themselves, which survived the companies' dissolutions, found buyers who were often in the coal trade, including some of the companies' shareholders.

IV

At least 70 screw colliers were built for the east coast and near-Continental coal trades in the 1850s (see Chapter 2). It could be expected that their owners would have grasped opportunities to exploit both their operating experience and their contacts with coal owners and shippers to expand their use of steam propulsion in order to compete with sailing ships in more distant trades. In his extensive survey of tramp shipowners, Thomas has identified a number of early owners of tramp steamers in London, on the Tyne and on the Wear who had their origins in the coastal coal trades, as screw collier operators, coal owners, coal merchants or coal factors (see Table 4.3).

---

[13]   TNA, London customs registers, CUST 130.

Table 4.3 Steam tramp owners originally involved in collier trades

Owner	First steamer	Involvement with coastal coal trade	Reference
London owners			
Commercial Steamship Co. Ltd (Young, Ehlers & Co.)	*Pelaw* 1869	In coastal coal trade	Macrae[a] Thomas[b]
Cory, Lohden	*Gazelle* 1869	Later Jackson Brothers and Cory	Thomas[c]
Dixon and Harris	*Hastings* 1864	Collier. Coal factors since 1796	Thomas[d]
Fenwick and Stobart	*Black Diamond* 1855	London agents for north-east collieries	Macrae[e]
Gordon and Co.	*H.P. Stephenson* 1871	Collier	Thomas[f]
E.T. Gourlay	*Admiral Kanaris* 1858		Thomas[g]
J. and C. Harrison	*James Southern* 1887	Related by marriage to Lambert family	Cooper[h]
Lambert Brothers	*Kenley, Medway* both 1879	Coal factors, screw collier owners	Thomas[i]
Mercantile Steamship Co. Ltd	*Nile & Neva* 1864	In coal trade to Baltic	Thomas[j]
Pyman	*Admiral Cator* by 1858	Earlier had collier brigs	Hogg & Appleyard[k]
Watts, Watts; Watts, Ward; Watts, Milburn	*Gosforth* 1856	Sailing colliers since 1850s	Thomas[l]
Newcastle owners			
William Dickinson	*South Tyne* 1871	Coal exporters from 1847	Thomas[m]
Elliot, Lowrey and Dunford	*Iduna* 1868	Coal fitters	Thomas[n]
Fenwick and Reay	*Pelton* 1876	Previously in coal trade	Thomas[o]
Lawes and Surtees	*Kielder Castle* 1868	Screw collier owner	Thomas[p]
John Morrison and Son	*Benmore* ex *Samson* 1874	Screw collier owner	Thomas[q]

Owner	First steamer	Involvement with coastal coal trade	Reference
Ridley, Sons and Tulley	*Linda* 1873	Coal exporters; coastal coal trade	Thomas[r]
Walter Runciman	*Dudley* 1885	Runciman was master in sailing colliers.	Thomas[s]
Sunderland owners			
Edward T. Gourley	*Samson* 1860	Owned 20/64ths of *Samson*; in coal trade	Thomas[t]
T. Kish	*Morehampton* 1873	Home and intermediate coal trades	Thomas[u]
James Laing	*Volunteer* 1868	Shipbuilders, colliers built on spec	Thomas[v]
James Westoll	1863	Early coal exporter remaining in coastal trade	Thomas[w]

[a] J.A. Macrae and C.V. Waine, *The Steam Collier Fleets* (Albrighton, 1990), 53.

[b] P.N. Thomas, *British Ocean Tramps*, vol. 2, *Owners and Their Ships* (Albrighton, 1992), 96.

[c] Thomas, *British Ocean Tramps*, vol. 2, 107.

[d] Thomas, *British Ocean Tramps*, vol. 2, 104.

[e] Macrae and Waine, *Steam Collier Fleets*, 41.

[f] Thomas, *British Ocean Tramps*, vol. 2, 101.

[g] Thomas, *British Ocean Tramps*, vol. 2, 154.

[h] M. Cooper, *J. and C. Harrison: The History of a Family Shipping Venture* (Preston, 2012), 5.

[i] Thomas, *British Ocean Tramps*, vol. 2, 108.

[j] Thomas, *British Ocean Tramps*, vol. 2, 98.

[k] P. Hogg, and A. Appleyard, *The Pyman Story* (Hartlepool, 2000), 3.

[l] Thomas, *British Ocean Tramps*, vol. 2, 114.

[m] Thomas, *British Ocean Tramps*, vol. 2, 132.

[n] Thomas, *British Ocean Tramps*, vol. 2, 133.

[o] Thomas, *British Ocean Tramps*, vol. 2, 135.

[p] Thomas, *British Ocean Tramps*, vol. 2, 138.

[q] Thomas, *British Ocean Tramps*, vol. 2, 139.

[r] Thomas, *British Ocean Tramps*, vol. 2, 140.

[s] Thomas, *British Ocean Tramps*, vol. 2, 142.

[t] Thomas, *British Ocean Tramps*, vol. 2, 154.

[u] Thomas, *British Ocean Tramps*, vol. 2, 154.

[v] Thomas, *British Ocean Tramps*, vol. 2, 155.

[w] Thomas, *British Ocean Tramps*, vol. 2, 158.

3: At 226 feet, *Medway* of 1879 was at the larger end of the size range for screw colliers. She was built at Sunderland for Lambert Brothers, who moved into deep sea tramps after selling their colliers to Cory in 1896. She retained her two-cylinder compound engine throughout her life, which ended in a Boulogne shipbreaking yard in 1910. *Author's collection*

V

To examine the sizes and characteristics of colliers and ocean-going tramps, surveys were made of around 25 representative of each type built during the 1860s, and in each of the years 1870, 1880 and 1890 or in years adjacent.[14] Candidate ships were identified either from the *Mercantile Navy List* or from the Starke/ Schell Registers, which give details of ships completed in each year from 1870 to 1890.[15] Hull dimensions and forms, details of the machinery originally fitted, and builders' names were taken from Lloyd's Register of Shipping. The major criteria for allocation to the category of tramp or collier was the known activities of their owners, whether tramping deep sea or in coastal and near continental coal trades.[16]

---

[14]   For several of the years surveyed the methods used did not provide the required total of 25 vessels, so vessels built during adjacent years were added to complete the sample. Even this was insufficient to provide examples for Table 4.4, for which the vessels whose details are summarised were built from 1857 to 1865.

[15]   T. Starke and W. Schell, *Register of Merchant Ships Completed in 1911–21* (Gravesend, various dates). Based largely on details in *Lloyd's Register* and other annual registers, these volumes list ships over 300 tons built in a particular year and have been published by the World Ship Society.

[16]   Macrae and Waine, *Steam Collier Fleets* and P.N. Thomas, *British Ocean Tramps*, vol. 1, *Builders and Cargoes* (Wolverhampton, 1992); vol. 2, *Owners and Their Ships* (Albrighton, 1992) were useful sources for identifying owners' activities, in conjunction with published histories of shipping companies.

Any details known of voyages, including those on which a ship was lost, were also taken into account when allocating steamers to types.[17]

Arrangements for carrying water ballast are important characteristics of both collier and tramp. These were not included in reports by surveyors for Lloyd's Register of Shipping on individual ships until 1865 and were not consistently recorded in the register book until 1880.[18] Thus, steamers built in the 1860s and around 1870 had to survive until 1880 and had to be classed by Lloyd's Register of Shipping to be included in the survey of the 1870 ships. Similarly, details of engines and boilers began to appear only in the mid-1870s, by when a number of ships had been re-engined or compounded, and had new boilers installed. From 1880 onward the *Register Books* includes ballast and engine details of a few ships not classed by Lloyd's Register of Shipping. It is not possible to know whether omission of water ballast details from the *Register Books* signifies their absence from the vessel, or simply the surveyor's failure to record them. For this reason the findings concerning water ballast arrangements for vessels built in the 1860 should be treated with caution.

The aims of this survey were first to discover whether colliers and tramps can be defined in terms of size, ballast arrangements, power or hull structure; second, whether there were significant differences between the two categories; and third, whether these changed over time.

According to Macrae and Waine's survey of owners and their vessels, screw colliers were built in increasing numbers from 1852, while steam tramps began to appear in the 1860s.[19] Table 4.4 compares samples of screw colliers built from 1857 to 1866 and tramp steamers built from 1861 to 1866. The vessels in Table 4.4 classed as tramps tend to be larger on average, although this is most apparent in terms of gross tonnage, which was 15 per cent higher in tramps.[20] The differences

---

[17]　Until the mid-1870s, entries in *Lloyd's Register* included a 'destined voyage' column. Given that a steamer would make multiple voyages in the year for which an edition of the register book was current, this information is of limited value, but does give an indication of the owner's intention. For instance, in the 1871 edition of the *Register Book*, the *Roxana*'s destined voyage is first shown as 'London coaster', and then 'London–Mediterranean'. The column was dropped around 1875.

[18]　Barbara Jones of Lloyd's Register Foundation kindly researched surveyors' records and register books to identify 1865 as the year surveyors were required to record water ballast arrangements in new ships. However, this data is available only for classed ships, and even for them, water ballast capacities are not always published. The situation improves with later editions of the *Register Book* but deteriorates after the Second World War as fewer ships are classed by the society.

[19]　Macrae and Waine, *Steam Collier Fleets*, 21–46.

[20]　Net tonnage gave a better representation of the cargo capacity of a steamer than gross tonnage, which took into account other enclosed spaces which had no revenue-earning potential. Owners were anxious to minimise net tonnage because dock, harbour and canal dues were usually calculated on this measurement.

Table 4.4 Characteristics of colliers and tramps built around 1860

Characteristic	Collier 1860s	Tramps 1860s	Comparison
Sample size	*25*	*26*	
Gross tonnage (average)	710	813	tramp + 15%
Gross tonnage (range)	393–1,578	420–1,235	
Net tonnage (average)	535	577	tramp + 8%
Net tonnage (range)	280–1,156	258–1,023	
Length feet (average)	197	213	tramp + 8%
Length feet (range)	155–245	153–247	
Beam feet (average)	28	28	equal
Beam feet (range)	26–35	17–32	
Depth feet (average)	16	17	tramp + 6%
Depth feet (range)	14–18	15–18	
Length/beam ratio	7.0	7.6	
Beam/depth ratio	1.75	1.6	
Length/depth ratio	12.3	12.5	
Water ballast tons (average)	323 (n = 3)	197 (n = 5)	
Water ballast tons (range)	188–500	90–260	
Horsepower (average)	88	97	tramp + 10%
Horsepower (range)	70–180	65–150	
Boiler pressure p.s.i. (average)	41 (n = 6)	55 (n = 4)	
Boiler pressure p.s.i. (range)	14–65	30–75	tramp higher
I. 2-cyl.	14/17 (82%)	11/14 (79%)	similar
D 4-cyl.	–	–	
C 2-cyl.	2/17 (12%)	3/14 (21%)	
C. 4-cyl.	1/17 (6%)	–	
T. 3-cyl. (number)	–	–	
Q. 4-cyl. (number)	–	–	
Double bottoms (number)	15	17	similar
Forecastle	2	8	
Bridge deck	1	0	
Raised quarter deck	10	13	
Poop	1	3	
Single deck	19/20	14/20	
Two decks	1	6	tramp higher
of which awning decks	–	–	
of which spar decks	1	2	

in net tonnage, length and depth were much smaller, invariably less than 8 per cent, and the average beam of both types was 28 feet. The ratios between lengths, breadth and depth are all close, with no clear differences emerging. Size alone cannot distinguish the collier built in this period from the tramp, and it is notable that, at the upper end of the tonnage range, one collier, *William Cory*, is larger than any tramp.[21] At the lower end of the range, the Cardiff tramp *Llandaff*[22] is the smallest vessel in the survey.

The majority of both types are single-deck vessels, as might be expected from the practice of having holds that are as large as possible. One collier (again the *William Cory*) and six tramps have more than one deck, two of these tramps having spar decks. Although more tramps than colliers have a raised quarterdeck, and more tramps have forecastles, there are no substantial differences which differentiate the two hull forms. Numbers of vessels recorded as having double bottoms or partial double bottoms are close, at 15 for colliers and 17 for tramps. However, the figures for water ballast capacity are too sparse to allow worthwhile comparisons.

A majority of colliers and tramps were built with simple two-cylinder engines but given the relatively small sample size (and the lack of data) the figures for both types are very close. Both types tended to be retrofitted with compound engines or had their engines compounded. Nominal horsepower is quoted for all ships, and is 10 per cent higher in the tramps, in parallel with their slightly greater size.

VI

The survey discussed above allows comparisons to be made between colliers and tramps built over the period 1860 to 1890. The results are summarised in Tables 4.5 and 4.6. Table 4.5 shows the change in sizes and other characteristics of steam colliers built from the 1860s to 1890. With the exception of gross tonnage, growth in size is modest over this 30-year period, with net tonnage increasing by 12 per cent, length by 7 per cent, and depth actually decreasing by 13 per cent. Other characteristics change more markedly. Fitting of double bottoms (or, at least, recording of them) is almost universal as early as 1870. All but two colliers (one each in 1860 and 1880) are single-deck vessels. There are just two compound-engined colliers built in the 1860s, yet by 1880 every vessel built this year has this machinery, but by 1890 it is largely replaced in popularity by triple-expansion machinery. Unsurprisingly, boiler pressures increase by over 200 per cent, with nominal horsepower growing by 34 per cent.

---

[21]   Built on the Tyne in 1857, *William Cory* was, at 245 feet, one of the largest colliers in the east coast coal trade. TNA, London customs registers, CUST 130/57.

[22]   Built on the Tyne, *Llandaff* was just 153 feet long, much the same size as the *John Bowes* of 1852. *Lloyd's Register*, 1871.

Table 4.5 Characteristics of colliers built 1860–1890

Characteristic	Collier 1860s	Collier 1870	Collier 1880	Collier 1890	Change 1860s–1890
Sample size	*25*	*26*	*25*	*25*	
Gross tonnage (average)	710	776	883	976	+ 37%
Gross tonnage (range)	393–1,578	500–1,103	495–1,904	390–1,671	
Net tonnage (average)	535	517	629	597	+ 12%
Net tonnage (range)	280–1,156	331–813	289–1,242	237–1,290	
Length feet (average)	197	203	211	212	+ 7%
Length feet (range)	155–245	166–247	165–276	161–260	
Beam feet (average)	28	29	31	32	+ 13%
Beam feet (range)	26–35	27–31	25–38	25–39	
Depth feet (average)	16	16	15	14	− 13%
Depth feet (range)	14–18	13–18	12–20	11–18	
Length/beam ratio	7.0	7.00	6.8	6.63	− 5%
Beam/depth ratio	1.75	1.81	2.1	2.3	+ 31%
Length/depth ratio	12.3	12.7	14.1	15.1	+ 23%
Water ballast tons (average)	323 (n = 3)	184 (n = 3)	221	289	
Water ballast tons (range)	188–500	121–260	49–530	67–505	
Horsepower (average)	88	99	116	118	+ 34%
Horsepower (range)	70–180	60–190	70–300	70–220	
Boiler pressure p.s.i. (average)	41 (n = 6)	53	78	154	+ 275%
Boiler pressure p.s.i. (range)	14–65	30–75	70–100	60–160	
I. 2-cyl.	14/17 (82%)	10	–	–	
D. 4-cyl.	–	2	–	–	
C. 2-cyl. (number)	2/17 (12%)	13	25	3	
C. 4-cyl. (number)	1/17 (6%)	1	–	–	
T. 3-cyl. (number)	–	–	–	22	
Q. 4-cyl. (number)	–	–	–	0	
Double bottoms	15	24/25	25/25	23/23	
Forecastle	2	14	24	25	
Bridge deck	1	2	18	22	
Raised quarter deck	10	20	18	22	
Poop	1	5	6	14	
Single deck	19/20	26	24/25	25	
Two decks	1	–	1	–	
of which awning decks	–	–	–	–	
of which spar decks	1	–	–	–	

**Table 4.6 Characteristics of tramps built in the 1860s
and in years 1870, 1880 and 1890**

Characteristic	Tramp 1860	Tramp 1870	Tramp 1880	Tramp 1890	Change
Sample size	*26*	*26*	*25*	*25*	
Gross tonnage (average)	813	1,099	1,723	2,393	+ 194%
Gross tonnage (range)	420–1,235	490–1,736	1,122–2,604	1,352–3,518	
Net tonnage (average)	577	748	1,114	1,591	+ 176%
Net tonnage (range)	258–1,023	326–1,412	859–2452	816–2,931	
Length feet (average)	213	224	265	290	+ 36%
Length feet (range)	153–247	175–266	235–511	230–347	
Beam feet (average)	28	31	35	39	+ 39%
Beam feet (range)	17–32	28–34	32–38	33–43	
Depth feet (average)	17	19	21	20	+ 18%
Depth feet (range)	15–18	14–26	14–29	14–21	
Length/beam ratio	7.6	7.2	7.5	7.4	
Beam/depth ratio	1.6	1.60	1.60	1.95	
Length/depth ratio	12.5	11.8	12.3	14.5	
Water ballast tons (average)	197 (n=5)	214	311	539	+ 174%
Water ballast tons (range)	90–260	155–250	218–820	263–1125	
Horsepower (average)	97	111	173	216	+ 123%
Horsepower (range)	65–150	70–150	90–300	130–300	
Boiler pressure p.s.i. (average)	55 (n=4)	60	79	160	+ 191%
Boiler pressure p.s.i. (range)	30–75	35–75	75–90	150–200	
I. 2-cyl.(number)	11/14 (79%)	7	–	–	
D. 4-cyl.	–	–	–	–	
C. 2-cyl. (number)	3/14 (21%)	19	25		
C. 4-cyl.	–	–	–	–	
T. 3-cyl. (number)	–	–	–	24	
Q. 4-cyl. (number)	–	–	–	1	
Double bottoms (number)	17	23	25	25	
Forecastle (number)	8	15	23	18	
Bridge deck (number)	0	2	13	18	
Raised quarter deck (number)	13	9	11	23	
Poop (number)	3	9	–	23	
Well decks	–	–	–	16	
Single deck	14/20	16	12	16	
Two decks	6	10	13	9	
of which awning decks	–	4	1	7	
of which spar decks	2	–	–	2	

VII

The data in Table 4.6 charts the development of the ocean-going tramp steamer. Over the 30 years covered, it grew in size and sophistication considerably more than did the collier. Gross and net tonnages of tramps grew in step with each other, both by over 150 per cent. Increases in hull dimensions were more modest, from an average size of 213 × 28 × 17 feet to 290 × 39 × 20 feet, the major factor being the growth in length by 36 per cent. The length to beam ratio remained fairly constant between 1860 and 1890, indicating that the two dimensions were increasing in step. It is notable that the increase in average depth of hulls ceased by 1880: further increases would have ruled out trading to ports with restricted water levels. The ranges of size recorded in terms of hull dimensions, gross and net tonnage deserves comment. As Craig has pointed out, it was not always the largest steamers that were the most profitable, as their size could act as a constraint in certain trades from ports where there were physical difficulties in accommodating large ships.[23] The shipment of iron ore from Bilbao was an important example of such constraints.

Of particular significance to this study is the growing proportion of tramps having capacity for water ballast in double bottoms and in fore and aft peak tanks. Water ballast capacity rises steadily, until at 1890 it is on average 174 per cent higher than the in 1860. Initially, the tanks for water ballast were included in tonnage measurements, making owners reluctant to fit them until this anomaly was addressed.[24]

Perhaps the most striking change is in engine type. Tramp owners were relatively quick to specify compound engines (and to have older machinery compounded) so that all 1880-built tramps were so fitted. An equally abrupt change was apparent by 1890, with 24 out of 25 tramps fitted with triple-expansion engines, with the remaining example having quadruple-expansion machinery. These machinery changes are accompanied over the 30-year period by a 191 per cent increase in average boiler pressure, and a growth in nominal horsepower of 123 per cent.

Various hull designs were developed to increase capacity while minimising the extra iron or steel work required. The growing popularity of multiple deck ships is apparent from Table 4.6, with the fitting of intermediate decks, to give spar, awning, shade and shelter-deck steamers. The simplest hull design, the flush-decked steamer, was built with 'full scantlings', i.e., with hull plates, frames, stringers, angles and brackets as laid down by a classification society for a vessel of a given length. Working in extra decks would involve additional scantlings of comparable strength, but various ways round this were devised and were authorised by classification societies. Spar-decked vessels were allowed

---

23   Craig, 'Aspects of Tramp Shipping and Ownership', 222.

24   Thomas, *British Ocean Tramps*, vol. 1, 28.

an upper deck, which had a lighter (and therefore cheaper) build, but no heavy superstructure could be placed upon it. The spar deck was intended to be used for lighter cargoes, and vessels so classed were required to have more freeboard than two-deck vessels. An awning deck was of even lighter construction than a spar deck, and ships so fitted were required to have even more freeboard. A shade deck above the upper strength deck might extend the full length of this ship but required openings in the side. These designs gradually gave rise to the shelter deck, which extended the full length of the ship but which was not counted for purposes of tonnage measurement if it had permanent openings. Shelter deck vessels with 'tonnage openings' were built alongside single-deck vessels throughout the remaining lifetime of the conventional steam tramp ship, and indeed in their last years, from about 1930, would become usual.[25] The 'tween deck in these vessels compromised the ability to load and to discharge a bulk cargo as hatches needed to be fitted in the intermediate decks to allow access to the holds beneath. However, tramp owners were always alert to the possibility of chartering their ships to liner operators. As well as reducing net tonnage and with it harbour dues, having a 'tween deck made tramps more suitable for liner trades, where, in contrast to the bulk trades, variously sized packets of cargo needed to be stowed.

Table 4.6 demonstrates the growing number of steamers which had raised structures above the weather or strength deck: forecastles, bridge decks, raised quarterdecks and poop decks. The raised forecastle reduced the risk of a head sea breaking over the vessel, and a raised poop reduced this risk in a following sea and was also useful in increasing the space aft to accommodate crew members. The bridge deck began as a casing to raise the wheelhouse. The need to run the tunnel for the propellor shaft through the after-holds significantly reduced their cargo capacity, and to compensate, the depth of these holds was raised, giving rise to the raised quarterdeck running from about amidships to the stern. Increasing the cargo capacity aft also had the benefit of improving trim, as without the raised deck the vessel tended to trim with her bows down. The combination of forecastle, bridge deck and poop became known as the 'three island hull', and, as the figures in Table 4.6 show, it had become almost universal by 1890. This design left two 'wells' between forecastle and bridge deck and bridge and poop. There was concern that in a seaway water could pool in the wells and so compromise stability, so freeing ports were fitted in the bulwarks along the well, and large hatch coamings reduced the space where water could accumulate. The issue of the breaks in the deck compromising the vessel's longitudinal strength was addressed by the inclusion of additional brackets to stiffen the hull at these points.

---

[25]   One of the more successful standard ships of post-Second World War years was Austin and Pickersgill's SD14 design, the designation meaning 'shelter deck, 14,000 tons deadweight'. J. Lingwood, *SD14: The Full Story* (Preston, 2004).

4: *Sybil* shows an early stage in the evolution of the steam tramp, retaining the raised quarterdeck of the screw collier, but enlarged to 266 feet, comparatively large for the year 1879. Compare her profile with the smaller *Medway*, completed in the same year. Built with a two-cylinder compound engine, *Sybil*'s machinery was replaced with a triple-expansion engine in 1893, extending her life considerably. Whilst under the Swedish flag as *Goosebridge*, she was captured and sunk by a U-boat on New Year's Day 1917. *Author's collection*

A significant change during the 1880s was the general move from iron to steel construction. Steel was stronger than iron, and thinner sections and thicknesses could be used to give the same strength, saving weight and increasing cargo capacity. Steel was initially more expensive than iron, but developments in steel making progressively reduced its cost so that by 1890 only smaller vessels continued to be built from iron.[26]

VIII

Building iron steamers required a great deal more in terms of plant, skills, manpower and investment than did wooden ships, which could and often were built by a river or harbour where there was a ready supply of timber. Investment in iron shipyard equipment and maintaining a skilled workforce required regular orders from shipowners. Hence yards building in iron needed to market

---

[26]   Thomas, *British Ocean Tramps*, vol. 1, 22.

Table 4.7 Major builders of screw colliers, 1860s–1890

	1860s	1870	1880	1890	Totals
S.P. Austin, Sunderland	0	0	2	2	4
R. Craggs, Tees	0	0	1	2	3
Denton, Gray, West Hartlepool	0	1	1	0	3
William Doxford, Sunderland	0	2	0	0	2
J.T. Eltringham, South Shields	0	0	2	0	2
Hodgson & Gardner, Sunderland	0	0	3	0	3
J. Laing, Sunderland	3	3	2	0	6
Charles Mitchell, Low Walker	3	2	0	0	2
T.R. Oswald, Sunderland	0	1	0	1	2
Palmer Brothers, Tyne	12	4	1	3	20
Pile, Spencer, West Hartlepool	2	0	0	0	2
Schlesinger, Davis, Wallsend	1	1	0	1	3
T. & W. Smith, North Shields	5	5	2	1	10
Strand Slipway, Sunderland	0	0	0	3	3
Robert Thompson, Sunderland	0	0	1	3	4
Watson, Sunderland	0	2	0	0	2
Alexander Withy/Withy, Hartlepool	0	1	3	0	4
Wood, Skinner, Bill Quay	0	0	0	2	2
Yards building one collier					16

themselves in terms of price, technology and delivery times, and to be alert for new opportunities. Those with experience of building screw colliers might be expected to exploit this by meeting the demand for progressively larger iron steam ships, and this expectation has been tested by listing builders of both types of craft.

Table 4.7 lists the builders of almost one hundred colliers from the 1860s to 1890 included in the surveys reported above. A total of 33 different builders are represented of which 17 built two or more colliers. Table 4.8 includes this data for the same number of tramps, for which there were 38 different builders, 16 of which built at least two. The major builder of both types was the yard of Palmer Brothers on the Tyne, which not only built the pioneering *John Bowes*, but was responsible for 24 of the colliers built up to 1859. Two other builders figure prominently in Tables 4.7 and 4 8. Charles Mitchell of Newcastle-upon-Tyne was responsible for seven colliers up to 1859 and had contributed two further colliers

Table 4.8 Major builders of steam tramps, 1860s–1890

	1860s	1870	1880	1890	Totals
John Blumer, Sunderland	0	0	2	2	4
Denton, Gray, West Hartlepool	2	4	2	2	10
Robert Duncan, Port Glasgow	0	0	1	1	2
James Laing, Sunderland	2	0	1	0	3
Charles Mitchell, Low Walker, Newcastle	0	4	1	0	5
Palmer Brothers, Tyne	12	3	4	0	19
Richardson, Newcastle	1	1	0	0	2
Richardson, Duck, Thornaby	1	2	0	1	4
Schlesinger, Davis, Wallsend	1	2	0	2	5
Short Brothers, Sunderland	0	0	1	2	3
T. & W. Smith, North Shields	1	1	0	0	2
Swan, Hunter, Newcastle	0	0	2	1	3
J.L. Thompson, Sunderland	0	0	1	2	3
Tyne Iron, Willington Quay	0	0	2	2	4
Withy, Alexander, West Hartlepool	0	1	1	5	7
Yards building one tramp					25

and nine tramps by 1890. With five colliers built to 1859, James Laing contributed six further colliers plus two tramps by 1890.

Just seven yards built both colliers and tramps: Palmer, T. & W. Smith, Laing, Withy, Denton, Schlesinger and Mitchell. It is significant that six of this seven were responsible for all but two of the earliest tramps surveyed, those built in the 1860s. The combined output of these seven yards represented 51 per cent of the colliers in this survey and 37 per cent of the tramps, indicating that collier builders could certainly turn their hands to larger tramps. However, any conclusions drawn from this aspect of the survey must also take into account the activities of the less prolific yards and especially the 16 which built just one collier and the 23 building just one tramp.

IX

Drawing the above strands together, some conclusions can be drawn as to the contribution of the early screw collier to the origins and development of the ocean-going steam tramp. There is a temptation to consider whether this was a matter of the tramp simply evolving from the collier. However (like the Darwinian evolution of species), this can never be conclusively proved, although it could be readily disproved, for instance, by the discovery of numerous tramps with double bottoms and compound engines built in the 1840s. Existence of these has not so far been demonstrated![27]

In the mid-1850s, the British government and early owners of screw colliers had shown that voyages as far as Constantinople and the Black Sea were quite feasible for the newly developed screw collier. With the steady proliferation of these steamers in that decade, their trading area was quickly expanded. Crew agreements surveyed indicate that in the late 1850s screw colliers were working outside the purely coastal collier trade for about 40 per cent of their time. To exploit the screw collier, two well-resourced joint stock companies were set up to trade around Great Britain and beyond: the General Iron Screw Collier Co. Ltd in September 1852 and the London Steam Navigation Co. Ltd in March 1864.[28] The 1860s also saw the origins of a number of enterprises which grew into substantial tramp ship operators, which were promoted or supported by individuals in London, Tyneside and Wearside who were established in the coal industry as colliery owners, factors, colliery agents, coal merchants and coal fitters. This was closely followed by similar businesses being founded in South Wales, where exporting of steam coal was becoming significant.[29] At this point it is worth recalling the dependence of the emerging steam tramp on coal as a staple cargo. As Craig points out, equally important to the success of tramp steamers loading coal outwards was their finding profitable return cargoes and thus minimising or eliminating ballast passages.[30] In the case of carrying coal to the Eastern Mediterranean, back cargoes of grain from the Black Sea to western Europe were available. On the shorter routes, to southern France or Spain, the mines around Bilbao provided cargoes of rich iron ore which was replacing that from British sources with the adoption of the Bessemer converter for steel making.[31]

It might be argued that the evidence cited above of the screw collier developing directly into the deep-sea tramp could be circumstantial. More concrete evidence comes from comparison of the characteristics of the two types at the point of emergence of the steam tramp in the 1860s. As Table 4.4 shows, dimensionally the hulls of the latter are simply a scaling up of the hull size of the collier by a modest 8 per cent. Examples of both types have facilities for

---

[27]   Craig cites the iron, screw steamer *Sarah Sands* of 1846 as a candidate for the first tramp steamer to reach and later to cross the Pacific, but there is no evidence of her having water ballast facilities. R. Craig. *British Tramp Shipping, 1750–1914* (St. John's, Newfoundland, 2003), 24.

[28]   TNA, company registration papers, class BT 31/916/1069c.

[29]   Craig, *British Tramp Shipping*, 27.

[30]   Craig, *British Tramp Shipping*, 28.

[31]   Craig, *British Tramp Shipping*, 28–9.

carrying water ballast, with double bottoms almost equally common. Perhaps unsurprisingly in view of the larger size and intended trading patterns, some tramps were fitted with the higher efficiency, more economical and powerful compound engine, while all but two colliers were built with simple two-cylinder machinery. Tramps had on average 10 per cent higher horsepower. However, numbers of both types were retrofitted with compound engines or had their engines compounded.

Tables 4.5 and 4.6 trace the development of these characteristics in the two types of steamer over the next 30 years. Comparison of the 'change' columns in these tables show the steam tramp increasing in size much more dramatically than the collier. The dimension of the latter were particularly limited by the size of the ports they used (especially in terms of draft), the docks in which they discharged, and in some cases by the limited needs of coal merchants, especially those in smaller ports. Deep-sea tramp steamers were also constrained in size by port facilities, but the economies they brought to trades such as coal, grain and iron ore obliged port authorities to arrange to accommodate, load and discharge increasingly larger vessels.[32] Interestingly, however, owners of both colliers and tramps were almost equally enthusiastic in embracing new technology, including dramatically increased boiler pressures and compound and later triple-expansion machinery. Double bottoms for carrying water ballast, along with fore and aft peak tanks, had become almost universal in both colliers and tramps by 1870, and became defining features of both types of steamer.

The most productive collier builder, Palmer Brothers on the Tyne, also topped the league table for tramp construction (see Tables 4.7 and 4.8). Other yards also figure prominently in both lists, also on the Tyne. Of these it is tempting to champion those, especially Palmer, as the yards that turned the collier into the tramp. However, the large number of shipyards involved must also be taken into account, the 33 that built at least one collier and the 38 that built one or more tramps. It is proposed that rather than simple evolution that might have occurred at the Palmer yard, technology transfer should be recognised as playing its part in turning the screw collier into the steam tramp, as the features of the screw collier were well described in the technical press.[33] In addition, the staff of shipyards on the north-east coast especially would be very familiar with the screw colliers themselves from their daily sailings from local collieries or coal tips and their visits to shipyards for surveys and repairs. Owners with experience of the coal trade would naturally instruct builders to incorporate water ballast capacity and large holds and hatches in steamers destined for longer-distance trades. The situation is not unlike that which

---

[32]   G. Jackson, *The History and Archaeology of Ports* (Tadworth, 1983), 73.

[33]   For instance, E.E. Allen, 'On the Comparative Cost of Transit by Steam and Sailing Colliers, and on the Different Methods of Ballasting', *Proceedings of the Institute of Civil Engineers*, 14 (1854–5), 318–73.

produced the steam coaster by adopting characteristics of the screw collier, except that with steam tramps the development happened over a much shorter period of time.

Rather than citing the shaky ground of evolution for colliers becoming tramps, it can safely be said that without the invention and development of the screw collier in the 1850s, the tramp steamer is very unlikely to have been ready to steam off in the very next decade to begin the revolution in deep-sea bulk carrying which was to have such wide-reaching effects on world trade.

X

Collier into tramp: a chronology

1840s   Attempts to build a screw-driven bulk carrier for coastal use. Most were technical or commercial failures.

1851   First successful screw colliers delivered – *John Bowes* by Palmer, *Lady Berriedale* by Scott Russell, *Haggerston* from Liverpool.

1851–60   At least 70 screw colliers built for the east coast coal trade.

1854   First compound engine fitted, in coaster *Brandon*.[34]

1854–6   Many colliers sent to the Black Sea during the Crimean War, establishing their ability to make extended voyages.

1857   Participants in the coal trade begin to build large screw colliers, 200 to 250 feet overall, to carry coal 'to Britain, Ireland and foreign'.

1860   Earliest steam tramps owned in Sunderland by Gourley and by Laing.[35]

1861   Earliest steam tramp owned in London by Watts.[36]

1865   Earliest steam tramp owned in Cardiff.[37]

1869   Suez Canal opened, considerably extending the operating range of the steam tramp.

---

[34]   R. Craig, *The Ship: Steam Tramps and Cargo Liners, 1850–1950* (London, 1980), 11.

[35]   Thomas, *British Ocean Tramps*, vol. 1, 154, 155.

[36]   Thomas, *British Ocean Tramps*, vol. 1, 114–18.

[37]   J.G. Jenkins and D. Jenkins, *Cardiff Shipowners* (Cardiff, 1986), 8. Although Cardiff was to become, along with London and Newcastle, one of the triumvirate of British tramp shipowning ports, its position in terms of coal shipments was successfully challenged by the better facilities at Barry. The first dock was opened there in 1889, and a second in 1898, allowing Barry to surpass its older rival in terms of coal shipments in 1913, when it became the busiest coal port in the world, loading 11,000,000 tons of coal. Jackson, *History and Archaeology of Ports*, 130; W.E. Minchinton, *Industrial South Wales, 1750–1940: Essays in Welsh Economic History* (London, 1969), xxi.

1870	Double bottoms for water ballast established in the design of both colliers and tramps.

1871	Earliest tramp steamer owned in Whitby.[38]

1874	First triple-expansion engine fitted, in *Propontis*,[39] to be widely adopted by tramps in the 1880s.

---

[38]	Thomas, *British Ocean Tramps*, vol. 1, 160.

[39]	D. Griffiths, 'Triple Expansion and the First Shipping Revolution', in B. Greenhill (ed.), *The Advent of Steam: The Merchant Steamship before 1900* (London, 1993), 107.

Chapter Five

Miniaturisation:
The birth of the steam coaster

I

Steam ship penetration of British coastal bulk trades other than those for east coast coal was comparatively slow, and it was not until the late 1870s that what became known as the steam coaster began to be built in substantial numbers. Thereafter these vessels quickly multiplied, with perhaps as many as two thousand eventually built, and completed in a range of sizes from 80 feet in length to around 180 feet, the latter examples rivalling screw colliers in terms of carrying capacity.[1] Although steam coasters found employment in trades all around the British coast and on short-sea routes to continental Europe, there was a notable preponderance of owners in ports on the west side of the United Kingdom, suggesting that these ships were particularly well suited to trades on the west, especially those around the Irish Sea.[2]

In this account, the widely used term 'steam coaster' refers to the smaller ships, often found working (although by no means exclusively) in bulk trades on the west coast of the United Kingdom.[3] The older term 'screw collier' is used for larger vessels, usually intended for the east coast coal trade.

The origin and early development of the steam coaster has been little studied. Armstrong, who has made a notable contribution to the academic study of coastal shipping and, with co-author Williams, to the development of steam shipping, has very little to say on bulk carrying by steam coaster. In an otherwise

---

[1]   C.V. Waine, *Steam Coasters and Short Sea Traders*, 1st ed. (Albrighton, 1976).

[2]   C.V. Waine and R.S. Fenton, *Steam Coasters and Short Sea Traders*, 3rd ed. (Albrighton, 1994), 128–74. Chapter 12 gives an overview of steam coaster owners organised by the ports in which they were based.

[3]   Coasting vessels divide into the same two types of cargo ship as are found in deep-sea trades: the liner and the tramp. Coasters were designed and built for both types of trade, those for the liner trade being slightly faster, with more decks and subdivisions and more extensive cargo gear. The coasters considered here were built for bulk carrying cargoes including barrels, bricks, china clay, coal, fertilisers, grain, lime, metallic ores, pig iron, railway rails, salt, slates, stone and timber.

useful volume on steam ship development, Craig virtually ignores the steam coaster while citing various screw colliers as exemplifying the development of steam ships in coastal bulk trades.[4] Waine, who has done more than any author to classify and chronicle the steam coaster, simply suggests that they evolved from screw colliers.[5] It is tempting to suggest that the Clyde 'puffer' may have contributed to the design of the steam coaster.

In attempting to chart the early design and development of steam coasters, several strands will be investigated. Timelines will be drawn for the emergence of the screw collier and steam coaster and comparison made of the size and other characteristics of the two types of vessel. Histories of the shipbuilders will be explored to decide if there was continuity between the building of screw colliers and steam coasters.

II

Craig refers by name to five steamers carrying bulk cargoes (iron and copper ore and coal) on the west coast of the United Kingdom in the 1850s, and the prominence he gives to them suggests that steam was relatively important in these trades.[6] However, the present author has surveyed steam coasters owned in ports from Pembroke to Liverpool and found that they did not become numerous until the 1880s.[7] This is in marked contrast to the timeline for the emergence of the screw collier.

Table 2.1 in Chapter 2 lists known attempts to build screw colliers up to 1859. To provide a comparison, Table 5.1 lists screw-propelled bulk carriers known to be working in west coast trades from 1849 to 1857. There were just 17 in total, with only 12 being built during the 1850s. A marked difference in the penetration of the east and west coast bulk trades by steam is apparent in Tables 5.1 and 5.2. Although building coastal bulk carriers for use outside the east coast coal trade began in the late 1840s, their numbers lagged seriously behind those of of screw colliers, and the steam coaster only began to be multiplied in the 1870s, at least two decades later. Although growth then levelled off, by 1900 the steam coaster was more numerous than the screw collier.

A comparison of the size and other characteristics of screw colliers and steam coasters would be expected to give an indication of how closely they are related and provide clues to whether the latter 'evolved' from the former, as

---

[4]   R. Craig, *The Ship: Steam Tramps and Cargo Liners, 1850–1950* (London, 1980).

[5]   Waine, *Steam Coasters and Short Sea Traders* (1st ed.), 7–11.

[6]   R. Craig, 'Aspects of Tramp Shipping and Ownership', in K. Matthews and G. Panting (eds), *Ships and Shipbuilding in the North Atlantic Region* (St. John's, Newfoundland, 1978), 210–11.

[7]   R.S. Fenton, *Cambrian Coasters* (Kendal, 1989); R.S. Fenton, *Mersey Rovers* (Gravesend, 1997).

Table 5.1 West coast bulk-carrying steamers, 1849–1869

Name	Registered	Builder	Intended trade
Dumbarton Youth	4 November 1847	Denny, Dumbarton	iron ore
Express	24 June 1847	Harvey, Hayle	Bristol Channel
John	3 February 1849	Price, Neath Abbey	Bristol Channel
Augusta	1 November 1849	Sturge, Swansea	iron ore
Collier	29 April 1850	Wood & Reid, Clyde	coal
Briton Ferry	17 September 1852	Renfrew	iron ore
Preston	1 October 1853	South Shields	coal/iron ore
Will O'th Wisp	15 February 1854	Mitchell, Newcastle	Dublin collier
Isabella Croll	6 July 1854	Palmers, Jarrow	coal
Iron Age	7 August 1854	Pearse, Stockton	iron ore
Arbutus	11 November 1854	Toward, Newcastle	Dublin collier
Alma	26 April 1855	Chepstow	Bristol Channel
Annie Vernon	11 April 1856	Vernon, Liverpool	coal/iron ore
Thomas Powell	6 August 1856	Stothert, Bristol	coal/iron ore
Deva	23 June 1857	Chester	coal
James Kennedy	5 September 1857	Liverpool	coal/iron ore
Windermere	16 September 1857	Poplar	iron ore

The primary sources for this data are the registration documents held at The National Archives, Kew classes BT 107 and BT 108 and at certain regional archives. These have been supplemented with data from the *Mercantile Navy List, Lloyd's Register, Liverpool Underwriters' Register of Iron Ships, Lloyd's Confidential Index, Lloyd's Casualty Returns* and *Board of Trade Wreck Returns*.

Table 5.2 Numbers of bulk carriers in service on the east and west coasts of the United Kingdom, 1860–1910

Year	1860	1870	1880	1890	1900	1910
West coast 'steam coasters'	12	37	184	233	272	332
East coast 'screw colliers'	58	135	280	260	258	259

Table 5.3 Net tonnages of steam coasters and screw colliers in service, 1860–1910

Year	1860	1870	1880	1890	1900	1910
Total net tonnage						
Steam coaster		7,316	34,019	47,786	48,698	70,260
Screw collier		65,880	125,826	123,186	136,985	157,989
Difference		11%	27%	39%	36%	44%
Number						
Steam coaster	12	37	184	233	272	332
Screw collier	58	135	280	260	258	259
Average net tonnage						
Steam coaster		197	184	196	178	212
Screw collier		488	447	476	533	612
Difference		40%	41%	41%	33%	35%
Average length						
Steam coaster		137 feet	140 feet	148 feet	152 feet	164 feet
Screw collier		185 feet	190 feet	196 feet	204 feet	212 feet
Difference		74%	74%	76%	75%	77%

Note: 'Difference' expresses the steam coaster figure as a percentage of the screw collier figure.

Waine proposed. A survey was carried out of the numbers and net tonnages of steam coasters and screw colliers found working in bulk trades in the years from 1860 to 1910. The results are shown in Table 5.3.[8]

Figures in Table 5.3 indicate substantial differences in both the average lengths and net tonnages of steam coasters and screw colliers. Over the period surveyed, length differences are maintained, while the average net tonnage of steam coasters falls in comparison with that of screw colliers. The figures point to significant differences between the two types of vessel.

---

[8]   The figures have been computed from contemporary lists of owners and their fleets published in three shipping registers: the *Liverpool Underwriters' Registry of Iron Vessels, Lloyd's Register* and *Lloyd's Confidential Register*. The owners surveyed were known to have specialised in either steam coasters (largely based in west coast ports) or screw colliers (based mainly in London, Newcastle and Sunderland).

III

The survey resulting in Table 5.3 aimed to take in all candidate steam coasters and screw colliers. As the sizes of these steamers varied very considerably, meaningful comparisons between the two types require separating steam coasters into different size bands and distinguishing the two widely adopted designs of screw collier. Waine found that vessels of different sizes had distinct characteristics, not least in terms of hull form.[9] To compare vessels in these size bands, ships were chosen at random to give building dates from the 1850s to 1914. In assigning ships to groups, reference has also been made to photographs and to general arrangement and other shipyard drawings of the vessels reproduced by Waine and Macrae and Waine.[10] Results are shown in Tables 5.4 to 5.8.

Table 5.4 Characteristics of steam coasters below 130 feet in length

Name	Date	Length	Beam	Depth	L:B	L:D	Ballast
Larry Bane	1875	115	20	9	5.8	12.8	?
Agate	1878	121	20	10	6.1	12.1	F 15t
Ada	1880	109	20	9	5.5	12.1	F 12t
Sodium	1887	100	20	8	5.0	12.5	F 20t
Velinheli	1892	95	19	9	5.0	10.5	F ?
James Tennant	1893	120	21	9	5.7	13.3	F 32t
Edith	1900	100	23	11	4.3	9.1	F+A 48t
Calatum	1908	121	22	10	5.5	12.1	F 25t
Saint Modan	1910	122	22	9	5.5	13.6	F+A 21t
Lucena	1913	114	24	11	4.8	10.4	F ?
Collin	1915	121	22	9	5.5	13.4	F+A 25t
Averages		124	21.2	9.5	5.8	12.0	25t

L = length; B = beam; D = depth; F = forepeak tank; A = aft peak tank.

Table 5.4 considers steam coasters in the smallest size range of 80 to 130 feet. These usually had a single hold served by one or rarely two hatches. A raised

---

9   Waine and Fenton, *Steam Coasters and Short Sea Traders*, 11.

10   J.A. Macrae and C.V. Waine, *The Steam Collier Fleets* (Albrighton, 1990). Dimensions and dates are from *Lloyd's Register*, *Mercantile Navy List* and The National Archives, Kew (TNA), registration documents, classes BT 107, BT 108, BT 110 and CUST 130. Ballast arrangements are not noted in *Lloyd's Register* for early colliers, and it has not been possible to discover the ballast capacity of many engines-aft vessels of this type.

5: *Edith* represents the smallest steam coasters: she was just 100 feet in length. Built by prolific west coast Scottish yard, Scott and Sons of Bowling for Merseyside owners in 1900, she survived to be fitted with an oil engine by Danish owners in 1947 and was not deleted from *Lloyd's Register* until the 1970s. *Ships in Focus*

forecastle and in the larger vessels a poop (it could also be regarded as a bridge deck or quarterdeck) helped sea-keeping properties. The well-deck, between forecastle and quarterdeck, was protected by bulwarks. The cargo gear was usually confined to a single derrick on the foremast which was usually stepped at the break of the forecastle. A smaller mizzen mast was fitted right aft but was intended mainly to carry navigation lights and a steadying sail (sails were also often rigged on the forestay). The engine was aft, with an often rudimentary open wheelhouse forward of this. The seamen and firemen were accommodated in the forecastle, the master, mate and engineer having cabins above the raised quarterdeck aft, where there was also a saloon and a galley.

These steamers had a very modest capacity for water ballast. Ballast tanks were usually fitted in the forepeak (i.e., right forward, below the accommodation in the forecastle) and in a few cases in the aft peak (right aft, usually just ahead of the stern post). None is known to have had double-bottom tanks. The water ballast capacity of the fore and aft peak tanks was very modest: just 24 tons on average, about 8 per cent to 9 per cent of their deadweight capacity. It is likely that in these small steam coasters water ballast capacity was provided merely to improve trim when steaming without a cargo.

Table 5.5 Characteristics of steam coasters 130 to 160 feet in length

Name	Date	Length	Beam	Depth	L:B	L:D	Ballast
Sapphire	1881	160	23	11	7.0	14.5	F+A 51t
Sylfaen	1883	160	23	11	7.0	14.5	F+A 51t
Primrose	1885	135	20	10	6.8	13.5	F 40t
Moss Rose	1890	150	23	10	6.5	15.0	F+A 60t
Lancashire	1892	160	23	12	7.0	13.3	F+A 55t
Queen's Channel	1894	153	24	9	6.4	17	DB+F 117t
Latchford	1897	160	24	9	6.7	17.8	DB+A 121t
Helmsman	1903	160	25	13	6.4	12.3	DB+F 129t
Inchbrayock	1909	140	24	11	5.8	12.7	?
Ashfield	1914	143	26	12	5.5	11.9	DT+A 39t
Average		148	23.5	10.8	6.5	14.25	74 t

L = length; B = beam; D = depth; DB = double bottom; F = forepeak tank; A = aft peak tank; DT = deep tank.

Once arrived at, this design proved remarkably durable. The earliest of this type for which Waine has a drawing is the *Agate* of 1878. In 1920, in what was amongst the last ships of this size built, the 120-foot-long *Doris Thomas* differed mainly in having a taller forecastle and quarterdeck. The cargo capacity (i.e., deadweight) had been raised from the 210 tons of the *Agate* to 270 tons in *Doris Thomas*, partly by increasing the beam and probably by making the underwater body of her hull fuller.

Characteristics of sample coasters over 130 feet in length are listed in Table 5.5. For steam coasters of this size, the usual arrangement was to have two holds and two hatches. It was normal for the aftermost hatch to be one deck higher than the forward hatch, so that a raised quarterdeck ran from about two-fifths of the length aft to the stern. The wheelhouse was usually positioned at the forward end of this quarterdeck, and below it was accommodation for master and mate. As in the smaller steamer, there was a forecastle forward, with basic accommodation for seamen and firemen. The engine was aft, with accommodation for the engineers and a galley in a deckhouse aft, above the engines. Each of the holds was served by a mast and derrick. A large number of this type fell in the length band 140 to 150 feet, with 142 feet being particularly popular.[11] This reflected the maximum dimensions of the entrance locks to

---

[11] Waine and Fenton, *Steam Coasters and Short Sea Traders*, 79.

6: The 142-foot *Ashfield* of 1914 is an example of the most numerous design of long raised quarterdeck steam coasters. She was built by the Lytham Shipbuilding and Engineering Co. Ltd for the Zillah Shipping and Carrying Co. Ltd of Liverpool, remaining with this owner until broken up in 1954. *Ships in Focus*

Ringsend Basin, the main dock used for the coal trade to Dublin, and of the Newry Ship Canal.

The smaller coasters in this size band mainly had compound two-cylinder steam engines, it being claimed that the additional economy of triple-expansion machinery was not worth the extra cost and that, in small vessels, the additional cylinder reduced space available for cargo.[12] The larger the steamer, the greater the likelihood of fitting a triple-expansion engine, and this machinery was usual in the 142-foot type.

The peculiarity of the hull form of these vessels, with a break or well between forecastle and quarterdeck, requires some explanation, especially as the omission of a continuous deck at this point would add to construction costs and reduce the overall strength of the hull. However, the raised quarterdeck design was favoured because it gave better trimming characteristics. The engine, boilers and bunkers occupied over a third of the vessel's length, but these were relatively light in comparison with a hold filled with coal or stone. Thus, when the hold was filled with cargo the weight was concentrated well forward, making the ship trim by the head, i.e., with the bow drawing more than the stern. This made steering more difficult, would allow the screw to come out of the water in a rough sea, and could cause draft problems when a loaded ship had to enter or leave a port, which, like many of those used

---

[12]   Waine and Fenton, *Steam Coasters and Short Sea Traders*, 35.

Table 5.6 Characteristics of steam coasters over 160 feet in length

Name	Date	Length	Beam	Depth	L:B	L:D	Ballast
Mersey	1891	173	25	12	6.9	14.4	F+A 45t
Brier Rose	1892	165	25	10	6.6	16.5	F+A 70t
Bass Rock	1892	165	26	12	6.3	13.8	DB+F+A 70t
Devonshire	1894	175	27	10	6.5	17.5	DB+F 180t
Fleswick	1899	179	28	11	6.4	16.3	DB+F+A 210t
British Empire	1902	168	27	12	6.2	14.0	DB+F+A 76t
Cheshire	1904	178	29	11	6.1	16.2	DB+F+A 183t
Wheatfield	1909	163	27	12	6.0	13.6	DB+F+A 135t
Primrose	1910	175	28	11	6.3	15.9	DB+F 188t
Allerton	1913	175	28	10	6.3	17.5	DB+F+A 232t
Average		188	27.0	11.1	6.4	15.6	139t

Note: All had a raised quarter deck and engines aft.
L = length; B = beam; D = depth; DB = double bottom; F = forepeak tank; A = aft peak tank; DT = deep tank.

by west coast bulkers, had restricted depth of water. The raised quarterdeck design ensured that the hold further aft, which was deeper thanks to the raised quarterdeck, took more of the cargo. Placing proportionally more of the weight aft enabled a loaded steamer to trim on an even keel.[13]

The raised quarterdeck configuration became very popular, and virtually all the larger, engines-aft steam coasters and many screw colliers eventually adopted the arrangement. Paucity of photographs and published plans of vessels built in the 1870s makes it very difficult to state with certainty when the design was applied to engines-aft vessels. The earliest known illustration of this arrangement is of William Robertson's 160-foot *Sapphire* of 1881,[14] a product of the Paisley yard of John Fullerton. This shipyard may well have been one of the pioneers of the design as it went on to build many more of this type, although the design was also constructed at other yards.

As well as a more sophisticated structure, these middle-sized steam coasters had greater provision for water ballast, most having a combination of fore and aft peak tanks, and the larger vessels also had double bottoms. The average ballast

---

[13] The author has published this explanation and it has not been challenged. See R.S. Fenton, 'Coastal and Short-sea Shipping', in R. Gardiner, *The Golden Age of Shipping: The Classic Merchant Ship, 1900–1960* (London, 1994), 81–96.
[14] Photograph in the collection of Glasgow University Archives.

7: The large, engines-aft collier *J.R. Hinde* of 1864 sails from Hull
well loaded. The Cory family were the biggest shareholders in the ship when
new, and she was in their ownership when broken up at Boulogne in 1910.
Ships in Focus

capacity was 74 tons, which, given a deadweight of about 450 tons, represented
16 per cent of its cargo capacity, a figure regarded by Allen as ideal.[15]

The steam coasters of over 160 feet in length whose details are included in
Table 5.6 were of the raised quarterdeck type, and their layout was generally
similar to those of 130 to 160 feet. There appears to have been relatively little
employment for vessels over 180 feet on the west coast in the period up to 1914;
no vessels of this size being built for recognised west coast owners in a large
series of vessels surveyed by the author.[16]

In eight out of ten vessels of 160 feet and above, double-bottom tanks were
fitted, as well as fore and often aft peak tanks. There was a wide variation in
ballast capacities, from 45 tons to 242 tons, the average being 139 tons. Waine
estimates their deadweight at 735 tons, so the ballast capacity of these ships is
equivalent to 19 per cent of their total cargo-carrying capacity.

Screw colliers are assigned to two groups: those with engines aft (Table 5.7)
and those with engines amidships (Table 5.8). Where possible, early colliers have

---

[15]   E.E. Allen, 'On the Comparative Cost of Transit by Steam and Sailing Colliers, and
on the Different Methods of Ballasting', *Proceedings of the Institute of Civil Engineers*,
14 (1854–5), 318–73.

[16]   Fenton, *Mersey Rovers.*

Table 5.7 Characteristics of screw colliers with engines aft

Name	Date	Length	Beam	Depth	L:B	L:D	Ballast
John Bowes	1852	149	26	16	5.7	9.3	?
Haggerston	1852	159	25	15	6.4	10.6	DB
Caroline	1853	141	26	15	5.4	9.4	DB –
Lady Alice Lambton	1853	159	17	15	9.4	10.6	?
William Cory	1857	245	35	18	7.0	13.6	DB –
Rouen	1857	204	30	15	6.8	13.6	?
Henry Morton	1860	230	32	18	7.2	12.8	DB –
J.R. Hinde	1864	199	28	17	7.1	11.7	?
Tanfield	1865	203	28	17	7.3	11.9	DB –
New Pelton	1865	180	28	17	6.4	10.6	DB –
Upton/Burham	1865	202	28	17	7.2	11.9	DB 188t
Northumbria	1869	221	28	17	7.9	13.0	DB 200t
Lord Alfred Paget/ Eastwood	1870	224	28	17	8.0	13.2	DB –
Average	–	194	28	16.5	8.6	10.1	–

L = length; B = beam; D = depth; DB = double bottom.

been selected, as the objective is to examine whether their design influenced that of west coast bulk carriers.

Table 5.7 includes some of the pioneering vessels according to plans published by Allan and by Waine,[17] including *John Bowes*, *Lady Berriedale*, *Black Prince*, *Firefly*, *Imperial*, *Eagle*, *Hawk* and *Falcon*. They had one or two holds and hatches ahead of the engine room. They were flush-decked, with a rudimentary steering position mounted at the forward end of a low casing around the engine. They were rigged as schooners, and gaffs on the fore and main masts were the only cargo gear fitted.

As the engines-aft design of collier grew in length, the navigating position was moved forward to between the two hatches. The masts and rigging were retained, with the main mast just abaft of the bridge. The aft part of the hull was built higher than that alongside the hatches, giving rise to a half-height quarterdeck. A forecastle also appears, although originally it was no higher

---

[17] Allen, 'Comparative Cost of Transit'; Waine and Fenton, *Steam Coasters and Short Sea Traders*, 45–53.

than the bulwarks which flank the hold and is only apparent in stern views. The *J.R. Hinde* of 1864 and *Trevethick* of 1866 have this arrangement in photographs taken around 1900.[18] At this date the vessels are still carrying sails. In later vessels, the forecastle was raised to a full deck height, and this is evident in photographs of *Upton* (later *Burham*). Two-cylinder simple steam engines were fitted in most colliers built until the early 1870s, with many colliers being either re-engined or compounded in the 1870s and 1880s, *J.R. Hinde* and *Trevethick* being so treated.[19]

Water ballast arrangements in these colliers varied, with a combination of McIntyre tanks in the holds and double bottoms gradually replacing the ballast bags originally popular. Ballast capacities are listed in *Lloyd's Register* for only two of the engines-aft colliers in Table 5.7, too few to draw conclusions.

The design of engines-amidships screw colliers sampled in Table 5.8 emerged early: the *Lambton* of 1857 being the earliest known example of this design.[20] One hold was ahead of, and one abaft of, the engines and superstructure. *Lambton* was flush-decked like many early engines-aft colliers, and this design was perpetuated until at least the *Fenham* of 1868.[21] However, within 12 months the yard which had built *Fenham*, Charles Mitchell of Low Walker on the Tyne, had completed the *Hugh Taylor*, a vessel with a raised quarterdeck extending from the navigating bridge about amidships right to the stern.[22] The raised quarterdeck design then became the norm, further engines-amidships vessels having this feature. One reason for the popularity of this arrangement may be that on an engines-amidships vessel the shaft tunnel reduces the space available for cargo in the after-hold. This will lead to the vessel trimming by the head when laden, making steering difficult and increasing draft.[23] Deepening the after-hold by adding a raised quarterdeck increased its capacity, and helped overcome the trimming problem.

The raised quarterdeck design was enlarged, and colliers such as *Medway* and *Kent* had two holds ahead of the bridge. Some later designs also had two holds aft. This sample includes a number of colliers built for the coal trade to Goole, which required shallower vessels than those loading on the Tyne or Wear.[24]

Water ballast was typically contained in double bottom tanks, with only one of the vessels sampled having an aft peak tank, and none a forepeak tank. This may have reflected the tendency of the vessels to trim by the head. Ballast capacity was considerable at an average of 244 tons.

---

[18]   Photographs taken by Marcus Barnard of Hull, active about 1900–20. The negatives are in the collections of John Clarkson and Hull Museums.

[19]   *Lloyd's Register*, various dates.

[20]   Macrae and Waine, *Steam Collier Fleets*, 4.

[21]   Macrae and Waine, *Steam Collier Fleets*, 20.

[22]   Macrae and Waine, *Steam Collier Fleets*, 18.

[23]   Waine and Fenton, *Steam Coasters and Short Sea Traders*, 109.

[24]   Waine and Fenton, *Steam Coasters and Short Sea Traders*, 106.

Table 5.8 Characteristics of screw colliers with engines amidships

Name	Date	Length	Beam	Depth	L:B	L:D	Ballast
Lambton	1857	168	27	14	6.2	12.0	?
Sherburn	1866	187	29	17	6.4	11.0	DB –
Warkworth	1869	160	27	14	5.9	11.4	DB 180t
Fenham	1868	225	29	18	7.6	12.5	DB 211t
Hugh Taylor (RQD)	1869	225	29	18	7.6	12.5	DB 230t
Broomhill (RQD)	1878	175	29	13	6.0	13.5	DB –
Joseph Rickett (RQD)	1879	186	28	14	6.6	13.3	DB 180t
Medway (RQD)	1879	226	31	14	7.3	16.1	DB+A 319t
Kent (RQD)	1881	226	32	14	6.6	13.3	DB 272t
Langdon (RQD)	1882	240	34	16	7.1	15.0	DB 317t
Average	–	202	30	15.2	6.8	13.3	244t

L = length; B = beam; D = depth; DB = double bottom; F = forepeak tank; A = aft peak
tank; RQD = raised quarter deck.

The engines-amidships screw collier proved less durable in the coastal coal
trade than that with engines aft. Although ships of this type continued to be built
up to and beyond the First World War,[25] the engines-aft design then reasserted
its supremacy. The *Fulgens* of 1912, the first collier built for the Gas Light and
Coke Company, was a large vessel, 305 feet long, and had two holds forward
of the bridge, and two between the bridge and engines right aft, with a raised
quarterdeck.[26] She set the pattern for coastal colliers until the last steamers
were built for this trade in the mid-1950s.[27] However, as the next chapter will
discuss, the engines-amidships screw collier was the immediate progenitor of the
ocean-going steam bulk carrier, the 'tramp'.

Considering the data in Tables 5.4 to 5.8, the most obvious difference
between steam coaster and screw collier beyond their size is their capacity to
carry water ballast. In the steam coaster, capacity rises with overall size, so
that in the smallest ships under 130 feet it is minimal and confined to small aft
and/or forepeak tanks. In the medium-sized steam coaster, older vessels only
have aft and forepeak tanks, with tanks in double bottoms being added in later

---

[25] Waine notes the *Cordene* of 1924 as one of last. Waine and Fenton, *Steam Coasters
and Short Sea Traders*, 118.

[26] From trials' photographs taken on behalf of the builder, Wood, Skinner. Copies are
held by the World Ship Society. *Fulgens* was torpedoed in August 1915. D.R. Chesterton
and R.S. Fenton, *Gas and Electricity Colliers* (Kendal, 1984), 45.

[27] Chesterton and Fenton, *Gas and Electricity Colliers*, 40–71, 91–115.

8: Large colliers like *Hurstwood* of 1906 tended to have their engines amidships with a long raised quarterdeck stretching to the stern. Built by S.P. Austin and Son Ltd, Sunderland for William Cory, she was torpedoed by a German submarine north-east of Whitby in February 1917. *World Ship Society Ltd*

vessels, although the average ballast capacity of 74 tons is still quite modest. This capacity is doubled when the steam coasters over 160 feet are considered, most of these having double bottoms. In screw colliers where ballast capacity is known, it tends to be larger, averaging 244 tons for the engines-amidships type. As most steam coasters fall into size bands below 160 feet, their ballast capacity is always lower than that of steam colliers.

Steam coasters were built in a broad range of sizes, from 80 feet up to 180 feet. In contrast, all east coast colliers exceeded 150 feet, and the averages for the two types studied, engines aft and engines amidships, was 194 and 202 feet. Many larger colliers tended to have their engines amidships, while steam coasters invariably had engines aft.

The steam coaster was shallower drafted than the screw collier, with an average depth of hold which in the smaller vessels was 9.5 feet, rising modestly to 11.1 feet in the biggest vessels. It is significant that designers of the most popular steam coasters in the 130 to 160 foot range were constrained by draft, and this produced a vessel which was little deeper than their smaller cousins. In contrast, screw colliers, early examples of which were of comparable length to the large steam coasters, the average depth of hold was 15.2 to 16.5 feet for the two groups. This difference is significant, representing about a third of carrying capacity.

The shallowness of steam coasters undoubtedly reflected conditions in the trades in which they invariably worked. Whereas the rivers Tyne, Wear and Thames habitually used by screw colliers presented no barriers to using relatively deep-drafted vessels, the steam coaster owner found himself trading to an enormous variety of usually smaller ports, harbours and some cases offshore jetties.[28] In addition, coal, although the commonest single commodity carried by steam coaster, was by no means the only cargo. Metallic ores, stone, slates, timber, fertilisers, barrels, grain, and other foodstuffs which could be carried in bulk, all provided cargoes for steam coasters from and to a wide geographical range of ports. A shallow draft and a modest length gave the coaster the flexibility to trade widely, a necessary condition in what were essentially tramp trades. It is not surprising that relatively few east coast colliers were sold to west coast owners for working in their local trades.[29]

IV

If steam coasters did evolve from screw colliers it could be expected that the yards that pioneered the latter would exploit their experience and expertise and have eagerly built steam coasters as the demand for them rose from the 1870s onwards. To investigate this, all known coastal bulk carriers built of iron up to 1870 have been listed by builder (Table 5.9).[30]

Table 5.9 shows that the expectations about east and west coast builders are completely reversed. Despite their considerable expertise in building screw colliers, east coast yards won very few of the orders for bulk carriers for the west coast, building only seven out of the known 31 vessels which traded on the west coast to 1870. Palmer are the most spectacular example: they built 55 east coast colliers (three out of every ten built in this period) but only one west coast steamer, the *Morfa*, despite their founder's aggressive marketing. The next most prolific collier builder, James Laing of Sunderland, built none for the west

---

[28]   Two important Irish ports receiving shipments of coal had severe size limitations. Newry was limited by the dimensions of the Newry Ship Canal, and Dublin, where coal was mostly destined for, by the Ringsend Basin. In both cases, steam coasters of 142 feet were the largest that could be used, and this size remained a benchmark for the steam coaster. T. O'Conalláin, 'Dublin Gas Boats', *Ships in Focus Record*, 7 (1998), 146–54.

[29]   The exceptions included vessels specifically built or bought to carry steam coal from South Wales to Liverpool for use in fast passenger ships and in power stations. Examples were owned by the Rea family and latterly by Monroe Brothers of Liverpool. R.S. Fenton and W. Harvey, 'Rea Colliers', *Ships in Focus Record*, 63 (2016), 138–46; R.S. Fenton, *Monroe Brothers, Shipowners* (Kendal, 1982).

[30]   The details of builders are taken largely from TNA, registration documents, classes BT 108, BT 100, BT 110 and CUST 130, but not all of these recorded the name of the hull builder.

Table 5.9 Known builders of bulk-carrying steamers up to 1870

(Steam coasters are shown in italics; screw colliers in roman type)

Bainbridge, Willington Quay-on-Tyne	Henderson, Renfrew
1865 Southampton	*1866 Dorset*
1865 Basingstoke	J.M. Hoby & Co., Renfrew
Barclay, Curle & Co., Glasgow	*1854 Iron Age*
1861 Jessie Brown	1856 William France
Bowdler, Chaffer & Co., Seacombe	Robert Irvine & Co., West Hartlepool
1865 Kirkless	*1866 Ogmore*
1865 Agnes Jack	James Laing, Deptford, Sunderland
1865 Jane Bacon	1854 Great Northern
1867 Lancaster	1855 Vulture
Candlish, Middlesbrough	1855 Wearmouth
1866 Sunderland	1855 Vedra
J. Clayton, Liverpool	1860 Samson
1855 Carbon	1860 Deptford
J. Coutts, Walker-on-Tyne	1861 Earl of Elgin
1844 Q.E.D.	1861 General Havelock
George Cramm, Dee River Yard, Chester	1861 Haswell
1854 Chester	1861 Lady Havelock
1855 Derwent	1861 Newburn
Denny, Dumbarton	1862 Medusa
1847 Dumbarton Youth	1863 George Elliot
Alexander Denny, Dumbarton	1863 Lady Beatrix
1853 Chanticleer	1864 Biddick
Gill, Sunderland	1865 Belmont
1868 Ottercaps	1865 Cambridgeshire
Harvey & Co., Hayle	1865 Hartlepool
1864 Bride	1865 Lumley
1865 Bessie	1866 Kelloe
1867 Hayle	1865 Primus
Haswell, Sunderland	1866 Sherburn
1865 Natalian	1867 Harraton
	1867 Weardale

Table 5.9 *continued*

<table>
<tr><td>

1868 Langley

1868 Tynedale

1868 General Codrington (2)

1869 Ryhope

1869 Finchale

1869 Frankland

1869 Resolute

London and Glasgow Engineering and
Iron Shipbuilding Co. Ltd, Govan

1865 Cromwell

1865 Fairfax

Charles Lungley, Deptford

1854 Union

1854 Norman

1855 Dane

1863 Blonde

1864 May Queen

McNab, Greenock

1866 William Coulman

C.J. Mare & Co., Blackwall,
London

1853 Rajah

Thomas D. Marshall, South Shields

1842 Bedlington

1847 Conside

1853 Lady Alice Lambton

1862 Volunteer

1866 Derwent (2)

Maudslay, Sons & Field, East
Greenwich

1865 Lady Derby

Millwall Iron Works

1864 Newton Colville

1866 Salisbury

</td><td>

C. Mitchell & Co., Low Walker,
Newcastle

1854 Earl of Durham

1854 Hetton

1855 Killingworth

1856 Eupatoria

1856 St. George

1857 William Cory

1857 Lyon

1857 Lambton

1863 John Liddell

1863 John Johnasson

T.R. Oswald & Co., Pallion,
Sunderland

1861 Edith

1865 Fatfield

1865 Wear

1866 Hampshire (1)

1866 Houghton

Palmer Brothers & Co., Newcastle

1852 John Bowes

1852 William Hutt

1853 Countess of Strathmore

1853 Northumberland

1853 Sir John Easthope

1853 Durham

1853 Jarrow

1853 Marley Hill

1854 Ross D. Mangles

1854 Nicholas Wood

1854 Cochrane

1854 Samuel Laing

1854 Black Boy

1854 Whitley Park

</td></tr>
</table>

Table 5.9 *continued*

1854 Black Sea	1865 Margam Abbey
1855 Normanby	1866 Boston
1855 Sardinian	1866 Merthyr
1855 George Hawkins	1866 Trevethick
1855 General Codrington	1867 JE McConnell
1855 Hutton Chaytor	1869 Beckton
1855 Earsdon	1869 Northumbria
1856 Marmora	**Ebenezer Pike, Cork**
1857 Seaton	*1860 Ibis*
1857 Rouen	**John Pile/Pile, Spence, West Hartlepool**
1859 James Dixon	1857 Londonderry
1860 Sentinel	1865 Wisbeach
1860 Henry Morton	**W. Pile, Sunderland**
1861 Sir James Duke	1862 Miriam
1861 Hawthorns	**J.T. Price, Neath Abbey**
1861 John Fenwick	*1849 John*
1861 Brunette	**J. Ray, Sunderland**
1862 Morfa	1845 Experiment
1863 John Mcintyre	**John Reid & Co., Greenock**
1863 James Joicey	1849 Collier
1863 Fanny Lambert	**Richardson Brothers, Hartlepool**
1864 Despatch	1856 Florence Nightingale
1864 John R. Hinde	1855 Rechid
1864 Orwell	**Richardson, Low Walker**
1864 Tanfield	1864 Bebside
1864 Thomas Lea	**Richardson, Duck & Co., South Stockton**
1865 Conservator	1855 Countess Of Durham
1865 Mary Nixon	*1866 Lady Alice Hill*
1865 New Pelton	*1860 Cuirassier*
1865 Berrington	**Samuda Brothers, Poplar, London**
1865 JM Strachan	1854 Saxon
1865 ME Clarke	1854: Briton
1865 CS Butler	*1857 Windermere*
1865 William Hunter	

Table 5.9 *continued*

1869 Dromedary	1865 Dudley
M. Samuelson & Co., Hull	1865 James Southern
1857 Velocity	1865 Wentworth
1861 Falcon	1867 Bradley
Schlesinger, Davies & Co., Wallsend	1869 Blue Cross
1867 Aston	**J.K. Stothert & Co., Bristol**
J. Scott Russell & Co., Millwall, London	*1856 Thomas Powell*
1852 Lady Berriedale	**Sturge, Swansea**
1853 Caroline	*1849 Augusta*
1853 Falcon	**Swan Brothers, Dumbarton**
1853 Eagle	*1867 Lady Alice Kenlis*
1854 Imperial	**Union Shipbuilding Co., Kelvinhaugh**
1854 Hawk	*1864 Norseman*
1855 New Pelton (1)	**T. Vernon & Son, Liverpool**
J.E. Scott, Cartsdyke, Greenock	1852 Hunwick
1855 Berwick	1852 Haggerston
T.B. Seath, Rutherglen	1854 Black Prince
1864 Vanderbyl	1854 Firefly
Simons, Renfrew	1856 *Annie Vernon*
1857 Contest	*1857 James Kennedy*
T. & W. Smith, North Shields	**Walpole, Webb & Co., Dublin**
1861 Tom John Taylor	*1866 Dublin*
1863 Black Duck	**Wingate, Glasgow**
1864 Black Swan	1866 Ludworth
1865 Hastings	1866 Thornley

coast. The only east coast yard found to have built more than a single west coast steamer was Richardson, Duck and Co. on the Tees, but their products – the specialist, shallow-draft china clay carrier *Cuirassier* of 1860 and the collier *Lady Alice Hill* of 1866 – suggest no continuity in design.

West coast builders contributed more ships (a total of 14) for east coast trades than east coast builders did for west coast trades. Thomas Vernon at Liverpool, for instance, built four colliers between 1852 and 1854, the *Haggerston* being completed only a month after the pioneer *John Bowes,* and employed novel double-bottom tanks. However, despite this lead, Vernons did not go on to become major suppliers of steam coasters to local owners, building only the *Annie Vernon* of 1856. Many of the bulk carriers built for west coast owners up to 1870 were one-offs, their builders not being known to have constructed others. The two exceptions are Harveys of Hayle, who built three for their own account, and Bowdler, Chaffer of Seacombe on Merseyside, who built four between 1865 and 1867. However, neither of these yards went on to become significant suppliers of coastal bulk carriers.

It remains to be asked, if not the screw collier yards, who did build steam coasters? Table 5.10 shows the location of yards responsible for 133 vessels built in the 1870s, which were considered to be true steam coasters from their ownership and/or trading patterns involving UK coastal/short-sea bulk trades. All candidate vessels had iron hulls, were screw propelled, fell in the range 90 to 180 feet (to exclude Clyde puffers) and had water ballast capacity.

Table 5.10 indicates the importance of Scottish yards in pioneering and refining the steam coaster. Yards on and around the Clyde – at Campbeltown, Dumbarton, Glasgow, Kirkintilloch, Maryhill, Paisley, Port Glasgow, Renfrew and Rutherglen – built twice as many steam coasters as the rest of the United Kingdom put together. Their only challengers were yards on the Tyne at just 11 per cent: yards which had developed the screw collier 20 years earlier. The entire output of east coast English yards – on the Tyne, the Tees and Hartlepool, the Wear and Humber – made up just 18 per cent of the total. Just three yards in one Scottish town, Paisley, built 33 per cent of the total: Fullerton, McIntyre and the Abercorn yard of Hanna and Donald.[31] This compares with the 30 per cent built by all English yards put together.

Work by Waine indicates that west coast Scottish dominance continued.[32] He assigned the steam coasters existing in 1927 to builders. Although the date is late, this is a useful comparison as many vessels he listed would have been built before 1914, and in any case most major builders of steamers were well established before the First World War.[33] Scottish yards contributed about 55 per cent of the total, although east coast Scottish yards had grown in importance. West coast Scottish yards' contribution is about 45 per cent.

It is likely that local owners were 'driving' the development and building of steam coasters. William Robertson of Glasgow was the most prolific British

---

[31]   R.S. Fenton, 'Was the Steam Coaster a Scottish Invention?' Annual Scottish Maritime History Conference, Glasgow, 2013.

[32]   Waine and Fenton, *Steam Coasters and Short Sea Traders*, 11.

[33]   Several yards were either newly set up to build coasters after the war or turned from building fishing vessels or purely ship repair work to coaster construction. In the very unfavourable economic circumstances which set in for shipbuilding early in the 1920s, their output was relatively small and they quickly went bankrupt or returned to repair work. See, for instance, R.S. Fenton, and M. Guegan, 'Hansen Shipbuilding, Bideford', *Ships in Focus Record*, 14 (2000), 75–81 and *Ships in Focus Record*, 15 (2001), 158–63.

Table 5.10 Steam coasters built 1870–1880 by region of build

(n = 133)[a]

Region	Number	Percentage
Western Scotland	83	62%
Tyne	14	11%
North-west England	8	6%
Bristol Channel	7	5%
Eastern Scotland	6	4%
Tees	6	4%
Belfast	4	3%
Wear	2	2%
Humber	2	2%
Southern England	11	1%

[a] Sources are Parliamentary Papers, Annual Parliamentary Returns of Steam Vessels, *Mercantile Navy Lists*, 1870–1880, *Lloyd's Register* (builders and other details), and registration documents at The National Archives, Kew; Mitchell Library, Glasgow; National Archives of Scotland, Edinburgh and other local record offices; and World Ship Society yard lists.

coaster owner.[34] He only ever ordered steamers from Scottish builders, and all but one came from west coast yards. He was clearly shopping around for favourable deals, continually looking for improvements, and his company almost certainly had an input into design. His fleet showed definite progress from sail, through basic steam lighters to more and more sophisticated steam and, finally, motor coasters.

It is instructive to ask why the steam coaster took so long to emerge, when the screw collier had established the basic needs of a bulk-carrying steamship two decades earlier. Trading opportunities for British coasters away from the east coast involved a very wide range of ports, whose physical properties often severely limited the size of vessels which could use them. In addition, there were not the huge and regular flows of cargo which characterised the east coast coal trade. The steam coaster needed to be small enough to give its owner the flexibility to trade widely, where relatively small cargoes were the norm. In turn, this placed considerable demands upon the marine engineering companies who supplied its machinery. To offer capacity for economical carriage of cargo to compete with sailing ships, smaller steam coaster required compact and therefore more efficient

---

[34]   R.S. Fenton and P. Robertson, *William Robertson and the Gem Line* (Preston, 2009).

machinery and, especially, a bunker capacity which did not unduly impinge on cargo space. Only with evolution of the steam engine, involving higher working pressures and more efficient boilers, could this be achieved and, as discussed in an earlier chapter, this evolution was not achieved until the late 1870s.

V

At least one yard which built steam coasters in the 1870s – Swan Brothers of Maryhill – had built small screw steamers known as Clyde 'puffers'. Initially developed for use on the Firth of Clyde and its connecting canal system, puffers frequently made coastal and short-sea passages despite their modest size.[35] Waine estimates that around 400 puffers were built, making them a very important, if localised, group of small steamers.

Did these small but effective steamers contribute to the development of the larger steam coaster? Puffers were strictly limited in length by dimensions of locks on the canals they used (to 88 feet in the case of the Crinan Canal, and just 66 feet for those using the Forth and Clyde Canal), and the experience of their designers in installing efficient steam plant in a small hull would have been valuable in designing seagoing bulk carriers. This view was expressed by an audience member during discussion of a paper presented to the Institution of Engineers in December 1953 by a descendant of William Robertson, a pioneer owner of coastal bulk carriers.[36] Pointing out that Robertson's first steam vessels were puffers, and the puffer was the first steam coastal tramp, a speaker from the floor went on to argue that yards at Maryhill (Swan) and Kirkintilloch (Hay, and McGregor) constructed 'extra long puffers', which were built in two parts and towed to Bowling to be put together. He felt that each half of the coaster was like a puffer, being very bluff and not at all like the schooners they superseded. In their reply, Robertson and Hagan doubted whether this was strictly accurate, and pointed out that the coastal tramp has proportions and hull form entirely

---

[35]   There have been several books about Clyde puffers, but they tend to be anecdotal, and at times romantic, rather than analytical. D. McDonald, *The Clyde Puffer* (Newton Abbott, 1977) is beautifully illustrated but light on text. L. Paterson, *The Light in the Glens: The Rise and Fall of the Puffer Trade* (Colonsay, 1996) scampers through the puffer's history to dwell at length on the post-Second World War fortunes and misfortunes of the last surviving puffer owner, Glenlight Shipping. Chapter 5 of Waine and Fenton, *Steam Coasters and Short Sea Traders*, is devoted to puffers, but is concerned mainly with constructional details of specimen craft. G.W. Burrows, *Puffer Ahoy!* (Glasgow, 1981) is anecdotal, rambling and disorganised. The author of this book has contributed a photographic essay in R.S. Fenton, 'The Clyde Puffer', *Archive*, 30 (2001), 49–64. The early history of this type of craft deserves further study.

[36]   J.C. Robertson and H.H. Hagan, 'A Century of Coaster Design and Operation', *Transactions of the Institution of Engineers*, 97 (1954), 204–56.

different from the puffer. 'The mere elongation of the original puffer form would not produce the desired sea-keeping qualities which were clearly apparent in the six coasting tramps constructed for the fleet analysed in the years 1877 to 1880, and immediately following on the puffers mentioned'.

There is much in the history of the puffer that supports Robertson and Hagan's separation of the puffer and the coastal bulk carrier. Throughout their long constructional life (they were built in very considerable numbers for use by the Admiralty during the Second World War), puffers remained a very distinct class of steamer, retaining much of their simplicity including a lack of a double bottom or indeed any facility to carry water ballast. Their trade was limited by their modest size, which was determined absolutely by the locks on the canals they habitually used. This led to the operation of puffers remaining distinct from that of larger coasters. Of the two major operators, Ross and Marshall of Greenock had only two coasters in their fleet but had many puffers.[37] The Hays of Kirkintilloch kept their puffer and coaster operations entirely separate, one side of the family being involved in running, building and repairing puffers, and the other in large coasters.[38]

The success of the puffer, the first of which is dated from 1857, may have encouraged builders and owners to exploit the potential of steam in the coastal bulk trades, but this small craft made minimal contribution to the design of the steam coaster.

VI

The typical steam coaster is dimensionally distinct from the screw collier. It is shorter, shallower and has a considerably smaller cargo capacity, all factors determined by the available cargoes and ports served. It was built in a wide range of sizes, but the typical steam coaster was around 150 feet in length, compared with around 200 for the screw collier. An important common feature was a capacity to carry water ballast, but this facility tends to be much smaller in the steam coaster, and in many was confined to fore and aft peak ballast tanks of relatively modest capacity. The double bottom, developed early in the screw collier's evolution, came relatively late to steam coaster construction, and then was mostly confined to the larger vessels.

The steam coaster began to be multiplied some two decades after the explosion of screw collier construction in the 1850s, and the yards that built

---

[37]   Paterson, *The Light in the Glens*, 48–57.

[38]   A.J. Bowman, *Kirkintilloch Shipbuilding* (Kirkintilloch, 1983) is devoted largely to a history of the Hay family's shipbuilding and shipowning activities. William Robertson had two vessels of puffer size (65 feet) but sold them well before moving on to his first steam coasters, the *Agate* of 1878. Fenton and Robertson, *William Robertson and the Gem Line*.

the latter played very little part in the development and multiplication of the steam coaster. Instead, the steam coaster was perfected in the late 1870s largely by yards around the River Clyde (notably those on the River Cart), which had no experience of building screw colliers, but were working with owners such as Robertson and the Hay family,[39] who thoroughly understood the needs and constraints of local trades. In collaboration were local marine engineering companies, such as William King and Company of Glasgow, who made most of the engines for the steam coasters built by the very successful Paisley yard of John Fullerton. Jackson has pointed out how the cotton industry in Glasgow stimulated the manufacturing of steam engines, helping explain the city's lead in marine engineering.[40]

It cannot be said that the steam coaster 'evolved' directly from the screw collier. However, it is apparent that there was ready and free interchange of ideas on construction. The water ballast arrangements of fore and aft peak tanks and, for larger vessels, double-bottom tanks, were taken from east coast yards to those on the west coast. Indeed, it is likely that the west coast actually influenced the east coast designs, in applying the ubiquitous raised quarterdeck arrangement to engines-aft colliers.

---

[39]   See Fenton and Robertson, *William Robertson and the Gem Line*. Members of the Hay family did not confine themselves to puffers. James Hay has been identified as the owner of 25 steam coasters before over-reaching himself and going out of business in 1888. Registry of Shipping and Seamen, closed registers for Glasgow. Mitchell Library, Glasgow.

[40]   G. Jackson 'From Coaster to Steamer', in J. Armstrong and A. Kunz, *Coastal Shipping and the European Economy, 1750–1980* (Mainz, 2002), 96.

CHAPTER SIX

Steam bulk carrying dominant

I

This chapter examines the period from 1890 until 1950 during which the steam tramp dominated the carriage of bulk cargoes, eliminating the sailing vessel in most long-distance trades, and itself growing in size, efficiency and sophistication.

Table 6.1 Tonnage of British steam and sailing ships, 1870–1890

Year	Total	Steam	Sail
1870	7,149,000	1,202,000 (17%)	5,947,000 (83%)
1880	8,447,000	2,949,000 (35%)	5,498,000 (65%)
1890	9,688,000	5,414,000 (56%)	4,274,000 (44%)

Table 6.1 has figures quoted by Hope showing that total steam tonnage for British ships surpassed sail tonnage during the 1880s.[1] This was accounted for partly by a modest decline in sail tonnage from 1880 to 1890, but also a 94 per cent increase in steam tonnage over the same period. The latter mainly comprised passenger and cargo liners and tramps, with fishing, tugs and other vessels of modest size adding little to the total.

Although it is an exaggeration to claim the steam tramp had matured by 1890, the basic features which were to serve it well for another 60 years were already established. These were an efficient and reliable triple-expansion engine served by boilers delivering high-pressure steam, a significant capacity for water ballast in various tanks, and usually four holds with wide hatches each served by one or two derricks. Over the six decades for which these features remained fundamentally unchanged, especially in British construction, growth in size, power and sophistication was significant.

---

[1]   R. Hope, *A New History of British Shipping* (London, 1990), 307. The figures appear to be from C.E. Fayle, *A Short History of the World's Shipping Industry* (London, 1933), 246. Note that the figures include all ships regarded as 'British', i.e., everything owned in the British Empire.

To track these changes, decennial surveys were made of the characteristics of a sample of tramps built in British yards at seven time points, beginning in 1890 and ending with the 1950s.[2]

II

Dimensions of ships included in Table 6.2 emphasise the wide size range of steamers classed as tramps built at each time point, reflecting the variety of trades, cargoes and ports which owners expected their ships to serve. Nevertheless, taking an average size does allow tracking the growth of tramps over time, with average gross tonnage increasing over some 60 years by 140 per cent, and net tonnage by 105 per cent. Growth in length, breadth and depth was significant but more modest, depth especially being constrained by the characteristics of the ports to be used. Increase in the horsepower of engines paralleled that of net tonnage at around 100 per cent. This was achieved by design improvements to the steam engine and particularly developments in design and construction of boilers. These meant that the pressure of steam supplied to the machinery increased from a minimum of 150 to a maximum of 250 p.s.i. The triple-expansion engine proved extremely durable, and with refinements discussed later in this chapter it saw off challenges from both pure turbine machinery and quadruple-expansion engines as the preferred power unit for steam tramps. Both of these were perceived as costing more but introducing extra complications for

---

[2]   The names of ships built were extracted from the Starke/Schell Registers, which were discussed previously. Candidate tramps were chosen mainly from knowledge of their owners' trades, assisted by – where known – details of final voyages, and with obviously multi-decked vessels eliminated. Dimensions and other details were taken from contemporary volumes of *Lloyd's Register*. Although for the period researched, this covers all merchant ships over a certain size, details of water ballast facilities are only recorded for vessels classed by Lloyd's Register of Shipping, and only these ships are included. Fortunately, this Society classed the majority of British ships, at least until the British Corporation was set up to challenge Lloyd's Register of Shipping in the 1890s. This polarised opinion amongst tramp shipowners with important fleets including Hogarths of Glasgow, Reardon Smith of Cardiff and Ropners of West Hartlepool loyally supporting the British Corporation. F.M. Walker, *Song of the Clyde: A History of Clyde Shipbuilding* (Cambridge, 1984), 51–2. Numbers in the survey vary depending on how many ships were built in the year in question. Given that building steam ships had almost finished by 1950, the column headed Tramp 1946–56 includes almost all the ships built between 1946 and 1956. For the years 1920, 1940 and the 1946–56 period, vessels known to have been built under the various wartime standard ship programmes were avoided if they were known to have been allocated a 'War' or 'Empire' name. However, in both years, vessels were completed which adhered, more or less, to designs of those laid down for the Shipping Controller in the First World War or government ministries in the Second World War.

9: The steam tramp *Runswick* was built at Sunderland for Headlam and Sons of Whitby in 1930, by when the well-deck type was all but obsolete. Her flag of convenience buyers in 1955 did not agree, and she steamed on until 1971. *Ships in Focus*

only marginal gains in efficiency and speed. Significant machinery developments were the general adoption of oil firing from 1930 onwards and the near-universal addition of an exhaust turbine after 1940.

Hull structures developed alongside increases in size. The most popular arrangement of decks until the 1920s was simply to have a weather deck, giving deep, capacious holds, readily filled with bulk cargo and relatively easily discharged by grabs and later suction-based elevators. A minority of ships had extra decks fitted, including the awning and spar decks referred to in a previous chapter. However, around 1930 the shelter-decker became the most frequent choice of the owner placing an order for a new ship. Although the need to move hatches in the intermediate or 'tween deck complicated and slowed loading and discharge, owners accepted this for the design's two other advantages. First, the shelter deck was not measured for tonnage purposes provided that a small 'tonnage opening' was left, thus reducing dock and other dues which were based on net tonnage. A further important reason for specifying a shelter deck was its popularity with liner companies. Tramp operators were well aware that liner trade companies needed to enhance their own fleets by chartering in, and even by buying in, additional tonnage when demand for space for general cargo exceeded capacity in their own fleet. Additional speed was also considered desirable for such charters, beyond the 10 knots at which tramps habitually steamed. In rare cases, a tramp might even have limited capacity

Table 6.2 Characteristics of steam tramps built from 1890 to 1956

Characteristic	Tramp 1890	Tramp 1900	Tramp 1910
Sample size	*25*	*25*	*25*
Gross tonnage (average)	2,393	3,693	4,040
Gross tonnage (range)	1,352–3,518	1,778–2,762	3,700–5,865
Net tonnage (average)	1,591	2,445	2,513
Net tonnage (range)	816–2,931	1,119–2,762	1,980–3,672
Length feet (average)	290	328	362
Length feet (range)	230–347	228–365	316–28
Beam feet (average)	39	46	51
Beam feet (range)	33–43	35–48	46–54
Depth feet (average)	20	21	25
Depth feet (range)	14–21	16–26	21–29
Length/beam ratio	7.4	7.4	7.1
Beam/depth ratio	1.95	2.2	2.04
Length/depth ratio	14.5	14.5	14.5
Water ballast tons (average)	539	821	1,190
Water ballast tons (range)	263–1,125	532–1,263	636–2,910
Horsepower (average)	216	292	360
Horsepower (range)	130–300	190–434	247–542
Boiler pressure p.s.i. (average)	160	169	178
Boiler pressure p.s.i. (range)	150–200	160–180	160–180
C. 4–cyl.	0	0	0
T.3–cyl. (number)	24	25	25
T. 3–cyl. + turbine			
Q.4–cyl. (number)	1	0	0
Turbine	0	0	0
Double bottoms	25	25	25
Forecastle (number)	18	25	24
Bridge deck (number)	18	25	23
Raised quarter deck (number)	23	1	1
Poop (number)	23	25	24
Well decks	16	–	–
Single deck	16	15	16
+ part deck			1
+ shelter deck			1
+ spar deck	2		
+ awning deck	7	9	1
Two decks	0	1	6

Tramp 1920	Tramp 1930	Tramp 1940	Tramp 1946–56	Growth 1890–1956	
25	*30*	*33*	*30*	No.	%
4,592	5,029	5,115	5,745	3,352	140%
2,445–6,695	3,443–6,675	3,168–7,628	2,946–8,053		
2,819	3,067	3,036	3,263	1,672	105%
1,467–4,122	2,038–4,059	1,841–5,595	1,948–4,791		
379	386	434	436	146	50%
300–450	338–436	357–458	364–458		
52	54	52	56	17	44%
45–55	48–60	48–60	49–60		
27	25	26	25	6	6 30%
20–34	22–29	21–36	19–29		
7.3	7.3	7.6	7.8	0.4	
1.9	2.2	2.2	2.2	0.25	
14.0	15.4	16.6	17.4	2.9	
1,349	1,783	1,723	2,584	2,045	379%
596–2,967	1,040–2,726	1,094–3,044	898–3,469		
440	431	430	–	214	99%
266–620	277–804	287–542	–		
181	206	221	223	63	39%
180–200	150–250	200–230	220–250		
0	1	0	1		
24	23 (1 oil fired)	33 (17 oil fired)	9 oil fired	–	
	1		20 oil fired		
0	6	0	0		
1	0	0	0		
25	30	33	28/28		
19	24	24	11		
15	15	3	1		
B+F x 1	0	0	0		
18	16	3	4		
–					
14	13	3	4		
1			2		
9	16	28	18		
1					
	1	2*	6		

for passengers.[3] The hull was invariably subdivided, with watertight bulkheads fitted forward (the collision bulk head) either side of each hold and of the machinery space.

Forecastles and poops were almost universal until 1930, with a central bridge deck of the time-hallowed three-island design peaking in popularity in 1900. Classification society rules on such deck erections reduced their attraction with the widespread adoption of the shelter-decker, as prior to 1930 such erections were not allowed to be built on such comparatively light decks. Forecastles seem to have been excepted, however, and continued to be specified for many ships.[4]

Over the six decades covered by the survey, arrangements for carrying water ballast became ever more sophisticated, and of considerably greater total capacity. By 1890, all tramps surveyed had cellular double bottoms for ballast, while a third had aft peak tanks, which, while contributing rarely more than 10 per cent to total capacity, helped in trimming the vessel. By 1900, aft peak tanks were universal and by 1910 began to be joined by forepeak tanks, which were usual by 1920. In the 1920s, tramps began to be fitted with additional water ballast capacity, with some having deep tanks which could be used either for water ballast or for liquid cargoes, and which were of a size to add significantly to overall ballast capacity. In the 1930s, additional but smaller tanks began to be fitted alongside the shaft tunnel and in the engine room. In steam tramps built from 1946 onwards, fore and aft peak tanks were universal, usually together with some combination of deep, side, engine room or midships tanks. A further sophistication involved wing tanks occasionally fitted high in the hull structure. These were fitted to the last of the turret and trunk deck designs and were later to become a particular feature of the bulk carrier. As Table 6.2 records, total water ballast capacity grew by well over 340 per cent, a figure considerably in excess of growth in tonnage. A double bottom could well extend the full length of the hull, itself subdivided into as many as seven separate tanks.

By 1940, growth in the size of tramps reached a peak, with average dimensions and engine power increasing only slightly until the last steam tramps were delivered almost two decades later. Partly, this was due to the Second World War, when the need to build ships in quantity far outweighed the desire to

---

[3]   A rare case of such accommodation being specified, in this case for six passengers, was Ropner's *Clearpool*, delivered by William Gray at West Hartlepool in 1935. She was also very unusual in a tramp fleet for having geared turbine machinery, which, following tank testing of her hull form, allowed her to cruise comfortably at 11½ knots. Yet she was essentially a single-deck ship, with five holds extending from weather deck to the tops of the double bottom tanks, but with a 'tween deck worked in beneath her 249 foot bridge deck. 'The Clearpool', *Shipbuilding and Shipping Record*, 47 (1936), 124–8.

[4]   Fine examples were the *Generton* and *Hermiston*, shelter-deckers built in 1939 for Chapman and Willan of Newcastle, which had relatively prominent forecastles, their height exaggerated by an unusually well-raked bow. J. Lingwood, *Chapman of Newcastle* (Kendal, 1985).

improve performance, and which saw designs developed in the 1930s enormously multiplied. The availability of so many wartime-built ships subdued the demand for new ships in peacetime, by when the motor tramp was accepted to have advantages and tramp steamer development inevitably stagnated. The 30 steam tramps surveyed for Table 6.2 in the 1946 to 1950 period represent practically all those built in the United Kingdom in this period.

III

Although the basic features of a steam tramp were generally agreed upon by 1890, competition between the growing number of builders resulted in considerable variations in hull structure, most of which were claimed to have advantages in terms of minimising tonnage, increasing fuel economy, ease of trimming cargoes such as coal and grain, improving seaworthiness and/or economy in construction. The popularity of these types waxed and waned with alterations in shipbuilding rules set by classification societies and the British Board of Trade (on the basis of which harbour and canal dues were calculated). Although the numbers of one type reached triple figures, few of these designs had a lasting influence on steam tramp ship construction. Nevertheless, the variants are part of the story of tramp ship development and exploring them illustrates the design issues which shipbuilders and owners had to confront.

Amongst the earliest and for a time the most successful of these variations was the Doxford turret ship. It was inspired by an unusual type of vessel which became popular on the Great Lakes of North America, referred to as the 'whaleback', designed by Alexander McDougall of Duluth, Minnesota.[5] 'Fluid' cargoes such as grain or coal tended to settle after loading; grain by as much as 6 per cent of its volume. Even when a hold was filled right to the hatch covers, settling meant that free space was created, which could allow the cargo to shift in rough weather with potentially serious consequences for stability. To help avoid this, coal needed to be trimmed manually, and bagged grain had to be laid on top of the bulk grain; both requiring extra work and extending loading times and labour requirements. When carrying these commodities, the holds of the 'whaleback' were self-trimming. The upper part of each hold was designed to funnel the cargo below, its shape minimising the empty space and the tendency for the cargo to shift. In 1891, the whaleback *Charles W. Wetmore* arrived in Liverpool and aroused interest amongst naval architects. The steamer's hull was rounded, and did not have a conventional deck, only a narrow gangway from the forecastle leading to the bridge and the machinery which was placed aft. There were no hatch coamings, the hatch covers being bolted on to form part of the hull. Machinery and deck houses were mounted

---

[5]   P.N. Thomas, *British Ocean Tramps*, vol. 1, *Builders and Cargoes* (Wolverhampton, 1992), 31–2.

on steel cylinders dubbed 'turrets'. With no bulwarks she was vulnerable to heavy seas, and her stability was questioned: rightly so as on her return to the west coast of North America she had problems rounding Cape Horn, and in September 1892 was wrecked on the coast of Oregon.

Despite the problems with *Charles W. Wetmore*, Arthur Havers, the Chief Draughtsman of William Doxford and Sons Ltd, saw some merit in the whaleback.[6] In Havers' design the concept of the whaleback was modified so that the 'turrets' were connected to give a trunk which ran the length of the ship and carried an elevated, narrow deck.[7] Viewed from the bow or stern, the hull plates rose vertically above the waterline for several feet, and were then radiused inwards to give a narrow, almost flat deck (the 'harbour deck'), and then rose up again to the turret. The trunk acted as a feeder to the hold, and Doxford's patent was worded to emphasise the design's qualities as a self-trimmer. Other advantages were claimed, including that an elevated deck provided righting buoyancy in a rough sea and was safer for the crew. The pioneer turret's ratio of gross tonnage to displacement was 2.53, better than the norm in contemporary tramp steamers, enabling her to carry a larger weight of cargo than a conventional ship with the same tonnage. As hulls grew in length, another advantage of the design proved itself, as the turret's structure gave great longitudinal strength facilitating longer, single-deck ships. The 440-foot turret *Grangesberg*, built in 1903 for a Rotterdam owner, was for a time the largest single-deck vessel in the world, and a precursor of the modern bulk carrier.

Owners were initially unconvinced about the concept, and some critics were downright pessimistic about its sea-keeping qualities. Doxford themselves financed the building of the first of the type, *Turret*, even accepting the risks of its loss, as insurance could not be obtained. They appointed Petersen, Tate and Company of Newcastle as managers, and its principal, Captain Petersen, took command of *Turret*. Petersen deliberately faced sea conditions which it was prophesied *Turret* could not survive, but she came through unscathed.[8]

---

[6]   In 1893, a ship similar to the whaleback was built under licence by Doxford, the *Sagamore*, for a company 50 per cent financed by the builders. Her co-owners and managers were William Johnston and Co. Ltd of Liverpool, who used her on the coal out, grain home trade to the Black Sea. Her master and crew were complimentary about her properties as a sea boat, and she remained with her first owner until 1911. L. Gray and J. Lingwood, *The Doxford Turret Ships* (Kendal, 1975), 3–4.

[7]   Havers attempted to patent the design of the turret, only to find that his employers, William Doxford and Sons Ltd, had pre-empted him. Havers' salary was increased and he was awarded a gratuity and given shares in the company. However, in view of the success of the turret design, Havers subsequently sued Doxford, who claimed that others had a hand in the design. Havers was awarded £1,250, an insignificant sum compared to Doxford's profits on the design. Gray and Lingwood, *Doxford Turret Ships*, 12.

[8]   The presentation of a 1895 paper by S.O. Kendall entitled 'Turret Deck Cargo Steamers' to the North East Coast Institution of Engineers and Shipbuilders was notable

10: The photograph of the Greek *Adelfotis* shows the unusual shape of a turret steamer's hull. She was built in 1908 as *Penrose* for R.B. Chellew of Truro, and was sold in 1927, the photograph being taken soon after her sale. Note the name of her port of registry, Andros, being painted on her stern. *Author's collection*

Eventually, owners began to take an interest in the turret concept, but only after two more ships were built for management by Petersen, Tate and Company. Three were completed in 1894, and nine in 1895, and eventually a total of 182 were built, including six constructed by other builders under licence. The very last, *Orangemoor*, was completed in 1911, 19 years after the original *Turret*.

By no means all ships built to the turret design were tramps. In 1896 and 1897, Cayzer, Irvine and Company, managers of Clan Line, bought two second-hand examples in order to evaluate them in their liner trade. They were clearly satisfied as they eventually ordered a total of 28 more, making Clan Line the largest operator of turrets. As these were multiple deck vessels intended for liner trades, stability with bulk cargoes was not an attraction to the owner, rather it was the reduced dues for passing through the Suez Canal on the line's route to India. At the time, Canal dues were calculated on the basis of the vessel's breadth at the upper deck, which was clearly smaller for turrets than conventional vessels. Not surprisingly, the Suez Canal authorities later changed this method of charging.

---

for the fierce debate which followed, extending over four sessions. The loss rates amongst the 182 turrets built have been equivalent to those of conventional ships. Gray and Lingwood, *Doxford Turret Ships*, 11.

There were a number of attempts to emulate the success of the turret, but only the Ropner trunk deck, introduced with the *Trunkby* in 1896, succeeded in attracting significant orders.[9] However, fully half of these orders were placed with the Stockton-on-Tees yard of Ropner and Son by its associated shipping company, the West Hartlepool-based Robert Ropner and Company.[10] The trunk deck design was similar to that of the turret, with a flat-sided trunk about seven feet high running the length of the ship from forecastle to poop deck. This trunk carried the hatchways and winches and was about half the width of the ship, being a continuation fore and aft of the engine and boiler casing amidships. Unlike the turret, the equivalent of the harbour deck lacked the curved plates connecting it to the ship's sides and to the trunk. Advantages claimed for the trunk deck over conventional hulls were similar to those of the turret: that the vessels were largely self-trimming, had an increased deadweight capacity, and that the trunk gave extra protection from heavy seas. The vertical sides of the trunk meant that its self-trimming properties were less than those of the turret, but to compensate the camber of the main deck was doubled.

Further iterations of the self-trimming principle followed. The tower deck design, built by the yard of John Priestman and Company at Sunderland, had a narrow upper deck similar to those on the turret and trunk, but from there the hull sloped down at 45 degrees to a narrow walkway extending the full length of the hull.[11] The *Enfield* of 1897 was the first of just three tower deck vessels. Shipowner Henry Burrell designed the straightback steamer, having a trunk but a very narrow side deck.[12] Just two were built, *Ocland* in 1907 for a Norwegian owner and *Ben Earn* for Burrell's own Straightback Steamship Co. Ltd. The engines-aft design of the latter plus deck cranes has prompted comparisons with modern bulk carriers.[13]

---

[9]   H. Appleyard, 'Ropner Trunk Deck Steamers, Part 1', *Ships in Focus Record*, 2 (1997), 82–91 and Part 2, *Ships in Focus Record*, 3 (1997), 154–9. See also Thomas, *British Ocean Tramps*, vol. 1, 34.

[10]   Neither the Ropner yard nor its shipowning associate placed complete faith in the trunk deck design. Over the trunk deck's production life from 1896 to 1909 the output of Ropner's Stockton yard also included 72 conventional steamers, 11 of which ended up in the fleet of Ropner and Company. L. Gray, *The Ropner Fleet, 1874–1974* (Kendal, 1975) and I. Dear. *The Ropner Story* (London, 1986). Dear refers to the trunk deck as a 'revolutionary design'. Doxford clearly did not think so and brought an action against Ropner for infringement of their patent, citing the *Clarissa Radcliffe* of 1904, which the British Board of Trade measured as a turret not a trunk.

[11]   Thomas, *British Ocean Tramps*, vol. 1, 35

[12]   Thomas, *British Ocean Tramps*, vol. 1, 35.

[13]   R. Craig, 'Aspects of Tramp Shipping and Ownership', in K. Matthews and G. Panting (eds), *Ships and Shipbuilding in the North Atlantic Region* (St. John's, Newfoundland, 1978), 219.

Having left Doxford following a disagreement over the poor reward for his part in the turret design, Arthur Havers began working with Petersen (who had captained the *Turret*) on hull designs that reduced water resistance.[14] It was found that a longitudinal grove in the hull sides along the waterline achieved this, the eventual outcome being a hull which viewed in cross section had two distinct bulges. It has been suggested that the groove between the bulges acted as a guide for the water passing along the hull, producing a smoother flow to the screw, thus consuming less power. Savings in fuel costs of up to 16 per cent were claimed, and also that the corrugations in the hull increased structural strength. The type was dubbed the monitor, the prototype *Monitoria* emerging from Osbourne, Graham's yard on the Wear in 1905. As with several such designs, building was modest and protracted, with the last of 30 being the *Rio Diamante* completed in 1928. Problems with the corrugated hull of the motor ship *King James* of 1925 may have helped to end sales. Despite being intended to maintain 11 knots, *King James* could barely manage 10, and in 8-knot wartime convoys she had difficulty maintaining station.[15] The corrugations were easily damage by contact with wharves while uneven flexing between the flat hull plates and the bulges caused frequent cracking of plates, eventually leading to the *King James* being laid up in 1949.

A turret deck and its imitations contributed to the longitudinal strength of a ship, allowing less steel to be used for a given strength. Several successors to the turrets and trunks adopted other means to achieve the same end, the most notable being the longitudinal framing introduced in 1908 by Joseph Isherwood. In contrast to the limited success of some designs, the Isherwood system quickly became very well established, with over one thousand vessels of varying types built within ten years.[16] The principle was relatively simple, with multiple longitudinal stringers allowing the numbers of frames to be significantly reduced. Whilst the stringers maintained or increased hull strength, fewer frames meant a greater hold volume available for cargo, increasing grain and bale capacity, and improving the deadweight to net tonnage ratio. A minor disadvantage with tramps carrying grain cargoes was that the stringers meant more ledges from which grain had to be swept during unloading.

The major characteristic of the arch-deck vessel which emerged with the *Edenor* in 1911 was that the upper part of the hull was radiused inwards.[17] The frames terminated at the point where the deck would be placed in a conventional ship and were joined to the deck beams by arched brackets. Stringers joined the arched brackets along the length of the ship, the combination acting like a girder

---

[14] Thomas, *British Ocean Tramps*, vol. 1, 41; Gray and Lingwood, *Doxford Turret Ships*, 12.

[15] A. Mallett, *Idyll of the Kings: The History of the King Line, 1889–1979* (Kendal, 1980), 14, 38.

[16] Thomas, *British Ocean Tramps*, vol. 1, 40–1

[17] R.S. Fenton and others, 'The Arch Deck Steamers', *Ships in Focus Record*, 29 (2004), 28–33 and *Ships in Focus Record*, 30 (2005), 92–104.

and contributing to longitudinal strength. Savings in steelwork of up to 14 per cent compared with a conventional vessel of the same dimensions were claimed by the designer, Maxwell Ballard.

Working with shipbuilder Wilfred Ayre, Ballard took advantage of the extra freeboard which the arch deck design gave to adopt reverse sheer. This was a sound engineering principle, as the inverse sheer better supported the weight of cargo, engines and deck erections than in a ship with normal sheer. It was possible to adopt reverse sheer and maintain the vessel's sea-keeping qualities because the weather deck was some seven feet higher amidships than that in a conventional vessel of the same size.

A total of 28 arch deck ships were built by seven shipyards over a long period, the last being completed by Swan, Hunter and Wigham Richardson Ltd in 1928.[18] Because the arched deck gave it excellent self-trimming properties, the design appealed most to owners operating modest-sized ships in the middle-distance coal trades. The most likely reason why more of the type were not built is the decline in these trades, especially after industrial unrest in British coalfields during the 1920s.

The First World War had two significant effects on shipbuilding in Britain. The scale of Allied loses to unrestricted U-boat warfare led, belatedly, to merchant shipbuilding recommencing after a period up to 1916 during which the Admiralty demanded maximum resources being put into warship construction, while themselves worsening merchant ship losses by refusing to adopt a convoy system. In previous wars, convoys had been shown to deter attacks on shipping. The building programme introduced involved ten standard types of ship, in most cases based on existing designs and often ordered from the builder responsible for the original design.[19] The single-deck types are listed in Table 6.3.

By 1917, it was belatedly realised that losses of merchant ships to submarine warfare were prejudicing the ability of Great Britain to prosecute the war, and even to feed its inhabitants, especially as its merchant fleet needed to serve its allies, including France and Italy, and finally the United States when it entered the war in April 1917. The previous month had seen the British government beginning to place orders with both Japanese and US yards. Japan had already begun an ambitious programme of increasing its shipyard capacity and building standard ships, which found a ready market. A number of these were bought by the British government, the majority being two-deck steamers, with just ten single-deck ships. Ordering in the United States was much more extensive, with an estimated three-quarters-of-a-million tons being contracted for, comprising mostly two-deck ships with some single-deckers, powered by

---

[18]   Fenton and others, 'The Arch Deck Steamers', *Ships in Focus Record*, 30 (2005), 92–104.

[19]   W.H. Mitchell and L.A. Sawyer, *British Standard Ships of World War 1*, 3 vols (Liverpool, 1968).

Table 6.3 Single-deck cargo ships built during the First World War

Type	Dimensions (feet)	Gross tonnage	Notes
A	400 × 52 × 31	5,030	the similar B type had two decks
C	331 × 46.5 × 25.5	3,000	intended as colliers
D	285 × 41.7 × 21.3	2,300	
E	376 × 51.5 × 29	4,400	
H	303 × 43 × 23	2,800	
N	428 × 55 × 28	6,500	prefabricated

turbine or reciprocating engines. After the US entry into the war in August 1917 all of these ships were requisitioned, with only the *War Sword* being released to serve Britain.[20] In total, the extraordinary number of 3,500 cargo ships ordered during hostilities were eventually completed in the United States, mostly after the Armistice, with relatively few being cancelled. However, relatively slow cargo ships were not what would best suit the US merchant marine in peacetime, when the country's trade required faster and more sophisticated ships for liner sailings. As a result, large numbers were laid up, a few were sold outside the United States, but many were prematurely scrapped. As the cost of operating ships under the US flag meant owners were neither willing nor able to compete in the tramp trades, the impact these ships had internationally was very small.

Of lasting significance was the adoption of prefabrication for the British N-type vessels. As far as possible, flat plates were used, with bilges being at a 45 degree angle and a triangular transom stern fitted.[21] Of the 33 ordered, only two were completed before the Armistice in November 1918. Prefabrication was then neglected for two decades and was not employed again until the Second World War. This might have reflected the diminished demand for ships during the bleak times between the wars, but it also demonstrated the conservative nature of British owners and constructors. Few owners were in a position to place a large enough order to justify a builder instituting prefabrication. However, designing and marketing such a ship might well have produced cost savings that would have benefited a yard desperate to win what few orders were available.

Hard times did stimulate several builders to look critically at the designs of tramp ships and come up with 'economy' designs.[22] The Burntisland Economy

---

[20]   Mitchell and Sawyer, *British Standard Ships of World War 1*, vol. 1, 1–27.

[21]   Mitchell and Sawyer, *British Standard Ships of World War 1*, vol. 1, 121–32.

[22]   At least three yards used 'Economy' as the name for their design, probably the most successful being Doxford, who built it round their own three-cylinder, opposed-piston oil engine.

types, of which the first was delivered in 1929, resulted from underwater refinements including careful design of the propellor and streamlining of the rudder to reduce drag.[23] But most significant was improved engine design, including insulation to reduce heat losses and attention to valve gear. The builders claimed that at 9 knots coal consumption was 18 tons per day compared with the 24 to 25 tons with a conventional tramp. Adding superheating of steam was claimed to lower consumption to 13.63 tons per day, but superheaters were unpopular with the conservative tramp ship engineer. The ultimate saving came at the expense of having a turbine which extracted some of the energy from exhaust steam, the addition of which, it was claimed, reduced coal consumption to 11.25 tons per day. Burning less coal not only significantly reduced the cost of bunkering, but also increased carrying capacity because less space needed to be allocated for bunker coal. Burntisland were not slow to calculate that these savings could make the difference between profit and loss on a typical tramp ship voyage from Northern Europe to the River Plate. The design helped to maintain a steady flow of orders to the Burntisland yard throughout a period during which a significant number of major British shipyards closed, some never to reopen. The Burntisland yard successfully diversified, and also built motor coasters and steam colliers, including up-river types for gas and electricity companies. It had a progressive management, but it is interesting to note that only two large ships it built up until the outbreak of the Second World War were propelled by oil engines, one for a Glasgow owner and one for a Norwegian.[24]

Not content with the success of his longitudinal hull design, Sir Joseph Isherwood, as he had become, developed the Arcform hull.[25] He was convinced that the traditional box-shaped hull prevented a smooth flow of water along the hull surface, contributing to drag and hence higher fuel costs. His novel hull design was almost circular in cross section, the rounding giving considerable tumblehome above the waterline, and extending below. Tank testing at Teddington gave credence to Isherwood's ideas on hull form, and three steamers to his design were ordered from three different yards to be delivered in 1934, each owned by a single ship company managed by Isherwood Arcform Ships Ltd. Unsurprisingly, the ships had Isherwood's longitudinal framing, and were also equipped with steel hatch covers to another of Isherwood's patents. Once again, Isherwood's idea was vindicated in practice, and reports on the early voyages of the steamers indicated that coal consumption was as much as 50 per cent lower than for conventional ships built in the mid-1920s. Two further ships of the type were ordered but following Isherwood's death these and the earlier three were sold, apparently finding willing buyers. Given the excellent reports on the ships' fuel consumption, it is perhaps disappointing to learn that in the next 20 years

---

[23]   Thomas, *British Ocean Tramps*, vol. 1, 50–1.

[24]   World Ship Society Yard List Team, Burntisland Shipbuilding Co. Ltd.

[25]   Thomas, *British Ocean Tramps*, vol. 1, 50.

just 50 ships were built with an Arcform hull, 31 of which were tankers and only 19 dry cargo ships.

As with the Burntisland design, the 'economy' type from the yard of J.L.Thompson on the Wear was built round an improvement to the triple-expansion steam engine, the adoption of the reheater, discussed below The Thompson yard had built no ships between 1931 and 1934,[26] but reopened with the building of the *Embassage* fitted with a reheater engine from the North Eastern Marine Engineering Co. Ltd. Completed in 1935, she was a commercial success, and more orders quickly followed. The individual ships, generally referred to as being of the 'North Sands' type, differed in dimensions according to the owners' specifications. Some 20 had been built with the completion of the *Dorington Court* shortly before the outbreak of the Second World War.

The importance of the North Sands design went far beyond saving a long-established Wearside shipyard. Ships of the type became the basis of a standard shipbuilding programme quickly instituted in British yards following the outbreak of the Second World War. Events in 1940 and 1941 also meant that this type became the basis of by far the largest group of standard ships ever built.

In 1940, with losses of merchant ships mainly to submarines outstripping the rates they could be replaced from British yards alone, a Shipbuilding Mission was sent to North America to negotiate building of similar ships.[27] This initially resulted in orders for 60 ships of the 'Ocean' type in the United States to a design based on drawings of the Thompson-built *Empire Wave*, itself essentially a 'North Sands' type. Further orders were placed in Canadian yards, which produced over 300 of the very similar 'Fort' and 'Park' and the related Canadian 'Victory' types.[28]

With the United States entering the war after the attack by Japan on Pearl Harbor and the subsequent declaration of war by Germany, an enormous expansion of an ongoing shipbuilding programme was instituted. Contrary to normal US practice, which favoured relatively fast and sophisticated turbine-driven ships suitable for liner trades, the model chosen for the major plank of this programme was a version of the 'Ocean' type. Redesigned to have a flush deck, a composite superstructure and oil-burning reciprocating steam engines fitted with reheaters, this resulted in what came to be called 'Liberty' ships, the largest standardised type of ship ever built, running to 2,710 units.[29]

British wartime construction comprised mainly a variety of designs of shelter-decker, all broadly similar to Thompson's 'North Sands' type, plus some privately ordered ships to existing designs.[30] Steam or oil engines were fitted,

---

[26]   N.L. Middlemiss, *British Shipbuilding Yards*, vol. 1, *North East Coast* (Newcastle-upon-Tyne, 1993), 174.
[27]   M. Cooper, *The Ocean Class of the Second World War* (Barnsley, 2022).
[28]   W.H. Mitchell and L.A. Sawyer, *The Oceans, the Forts and the Parks* (Liverpool, 1966).
[29]   W.H. Mitchell and L.A. Sawyer, *The Liberty Ships*, 2nd ed. (London, 1985).
[30]   W.H. Mitchell and L.A. Sawyer, *The Empire Ships*, 2nd ed. (London, 1990).

largely according to the availability of each type and the particular builder's experience. Together, wartime construction in North America and Britain produced a large pool of well over three thousand steam ships, which more than ensured that extensive war losses were replaced and allowing owners worldwide to rebuild their tramp fleets.

The war years saw no significant developments in the design of steam cargo ships, but did belatedly encourage two advances in ship construction: the replacement of riveting by welding and the adoption of prefabrication techniques pioneered in British yards during the First World War. Both were adopted readily in US yards, welding because it was easier to train operatives. Prefabrication with units as large as an entire accommodation block built in a shed and lifted aboard was possible only with massive investment in plant and craneage, but did achieve meaningful efficiencies, not to mention some of the spectacularly short building times achieved in the Liberty ship programme. Both welding and prefabrication were widely adopted post-war, although somewhat reluctantly in the more conservative British yards. Overseas competitors were less inhibited (and often less restrained by financial issues), contributing to the slow decline and eventual extinction of major cargo shipbuilding in Britain and later in Europe.

IV

In the period covered in this chapter, from 1890 to the end of steam tramp building in the 1950s, refinements of the propelling machinery were gradual and incremental rather than spectacular. Economy and reliability were of utmost importance, while tramp shipowners' rather dismal view of the capabilities of their engineers meant simplicity of operation and maintenance was favoured over innovation. Yet as the figures in Table 6.2 demonstrate, average engine power more than doubled over six decades, keeping pace with growth in the size and capacity of hulls.

A major factor was the increased temperature and pressure of the steam generated in the ship's boilers, Table 6.2 showing how average pressure rose from a minimum of 150 p.s.i. in 1890 to an ultimate maximum of 250 p.s.i. Superheating of steam also contributed to greater efficiency, although it increased complexity, cost and maintenance of engines. With the traditional Scotch boiler universal in tramps,[31] steam temperatures of 550 degrees Fahrenheit could be achieved.[32] Higher steam pressure and temperature improved the efficiency of transferring energy from the combustion of coal to the cylinders. Improvements in the design and construction of boilers to provide these increases were quite as significant as developments of the engine itself. It also helped that boilers needed to be replaced at intervals, enabling owners to specify the latest boiler technology.

---

[31] D. Griffiths, *Steam at Sea: Two Centuries of Steam-powered Ships* (London, 1997), 66.

[32] Griffiths, *Steam at Sea*, 112.

A logical development, realised in the last years of the nineteenth century, was to move from triple- to quadruple-expansion of steam. This meant greater complexity, cost and maintenance requirements, and was mostly employed for large passenger ships where high speed was a commercial imperative. Some cargo liners adopted this machinery, but its use in tramps was rare: the only example encountered in the random sampling of some 150 ships for Table 6.2 was a very early example, the *Beechdene* of 1890.[33]

A significant improvement in steam engine efficiency came in the 1930s with the development of the reheater.[34] Steam passing through an engine lost energy in each cylinder because of condensation on the cylinder walls, but this could be minimised by reheating the steam between cylinders. The simplest and most successful application of reheat was developed by the North Eastern Marine Engineering Co. Ltd and involved reheating only the steam that emerged from the high-pressure cylinder. This was done by passing the steam through a tubular heater which itself took superheated steam from the boiler.

Oil firing of boilers had a number of advantages over burning coal. Whereas coal was best stored close to the furnaces, and otherwise had to be laboriously wheelbarrowed from distant bunkers, liquid fuel could simply be pumped from any available and otherwise inaccessible space on the ship. Elimination of coal bunkers thus increased available cargo space. Although making more work for engineers and other hands in the machinery department, oil firing reduced the crew by eliminating firemen. However, adoption of oil burning was held back, in practical terms by the higher price of oil than coal and poor availability of bunkering facilities for oil until a world-wide network of oil bunkering stations had been established.[35] Once again, the conservatism of tramp owners meant their steamers continued to rely mainly on coal: Table 6.2 has only one oil burner built in 1930. The subsequent decade, and the imperative of economical operation, saw the situation reversed so that in 1940 almost half of those built in that year were oil burners. However, the need to import oil into Britain saw a reversion to coal-firing for wartime construction – on the principle that coal could simply be dug up in the British Isles.[36]

The major development in marine steam machinery in the twentieth century,[37] the turbine, had only a limited influence on tramp ship design. Quickly grasped by engineers as a means of achieving high speeds, the turbine

---

[33]   *Lloyd's Register*, 1891.

[34]   Griffiths, *Steam at Sea*, 181.

[35]   To provide for bunkering, steam coal from the United Kingdom had to be shipped out to the many ports around the world where coal was either not available locally or not of a quality deemed acceptable. An irony is that in the early days of ocean-going steam ships, much bunker coal was carried by sailing ship. Griffiths, *Steam at Sea*, 114.

[36]   Coal-firing was insisted upon for the Ocean class of 60 ships ordered by Britain from US yards early in the war. Cooper, *Ocean Class of the Second World War*.

[37]   Griffiths, *Steam at Sea*, 140–53.

became the machinery of choice in high-end passenger ships and cargo liners. As ever, higher speed at sea came at a very considerable cost in terms of fuel burnt; typical figures were that a modest increase from 9 to 12 knots doubled fuel consumption. Relatively few tramps were fitted with turbines, and these, such as the *Clearpool* referred to above, were built with the possibility of charters to liner companies in mind. However, the technology figured in what was arguably the last advance in the design of steam machinery for tramps, the exhaust turbine.

The steam emerging from the low pressure cylinder in a triple-expansion engine still had some residual energy, and this could be used to drive a modest-sized turbine. Harnessing this power to help turn the propellor required some ingenuity. A device by turbine pioneers Parsons used a flexible coupling to the propellor shaft, comparable to a car's clutch. An early installation was in the tramp *Kingswood* in 1931, increasing her triple-expansion engine's power from 1,750 to 2,100 indicated horsepower.[38] However, the most popular system proved to be the Bauer-Wach design, which also incorporated a clutch, but one which allowed a smooth coupling and uncoupling of the turbine. Trials, admittedly on the quadruple-expansion-powered cargo liner *Britannia*, showed the Bauer-Wach system cut fuel consumption by 20 per cent.[39] Eventually, the exhaust turbine become so popular that most of the last 49 tramp steamers built in Britain were fitted (Table 6.2). The combination of high pressure, superheated steam, oil firing, a reheater and an exhaust turbine was the culmination of a century and a half of development of the reciprocating steam engine. However, it was not enough to defeat the rise of the motor ship.

V

This and previous chapters have been unrepentant in concentrating on the design, building and ownership of tramp steamers in the British Isles. The British were the most prolific operators of steam tramps and British yards were largely unchallenged in producing them. Much of the literature on tramps and their engines was produced in Britain. Around 1890, this dominance began to be eroded (although throughout the long reign of the steam tramp the British were to remain pre-eminent as both builders and owners). Table 6.4 lists by nationality of the shipyard steamers over 300 gross tons built in 1914 which can be categorised as tramps or colliers.[40]

---

³⁸ Griffiths, *Steam at Sea*, 180.

³⁹ Griffiths, *Steam at Sea*, 180.

⁴⁰ The list is based on W. Schell and T. Starke, *Register of Merchant Ships Completed in 1914* (Gravesend, 2004), which gives dimensions, builders and lifetime owners of all seagoing vessels over 300 gross tons built in a particular year. Assignment to tramp or collier status is based on knowledge of the owner's trades, the career of the ship and

Table 6.4 'League table' of world tramp steamer building in 1914

Country	Total	Ownership	
		Domestic	**Foreign**
1 United Kingdom	143	117	26
2 Norway	26	24	2
3 Netherlands	13	8	5
4 United States	11	11	0
5 Japan	9	9	0
=6 Denmark	8	8	0
=6 Sweden	8	7	1
=8 Italy	5	5	0
=8 Belgium	5	0	5
=10 Canada	2	2	0
=10 France	2	2	0
=10 Spain	2	2	0
Totals	234	195 (83%)	39 (17%)

Table 6.4 confirms the pre-eminence of British yards and British tramp owners in 1914. The former built 143 of the 234 tramp steamers completed, 59 per cent of the total. Of these, 26 were for owners in 11 countries, most of which had domestic shipbuilders. The total of 117 built for British owners compares favourably with the 125 built for owners in the rest of the world. All but two of the British ships came from British yards, stressing either the uncompetitiveness of foreign yards or the reluctance of British owners to place orders abroad.[41] Of 11 countries for which the United Kingdom, built, the largest orders were six from Greece, which was yet to have a domestic shipyard, and the four from the Netherlands, which did.

The league table of builders in Table 6.5 puts Norway, a country not at the time noted for its industrialisation, second only to Britain in 1939. This may well reflect the importance of the tramp trade to the Norwegian shipping industry, for which this sector was of overwhelming importance.[42] The combined output

---

construction details in contemporary *Lloyd's Registers*, with single-deck or shelter-deck vessels being given preference for inclusion over multi-decked ships.

[41] One of the two exceptions, the large shelter-decker *Lowther Castle*, built in Belgium, is difficult to categorise as it was ordered by Chambers, a rare British company which operated both tramps and liners. Thomas, *British Ocean Tramps*, vol. 2, 84–6.

[42] With a very small domestic market for shipping services, Norway expanded its

Table 6.5 'League table' of world tramp steamer building in 1939

Country	Total	Ownership	
		Domestic	**Foreign**
1 United Kingdom	20	17	3
3 Norway	10	7	3 (Sweden)
4 Germany	7	7	0
2 Japan	3	3	0
6 Denmark	2	2	0
Totals	42	36 (86%)	6 (14%)

of 13 vessels built in North America includes a number built for trading on the Great Lakes and also intended for the US east coast domestic coal trade, both the United States and Canada producing examples of the largest individual ships appearing in the table. Already dubbed bulk carriers by some, these ships will be examined in due course. Japanese shipbuilding appears quite prominent, but in 1914 was entirely concerned with building for domestic owners. In contrast, tramp steamer building in Belgium was purely for export. The relatively low numbers of tramps built in the Netherlands, Germany, Italy and France reflect the importance of the liner sector in shipowning in these countries, with local builders apparently concentrating on winning orders for what were usually more sophisticated and hence valuable vessels for these trades.

Data in Table 6.5 was compiled for 1939, which like 1914 was a year on the brink of war. British yards still headed the league table, but this may reflect the rather narrow criteria for inclusion of steam tramps, whose building elsewhere had declined in favour of motor ships.[43] Also apparent is the continuing importance of domestic orders, with only 6 of 22 vessels built being for foreign

---

fleet largely through cross trading between other countries. Tenold characterises the interwar period as being one of transition for Norwegian owners from 'classic tramp' to tanker and liner shipping. S. Tenold, 'Norwegian Shipping in the Twentieth Century', in L.R. Fischer and E. Lange, *International Merchant Shipping in the Nineteenth and Twentieth Centuries: The Comparative Dimension* (St. John's, Newfoundland, 2008).

[43]   The method used to compile this data was similar to that for Table 6.1. Unfortunately, some details, such as water ballast capacities, nominal horsepower and boiler pressures were not published in contemporary editions of *Lloyd's Register* because the Society had not classed the ships concerned. Japanese numbers are probably underestimated, as details for some ships believed to have been completed this year cannot be found in *Lloyd's Register*. There was considerable official secrecy about maritime matters in Japan in the 1930s. For instance, although the country had a significant shipbreaking industry, details of ships scrapped were treated as a state secret.

owners. The United States does not figure on the list, as its steamer completions in this year were all of turbine-engined vessels, with the emphasis on cargo liners and faster ships with a military potential, reflecting the Government's shipbuilding policy in the immediately pre-war years.

Table 6.6 takes data from the survey described above to compare the characteristics of British and non-British completions in 1939. Overseas yards tended to be producing vessels which were, on average, smaller in terms of tonnage and other dimensions. This may reflect their intended trades, especially for ships built in or for Scandinavian countries. However, the figures for size ranges show that the maximum sizes built were much closer, although with British vessels still larger. Figures for horsepower need to be treated with circumspection, as the lowest figures quoted in *Lloyd's Register* are suspiciously small. Again, the maximums are closer, and – allowing for a paucity of data – boiler pressures are similar. As expected with the average size of non-British-built ships, single-deck configurations are more numerous, with British ships more likely to be built as shelter-deckers. The two-deck ships, one each of which was built in Denmark and Germany, may have been intended for liner trades. The 16 out of 22 non-British examples with compound engines reflect the vessels' lower average size. Two-cylinder compound engines tended to be more compact, allowing more space for cargo. It is noticeable that all eight two-cylinder and three-cylinder compound engines were equipped with exhaust turbines. Few figures for ballast arrangements and capacities are available for non-British ships, precluding any meaningful comparison.

British builders still led in their output of steam tramps, with their size and relative sophistication maintaining a small lead over the larger non-British designs. This is not to say that overseas builders were inactive in development work, but in many cases their energies went into motor ships rather than steamers.

An innovative design of steamer originating in 1932 with K.G. Meldahl in Denmark deserves highlighting for its relative success was the boilers-on-deck design.[44] Relocating boilers to the weather deck freed up space for cargo at the point amidships where the cross-sectional area of the hull was greatest. With timber cargoes, where a substantial part of the cargo was almost invariably stowed on deck, the additional inside space was valuable as timber stowed there obtained a higher freight rate than deck cargo. The design was also a particular advantage in trades where the ship's length was restricted, for instance when running from Europe to the Great Lakes of North America before the opening of the St. Lawrence Seaway in 1953. British owners were seemingly reluctant to embrace the boilers-on-deck design, only 11 examples being built, all by William Gray at West Hartlepool. First was the *Elmdene* in 1939, production continuing after the war with seven others, concluding with the *Silverburn* in 1952.

---

44   Thomas, *British Ocean Tramps*, vol. 2, 52.

Table 6.6 Comparison of British and overseas-built steam tramps completed in 1939

Characteristic	British	Overseas	Overall
Sample size	*20*	*22*	
Gross tonnage (average)	4,651	2,380	4,823
Gross tonnage (range)	2,019–5,643	1,258–5,956	
Net tonnage (average)	2,731	1,347	2,006
Net tonnage (range)	1,307–3,364	698–3,020	
Length feet (average)	418	299	356
Length feet (range)	282–457	237–443	
Beam feet (average)	54	45	49
Beam feet (range)	44–58	38–59	
Depth feet (average)	25	18	21
Depth feet (range)	19–29	13–24	
Length/beam ratio	7.8	6.6	7.3
Beam/depth ratio	2.2	2.5	2.0
Length/depth ratio	16.7	16.6	17.0
Water ballast tons (average)	1,778	1,357 (n = 4)	
Water ballast tons (range)	999–2,685	940–2,609	
Horsepower (average)	408	222	
Horsepower (range)	234–524	54–478	
Boiler pressure p.s.i. (average)	217	220	
Boiler pressure p.s.i. (range)	200–230	220	
C. 2-cyl. + LP turbine	0	5	5
C. 3-cyl. +LP turbine	0	3	3
C. 4-cyl. engine	0	8	8
T.3-cyl. engine	20	6	26
Double bottoms	19/19	4/4	
Forecastle (number)	15	7	
Bridge deck (number)	3	6	
Raised quarter deck (number)	1	1	
Poop (number)	2	6	
Single deck	5	11	16
+ shelter deck	15	9	24
Two decks	0	2	2

German engineers had made a significant contribution to the marine steam engine, including the introduction of higher boiler pressures and poppet valve gear, whose adoption was desirable with greater steam temperatures. Innovations already mentioned include the exhaust turbines, with the German Bauer-Wach type being the most successful. The large-scale licensing of this system and its widespread adoption by British builders and owners contrasts with their indifference to other foreign innovations. As the details in Table 6.6 demonstrate, the period also saw a temporary resurgence in compound engines, particularly notable being the high-speed four-cylinder engines developed in Germany by Christiansen and Meyer, the compactness and efficiency of which made them particularly suitable for smaller tramps. Adoption of this machinery in the United Kingdom was extremely tardy, but it was used in what was the swansong of the British steam tramp, the 337-foot *Uskbridge* delivered by Ailsa Shipbuilding in 1959 with a Christiansen and Meyer engine.

The reciprocating marine steam engine might have been dead in the country which developed and nurtured it. But steam colliers, from which type the steam tramp developed, outlived them in service for a number of years. In the 1950s, Polish yards were building steam vessels intended for their coal export trade, and in 1954 and 1955 the British gas and electricity industries took delivery of ten large oil-burning steam colliers. The last of these, the *James Rowan*, was retired and broken up as late as 1984.

VI

The ocean-going steam tramp had a long reign. Well established by 1890, over the period to the late 1950s hull and machinery were successively developed and enlarged. By 1890, the triple-expansion engine had become established as the machinery of choice, offering a combination of fuel economy, reliability and relative ease of operation and maintenance, and it remained unchallenged for 40 years, although the next 30 saw a gradual decline in numbers. Driven by competition between shipbuilders, there were numerous developments in hull form, but enthusiasm for even the most successful was usually short-lived. The overall trend, however, was to improve longitudinal strength, enabling the average length of the tramp to be increased by 50 per cent, with a doubling of net tonnage, and hence carrying capacity. Only with the belated acceptance of tank testing in the period between the wars were hydrodynamically efficient underwater hull forms realised.

Improvements in engine and boiler design were instrumental in improving efficiency, reliability and fuel economy, with the average horsepower of steam machinery doubling over the review period. These developments tended to be gradual and incremental, at least until the 1930s when an industry-wide depression encouraged the widespread adoption of two significant innovations – the reheat engine, developed in Britain, and the exhaust turbine, largely developed in Germany. Perhaps the ultimate accolade for the steam tramp was that the period of its maturation from the 1870s to the outbreak of the First World War was accompanied by a reduction in tramp shipping rates by a figure of between 33 per cent and 45 per cent, according to indexes quoted or compiled by Kaukiainen.[45]

Although gradually losing their established dominance after 1914, the British owners and builders of tramp steamers remained pre-eminent. Even by the outbreak of the Second World War, British yards were building half of the world's tramp steamers, although the British industry's position was being challenged by the emergence of the motor tramp. Aided by a quirk of history, the British-developed shelter-deck steamer was massively multiplied during the Second World War, mainly by US shipyards, and the many survivors formed the basis of post-war tramp fleets throughout the world.

---

[45] Y. Kaukiainen, 'Growth, Diversification and Globalization: Main Trends in International Shipping Since 1850', in Fischer and Lange, *International Merchant Shipping*, 37.

Chapter Seven

Steam tramp to motor tramp

I

There were compelling theoretical reasons to replace coal-fired steam machinery with internal combustion engines. The latter were inherently more efficient, as significantly more of the energy from the combustion of oil fuel was translated into power. Efficiency is the proportion of energy supplied to the power plant which is turned into mechanical power. A widely quoted efficiency figure for modern oil engines is 45 per cent compared with a mere 10 per cent for the steam reciprocating engine fitted to the majority of steam tramps.

Adoption of liquid fuel also allowed some reduction in crew compared with the traditionally coal-fired ship, as firemen were no longer needed. Importantly, oil fuel could be stored in any available space within the ship, in contrast to coal, which, ideally, was stored adjacent to the boilers that were in the part of the ship which was most useful as cargo space. However, progress in adopting oil engine technology was hampered by technical problems which had to be overcome to ensure machinery was reliable enough to be used for prolonged voyages. There were also cost issues, as oil was initially more expensive than coal, and oil bunkering facilities had to be provided worldwide. There was also an unwillingness, particularly amongst certain British tramp shipowners, to adopt the new technology, a reluctance stemming from, or at least attributed to, the lack of engineers with the necessary experience.[1]

This chapter will cover three strands in the transition from steam-powered tramps to those with internal combustion engines. First is the timeline of the introduction of the oil engine for ocean-going tramps, which was delayed compared with its adoption for coastal and estuarial craft. Second, it is considered whether the change in machinery was accompanied by developments in hull form and equipment. The third and most important strand is a discussion of the technology that led to the almost universal adoption of oil engines for tramps.

---

[1]   It should be noted that liner companies had no such inhibitions, including the Danish East Asiatic company from 1912 and the Alfred Holt group, which embraced the motor ship in the early 1920s. Holts were, however, training their own personnel at their college in Liverpool.

II

Which was the first marine use of the oil engine is a vexed question, and Denmark, France, Germany, the Netherlands, Russia, Sweden, Switzerland and the United Kingdom can all make good claims.[2] Oil-engined vessels were initially used on lakes,[3] canals[4] and rivers.[5] As to the first use in a seagoing vessel, there is some uncertainty, and it is difficult to identify the first oil-engined tramp. Hardy cites as the earliest example the Italian cargo ship *Romagna* (678/1910), which had twin Sulzer engines.[6] Her completion date and other details in register books are incomplete, not helped by her foundering when little more than a year old on 24 November 1911.[7] On her final voyage she was crossing the Adriatic on a trip from Ravenna to Trieste with general cargo, which suggests she was intended as a cargo liner. *Romagna* was quickly followed by the small Dutch tanker *Vulcanus* (1,179/1910), completed at Amsterdam in December 1910. Her Werkspoor four-stroke engine took her out to the East Indies, and even survived the ship: on her being broken up in December 1931 the machinery was taken out and used ashore.[8] The next, and the first British-built example, was the *Toiler* (1,659/1911), completed by Swan, Hunter in March 1911, which can claim to be ocean-going on the basis of her trans-Atlantic delivery voyage to work on Canadian canals and lakes. Swan, Hunter built a further example

-----

[2]   The British example was the Thames sailing barge *Spinaway C*, which was completed at Ipswich in 1899 and sent round to the Isle of Wight to be fitted with a Vosper hot-bulb engine. Returning to its east coast trading area, voyages were made along the River Blackwater, where weed fouled its propellor, much to its master's annoyance, so that the oil engines was quickly removed. A.C. Hardy, *History of Motorshipping* (London, 1955). Despite the experience of *Spinaway C*, oil engines came to be fitted to many sailing barges and to larger coastal schooners and ketches, in many cases prolonging their working lives. See, for instance, R.J. Scott, *Irish Schooner Twilight: The Last Years of the Western Seas Traders* (Lydney, 2012).

[3]   In 1904, the Sulzer Brothers' first marine engine was installed in the cargo vessel *Venoge*, built to operate on Lake Geneva. Hardy, *History of Motorshipping*, 13. Although useful, and written by a contributor to the journal *Motorship*, Hardy's book was obviously put together hastily, with dates and other information being inadequately checked, with numerous errors and contradictions, and is poorly indexed.

[4]   A small engine designed by Dr Rudolf Diesel was fitted in a French canal barge some time before 1903. Hardy, *History of Motorshipping*, 13.

[5]   From 1904, a number of tankers, some surprisingly large, were built in Russia for use on local waterways and the Caspian Sea. Hardy, *History of Motorshipping*, 13.

[6]   Hardy, *History of Motorshipping*, 310.

[7]   Hardy quotes 24 June 1909 as her delivery date on page 22, but elsewhere has her completed in both 1910 and 1911. Hardy, *History of Motorshipping*, 22, 310. *Lloyd's Register*, 1911 maintains that her building date was 1910, so she almost certainly pre-dated *Vulcanus*.

[8]   Hardy, *History of Motorshipping*, 18.

for Canada in 1912, the *Calgary*, which was also fitted with their 'Neptune' engine, a development of the Swedish 'Polar' design from A/B Diesel Motorer. The 'Neptune' engine clearly needed further development: that in *Toiler* was replaced with a compound steam engine in 1914, with *Calgary*'s example lasting only until 1921. A further Swan, Hunter completion for Canadian lake service, the *Tynemount* (1,744/1913), was fitted with two Mirrlees, Bickerton and Day oil engines, which drove generators powering an electric motor. This novel diesel–electric installation had an even shorter life than the previous two examples and was replaced by a steam engine in 1914.[9]

The ocean-going motor ship came of age in December 1912 with the commissioning of the two-deck cargo liner *Selandia* for the Danish East Asiatic Company, driven by a pair of Burmeister and Wain four-stroke engines coupled to twin screws. *Selandia* was built in the Burmeister and Wain yard in Copenhagen, with her sister *Jutlandia* and her licence-built engine being completed in parallel by Barclay, Curle in Glasgow.[10] *Selandia* is reported to have made a highly successful maiden voyage to Bangkok, where her machinery was overhauled by her own engineers.[11] The design was quickly replicated, and a whole generation of distinctive, funnel-less motor ships followed from Burmeister and Wain, also helping to ensure the success of the builder's four-stroke engines.[12]

---

[9]   The Clyde Shipbuilding and Engineering Co. Ltd of Port Glasgow were somewhat more successful with their *Fordonian* (2,368/1912), also built for Canadian service. The builder's own four-cylinder engine served her under the Canadian and US flags until replaced by diesel–electric drive in 1925. Details of all four Canadian ships are from T. Starke and W. Schell, *Register of Merchant Ships Completed in 1911–1921* (Gravesend, various dates).

[10]   The two ships were launched just six days apart in November 1911. However, there are rumours that work in Glasgow was delayed because the drawings of the Burmeister and Wain engines were dimensioned in metric units, causing some headaches to the Scottish fitters accustomed to imperial measures. In the event, both *Jutlandia*'s engines broke down during trials on the Clyde and she was not delivered to Copenhagen until August. R.S. Fenton, 'Three Stick Bamboo', *Ships Monthly* (July 2008), 22–5. Despite this experience, in 1913 Burmeister and Wain established their own engine works on Clydeside, the Lancefield Engine works. Initially they were in partnership with Barclay, Curle and with Swan, Hunter, but the two British partners later sold their interests, rather reluctantly, to Harland and Wolff. Hardy, *History of Motorshipping*, 161. M. Moss and J.R. Hume, *Shipbuilders to the World: 125 Years of Harland and Wolff, Belfast, 1861–1986* (Belfast, 1986), 156.

[11]   Anon., *Three Sticks Bamboo: The Story of the First EAC Motor Ship* (Copenhagen, 1991). Hardy agrees that her first round trip was indeed successful. Hardy, *History of Motorshipping*, 34.

[12]   The Burmeister and Wain engine design was licensed widely, perhaps most significantly by Harland and Wolff, who chose to modify the design considerably. Moss and Hume, *Shipbuilders to the World*, 156, 310.

A good candidate for the first motor tramp is the single-deck *Eavestone* (1,781/1912), completed by Raylton, Dixon and Co. Ltd, Middlesbrough in July 1912, with the builder's own version of a two-stroke, four-cylinder engine licensed from Carel Frères of Ghent.[13] She was ordered by Furness, Withy who operated both liner and tramp services, but her single deck suggests she was indeed the earliest motor tramp. She was a pioneer, but not a particularly successful one: in 1915, her oil engine was replaced with a steam engine.[14]

The Flower Motor Ship Co. Ltd was a determined attempt to introduce motor ships spearheaded by Marcus Samuel, founder of the Shell oil company, although oddly its three sister ships were dry cargo carriers rather than tankers.[15] Samuel's aim was to encourage the building of motor vessels that would benefit the oil industry, and particularly Shell. Unfortunately, the licence-built 'Polar' machinery fitted to *Arum, Arabis* and *Abelia* yet again proved unsatisfactory, with two of the ships being handed back to the builders and licence-holders Swan, Hunter. All three ships were sunk by submarines during the war. The peacetime careers of these two-deck ships would have been interesting; with their considerable water ballast capacity they were serious candidates as pioneering motor tramps.

Although development of the oil engine continued apace during the First World War, work was aimed largely at producing better machinery for submarines rather than for merchant ships.[16] Both during and immediately after the conflict merchant ships were built in large numbers, but almost all had steam-reciprocating or steam turbine engines. One of the very few exceptions, the single-deck *Svealand* of 1917, suggested that the native Swedish 'Polar' engine was more successful than its development by Swan, Hunter.[17]

Five single-deck Italian ships completed from 1918 to 1921 were the first with locally built machinery, including the Fiat-type engines in *Ansaldo San*

---

[13]   *Lloyd's Register*, 1913.

[14]   *Eavestone* was sunk by a German submarine on 3 February 1917 west of the Fastnet while on a typical tramping voyage from Barry to Gibraltar with coal. Starke and Schell, *Register of Ships Completed in 1912*, 21.

[15]   R.S. Fenton, 'Flowering Too Soon? A Saga of Pioneering British Motor Ships', *Ships in Focus Record*, 61 (2015), 30–4.

[16]   Such was the success of this work that the engines of both British and German submarines were quite capable of taking them on war service from their west European building yards to the Mediterranean and the Dardanelles. German manufacturers capitalised on this development work and became leading suppliers of oil engines for coastal craft. See, for instance, Hardy, *History of Motorshipping*, 262.

[17]   After serving as a cargo liner for the Swedish East Asiatic Company, she was converted to a yacht in 1924 and re-engined in 1926, reverting to a cargo vessel in 1940, and surviving until broken up in 1954, by which time she was working as a pilgrim ship in the Indian Ocean. Starke and Schell, *Register of Merchant Ships Completed in 1917*, 81.

11: The Swedish-flag *Yngaren* of 1921 was the outcome of development work by Sunderland shipbuilder William Doxford and Sons Ltd to produce a reliable oil engine for ocean-going ships. *Yngaren* was torpedoed and sunk in an Atlantic convoy on 12 January 1942. *Ships in Focus*

Giorgio I, *II* and *III* – which ships, according to Hardy, 'ran in the coal trade'.[18] The other Italian single-deckers, *Ardito* and *Primula*, had substantial water ballast capacity and were fitted with engines by Cantieri Navali Tosi of Taranto.

The *Strassa*, *Laponia* and *Lulea* were completed in 1921 and 1922 by Gotaverken with their own design of oil engines. At 394 feet, these single-deck ships with substantial water ballast capacity are significant in being built to carry iron ore.[19] Their owner, Trafik A/B Grängesberg-Oxelösund, was essentially a railway company which moved ore from mines in central Sweden to the Baltic.

A cargo liner for the Australian services of Rederi A/B Transatlantic of Gothenburg, *Yngaren* of 1921 saw the first use of an oil engine developed over some years by the shipbuilder Doxford.[20] She was the world's first single-screw, ocean-going motor ship. Doxford machinery came to be very widely used and licensed, especially for tramps, and was indeed the only native British oil engine which was truly successful internationally.

---

[18] Hardy, *History of Motorshipping*, 364–5.

[19] Starke and Schell, *Register of Merchant Ships Completed in 1921*, 102.

[20] P. Richardson, *William Doxford and Sons Ltd of Sunderland: Shipbuilders and Engineers, 1837–1988* (West Malling, 2019), 116–18.

Table 7.1 Candidate ocean-going tramp ships, 1910–1924

(Does not include auxiliaries or vessels converted to steam propulsion before entering service)

Date	Name	Flag	Hull	Engine type	Feet	Notes
1910	*Romagna*	Italy	Cantieri Navali Riuniti, Ancona, Italy	Sulzer 8-cyl.	175	Foundered 24 November 1911
31 March 1911	*Toiler*	Canada	Swan, Hunter and Wigham Richardson, Ltd, Newcastle	'Polar' A/B Diesel Motorer 8-cyl. 2SC	248	Canadian lakes. Converted to steam 1929
16 July 1912	*Eavestone*	Britain	Raylton, Dixon & Co. Ltd, Middlesborough	Richardson, Westgarth 4-cyl. 2SCSA	276	Water ballast capacity unknown Converted to steam 1915
4 September 1912	*Calgary*	Canada	Swan, Hunter and Wigham Richardson, Ltd, Newcastle	Twin 'Polar' A/B Diesel Motorer 4-cyl. 2SCSA	248	Canadian lakes
25 September 1912	*Fordonian*	Canada	Clyde S.B. & Eng. Co. Ltd, Port Glasgow	Clyde S.B. & Eng. Co. Ltd; 4-cyl. 4SCSA	250	Canadian lakes. Converted to diesel electric 1929
2 December 1913	*Tynemount*	Canada	Smith's Dock/Swan, Hunter and Wigham Richardson Ltd, Newcastle	Twin Mirrlees, Bickerton & Day Ltd; 12-cyl. 4SCSA with electric motor	250	Diesel electric. Converted to steam 1914. Canadian lakes

Date	Name	Flag	Hull	Engine type	Feet	Notes
14 May 1914	*Arum*	Britain	Smith's Dock/Swan, Hunter and Wigham Richardson Ltd, Newcastle	Twin Swan, Hunter and Wigham Richardson Ltd; 4-cyl. 2SCSA 'Neptune'*	350	Two decks. WB: 965t Torpedoed 4 September 1918
9 February 1915	*Arabis*	Britain	Smith's Dock/Swan, Hunter and Wigham Richardson Ltd, Newcastle	Twin Wallsend Slipway Co. Ltd, Wallsend; 4-cyl. 2SCSA 'Neptune'*	350	Two decks. WB: 1,224t Torpedoed 16 September 1917
12 July 1915	*Abelia*	Britain	Armstrong, Whitworth and Co. Ltd, Newcastle	Twin Wallsend Slipway Co. Ltd, Wallsend; 4-cyl. 2SCSA 'Neptune'*	350	Two decks. Sunk by U-boat 30 December 1915
1917	*Svealand*	Sweden	Sodra Varv. A/B, Stockholm, Sweden	Twin 'Polar' A/B Diesel Motorer 4-cyl. 2SCSA	221	One deck. b/u 1954
1918	*Ansaldo San Giorgio I, II & III*	Italy	Ansaldo San Giorgio, Spezia	Twin Fiat San Giorgio 4-cyl. 2SCSA	378	Three sisters. One deck. 'Later in coal trade'
1921	*Ardito*	Italy	Cant. Nav. Tosi, Taranto	Twin Tosi 12-cyl. 4SCSA	384	One deck. WB: 3,570t
March 1921	*Yngaren*	Sweden	Doxford, Sunderland	Doxford 4-cyl. 2SCSA	429	One + shelter deck WB; 1,531
July 1921	*Primula*	Italy	Flli Migliardi, Savona	Twin Tosi 12-cyl. 4SCSA	290	One deck. WB: 770t

Table 7.1 *continued*

Date	Name	Flag	Hull	Engine type	Feet	Notes
November 1921	*Strassa*	Sweden	Akt. Gotaverken. Gothenburg	Twin Gotaverken 12-cyl. 4SCSA	394	One deck. WB: 2,302t
March 1922	*Laponia*	Sweden	Akt. Gotaverken. Gothenburg	Twin Gotaverken 12-cyl. 4SCSA	394	One deck. WB: 3,032t
September 1922	*Lulea*	Sweden	Akt. Gotaverken. Gothenburg	Twin Gotaverken 12-cyl. 4SCSA	394	One deck. WB: 3,032t
October 1922	*Dordrecht*	Dutch	Burgerhout, Rotterdam	Twin Bolinders 8-cyl. 2SCSA	250	One deck. WB 711t
April 1923	*Arantza-Mendi*	Spain	Euskalduna, Bilboa	Harland & Wolff 6-cyl. 4SCSA	345	One + shelter deck. WB: 976t
June 1923	*Steelmotor*	USA	Federal, Kearny, N.J.	McIntosh & Seymour 6-cyl. 4SCSA	250	One deck
July 1923	*Chastine Maersk*	Danish	Odense, Denmark	B&W 12-cyl. 4SCSA	378	One + shelter. WB 1,367t
November 1923	*Margretian*	British	Charles Hill, Bristol	Twin Beardmore 12-cyl. 2SCSA	298	One + shelter deck
October 1924	*Silurian*	British	Blythswood, Glasgow	Twin Beardmore 12-cyl. 2SCSA	431	One deck. WB 4,488t

* Built by the associated Wallsend Slipway Co. Ltd., Swan, Hunter's 'Neptune' engine was licence-built and based on the 'Polar' engine by A/B Diesel Motorer, Stockholm.
WB = water ballast.

12: Owen and Watkin Williams' ill-judged venture into new technology began with *Margretian* in 1923, an early British motor tramp. After being twice re-engined, she lasted until the 1960s, long outlasting her unfortunate owners. *Author's collection*

The shelter-decker *Margretian* of 1923 and the larger, single-deck *Silurian* of 1924 were the first oil-engined vessels built for the many fleets owned in Cardiff. Unfortunately, their twin Beardmore oil engines proved to be a poor choice, and their unreliability was a significant factor in the failure of the owner, Owen Williams.[21] Nevertheless, *Silurian* was notable in being the world's largest single-deck motor ship when built in 1924, a year in which production of motor tramps almost doubled (see Table 7.2). In this year, 12 of the 30 vessels identified as motor tramps built worldwide came from British yards, eight of these for British owners (see Table 7.3).

The sudden interest in the oil-engined tramp challenges the widely held view that the British industry was held back by its reluctance to embrace the oil engine. Indeed, Andrew Weir's Bank Line, which ordered seven in 1924, and Harland and Wolff which built and engined most of them, were significant pioneers in demonstrating the efficiency and reliability of this machinery.[22] As

---

[21] D. Jenkins, *Owen and Watkin Williams of Cardiff: The Golden Cross Line* (Kendal, 1991), 37–41. Watkin Williams had withdrawn from the partnership in 1919.

[22] As discussed elsewhere in this volume, the Harland and Wolff engine was licensed from Burmeister and Wain, although undergoing such significant development that it was regarded as their own design. In turn, they sublicensed it to Kincaid. Moss and Hume, *Shipbuilders to the World*, 310; Hardy, *History of Motorshipping*, 77.

Table 7.2 Numbers of ocean-going motor ships built, 1910–1924

(Over 170 feet, excluding auxiliaries and conversions from sail to steam)

Year	Cargo liners	Other dry cargo	Tankers	Total
1910	0	1	1	2
1911	0	1	0	1
1912	0	3	0	3
1913	5	1	6	12
1914	9	1	9	19
1915	13	2	1	16
1916	3	1	3	7
1917	4	0	2	6
1918	7	0	1	8
1919	7	0	1	8
1920	15	2	4	21
1921	31	4	9	44
1922	36	3	2	41
1923	31	6	5	42
1924	41	25	12	78

Palmer has pointed out, it is difficult 'to argue that British shipowners were particularly resistant to the technology considering that in 1939 Britain owned 1500 motor vessels, the largest such fleet on any register'.[23]

III

To examine how the motor tramp developed from its *annus mirabilis* of 1924, random samples have been taken for those built in 1924, and at ten year intervals to 1970. The results of these surveys are summarised in Table 7.3, which looks at how deliveries in 1929 and 1930 compared with contemporary steamers, and Table 7.4, which traces the motor tramp's development over a half-century.

---

[23]   The figures are from the report of the Rochdale Committee, cited in S. Palmer, 'British Shipping from the Late 19th Century to Present', in L.R. Fischer and E. Lange, *International Merchant Shipping in the Nineteenth and Twentieth Centuries: The Comparative Dimension* (St. John's, Newfoundland, 2008), 133–4.

Table 7.3 Comparison of steam and motor tramps built in 1930

Characteristic	Steam 1930	Motor 1930	Comparison
Sample size	*30*	*30*	
Gross tonnage (average)	4,989	4,656	mv < ss
Gross tonnage (range)	3,433–6,675	1,040–8,036	mv > ss
Net tonnage (average)	3,038	2,801	mv < ss
Net tonnage (range)	2,038–4,059	510–4,663	mv > ss
Length feet (average)	386	387	mv = ss
Length feet (range)	338–436	230–455	ss > mv
Beam feet (average)	54	53	mv = ss
Beam feet (range)	48–60	34–59	ss > mv
Depth feet (average)	25	24	mv = ss
Depth feet (range)	22–29	14–35	mv > ss
Length/beam ratio	7.14	7.26	mv = ss
Beam/depth ratio	2.16	2.17	mv = ss
Length/depth ratio	15.44	15.8	mv = ss
Water ballast tons (average)	1,646	2,312 (of 19)	mv > ss
Water ballast tons (range)	1,040–2,726	556–3,240	mv > ss
Horsepower (average)	431	647	mv > ss
Horsepower (range)	277–604	257–1,246	mv > ss
Double bottoms (number)	30	19/30 11/30?	mv = ss
Forecastle	25	16	
Bridge deck	15	3	
Raised quarter deck	0	0	
Single deck	13	9	ss > mv
One deck + shelter decks	16	21	mv > ss

The average length of the 1930s motor ship was almost exactly the same as that of its steam contemporaries, with beam and depth similarly comparable, and the ratios of these three dimensions were very close. However, the averages of both gross and net tonnages were some 7 per cent to 8 per cent *lower* in motor ships. This is perhaps surprising, given that eliminating coal bunkers and storing oil fuel elsewhere in the hull would be expected to increase space available for cargo. It may be partly accounted for by the average water ballast capacity of

Table 7.4 Characteristics of motor tramps built 1924–1970

Characteristic	1924	1929/30	1940	1950	1960	1970	Growth
Sample size	25	30	25	29	35	25	
Gross tonnage (average)	4,577	4,656	5,453	4,794	7,876	9,083	98%
Gross tonnage (range)	1,314–6,903	1,040–8,036	2,937–10,224	1,900–9,115	3,369–11,512	5,570–13,020	
Net tonnage (average)	2,758	2,801	3,267	2,624	4,463	5,988	117%
Net tonnage (range)	681–4,345	510–4,663	1,605–6,139	1,012–5,262	1,787–7,960	3,329–9,399	
Length feet (average)	379	387	439	424	480	465	23%
Length feet (range)	231–431	230–455	374–516	263–506	414–518	409–525	
Beam feet (average)	52	53	57	55	62	67	29%
Beam feet (range)	36–57	34–59	52–64	41–62	53–70	57–75	
Depth feet (average)	26	24	27	24	27	28	8%
Depth feet (range)	15–24	14–35	18–39	16–35	20–32	21–32	
Length/beam ratio	7.3	7.3	7.7	7.7	7.7	6.9	
Beam/depth ratio	2.0	2.2	2.1	2.3	2.3	2.4	
Length/depth ratio	14.6	15.8	16.3	17.7	17.8	16.6	
Number of cylinders	9 (3–12)	9 (3–16)	4.4 (3–12)	6.4 (4–16)	6 (3–12)	8 (5–16)	
Horsepower (average)	550 NHP	647 NHP	530 NHP	–	–	6,547 BHP	–
Horsepower (range)	223–862	257–1,246	378–1,030	–	–	3,400–9,900	
Two-stroke	8	11	19	27	35	16	100%
Four stroke	17	19	6	1	0	9	-47%
Engines aft	0	0	0	0	10	19/25	
Twin screw	14	5	0	0	0	0	
Single deck	7	9	1	2	1	2	
+ shelter deck	15	21	22	27	15	2	
Two decks	2	0	2	0	17	18	

motor ships being about 40 per cent higher than that of steamers. There may also be a sampling bias as, at the lowest size range, the motor ships included in the survey tended to be smaller. All the steamers, and all the motor ships for which this detail is available, were fitted with double bottoms.

Engines of motor vessels tend to be more powerful, although this finding needs treating with caution as nominal horsepower, widely quoted by *Lloyd's Register* and the British *Mercantile Navy List*, is a figure calculated by a formula, and not directly measured, as is brake horsepower, a figure later quoted by *Lloyd's Register*.[24]

For both types of tramp the shelter deck was highly popular, and more so in motor ships. It meant the upper deck space was not included when tonnages were being measured, although it was a less handy configuration when bulk cargoes are loaded or discharged, as there were hatches in the intermediate deck.

Comparison of photographs, particularly of vessels belonging to Bank Line, which began strongly favouring motor ships in 1925, reveal that motor vessels could be distinguished only by their shorter, fatter funnels, as there was no need for tall funnels to provide increased draught for furnaces.[25] The elimination of a conventional funnel and its replacement by a spindly exhaust, as pioneered by Burmeister and Wain and their clients East Asiatic, was not to last. Owners liked to show their colours on a decent-sized funnel, while the unused space inside was useful for non-perishable stores. The hatch between bridge/officers' accommodation and the boiler casing/engineers' cabins, which in steamers had allowed coal to be loaded directly into the bunkers, was retained, the hold below adding usefully to cargo space. Amongst British motor tramps especially, this archaic split superstructure arrangement was perpetuated up until at least 1945, despite it meaning that water, plumbing and electrical services for the accommodation had to be duplicated.[26]

The similarity between steam and motor tramps is not surprising, as the latter were predominantly built by yards which had turned out steam tramps, and usually continued to do so.[27] Figures in Table 7.4 indicate that the average size of motor tramps sampled, measured by dimensions and by tonnage, doubled from 1924 until 1970, although with an apparent decrease from 1940 to 1950.

---

[24]   Annoyingly, in post-war years, *Lloyd's Register* moved from nominal horsepower to quoting a 'machinery number', derived by an artificial formula, before finally embracing brake horsepower.

[25]   In fact, the provision of particularly tall funnels for steam ships was fast fading, as electrical fans were being fitted to increase natural draught.

[26]   Anecdotally, it has been suggested that a physical separation suited both the deck officers and the engineers, although such 'class distinction' was rather more prevalent in liner companies than the more democratic tramp ships. For a discussion, see the excellent T. Lane (ed.), *Grey Dawn Breaking: British Merchant Seafarers in the Late Twentieth Century* (Manchester, 1986), 151–80.

[27]   Hardy, *History of Motorshipping*, 243.

This growth reflects not just the increase in ships' capacity but also changes in how tonnages were measured. There was also the changing popularity of shelter decks, which did not count for tonnage measurement purposes. By 1960, half the ships sampled had two full-strength decks, with a consequent increase in the measured tonnage compared with shelter-deckers. Better indications of growth come from length, beam and depth, which all increased significantly, and by almost a third in the case of beam. Increases in depth were constrained, as ever, by the ports, channels and harbours expected to be used. This resulted in length to depth ratios increasing from 14.6 in 1924 to 16.6 in 1970. The longest vessel in the survey, at 525 feet, probably represented the practical maximum size for a conventional, midships-engined tramp, with six holds being worked into its hull, three forward and three aft of the superstructure.[28]

As with steam tramps, arrangements for carrying water ballast became more complex over time, with the number of individual tanks proliferating. Double bottom tanks divided by transverse bulkheads and fore and aft peak tanks remained usual. These could be accompanied by tanks in the engine room, alongside the screw shafts (at least in engines-amidships vessels) and wing tanks alongside the upper part of the holds. Deep tanks, although mainly intended for carrying liquids such as edible oils as part of general cargoes, could also be used for water ballast, significantly increasing the vessel's total ballast capacity in parallel with growth in the average size of ships.[29]

A major change in hull structure was the move from one deck plus shelter deck to a two-deck configuration, apparent between the 1950 and the 1960 sample. This partly reflects the elimination of arcane practices like tonnage openings, and more importantly changes in methods of measuring tonnage which were agreed internationally to avoid some of the anomalies in measurement methods between countries. It may also reflect that, with increased length, two decks were necessary to maintain longitudinal strength.

Not surprisingly, the engine room saw the biggest changes. This included its actual position, as after 1950 there was an almost unstoppable trend in dry cargo vessels to move the engines further aft from their time-honoured amidship position.[30] Advantages included a much shorter propellor shaft, which was not only cheaper but eliminated the shaft tunnel through the aftermost holds, gave more cargo space and avoided the possibility of grab damage to the tunnel while

---

[28]   An example was the 571-foot *Virginia Bolten*, built by Lübecker Flenderwerke in 1958. A shelter-decker, she was employed for part of her career carrying ore for steel company Thyssen-Krupp. *Lloyd's Register*, 1959.

[29]   It is difficult to plot other trends in ballast arrangements because *Lloyd's Register* continued to quote water ballast figures only for vessels which had been surveyed by the parent classification society, and the number of such ships declined considerably over the period of the survey.

[30]   It is surprising that this took so long. From their inception in the nineteenth century, oil tankers had engines aft, as did smaller coasters and most colliers.

unloading. The trend gathered pace through the 1960s, and by the 1970 sample 19 out of 25 vessels had engines fully aft, while some others had engines approximately three-quarters aft.[31]

Between 1924 and 1960, the four-stroke oil engine declined in importance to the extent that none of the 1960s-built sample was given one. But by 1970 it was coming back into favour, probably due to the widespread adoption of supercharging in such engines, although the two-stroke still dominated the market.[32] The figures for horsepower are incomplete, given that Lloyd's Register of Shipping changed the way it measured this parameter twice in the period. However, power output of engines grew at least in line with size, with the number of cylinders increasing. The improved reliability of oil engines is apparent in the decline in completions of twin-screw craft from 20 out of 25 in 1924 to none by 1940.

A total of 34 types of engines are represented in the lists, and their popularity waxes and wanes over the half-century of this survey. The Burmeister and Wain four-stroke was easily the engine of choice in 1924 and in 1929/1930, and in the latter years examples from the builder's own works, plus licensed examples from Harland and Wolff and Kincaid, propelled over half the motor tramps surveyed. The results from the year 1940 need treating with caution, as British ships and builders were almost certainly over-represented, with a government programme of standard ships getting under way, while the conflict had put a brake on merchant ship completions (and information about them) elsewhere in Europe. Licence-built Burmeister and Wain engines were still represented, but outnumbered by Doxford engines, whose popularity had been increasing throughout the 1930s, linked with the success of this builder's 'Economy' motor tramp. Doxford engines were still leading the league table in 1950, with Burmeister and Wain lagging, only for the latter to show a revival in 1960, when the type was sharing first place with the long-established Sulzer two-strokes. Maschinenfabrik Augsburg-Nürnberg (MAN) was in third place but set to move to joint first with Sulzer in 1970, by when Doxford engines were not represented, and only one Burmeister and Wain engine features. In 1980, MAN were to take over Burmeister and Wain, establishing the German marque as the leading builder and licensor of large marine oil engines.

A total of 74 building yards are represented in the samples. The distribution of these hull builders is of less interest than the engine builders, as any competent yards could install an oil engine. The overall leader is Doxford, again for their combination of a successful design of oil engine and their 'Economy' hull. Harland and Wolff and Burmeister and Wain virtually tie for second place, building ships with versions of the same engine. Of the others, 18 yards are British, building

---

[31]   Three of the sample were of the Austin and Pickersgill-designed SD14 type, which had just one cargo hold aft of the engine room and superstructure. J. Lingwood, *SD14: The Full Story* (Preston, 2004), 8–9.

[32]   Supercharging was first applied to four-stroke engines, Hardy, *History of Motorshipping*, 66.

mostly for British owners, reflecting how the dominance of British tramp owners continued into the 1950s, with well over half of all completions of motor tramps in this period being for British owners. This is further evidence of flaws in the view that British tramp owners failed because they did not embrace oil engines. After 1950, no one nation could show such dominance in tramp shipping, with Norway, Greece and Germany the most prominent flags.

IV

Shipping registers do not tell the full story so the results of the survey need to be supplemented by a narrative account of the development of the motor tramp.

The first commercially successful attempt to design and market a 'standard' motor tramp was the Doxford 'Economy' type.[33] The 1920s and 1930s had not been easy times for the Sunderland yard, as for shipbuilding in general, and after delivery of the motor tanker *Lise* for Norwegian owners in March 1931 it closed for a second time since the First World War. Managing director J. Ramsay Gebbie took the opportunity to have the drawing office design a combination of shelter-deck hull and Doxford's three-cylinder, opposed-piston, two-stroke diesel engine. Three years of idleness ended for the yard when yard number 612, *Sutherland*, was laid down for Newcastle shipowner Sir Arthur Sutherland.

The 'Economy' embraced novel construction methods, with the hull plates being electrically welded although decks were still riveted. The design also employed waste gas from the cylinders to fire a boiler which gave steam for auxiliary equipment. In port with the main engine shut down, this boiler could be oil-fired, giving steam to power cargo gear. At £100,000, the Doxford 'Economy' was more expensive than a new steam tramp, but offered lower operating costs, consuming just 6.5 tons of fuel per day at 10 knots. The design successfully rebuilt Doxford's order book, and 30 of the type were eventually delivered with the three-cylinder engine, all for British owners. This was undoubtedly helped by the British government's 'Scrap and Build' scheme of 1935, which gave owners inexpensive loans to build new ships if they scrapped old tonnage, even that which they bought abroad simply to sell for breaking up.[34] Ten Doxford 'Economies' were financed in this way.[35]

Doxford offered engines other than the three-cylinder type, and a number of almost identical hulls to the 'Economies' were delivered with four-cylinder Doxford machinery, including the unusual twin-screw *Nonsuco* for a sugar company in the Philippines.[36] The three-cylinder engine remained in production and at least 140 were built over the next 20 years, with more being constructed

---

[33]   R.S. Fenton, 'Doxford and the Economies', *Ships Monthly* (June 2012), 28–31.

[34]   D.C.E. Burrell, *Scrap and Build* (Kendal, 1983).

[35]   Burrell, *Scrap and Build*.

[36]   *Lloyd's Register*, 1938.

13: The Doxford 'Economy' type motor tramp *Fernmoor* was built in 1934 for W. Runciman and Co. Ltd of Newcastle She was wrecked in the Philippines in February 1954. *Ships in Focus*

under licence. In 1938, an improved and larger version of the 'Economy', was introduced, 443 rather than 428 feet long, with the three-cylinder engines uprated to give 12 knots at the cost of increased fuel consumption. This extra speed made these tramps attractive to liner companies needing to charter additional tonnage. The 'Improved Economies' proved very successful, with at least 85 being built over the 16 years to 1954.

Choice of steam or oil engines in British wartime construction of standard ships was governed by how many engines the small pool of UK engineering works could supply. For instance, Bartram's yard at South Dock, Sunderland built 15 standard ships to three different hull designs, but all with steam engines. In contrast, Doxford's 23-ship output included just three with steam engines. Identical hulls were built with both steam and diesel engines. For instance, *Empire Canning* from the Caledon yard at Dundee delivered in November 1944 had a Hawthorn, Leslie four-stroke oil engine. The yard's next completion to the same standard 'B' type hull design, *Empire Favour*, had a triple-expansion steam engine. Sold by the Ministry in 1946 and 1947, both went to the same London tramp shipowner, Watts, Watts and Co. Ltd,[37] although the motor ship was probably more expensive. This further supports the conclusion drawn from Table 7.3 that the hulls of motor and steam tramps did not need to be fundamentally different.

---

[37]   W.H. Mitchell and L.A. Sawyer, *The Empire Ships*, 2nd ed. (London, 1990), 36.

14: *Eucadia* was one of the last generation of British motor tramps, built for Walter Runciman and Company as *Linkmoor* in 1961, but seen here in November 1974 masquerading as a cargo liner for the associated Anchor Line. She came from the yard of Hawthorn, Leslie (Ship Builders) Ltd with a licence-built Doxford engine. Note the antiquated split superstructure. Sold to Sri Lankan owners in 1981, she was broken up in 1983. *Author*

The relatively small output of motor tramps around 1950 and the lack of much in the way of innovation in their design during that period may well reflect the large number of standard ships laid down in wartime that were still being completed and satisfying pent-up demand from owners. Delivery of these standard hulls from British yards continued well into post-war years, reducing the need for further orders.[38]

The equipment of tramp ships saw more development than did their hulls. In steam ships, auxiliary machinery such as cargo gear and capstans were steam driven, with steam bled from the boilers. Some early motor ships had donkey boilers to supply this steam. Gradually, electric winches and capstans became available, driven by a generator coupled to the engine. Although amongst tramps many examples could be found with pole masts and derricks, bipod masts were often specified, their two legs requiring less staying and reduced rigging and maintenance, also lessening deck obstructions when working cargo.[39] Twin kingposts and goalpost masts provided additional anchorage points for derricks, with their associated winches allowing two derricks to work alongside each other.

---

[38]   See the histories of ships ordered in wartime in Mitchell and Sawyer, *Empire Ships.*
[39]   R. Fenton, *Tramp Ships: An Illustrated History* (Barnsley, 2013), 138.

A variety of electric cranes were developed, although these were more usual on cargo liners, where speed of unloading was important. Also facilitating loading and unloading was the size and design of hatch covers. Steel covers became universal post-Second World War. They not only offered secure covering but being mechanically opened and closed they saved much time before and after working cargo compared with the traditional hatch boards and canvas hatch cloths, which had to be handled manually.

Rather stretching the definition of the tramp were vessels designed for particular cargoes, as the essence of the traditional tramp ship was that it could carry practically any dry, bulk cargo on offer. However, the relatively few specialist ships had more in common with the tramp than the cargo liner.

Scandinavian operators and designers showed considerable interest in ships designed for lumber carrying. In 1932, Gotaverken in Sweden built and engined the *Aurora*. She had three particularly wide hatches and long holds for lengths of timber, the second hold noticeably splitting the superstructure, plus goalpost masts.[40] Her initial owners were Swedish, although in 1936 she was sold to Norwegians who were more interested in operating tramp ships than their Scandinavian neighbours. Danish yards also made contributions, Burmeister and Wain building *Tureby* for Danish owners in 1936, along similar lines to *Aurora*, but with a long bridge deck. The same yard's *Skagerak* and *Kattegat*, delivered to Norway in 1936, took the same layout and design to extremes, with five sets of twin kingposts and goalpost masts serving the three holds.[41] The Burmeister and Wain ships had early examples of the builder's two-stroke engines, that in *Tureby* pre-dating its hull by five years, and presumably being a development model.

Newsprint carriers were built to work between the mills in Canada and the United Kingdom and down the Atlantic seaboard of the United States. Newsprint rolls are large and heavy, but also very vulnerable to damage: a one-inch tear could make a mile of paper unusable. To reduce this risk, pillars were eliminated from the holds, and wherever possible other obstructions were avoided, while sparring was covered with rubber. In winter the ships had to sail through ice up to 18 inches thick, and so they were ice strengthened and had well-rounded forefoots.

Grain has long been a staple of the tramp trades, but only a minority of ships have been designed specifically to carry this cargo. Being much less dense than cargoes such as coal or iron ore, grain could fill the holds before a tramp was down to its load line, so ships dedicated to the grain trade had larger holds, giving what was referred to as a 'high cubic capacity'. Some such ships were owned by the large international grain traders, who could guarantee that their ships would be largely carrying grain.

---

[40]   Hardy, *History of Motorshipping*, 244. *Aurora* is illustrated as *Nordnes* in E.C. Talbot Booth, *Merchant Ships, 1949–1950* (London, 1949), 30.

[41]   *Tureby* and *Skagerak* are illustrated and described in Fenton, *Tramp Ships*, 90–1.

Ships designed for carrying ore were an important strand in the development of the bulk carrier, discussed in a later chapter. However, conventional tramps were also involved in the ore trade, with strengthened hulls to minimise damage when loading and to avoid grab damage during unloading.

The success of 'production line' methods employed during wartime, often in conjunction with prefabrication, in turning out identical ships in quick time was not lost on some shipbuilders post-war. The enormous growth in the fleet operated by the Soviet Union was partly thanks to yards in Finland and in several Warsaw Pact countries building to standard designs.[42] Most of these were also delivered to state-owned national fleets, especially in Poland, Eastern Germany and Yugoslavia, with a few going to commercial owners elsewhere. Yards in the USSR also contributed to this growth, although the attraction of earning hard currency meant that orders from western owners were not turned away.[43]

Yards elsewhere were rather slower at offering standard ships, but a surge of interest in the 1960s saw Japanese, British, West German and Spanish yards offering what were deemed 'Liberty replacement' designs.[44] First off the mark was Ishikawajima-Harima Heavy Industries (IHI) with their 'Freedom' type, a name clearly inspired by its illustrious and numerous US-built predecessor.[45] The six-hatch vessel measuring 467 feet was designed by Canadian consultants G.T.R. Campbell, with the first example delivered to Greek owners in September 1967. With its engines aft and goalpost masts, it did resemble a bulk carrier, but its two-deck structure disqualified it from this designation. A total of 168 was built, mostly by IHI, with some by licensees in Singapore, Taiwan and Spain.

Even more successful than the 'Freedom' was the Austin and Pickersgill-designed SD14, many of which were built in the Southwick shipyard on the Wear which had been laid out post-war to facilitate series building.[46] Its initials stood for shelter-decker, with the 14 indicating a deadweight of 14,000 tons, although in practice this was nearer 15,000 tons.[47] With its hull configuration of four

---

[42]   A. Greenway, *Soviet Merchant Ships* (Emsworth, 1989) and A. Greenway, *Comecon Merchant Ships* (Emsworth, 1989).

[43]   The Poltava type cargo liner built by yards at Nikolayev and Kherson proved popular outside Warsaw Pact countries, at least 14 flying the flags of India, Iraq, Malta, Greece or Panama. Greenway, *Soviet Merchant Ships*, 52.

[44]   The rationale for 'Liberty replacements' was that wartime standard ships were reaching the end of their lives and that economical replacements were needed. This was a flawed argument as those owners who could afford nothing more than 20-year-old, war-built tonnage could rarely raise the million pounds or so needed to order a new vessel. Indeed, analysis of the owners who ordered some 700 'Liberty replacements' indicates that only a minority had ever owned a 'Liberty', and most were simply taking the opportunity of acquiring a useful vessel at an economical price. Lingwood, *SD14: The Full Story*, 11 quotes the builder's initial cost estimate for an SD14 at £915,000.

[45]   Fenton, *Tramp Ships*, 156.

[46]   Lingwood, *SD14: The Full Story*, 6.

[47]   Lingwood, *SD14: The Full Story*, 11.

15: Although Austin and Pickersgill's SD14s were designed to replace ageing tramps, a number like the *Arrino* were built for liner companies, in her case the Australind Steam Shipping Co. Ltd. However, she was soon sold and passed through four other ownerships before being broken up at Alang, India in 1998. *Author's collection*

holds forward and one aft of the machinery, and mostly with simple and more conventional cargo gear, it was nearer the traditional appearance of a tramp. Its relatively inexpensive basic specification appealed particularly to Greek owners, who took the first deliveries in 1968, while a number were sold to Germany, despite local yards offering their own designs. With licence-building in four other British yards, in Greece, Brazil and Argentina (some with modifications), a total of 198 examples of the SD14 were completed over two decades. Most of the British-built examples had Sulzer engines, mainly licence-built.

IHI and their consultants succeeded in building on their success by developing their 'Freedom' design to produce a handy-sized bulk carrier dubbed the 'Fortune' type, plus a 'Freedom II' and a 'Friendship' design, giving a grand total of 282 ships.[48] In contrast, Austin and Pickersgill struggled to exploit their success with the SD14, and it fell to a yard in Rio Janeiro to produce a development known as Prinasa-121, of which 43 examples were delivered, all initially to Brazilian companies.[49]

---

[48]   Fenton, *Tramp Ships*, 156.

[49]   This raises suspicions of state involvement, either in subsidising the national shipbuilding industry or leaning on Brazilian companies to place orders. All Prinasas had subsequent careers, mostly under flags of convenience, and bizarrely several were given names redolent of the town of their birth, including *Sunderland Endeavour*. Lingwood, *SD14: The Full Story*, 232 et seq.

The most successful German-designed Liberty replacement was the 'Weser 36', conceived at Bremerhaven by A.G. Weser, but also built by yards in Vegesack and Flensburg.[50] German owners, who had operated very few Liberty types, took half the total of over 70 built between 1970 and 1978. To tempt owners, various permutations of cargo gear were offered and – undoubtedly more important – favourable credit terms were available, as they were for other contemporary standard types.

The 'Santa Fe' type 'Liberty replacement' was built by four Spanish yards, with Astilleros Españoles SA at Bilbao building by far the biggest share, a total of 43. The total ordered was 51, although this is not quite so impressive when 35 ended up with just two owners, including the Argentinean state shipping line, Empresa Líneas Marítimas Argentinas. It is noteworthy that the lead yard, Astilleros Españoles, did not put all their 'Liberty replacement' eggs in one basket, but also built eight of the 'Hispania' type variants of the IHI 'Freedom' design.

As the Liberty replacement programmes completed their course in the 1970s, and the European yards that built them closed one after another, building of recognisably conventional tramps also petered out. But this was not to say that tramping ceased. As a further chapter will demonstrate, this aspect of shipping changed so that the tramp ship's natural successor, the bulk carrier, sometimes highly specialised, continued to provide the bulk shipping on which mining, quarrying, agriculture, forestry and the chemical industry depended.

V

The principle on which all oil engines are based is that combustion of a fuel and air mixture takes place within the engine's cylinder, directly pushing the piston, which by a variety of rods, cranks and shafts turns the ship's propellor. In a steam engine, which relies on the expansion of hot, pressurised steam to operate the piston, combustion of the fuel occurs remote from the cylinders in a boiler, and heat losses here and while transferring the steam to the cylinders seriously reduce its efficiency. Early oil engines ran on highly volatile hydrocarbon-based fuels, including paraffin, which were ignited by either a spark or by a glowing plug fixed in the head of the cylinder. The marine oil engine quickly developed to use compression ignition where the air in the cylinder was compressed to such an extent that, when fuel was introduced, spontaneous ignition occurred.

Origination of the compression-ignition engine is usually attributed to Rudolf Diesel in the 1890s, although some historians will mutter that earlier inventors deserve some credit.[51] Diesel worked in conjunction with MAN in

---

[50]   Fenton, *Tramp Ships*, 156.

[51]   In particular, the name of Herbert Ackroyd-Stuart is mentioned. Hardy, *History of Motorshipping*, 9.

Germany and to a lesser extent with Sulzer Brothers in Switzerland, giving both companies a head start in producing successful marine oil engines.

The main distinction between marine oil engines is whether they operate on a four-stroke or two-stroke cycle. Then there are divisions between single- and double-action, between low, medium and high speed engines, and large variations in the numbers of cylinders fitted. This account will not cover the considerable list of patented variations tried in ocean-going ships, which almost invariably proved failures in service. An important exception, which was successful and became widely used, was the Doxford opposed-piston engine. The operation of the major successful types will be discussed, with a brief commentary on the significance and the longevity of each.

The first successful marine oil engines used the four-stroke cycle, including those developed by MAN and, under licence, by Burmeister and Wain in Copenhagen.[52] During the first of the four cycles, air in the cylinder is compressed as the piston moves upwards. Compression raises the temperature of the air, and when it is above the ignition temperature of the fuel, oil is injected into the cylinder which spontaneously ignites. This pushes the piston downwards providing the power stroke, which represents the second cycle. The third cycle sees the piston returning upwards, during which time exhaust valves open to allow the gases from the combustion to be ejected from the cylinder. As the piston descends on the fourth cycle, fresh air is admitted, ready to be compressed as the cycles begin again.

In the two-stroke cycle, the air is compressed during the initial stroke, fuel being injected which as it ignites drives the piston downwards. But towards the end of this second stroke, the exhaust valves open so that the pressure in the cylinder begins to fall. At this point uncovered scavenge ports admit air which helps to expel the exhaust gases. These ports are covered during the succeeding power stroke of the cycle.

The main advantage of two-stroke over four-stroke machinery is that power is not expended moving the piston during the third and fourth strokes. Thus it is more efficient in delivering power to propel the ship and is also 12 per cent to 15 per cent lighter,[53] but at the cost of extra complexity, for instance in needing a pump to deliver scavenge air.

The prominence and prestige of two major manufacturers, Burmeister and Wain and their main licensee Harland and Wolff, helped to keep the four-stroke engine dominant in tramp ships for many years. They were challenged by Sulzer and Fiat, joined later by Doxford, who all developed successful two-stroke machinery. What was probably the first motor tramp, *Eavestone*, had a two-stroke engine. A turning point came in 1930, when Burmeister and Wain and Harland and

---

[52]   The principles are described, in relatively easily understood language, in A.J. Weddle, *Marine Engineering Systems: An Introduction for Merchant Navy Officers* (London, 1976).

[53]   Hardy, *History of Motorshipping*, 23.

Wolff introduced their own two-stroke engines, tacitly admitting its advantages over their own four-stroke.[54] The increasing popularity of two-stroke machinery is seen in its growing use in tramp ships from the 1930s to 1970 (see Table 7.4.) However, in the 1950s, Hardy was writing that, although receding from the picture, the four-stroke engine 'is still popular in tankers and tramps'.[55]

The output of an oil engine can be considerably enhanced by compressing the air that is admitted to the cylinder, and in turn introducing more fuel.[56] Generally known as supercharging, this increases the energy generated and hence the power delivered, but at the cost of building a more robust engine to withstand the extra pressure or accepting that the machinery will wear more quickly. Supplying air at a higher pressure involves either an air compressor which takes its power from the engine or more commonly by adopting a gas turbine powered by the exhaust gases leaving the engine, a system known as turbocharging. First employed in the early 1920s, with the Swedish ore-carriers *Svealand* and *Amerikaland* of 1925 being notable pioneers,[57] turbocharging allows more power to be extracted from a given size of engine, which enables the engine room to be more compact, offering more space within the hull for cargo-carrying.

Early oil engines used compressed air to force fuel into the cylinder, referred to as air- or blast-injection. To be admitted, the air had to be at a very high pressure, as that already in the cylinder was being compressed by the upward piston stroke.[58] A powerful compressor was required, and this absorbed a significant proportion of the engine's power output and was also very greedy of space. The alternative developed was air-less or solid injection, whereby a fuel pump is fitted to each cylinder. Still mechanically driven from the main crankshaft, the pump required much less power than air injection. According to Hardy, by 1933 such solid injection was established practice for all new engines, increasing the power available to propel the ship and saving the space occupied by the compressors. So well established did the system become that many existing oil engines with blast injection were converted to solid injection.

Most marine steam engines were double-acting, with steam being introduced alternately into the cylinder above the piston and then below it. The principle appealed to designers of oil engines in their search for increased power from each cylinder, but there were problems to be overcome.[59] Given the high cylinder

---

[54]   Hardy, *History of Motorshipping*, 69.

[55]   Hardy, *History of Motorshipping*, 68.

[56]   Hardy, *History of Motorshipping*, 63.

[57]   Hardy, *History of Motorshipping*, 66.

[58]   Hardy, *History of Motorshipping*, 68.

[59]   Hardy, *History of Motorshipping*, 82 et seq. In his chapter 9, Hardy is mainly concerned with engines for large and usually high-speed passenger liners, in which double-acting engines of both two- and four-stroke design were successfully employed. Although having written a tour de force in examining the intimate development of the oil engine, Hardy is not always consistent. At the end of the chapter on double-acting

pressures generated with oil fuel, the aperture by which the piston rod passed through the lower cylinder cover had to be made gas-tight. Double-action was first applied in the early 1920s to four-stroke engines, whose manufacturers (especially Burmeister and Wain and Harland and Wolff) wanted to increase power to challenge two-stroke machinery. Design of the lower cover in a four-stroke had to accommodate the necessary valves, allow space for a combustion chamber and incorporate a stuffing box to seal the exit of the piston rod, so was particularly complex and posed maintenance problems. However, the principle of double-action was equally applicable to two-stroke engines and was easier to apply to this type of cylinder. Both MAN and Sulzer successfully developed double-acting two strokes in the late 1920s. Writing in 1957, Hardy claimed that the double-acting two stroke was the accepted method of propulsion when high power output was needed. This clearly did not apply to tramp ships, and in the survey of over 150 tramps built from 1924 to 1960, double-action engines were rare. This is a reflection of the additional maintenance required with more powerful machinery.

Doxford's opposed-piston, two-stroke engine was ultimately a dead end, eventually passing out of production. However, they were significant, in combination with their builder's 'Economy' design, in encouraging investment in motor ships, especially amongst British tramp owners. In this engine each cylinder housed two pistons, facing in opposite directions.[60] Air and then fuel were introduced into the space between the two pistons, driving them apart during firing. The pistons were arranged so that their movements exactly balanced each other, reducing the stresses inherent in conventional engines and allowing the structure to be lighter. There was no cylinder head as in a conventional oil engine, avoiding a frequent source of problems. Originally developed in three-cylinder form, the number of cylinders was increased to offer a higher power output. The drawback of the opposed-piston arrangement was its complexity, as the drive from the upper pistons had to be taken to the crankshaft by side-connecting rods that were almost the same height as the engine, which itself was particularly tall. However, the Doxford engine received Hardy's praise as being as easily operated as steam machinery while also proving reliable, highly economical and accessible for maintenance.[61]

The first heavy marine oil engines, like their steam predecessors, ran at slow speeds, between 120 to 300 revolutions per minute (r.p.m.), matching the ideal range of rotational speeds of the propellor, and so could drive the propellor directly. Efforts to increase engine output involved designing medium (300 to 1,000 r.p.m.) and high speed (over 1,000 r.p.m.) engines, but these needed a method of transmitting the drive to the propellor shaft. Gearing was an obvious answer but

---

engines, he admits that owners are moving away from double-acting engines because of the expense of overhauling such complex machines.

[60]   J.W.M. Sothern, *Marine Diesel Oil Engines*, vol. 1, 7th ed. (Glasgow, 1944).

[61]   Hardy, *History of Motorshipping*, 41.

increased the complexity and cost of the machinery installation. However, gearing did allow more than one engine to be fitted to drive a single screw, overcoming concerns about reliability. It also allowed one engine to be closed down for maintenance while its companion propelled the ship at reduced speed.[62] A solution which excited considerable interest was for the engine to be coupled to a generator which in turn drove an electric motor connected to the propellor. The *Tynemount* of 1913 adopted this principle. Again, increased cost and complexity have meant that medium and high-speed engines have proved unpopular in motor tramps.

VI

The transition from steam engine to oil engine was a logical progression in the design of tramp ships, albeit one which took over a half-century to be completed. It provided improved economy, additional space in the hull for cargo, and – eventually – the basis for the automation of the engine room. However, there was little concomitant development of the hull, and for instance not until the late 1950s did the trend begin for placing engines aft. Size of the motor tramp increased in step with that of the steam tramp, as did the provision and sophistication of cargo gear, the size and comfort of crew accommodation and changes in overall appearance. The last-named was apparent in the straight stem and counter stern giving way to a raked stem and a cruiser stern (or, in later examples, a transom stern), and the modelling of superstructures and funnels. Despite experience of standardisation and prefabrication pre-dating the motor tramp itself, building of standard tramps was slow to start. Revived during the Second World War, it blossomed in peacetime, with many standard classes built for the USSR and its satellites, and the 'Liberty replacement' designs of the late 1960s and early 1970s.

The machinery of motor tramps remained relatively uncomplex. The major changes over the half-century surveyed were the transition from single-acting, air-blast, four-stroke engines driving twin-screws, to turbo-charged, double-acting, solid-injection two-strokes with single screws. Complications, such as double-action, and especially gearing, were unpopular with tramp engineers, and therefore with company engineering superintendents. The following chapter will include consideration of the machinery in the motor tramp's successor, the bulk carrier.

---

⁶² Examples of such an installation included the twin-screw, German-built, Swedish-flag ore carriers *Svealand* and *Amerikaland* of 1925. With very short turnround times at both loading and discharging berths, provision was made to stop one engine while at sea to allow it to undergo valve-replacement and other maintenance. Hardy, *History of Motorshipping*, 180–1.

Chapter Eight

Steam coaster to motor coaster

I

Once developed, steam coaster designs proved very resilient.[1] Although the heyday of the steam coaster ended with the First World War, the last ones were constructed in the late 1940s,[2] and steam colliers even later.[3] Steam coaster construction showed little change after about 1890, with minor improvements to the triple-expansion engine which by then had become ubiquitous, with most boilers remaining coal-fired. Boilers had to be replaced at intervals, and this offered some opportunity for updating, but Scotch boilers of modest working pressures remained standard. In most cases, minor refinements in terms of crew comfort including an enclosed wheelhouse had to wait until the Second World War, while accommodation for deckhands and firemen remained in the oil-lamplit forecastle.

In contrast to steam coasters, the screw collier did evolve, becoming larger and turning to oil-firing, with more efficient boilers working at higher pressures, while crew accommodation was improved in line with general raising of standards in deep-sea vessels.[4] A significant early development was the up-river or 'flatiron' collier, very carefully designed with minimum air and water drafts to serve gas works and power stations above Thames bridges.[5]

---

[1]   C.V. Waine and R.S. Fenton, *Steam Coasters and Short Sea Traders*, 3rd ed. (Albrighton, 1994).

[2]   The last conventional steam coasters built, *Balsa* and *Ebony*, launched in 1947 for Joseph Fisher and Sons Ltd of Newry were distinguishable from this owner's *Oak* of 1906 only by the provision of a wheelhouse. They had counter sterns, and lighting for the crew accommodation was provided by oil lamps. R.S. Fenton, and S. Patterson, 'Joseph Fisher and Sons', in *British Shipping Fleets* (Preston, 2000), 79.

[3]   A class of four were built for the UK's state-owned Central Electricity Authority in 1954 and 1955, the last of which, *James Rowan*, worked until 1984. D.R. Chesterton and R.S. Fenton, *Gas and Electricity Colliers* (Kendal, 1984), 106–8. The last steam collier built for Stephenson Clarke, one of the biggest independent owners of these ships, was the *Arundel* of 1956, which was sold to an Italian owner in 1972, steaming on until 1983. C.J.M. Carter, *Stephenson Clarke* (Kendal, 1981), 35.

[4]   J.A. Macrae and C.V Waine, *The Steam Collier Fleets* (Albrighton, 1990).

[5]   Macrae and Waine, *Steam Collier Fleets*, 172–8.

From about 1890, steam coasters were built which were dedicated to carrying liquids, most usually petroleum products, very much following the principles used to design ocean-going tankers.[6] For both these subspecies, tanker and up-river colliers, coal-fired steam engines initially remained the machinery of choice.

British yards had little competition in building steam coasters, and largely fulfilled the needs of owners in the British Empire and, to a lesser extent, continental Europe. Until the First World War, only a few yards in Germany, Scandinavia and France built steam coasters or colliers, and their influence on design was small. During the First World War, Dutch builders grasped the opportunity to build steam coasters provided when British yards were turned over to naval construction but produced steamers very much along the lines of British vessels. In the panic to buy coasters apparent in the United Kingdom at the end of this conflict, many of these passed into British hands: Dutch owners rightly believed steam was becoming obsolete.

The major development in coastal shipping was the fitting of oil engines, although embracing this machinery was for British owners and builders an agonisingly slow process, and largely forced on them by the more economical Dutch and German motor coasters that made significant inroads into the steam coaster's trades. Initially, at least, the advantages of oil engines were most apparent for vessels at the smaller end of the scale.[7] Advantages included the elimination of boilers, while fuel bunkers had no longer to be situated adjacent to the engine as oil was capable of being stored in almost any convenient compartment in the hull, giving more capacity for cargo. Although oil was initially considerably more expensive per ton than coal, the growing efficiency of oil engines meant that their fuel costs were usually lower.[8] The reduced weight of oil engines compared with steam machinery and boilers meant that draughts were usually shallower, a major advantage in allowing access to ports with limited water, or where tidal conditions precluded vessels arriving or departing before or after high water. Oil engines meant firemen could be dispensed with, and the overall engine room crew reduced. In his final book on coasters, Waine adopted a very useful chronological approach to the development of motor coasters, although the book is largely confined to British-built and owned ships.[9] This chapter will concentrate on the principle developments, with reference to overseas, although predominantly European, practice.

---

6   Waine and Fenton, *Steam Coasters and Short Sea Traders*, 123–7.

7   C.V. Waine, *British Motor Coasters* (Lydney, 2018).

8   Waine quotes figures published in *Shipbuilding and Shipping Record* which compares an oil engine weighing 24 tons with the steam machinery of the same power weighing 35 tons. Oil was priced at over £4 per ton compared to £1 for coal, but the greater economy of the oil engine meant that fuel costs were significantly lower. Waine, *British Motor Coasters*, 9.

9   Waine, *British Motor Coasters*.

Before tracing the evolution of coasters from the beginning of the twentieth century, the vexed question of defining a coaster needs to be addressed.[10] Although coasters on average tend to be considerably smaller than ocean-going ships, it is the vessel's geographical trading pattern rather than its size which is important. An average-sized coaster is quite capable of crossing the Atlantic, and delivery voyages from Europe to the Antipodes were common. It was not unusual that in summer when voyages with bulk cargoes such as coal were less frequent, some vessels were switched from European trades to the Great Lakes of North America. At the other end of the size scale, ocean-going bulk carriers have been carrying roadstone from Scottish quarries to English south coast ports since the late twentieth century. The size of a coaster is therefore determined by the physical characteristics of the ports and waterways it is expected to use and by the anticipated sizes of cargoes in the trades for which it is intended. There may also be national regulations on size, which usually set manning levels on the basis of size and voyage. It is simplest, if rather facile, to define a coaster as a vessel which runs regularly in coastal or short-sea trades.

II

The first use of internal combustion engines at sea was in coastal sailing vessels, where an auxiliary motor of modest power would greatly help in calm conditions, and especially in entering or leaving port. Adding such machinery, which was not deemed to require a dedicated engineer, significantly increased the life expectancy of many wooden schooners and ketches. Most of those fitted with oil engines had been built as pure sailing ships, often of wood. However, a minority were built with auxiliary power, an example being the schooner *Eilian*, built at Amlwch in Anglesey in 1908 and fitted with a Dutch-built Kromhout oil engine.[11] *Eilian* was unusual for a coastal sailing vessel in having a steel rather than a wooden hull.

The term oil engine covers at least three rather different species of machinery. In the engine developed by Rudolf Diesel, the air/fuel mixture was ignited purely by compression within the cylinder,[12] which required a very high cylinder pressure. Somewhat less demanding to design and build were those in which the fuel/air mixture is ignited by a spark in the cylinder, as in the engines typically fitted to smaller motor vehicles and referred to by Hardy as a 'paraffin' engine. In the third category, the hot-bulb engine which was particularly popular in early applications for marine use, a heated element set off combustion.[13]

---

[10]   See, for instance, R.S. Fenton, *Coasters: An Illustrated History* (Barnsley, 2011), 8.

[11]   R.S. Fenton, *Cambrian Coasters* (Kendal, 1989), 182.

[12]   A.C. Hardy, *History of Motorshipping* (London, 1955), 11.

[13]   Hardy, *History of Motorshipping*, 62.

The last-named proved particularly popular for motorising small coastal craft, particularly the machinery manufactured by J. and C.G. Bolinder M/V A/B of Stockholm.[14] To start this engine, a bulb on top of each cylinder was heated by a blow lamp. When running, the heat generated by fuel combustion would keep the bulb hot. In contrast to the engine patented by Diesel in 1892, where a pressure of around 500 p.s.i. was needed to ignite the fuel, the hot bulb engine worked in the range 30 p.s.i. to 200 p.s.i., making it simpler to build and requiring considerably less maintenance. However, a distinct disadvantage of the hot-bulb engine was the need to heat the bulb for several minutes before the engine could be started. Compression-ignition engines, built to Diesel's principles, generally replaced hot bulb engines in marine use during the 1920s and 1930s.

The boilers of steam coasters produced an abundance of steam which could power auxiliaries, including winches, pumps and dynamos. A motor ship had either to be fitted with a donkey boiler to provide steam, to have auxiliaries which were themselves driven by oil engines or be electrically powered from a dynamo or alternator turned by the main engine. All options meant further expense for the owner and more maintenance for the engineers. These ships also needed a compressor and a reservoir to provide air to start the main engine.

III

Claims as to the first British examples of vessels built as coastal motor ships are hazy. Frank Bevis of Portsmouth had the Bolinder-engined *Ogarita* (95/1911) built at South Shields in 1911, probably for work in the Solent.[15] However, the first serious attempt to build a fleet of pure motor coasters in Britain is attributable to John M. Paton, a partner with a Peter D. Hendry in a large Glasgow-based steam coasting fleet.[16] Paton resigned from the partnership, clearly intending to put his energies and capital into the Coasting Motor Shipping Co. Ltd, which was incorporated on 16 January 1912 with a nominal capital of £50,000. Paton was nothing if not adventurous, and placed initial orders for 12 vessels, later following up with a further six. There were six length variations, the smallest being of a size with Clyde puffers, and four types of engine fitted, built respectively in Scotland, Sweden, the Netherlands and Denmark. These variations meant that the largest homogeneous group was just three strong (see Table 8.1). Water ballast capacity was minimal, which meant that in light conditions in open waters the screw could come out of the water, causing the engine to race. The governor would automatically cut the speed of the engine, so that the engine could stall when the screw re-entered the water. *Shipbuilding and Shipping*

---

[14]   Hardy, *History of Motorshipping*, 45.

[15]   Fenton, *Cambrian Coasters*, 157, 164.

[16]   R.S. Fenton, 'The Innis Boats: A Reappraisal', *Ships in Focus Record*, 26 (2003), 86–98.

Table 8.1 Types ordered by the Coasting Motor Shipping Co. Ltd

Dimensions (feet)	Builder	Engine type	Name
65.6 × 18.4 × 8.6	McGregor, Kirkintilloch	2-cyl. 2SCSA Bolinder	*Innisagra* *Inniscroone* *Innisdhu*
65.6 × 18.4 × 8.6	McGregor, Kirkintilloch	4-cyl. 2SCSA Beardmore	*Innisbeg*
65.6 × 18.4 × 8.6	McGregor, Kirkintilloch	2-cyl. 2SCSA Kromhout	*Inniseane* *Innisfree*
74.7 × 18.3 × 8.7	McGregor, Kirkintilloch	2-cyl. 2SCSA Kromhout	*Innisglora* *Innishowen*
74.2 × 18.7 × 8.8	Jeffrey, Alloa	2-cyl. Tuxham	*Innisinver* *Innisjura*
93.0 × 18.7 × 9.5	Cran, Leith	2-cyl. 2SCSA Bolinder	*Inniskea*
99.0 × 18.8 × 8.4	Cran, Leith	4-cyl. 2SCSA Beardmore	*Innislargie*
100.1 × 18.9 × 8.6	Jeffrey, Alloa	4-cyl. 2SCSA Beardmore	*Innismurray* *Innisnee*
115.7 × 21.6 × 9.6 bridge forward	Chalmers, Rutherglen	4-cyl. 2SCSA Beardmore	*Innisshannon* *Innistrahull*
115.7 × 21.6 × 9.6 bridge aft	Chalmers, Rutherglen	4-cyl. 2SCSA Beardmore	*Innisulva* *Innisvera*

Record published plans of an even larger type, with dimensions of 149.3 × 25.5 × 11 feet and Bolinder engines, and which looked like a conventional small coaster, but these were never built.

The four built by Chalmers were not uniform in design, although they had the same dimensions and engines. *Innisshannon* and *Innistrahull* initially had their bridge mounted right forward on the forecastle, while *Innisvera* and *Innisulva* had theirs on the poop. By the mid-30s, *Innisshannon* had lost her forward bridge in favour of an open structure conventionally placed aft.

Paton's initiative proved to be wildly overambitious. There was, for instance, insufficient time to modify individual designs in the light of experience with prototypes. But the biggest difficulty was recruiting engineers who had sufficient experience of oil engines to deal with their idiosyncrasies, especially in the arcane art of starting. Steam engineers were appointed who simply had to learn new skills on the job, but who often failed to do so. There were breakdowns, three contributing to the loss of a ship, so they received a bad press and set back the cause of the motor coaster by many years. Yet many of them had long lives

16: *Innisshannon* was one of two motor vessels of the Coasting Motor Shipping Co. Ltd with a wheelhouse right forward but was rebuilt to move it aft. She was one of the longer-lived of the company's ships, wrecked in the Red Sea in 1953. *Author's collection*

when sold on after the death of Paton in 1917 and the winding up of his Coasting Motor Shipping Co. Ltd in 1919. The McGregor-built *Innisfree* of 1913 was the longest lived, surviving until broken up in Denmark in 1980, by when she was on her third engine and had been rebuilt twice.

Perhaps the ship that most closely resembled the eventual concept of the motor coaster was the *Isleford*, completed in 1913 for another Glasgow concern, Mann, MacNeal and Company. At 150 feet, she was considerably larger than any of the *Innis-* vessels, with a substantial forecastle and a raised bridge deck. She had been designed as a steamer, but altered during construction to take a Bolinder hot bulb engine, but still needed a donkey boiler to power auxiliaries.[17] Her trials proved very successful but little is recorded of her subsequent performance, her registration documents noting that she passed to the Admiralty in 1918. She was wrecked in Wick Bay during January 1942.

As Table 8.2 indicates, building of motor coasters for commercial use was virtually halted by the outbreak of the First World War. However, vessels propelled by internal combustion engines were built for the Admiralty, dubbed 'X-lighters' from their pennant numbers. Of around 106 feet in length, the choice of oil engine (from a variety of makers) was to ensure a minimal draft, with the intention of using them as landing craft. Disposal by the Admiralty in the 1920s

---

[17]   Waine, *British Motor Coasters*, 14.

Table 8.2 Chronological list of early British motor coasters, 1911–1929

Registered	Name	Builder	Engine	Feet	First owner
18 November 1911	*Ogarita*	Hepple	Bolinder	88	Bevis
24 May 1912	*Innisagra*	McGregor	Bolinder	66	Coasting Motor Shipping
3 July 1912	*Inniskea*	Cran	Bolinder	93	Coasting Motor Shipping
3 July 1912	*Inniscroone*	McGregor	Bolinder	66	Coasting Motor Shipping
10 July 1912	*Innisbeg*	Beardmore	Beardmore	66	Coasting Motor Shipping
22 October 1912	*Innismurray*	Jeffrey	Beardmore	100	Coasting Motor Shipping
10 December 1912	*Innisdhu*	McGregor	Bolinder	66	Coasting Motor Shipping
27 December 1912	*Innisnee*	Jeffrey	Beardmore	100	Coasting Motor Shipping
20 January 1913	*Innislargie*	Cran	Beardmore	99	Coasting Motor Shipping
24 February 1913	*Isleford*	Ardrossan	Bolinder	150	Mann, MacNeal
29 March 1913	*Inniseanne*	McGregor	Kromhout	66	Coasting Motor Shipping
15 April 1913	*Innisfree*	McGregor	Kromhout	66	Coasting Motor Shipping
23 June 1913	*Innisshannon*	Chalmers	Beardmore	116	Coasting Motor Shipping
9 July 1913	*Innisinver*	Jeffrey	Tuxham	100	Coasting Motor Shipping
6 August 1913	*Innisjura*	Jeffrey	Tuxham	74	Coasting Motor Shipping
21 August 1913	*Innistrahull*	Chalmers	Beardmore	116	Coasting Motor Shipping
24 September 1913	*Carita*	Abdela & Mitchell	Bolinder	96	Summers
17 October 1913	*Innisglora*	McGregor	Kromhout	75	Coasting Motor Shipping
4 November 1913	*Innishowen*	McGregor	Kromhout	75	Coasting Motor Shipping

Table 8.2 *continued*

Registered	Name	Builder	Engine	Feet	First owner
24 November 1913	*Fleurita*	Abdela & Mitchell	Bolinder	103	Summers
28 May 1914	*Innisvera*	Chalmers	Beardmore	115	Coasting Motor Shipping
17 June 1914	*Red Hand*	Jeffrey	Beardmore	76	Allsup
9 November 1914	*Sir William*	Abdela & Mitchell	Bolinder	98	Vernon
3 December 1914	*Innisulva*	Chalmers	Beardmore	116	Coasting Motor Shipping
9 October 1915	*Swastika*	Yarwood	Lysekils	76	W. Gossage
11 April 1916	*Cristo*	Rennie Forrest	Bolinder	140	Christopherson
3 February 1917	*Lee Lee*	Rennie Forrest	Bolinder	140	Pollock
11 June 1917	*Lutona*	Pollock	Bolinder	116	Pollock
13 February 1919	*Molliette*	Pollock	Bolinder	131	Oppenheimer
18 September 1919	*Violette*	Pollock	Bolinder	131	Pollock
29 April 1920	*Warita*	Abdela & Mitchell	Bolinder	127	Summers
18 June 1920	*Georgita*	Crichton	Bolinder	126	Summers
26 June 1920	*Wilita*	Crichton	Bolinder	126	Summers
2 July 1920	*Fullagar*	Cammell, Laird	Beardmore	150	T&J Brocklebank
20 October 1920	*Marcita*	Crichton	Bolinder	126	Summers
15 January 1921	*Ben Truman*	Pollock	Bolinder	80	Truman, Hanbury & Buxton
28 January 1921	*Harparees*	Wills & Packham	Vickers-Petter	94	Rees, Parry & Harris
7 February 1921	*Stratum*	Livingstone & Cooper	Bolinder	103	Builder's account

Registered	Name	Builder	Engine	Feet	First owner
12 February 1921	*Admiral Vernon*	Pollock	Bolinder	127	Vernon
14 February 1921	*Indorita*	Abdela & Mitchell	Bolinder	109	Summers
16 February 1921	*Fer*	Crichton	Bolinder	130	Mostyn Iron Works
13 April 1921	*Eldorita*	Abdela & Mitchell	Bolinder	109	Summers
13 July 1921	*Polita*	Lytham	Bolinder	99	Summers
13 July 1921	*Dorita*	Lytham	Bolinder	99	Summers
3 September 1921	*Stoneboat*	J. Samuel White	Vickers-Petters	121	Road Maintenance & Stone Supply Co.
9 September 1921	*Carmenita*	Lytham	Bolinder	99	Summers
12 October 1921	*Alita*	Lytham	Bolinder	99	Summers
1 November 1921	*Arran Firth*	Hepple	Bolinder	138	Gillie & Blair
16 November 1921	*Jonita*	Crichton	Bolinder	126	Summers
3 August 1921	*Heather Pet*	Wills & Packham	Vickers-Petters	94	Vickers-Petters
17 January 1928	*Ability*	Fellows	Plenty	115	Everard
1 August 1928	*Amenity*	Fellows	Plenty	115	Everard

saw a number being sold to commercial owners who adapted them for estuarial and coastal work. They were to give a number of owners such as Metcalf Motor Coasters Ltd and F.T. Everard and Sons their first experience with motor ships.

An early owner who exploited the shallow draft possible with motor coasters was John Summers and Sons. This steel company's Deeside works needed to bring in pig iron and send out galvanised steel sheets and basic slag in spite of the limited depth of water in the River Dee. Their *Carita* of 1913 drew just two feet forward and five feet aft. As early as 1913 they had bought the *Ogarita* and supplemented it with a procession of Bolinder-engined vessels mainly from a nearby yard, that of Abdela and Mitchell Ltd at Queensferry, also buying two of the *Innis* ships built for Paton's venture.[18]

The British agents for Bolinder engines were James Pollock and Co. Ltd of Faversham and although building few motor coasters themselves they were instrumental in designing many pioneering vessels built elsewhere, including the *Sir William* of 1914 which went on to serve Summers as *Felita*.[19] They also had a hand in the design of the Admiralty X-lighters, for many of which they supplied engines. Built at their yard during a steel shortage at the end of the First World War, the Bolinder-engined *Molliette* and *Violette* of 1919 had concrete hulls, but had very short lives.[20] The yard's steel coaster designs were more successful, and Pollock was a rare example of a builder operating its own small fleet of coasters, although these were sold, reportedly because Pollock did not want to compete with possible customers.[21] Table 8.2 is believed to be a complete list of British-built motor coasters up to 1929.[22]

IV

Although merchant shipbuilding quickly resumed in the United Kingdom after the First World War, during which construction for the Admiralty took precedence, the numbers of motor coasters completed in the United Kingdom was relatively small compared with the volume of steam coaster production. The pent-up demand for steamers spawned several new steel shipyards either built on greenfield sites or adapted from yards hitherto building in wood.[23] The inevitable result was an oversupply of steam coasters, with a consequent drastic

---

[18]   Fenton, *Cambrian Coasters*, 157–71.

[19]   A. Salmon, *A Sideways Launch* (Rainham, 1992).

[20]   The National Archives, Kew (TNA), registration documents, classes BT 110/576 and BT 110/651.

[21]   Salmon, *A Sideways Launch*, 66.

[22]   TNA, registration documents, class BT 110.

[23]   Three of these arose in North Devon, the yards of Cock at Appledore, Hansen at Bideford and the Taw Shipyard at Barnstaple. Neither the Bideford nor Barnstaple yard prospered. G. Farr, *Shipbuilding in Devon* (NMM Monograph No. 22) (Greenwich, 1976).

fall in freight rates, leaving owners with expensively built steamers unable to operate them profitably. There was thus little incentive to invest in motor ships, especially as relatively new steamers were coming on the market at knock-down prices when the lenders who had financed them foreclosed on their loans. From 1921 to 1929 there were just two additions to the list in Table 8.2, both built for Everard of Greenhithe.[24]

Dutch coaster owners successfully grasped the opportunity presented by the situation on the British coast.[25] As neutrals, many had profited from high freight rates available from both sides during the war and took the opportunity to invest in oil engines to equip their predominantly sailing fleets. Reliable engines were being built by several Dutch manufacturers, including Kromhout, Stork and Brons, while German machinery also became popular, especially that built by Deutz (latterly Humboldt-Deutz). The progression to purpose-built powered coasters was achieved quickly, exploiting the lightness of the oil engine to offer a shallow draft, useful not just on continental waterways but also when trading to small ports around Great Britain and Ireland. With coasters often owned by their masters, who lived on board and employed family members as a highly economical crew, the Dutch were able to undercut ruling freight rates, to the distress of their British competitors.

The pressing need for economy in operation led a few enterprising British owners to emulate the Dutch and build motor coasters locally or buy the products of Dutch yards. Few owners exploited this earlier or better than F.T. Everard and Sons of Greenhithe. They gained experience with a Kromhout hot-bulb engine fitted as an auxiliary in one of their sailing barges and went on to build up a fleet of converted X-lighters and other small motor-driven craft.[26] Their first ship recognisable as a motor coaster was the appropriately named *Ability* of 1928, powered by a hot-bulb engine built by Plenty and Sons of Newbury. This was an engineering company which Everards were later to acquire to ensure the supply of engines and spares, and which supplied engines for many of their ships. The Newbury yard also fulfilled a vital role by offering training to Everard's engineers. *Ability* was followed into the fleet at regular intervals by dry-cargo motor coasters of increasing size.[27] Designs emerged which were to become very familiar amongst British motor coasters. *Ability* had a raised forecastle and bridge deck, with her

---

[24]   These were *Ability* and *Amenity* of 1928, both built by Fellows of Great Yarmouth. K.S. Garrett, *Everard of Greenhithe*, 2nd ed. (Windsor, 2017), 85–6.

[25]   A. Boerma, *Schepen van de kustvaart toen en nu* (Alkmaar, 1985).

[26]   Garrett, *Everard of Greenhithe*, 85.

[27]   *Ability* and her sister *Amenity* were built to a modest length of 115 feet but were lengthened in the 1930s to 136 feet. *Amenity* also had her hot bulb engine replaced by a diesel, a frequent procedure amongst Everard's vessels. For instance, the 1917-built *Leelee*, bought and renamed *Assurity*, had her Bolinder engine replaced in 1933 by one made by their own engineering subsidiary. A second replacement made in 1952 extended her life to 1960. Garrett, *Everard of Greenhithe*, 85–8.

17: Everard's *Ability* of 1928 was a development of earlier motor ships, one of the first of a recognisably British design with her raised forecastle and poop. Just 115 feet in length when built at Great Yarmouth, she was lengthened to 137 feet in 1939. She was lost when mined in the North Sea during November 1940. *Ships in Focus*

one hatch occupying the well between. With the 135-foot *Assiduity* of 1930 came another distinctive outline, emulating the medium-sized steam coaster with a raised quarterdeck with a bridge perched at its forward end. A two-hatch ship, she had just one long hold, whereas larger ships generally had two. Water ballast capacity was similar to that in steam coasters, for instance the 142-foot *Acrity* of 1934 could carry 62 tons in her forepeak tank and 32 tons in her aft peak.[28]

Few British shipyards showed much interest in building motor coasters. Everard's *Ability* and *Amenity* were built by Fellows and Co. Ltd at Great Yarmouth, in whom Everard had a financial interest, while others including *Acrity* came from George Brown and Co. Ltd at Greenock. This paucity of interest left some owners to buy directly from Dutch yards: for instance, Metcalf Motor Coasters had their first true dry cargo motor ship, the *Ellen M*, built in 1930 by Scheepsbouwwerf De Gideon of Groningen.[29]

One of the first British yards to wake up to the potential market for motor coasters was the Goole Shipbuilding and Repairing Co. Ltd. Encouraged by

---

28   From plans reproduced in Waine, *British Motor Coasters*, 32.

29   P.N. Quartermaine, *Metcalf Motor Coasters Limited* (Kendal, 1965), 2.

an order from David Williamson Ltd of London, they took the unusual step of using the National Physical Laboratory's model testing tank at Teddington to determine the best lines for a motor coaster, aiming to at least equal the performance of Dutch coasters.[30] With oil engines like the Deutz model selected for Williamson's two ships, *Affaric* and *Arrivaine*, the propellor turned at a much higher speed than with a steam engine. Tests indicated the optimum shape of cruiser stern for the chosen combination of engine and propellor. A useful water ballast capacity of 120 tons was achieved by fitting a cellular double bottom plus fore and aft peak tanks. Bridge control of the engine was another innovative feature. The Goole yard marketed their design strongly, naming it the 'Proficient' type. It was built in various lengths and at least three hull configurations, but all with a strongly raked stem. This design even seduced Everards away from their regular builders for their *Sequacity* of 1937 and *Ability* and *Amenity* of 1943, which were impressively large for a pre-Second World War motor coaster design.[31]

In the mid-1930s, several 'traditional' British owners and builders who had grown up with steam decided, at last, to embrace the motor coaster. William Robertson of Glasgow was a very early adopter of steam coasters, and during the 1930s had the largest British fleet of bulk-carrying coasters.[32] They hedged their bets during fleet renewal in the late 1930s, ordering both a motor ship, *Sapphire*, delivered in September 1935 by Ailsa as their first vessel of the type,[33] and a traditional steamer, *Pyrope*, delivered in July 1936.[34] Although the motor ship was particularly large at 200 feet, it is surprising that it was considerably more expensive at £24,350 compared with £15,630 for the 171-foot *Pyrope*. Part of Robertson's caution was over the lack of a diesel engine powerful enough for a vessel the size of *Sapphire*, the eventual decision being to install a Swedish engine from Atlas Diesel M/V. As *Sapphire* was lost following a collision in April 1939 the engine's longevity cannot be assessed. Three further motor ships followed from other Scottish yards, but Robertson then took four from yards in the Netherlands with German engines, this machinery proving so successful that Robertsons ordered no more steamers.

Scottish owners had reason to be wary of oil engines. Not only was the fate of Paton's Coasting Motor Shipping venture still remembered, but also that of the locally engined *Kindiesel* of 1936.[35] She was the result of a joint venture between Greenock coaster owner P. MacCallum and Sons Ltd and John G. Kincaid and Co., licence-holder for large Burmeister and Wain engines, but who designed

---

[30]   Waine, *British Motor Coasters*, 36.
[31]   Garrett, *Everard of Greenhithe*, 99, 104.
[32]   R.S. Fenton and P. Robertson, *William Robertson and the Gem Line* (Preston, 2009).
[33]   Fenton and Robertson, *William Robertson and the Gem Line*, 20–1.
[34]   Fenton and Robertson, *William Robertson and the Gem Line*, 90.
[35]   R.S. Fenton, 'Ard Coasters', *Ships in Focus Record*, 64 (2018), 2–14.

their own small oil engine which went into *Kindiesel*. After prolonged periods out of action for repairs, rebuilding and lack of work, the little coaster was sold to a Cardiff owner in 1941. Rebuilding the engine appears to have been reasonably successful, as she ran for Norwegian owners until wrecked in the Baltic during January 1969, ironically after a problem with her engine.

However, as an established and successful owner, Robertson's faith in motor coasters appears to have reassured other coaster owners and builders. Another significant Glasgow coaster owner, J. and A. Gardner and Co. Ltd, went to Scotts of Bowling for their *Saint Angus* and *Saint Bedan*, in 1936 and 1937, but like Robertsons then patronised Dutch yards for *Saint Ronaig* and *Saint Kentigern*, in 1937, both engined like *Sapphire* by Atlas Diesel M/V.[36] Other long-established Scottish coaster builders were by now building motor coasters, including the Ardrossan Dockyard, Caledon, A. and J. Inglis of Glasgow, Henry Robb of Leith and Scotts of Bowling.

The 1930s closed with most British coaster builders and a number of owners having been finally converted to the motor coaster (see Table 8.3). However, Dutch builders, with their considerably greater experience of the type, were able to offer serious competition. Where the United Kingdom seriously lagged behind, however, was in the development of convincingly reliable diesel engines for coasters, whereas Dutch, German and Swedish builders had established excellent reputations, and profited from them.

It needs to be asked why steam coasters were not converted to motor coasters, especially when there was a glut of them on the market after 1921. The expense would be high, especially at a time when freight rates were too low to offer a chance of paying off loans. Not only new engines needed to be fitted, but the steam auxiliaries, including winches, capstans and pumps, also needed to be replaced by diesel or electric units. In addition, a major benefit of a motor coaster, its relatively shallow draft, could not be realised in a conversion as steam coaster hulls were usually deeper. The Liverpool owners of the steamer *Hazelfield* rejected the idea of converting her to diesel as she was too deep for several ports to which the company's motor ships traded.[37] In addition, classification societies appear to have been opposed to such a rebuild. An anecdote tells of the North Wales-based owner of the 47-year-old steam coaster *Hove* who considered fitting her with a Crossley oil engine, using the boiler as an oil fuel tank and extending the after-hold into the bunker space. The local Lloyd's Register of Shipping surveyor disapproved, so the idea was dropped and *Hove* was sent to breakers at Dublin in 1961.[38]

---

[36]   G. Atkinson, *J. & A Gardner and Co. Ltd* (Portishead, 2002), 68–70.

[37]   The oil-fired *Hazelfield* was completed at Lytham in April 1948. After her sale to Greek owners she did become a motor ship. R.S. Fenton, *Mersey Rovers* (Gravesend, 1997), 274, 304.

[38]   Fenton, *Cambrian Coasters*, 81.

Table 8.3 Chronological list of early British motor coasters, 1930–1939

(This list includes shelter-deck coasters used predominantly in the liner trade and, for completeness, two-deck Coast Lines ships, indicated by*)

Registered	Name	Builder	Engine	Feet	First owner	O.N.
25 November 1930	*Assiduity*	Brown	Plenty-Still	135	F.T. Everard & Sons Ltd	162508
2 July 1931	*Aridity*	Fellows	Plenty-Still	130	F.T. Everard & Sons Ltd	162607
20 October 1931	*Activity*	Brown	Plenty-Still	135	F.T. Everard & Sons Ltd	162654
30 November 1931	*Acclivity*	Brown	Plenty-Still	164	F.T. Everard & Sons Ltd	162667
17 November 1932	*Fife Coast*	Ardrossan	Kincaid (B&W)	136	Coast Lines	162394
6 February 1933	*Actuality*	Fellows	Newbury 'SBD'	129	F.T. Everard & Sons Ltd	163314
17 February 1933	*Actuosity*	Brown	Newbury 'SID'	135	F.T. Everard & Sons Ltd	163316
3 October 1933	*Apricity*	Brown	Newbury 'SBD	143	F.T. Everard & Sons Ltd	163393
25 October 1933	*Antiquity*	Fellows	Newbury 'SID'	129	F.T. Everard & Sons Ltd	163400
4 January 1934	*British Coast*	Robb	British Auxiliaries	232	Coast Lines	162399
2 February 1934	*Acrity*	Brown	Newbury 'SBD'	143	F.T. Everard & Sons Ltd	163438
12 June 1934	*Angularity*	Brown	Newbury 'SBD'	161	F.T. Everard & Sons Ltd	163479
26 June 1934	*Atlantic Coast**	Robb	British Auxiliaries	242	Coast Lines	162405
11 August 1934	*Carrick Coast*	Ardrossan	Atlas-Diesel	136	Coast Lines	162409
5 September 1934	*Grit*	Brown	Newbury 'SBD'	161	F.T. Everard & Sons Ltd	163519
28 September 1934	*Affaric*	Goole	Humboldt-Deutzmotoren	118	D. Williamson Ltd	163528
2 November 1934	*Arrivaine*	Goole	Humboldt-Deutzmotoren	118	D. Williamson Ltd	163540
23 November 1934	*Lowestoft Trader*	Goole	British Auxiliaries	131	Gt. Yarmouth Sg Co. Ltd	164156
30 November 1934	*Aqueity*	Fellows	Newbury SBD	116	F.T. Everard & Sons Ltd	163551

Table 8.3 *continued*

Registered	Name	Builder	Engine	Feet	First owner	O.N.
13 December 1934	*Camroux I*	Pollock	Allen	136	Newcastle Coal & Shg	163555
2 January 1935	*Fauvette*	Furness	British Auxiliaries	183	General Steam	163558
3 January 1935	*River Trent*	Goole	Gardner	117	R.H. Hunt	163960
16 January 1935	*Charles M*	Burntisland	Humboldt-Deutzmotoren	142	T.J. Metcalf	163562
9 March 1935	*Lady Sheila*	Pollock	Allen	105	Watson	163581
28 January 1935	*Camroux II*	Pollock	Allen	136	Newcastle Coal	163567
22 February 1935	*Jolly Nights*	Lewis	British Auxiliaries	131	Horlock	163010
28 February 1935	*Aseity*	Brown	Newbury 'SBD'	116	F.T. Everard & Sons Ltd	164509
10 April 1935	*Jolly Days*	Lewis	Petters	131	Horlock	163011
23 May 1935	*Pacific Coast**	Ardrossan	British Auxiliaries	262	Coast Lines	164258
22 June 1935	*Andoni (1)*	Goole	Humboldt-Deutzmotoren	140	T.E. Evans & Co. Ltd	164495
15 July 1935	*Glen*	Hawthorn. Leslie	Humboldt-Deutzmotoren	165	Tyne-Tees	161584
31 July 1935	*Arduity*	Brown	Newbury 'SBD'	116	F.T. Everard & Sons Ltd	164509
30 August 1935	*Ocean Coast**	Robb	British Auxiliaries	252	Coast Lines	164266
2 September 1935	*Sapphire*	Ailsa	Atlas-Diesel	200	William Robertson	164062
19 September 1935	*Arbroath*	Caledon	British Auxiliaries	176	Dundee, Perth & London	144715
4 October 1935	*Anglian Coast**	Austin	British Auxiliaries	196	Coast Lines	164270
18 October 1935	*Accruity*	Brown	Newbury 'SBD'	151	F.T. Everard & Sons Ltd	164548
21 October 1935	*Adaptity*	Fellows	Newbury 'SBD	136	F.T. Everard & Sons Ltd	164549
15 November 1935	*Camroux III*	Smith's Dock	Humboldt-Deutzmotoren	162	Newcastle Coal & Shg	164554
8 January 1936	*Lady Stella*	Pollock	Allen	105	Watson	164567

Registered	Name	Builder	Engine	Feet	First owner	O.N.
24 February 1936	*Anonity*	Brown	Newbury 'SBD'	116	F.T. Everard & Sons Ltd	164587
4 March 1936	*Benguela*	Goole	Humboldt-Deutzmotoren	184	T.E. Evans & Co. Ltd	164641
11 April 1936	*Saint Angus*	Scott	British Auxiliaries	151	Gardner	164072
16 April 1936	*Conida*	Goole	Humboldt-Deutzmotoren	156	S.J. Jenkins	164614
6 May 1936	*Ashanti*	Goole	Nydqvist & Holm	184	T.E. Evans & Co. Ltd	164622
6 May 1936	*Sagacity*	Brown	Newbury 'SBD'	153	F.T. Everard & Sons Ltd	164623
29 June 1936	*Sedulity*	Brown	Newbury 'SBD'	153	F.T. Everard & Sons Ltd	164663
9 July 1936	*Cabenda*	Goole	Mirrlees	184	T.E. Evans & Co. Ltd	164672
23 July 1936	*Pembroke Coast**	Robb	British Auxiliaries	202	Coast Lines	164296
24 July 1936	*Devon Coast**	Ardrossan	Kincaid (B&W)	199	Coast Lines	164297
7 August 1936	*Loanda*	Goole	Mirrlees	184	T.E. Evans & Co. Ltd	164698
12 August 1936	*Jolly Girls*	Smith's Dock	Atlas-Diesel	158	Horlock	163012
25 August 1936	*Kindiesel*	Ardrossan	Kincaid	143	Kindiesel Shipping	165219
14 September 1936	*Kestor*	Goole	Humboldt-Deutzmotoren	135	H. Harrison (Sg) Ltd	164716
25 September 1936	*Glamis*	Caledon	British Auxiliaries	168	Dundee, Perth & London	144717
12 October 1936	*Sincerity*	Brown	Newbury 'SBD'	175	F.T. Everard & Sons Ltd	164732
16 October 1936	*Crescence*	Goole	Humboldt-Deutzmotoren	114	London & Rochester	163255
19 October 1936	*Rookwood*	Robb	Humboldt-Deutzmotoren	177	France, Fenwick	164738
9 November 1936	*Lockwood*	Robb	British Auxiliaries	177	France, Fenwick	165336
19 November 1936	*Boston Trader*	Goole	British Auxiliaries	144	Gt. Yarmouth Sg Co. Ltd	164171
27 October 1936	*Castle Combe*	Hill	Ruston & Hornsby	155	Ald Shipping	163872

Table 8.3 *continued*

Registered	Name	Builder	Engine	Feet	First owner	O.N.
22 August 1936	*Lairdscrest*	Harland & Wolff	Harland & Wolff	229	Burns and Laird	164091
7 August 1936	*Lairdswood*	Harland & Wolff	Harland & Wolff	229	Burns and Laird	165153
15 September 1936	*Lairdsbank*	Harland & Wolff	Harland & Wolff	229	Burns and Laird	164095
20 October 1936	*Dorset Coast*	Ardrossan	Kincaid (B&W)	199	Coast Lines	164303
17 February 1936	*Beal*	Hawthorn. Leslie	Humboldt-Deutzmotoren	165	Tyne-Tees	161591
6 May 1936	*Alnwick*	Hawthorn. Leslie	Humboldt-Deutzmotoren	165	Tyne-Tees	161595
21 May 1936	*Wooler*	Smith's Dock	Humboldt-Deutzmotoren	165	Tyne-Tees	163048
14 February 1936	*Daniel M*	Burntisland	Humboldt-Deutzmotoren	150	Metcalf	164586
13 May 1936	*Plover*	Caledon	British Auxiliaries	163`	General Steam	164627
29 April 1936	*Mallard*	Caledon	Atlas-Diesel	163	General Steam	164619
24 July 1936	*Devon Coast*	Ardrossan	Kincaid (B&W)	199	Coast Lines	164297
7 January 1937	*Chagford*	Goole	Humboldt-Deutzmotoren	135	H. Harrison (Sg) Ltd	165380
27 January 1937	*Cameo*	Inglis	Harland & Wolff (B&W)	211	William Robertson	164109
29 January 1937	*Hullgate*	Clelands	Humboldt-Deutzmotoren	156	Hull Gates	165002
12 February 1937	*Cornish Coast*	Ardrossan	Kincaid (B&W)	120	Coast Lines	164313
18 February 1937	*Antrim Coast*	Ardrossan	Kincaid (B&W)	199	Coast Lines	164314
19 February 1937	*Saint Bedan*	Scott	British Auxiliaries	163	Gardner	164110
1 March 1937	*Suavity*	Brown	Newbury 'SBD'	175	F.T. Everard & Sons Ltd	165417
7 April 1937	*Brendonia*	Goole	Humboldt-Deutzmotoren	149	J. Wharton	164894
30 June 1937	*Serenity*	Brown	Newbury 'L'	158	F.T. Everard & Sons Ltd	165499
12 July 1937	*Begerin*	Goole	Humboldt-Deutzmotoren	171	H. Wilson	164896+

Registered	Name	Builder	Engine	Feet	First owner	O.N.
26 August 1937	*Lochee*	Robb	British Auxiliaries	227	Dundee, Perth & London	144719
2 September 1937	*Signality*	Brown	Newbury 'L'	158	F.T. Everard & Sons Ltd	165568
13 September 1937	*Andoni (2)*	Goole	British Auxiliaries	187	T.E. Evans & Co. Ltd	165575
19 October 1937	*Spinel*	Robb	British Polar	185	William Robertson	165917
3 November 1937	*Norfolk Coast*	Ardrossan	Kincaid (B&W)	210	Coast Lines	164344
8 December 1937	*Sequacity*	Goole	British Auxiliaries	196	F.T. Everard & Sons Ltd	165616
9 December 1937	*Jacinth*	Robb	British Polar	185	William Robertson	165923
17 January 1938	*Welsh Coast*	Ardrossan	Kincaid (B&W)	210	Coast Lines	164349
26 January 1938	*Mytongate*	Clelands	Humboldt-Deutzmotoren	156	Hull Gates	165696
2 February 1938	*Brockley Combe*	Hill	Ruston & Hornsby	173	Ald Shipping	166039
8 February 1938	*Coxwold*	Goole	British Auxiliaries	216	Atkinson & Prickett	165698
6 September 1938	*Karri*	Scott	British Auxiliaries	147	Fisher, Newry	160298
9 September 1938	*Sodality*	Williamson	Newbury 'L'	188	F.T. Everard & Sons Ltd	166564
13 October 1938	*Lady Sophia*	Pollock	Atlas-Diesel	111	Watson	166591
12 December 1938	*The Lady Mostyn*	Goole	Humboldt-Deutzmotoren	128	Darwen & Mostyn	162046
11 January 1939	*Yewmount*	Scott	Atlas-Diesel	211	John Stewart	165957
2 May 1939	*Summity*	Brown	Newbury 'L'	169	F.T. Everard & Sons Ltd	167243
29 July 1939	*Gladonia*	Goole	Humboldt-Deutzmotoren	150	J. Wharton	164905
30 October 1939	*Supremity*	Brown	Newbury 'L'	169	F.T. Everard & Sons Ltd	167360
17 November 1939	*Arawai*	Yarwood	Widdop	125	Booker	92938
17 November 1939	*Spirality*	Brown	Newbury 'L'	169	F.T. Everard & Sons Ltd	167364

Source: National Archives, Kew, Registration documents in classes BT 110 and CUST 130.

Several steamers were converted, but relatively late in their lives. The coal-fired *Ebony* has a good claim to be the last classic steam coaster built in the United Kingdom, completed by Scotts of Bowling with her sister *Balsa* in 1947.[39] Both sisters were sold by their Northern Ireland owner in 1957, and in 1963 the *Ebony*, having been renamed *Monksville*, passed to Greece. She changed hands several times, and in 1967 had a Klöckner-Humboldt-Deutz oil engine fitted, which was purported to give a speed of 12 knots. Following various sales, she sank at Piraeus in 1995, so the new engine had more than doubled her working life.

Another conversion involved the steam collier *Pompey Power*, built in 1949. In 1960, she was retired and sold to Norwegian owners who, in 1963, fitted an oil engine built in Norway by Wichmann Motorfabrikk AL.[40] Renamed *Hamen*, she worked until laid up in 1986, and is currently the subject of a preservation attempt. However, such conversions were rare.

The pioneer *Isleford* of 1913, listed in Table 8.2, was designed as a steam coaster but completed with a Bolinder engine.[41] The design of the *Jolly Nights* and *Jolly Days*, built by Lewis, Aberdeen in 1935 for the barge- and coaster-owning Horlock family of Mistley, Essex suggests they too were planned as steamers but were given engines by Petters or British Auxiliaries. *Jolly Days* had a particularly long career, extended by two replacements of her engines over her 45 years.[42]

V

Notwithstanding the United Kingdom's dominance of the market, during the nineteenth and early twentieth centuries iron- and steel-hulled steam coasters were built in small numbers by other industrialised European nations, notably Germany, the Netherlands and Sweden. In their basic design if not in their profile they adhered to the same principles established by British yards. However, the first quarter of the twentieth century saw Dutch yards making perhaps one of the most important and lasting contributions to the design of the coaster.

Concentrated as it was in the north of the Netherlands, especially around Groningen and Delfzijl, the Dutch coastal shipping industry was second only in importance to that of the United Kingdom. It mainly comprised two- and three-masted topsail schooners, plus a number of the single-masted, bluff-bowed

---

[39]   Fenton and Patterson, 'Joseph Fisher and Sons', 79, 103. It was intended to fit both *Balsa* and *Ebony* with oil engines as the company already had one motor ship trading, but this was over-ruled by board members who pointed to delays in supplying oil engines and the shortage of engineers to operate them. In the event a company which ran some of its steamers for 45 years had just ten years of service from *Balsa* and *Ebony*.

[40]   Chesterton and Fenton, *Gas and Electricity Colliers*, 90.

[41]   Waine, *British Motor Coasters*, 17.

[42]   *Lloyd's Register*, 1935–80.

local craft large enough to be seaworthy, the zeetjalks.[43] The owners of small
Dutch coastal ships had shown little interest in adopting steam engines,[44] as they
would have significantly reduced cargo space and increased draft, an important
consideration with craft using inland waterways and shallow coastal waters.
However, the internal combustion engine was adopted with alacrity, and about
1910 began to be fitted in sailing vessels, mainly with locally built machinery.
This trend was accelerated by the First World War, during which the neutral
Dutch, accepting the risks, benefited from the enhanced freight rates offered
by Great Britain, France and Germany.[45] Many sailing vessel owners invested
their profits in fitting internal combustion engines, especially into steel-hulled
craft. The number of auxiliaries in service leapt from 43 at the end of 1917 to
89 a year later.[46] The hull form often revealed their sailing ship origins, with an
overhanging counter stern, strong sheer and a curved bow from which it was
obvious that the bowsprit had been cut off.

In 1911, a Dutch vessel appeared which had been designed as a motor
ship, the twin-screw *Zeemeeuw*, built by N.V. Werf De Noord on the Rhine at
Alblasserdam and powered by two Dutch-built gas engines.[47] In 1913, a modified
hull was built to the same length of 148 feet as *Zeearend*. Although *Zeemeeuw*
survived in the Mediterranean until 1969, the design appears to have been a dead
end, Dutch owners preferring smaller vessels. Auxiliaries continued to be built
into the 1920s, but there was then a trend towards 'pure' motor ships, to which at
least one Dutch author gives the title 'Wad- en Sontvaarder', roughly translated
as a ship capable of working in both shallow waters and sounds.[48]

The year 1924 saw the delivery of the *Gideona* by the yard of J. Koster
Hzn. of Winschoterdiep near Groningen. She was regarded by Lloyd's Register
of Shipping as an auxiliary, and indeed her builder's drawings show her with
sails rigged on her single mast amidships,[49] but she was an important stage in the

---

[43] Boerma, *Schepen van de Kustvaart.*

[44] Exceptions were made during the First World War, when Dutch shipbuilders became
aware that British yards hitherto constructing steam coasters had largely turned to naval
work. The opportunity to build steam coasters was grasped and once completed they were
for a time in Dutch ownership. However, the demand for tonnage immediately post-war
saw most being sold at a profit to British owners.

[45] Boerma, *Schepen van de Kustvaart*, 24–9.

[46] Boerma, *Schepen van de Kustvaart*, 92.

[47] Boerma, *Schepen van de Kustvaart*, 67.

[48] Boerma, *Schepen van de Kustvaart*, 96.

[49] A. Boerma, *Coasters: De laatste 50 jaar van de KHV* (Alkmaar, 1992), 27. Until
1914, most coasters left the shipyard with a suit of sails. The crew usually had experience
of handling sails, and – while they rarely added as much as a knot to the coaster's speed
– they had a steadying influence on the ship and were a fallback in the rare event of an
engine breakdown. Photographic evidence suggests that, when the original suit was no
longer fit for purpose, they were not replaced. However, there are photographs of small
Dutch motor coasters setting a single sail while in the English Channel in the 1960s.

development of the 'pure' motor coaster. Her builders enumerated her advantages as having a generous cargo capacity on a relatively short length of 106 feet, yet still having a spacious engine room and comfortably sized cabins. She was promoted as offering good stability and seaworthiness for her size. Externally, she broke with tradition in having a rounded, cruiser stern, which was an advantage in following seas, a feature slowly adopted by other Dutch builders. Her single hold was served by two hatches, between which a mast was stepped. An enduring feature of Dutch designs, her two derricks were offset horizontally, enabling the hinged mast to be lowered when passing under bridges on inland waterways. As the design was multiplied, the titles 'Gideon-type' or 'Koster-ship' were bestowed, the shipyard adopting the ship's name as part of its title and trading as J. Koster Hzn. Scheepsbouwwerf De Gideon. The term 'type' rather than 'class' was appropriate, as length varied and features were not standardised, but met individual owners' requirements. For instance, some ships had a large box-like cabin added ahead of the bridge, giving additional crew accommodation. There was a choice of engine, with the German-built Deutz the most common. Although the Koster-type proved very popular, other Dutch builders clung to older design features including the counter stern, and – belying the builders' experience with inland vessels – the accommodation sometimes had rectangular 'windows' rather than ports.

The single-masted design was disadvantageous when carrying a deck cargo, for instance in the Baltic timber trade, in which Dutch owners freely participated. Rather negating this, during the 1930s the raised quarterdeck design also became popular, increasing cargo capacity and improving trim. From 1930, two masts were often fitted, one immediately aft of the forecastle and one ahead of the bridge. To improve accommodation, an extra deck was added which raised the bridge and improved visibility, but at some cost in terms of the coasters' low air draft capability.

The bridge did not always remain aft, and in 1935 the Koster yard introduced the 'New Koster' type, with the engine room, bridge and accommodation amidships. However, this did not reassert the yard's design leadership as relatively few were built, although these included several larger examples completed as shelter-deckers for liner companies. The relatively large, 1938-built *Alouette* and *Drake* were built for the services to Rhine and near-Continental ports of London's General Steam Navigation Company.[50] Placing the bridge amidships while retaining the engines-aft configuration proved somewhat more popular, although this configuration increased complexity and therefore cost as plumbing and other services had to be provided for both the midships and aft superstructures.

The Dutch coaster designs that emerged by 1939 proved remarkably durable, with recognisable examples being built right into the 1960s. New and especially second-hand examples remained in considerable demand from owners outside the Netherlands, including those in Great Britain and Ireland.

---

[50]   N. Robins, *Birds of the Sea: 150 years of the General Steam Navigation Company* (Portishead, 2007), 63.

18: The *Antilope* of 1939 exemplifies the single-masted Dutch coaster, with derricks offset to allow the mast to be folded. Note that she has accommodation for a captain/owner's family ahead of the wheelhouse, and that she has a modern, cruiser stern. She was heavily damaged during a collision with another Dutch coaster in August 1971 and was subsequently sold for scrap. *World Ship Society Ltd*

Several factors beyond constructional features helped the owners of Dutch coasters to mount a serious and lasting challenge to the British steam coaster. Perhaps most important was the structure of the Dutch coastal shipping industry, in which a large proportion of the craft were owned by their masters. The profits from trading were all theirs, encouraging long working hours, while the tendency to make the ship their home with their families helping to crew them kept wage bills low. The master may well have acted as his own engineer, perhaps assisted by a deckhand designated 'motor-driver', whose duties included greasing. As the master had a mortgage to pay off, he did not have the option of laying up his ship when economic times were hard, and so he accepted low freight rates rather than be idle. Finance for a ship could be provided by a Scheepshypotheekbanken, specialising in offering mortgages to potential shipowners and represented in Rotterdam, Groningen and Delfzijl.[51] The third factor was the liberality of Dutch surveyors and registration authorities in

---

[51] Boerma, *Coasters*, 25. Mortgages were available not just to Dutch owners: several British owners, including Liverpool-based Richard Hughes, ordered steam coasters from Dutch yards around the time of the First World War and took out mortgages with Dutch banks. Fenton, *Mersey Rovers*, 84–123.

assigning low tonnages to ships whose dimensions would have merited higher figures elsewhere. British or Irish owners who bought second-hand coasters from the Dutch could be surprised when a survey on re-registration saw an increase of around 10 per cent on the net tonnage. Tonnage was a very critical factor with coasters in Dutch ownership as, if it could be kept below 500 gross, the statutory size of the crew was minimised. Hence, the largest Dutch coasters for many years had a declared gross tonnage of exactly 499.

The Second World War proved a disaster for Dutch coaster owners, with over 130 of their vessels lost, some 25 per cent of the 1940 fleet. Rebuilding, even assisted by war loss insurance payments from Great Britain, was a slow process, as yards had been badly damaged by air raids, sabotage and destruction by retreating German troops. In 1946, eight ships were added to the fleet, 17 in 1947, but in 1948 over one hundred arrived. The Dutch coaster fleet peaked at about 700 ships in the 1950s. Ingenuity was seen in the conversion into coasters of British- and American-built landing craft, of which there was an ample supply left over from the war.[52] Externally, the results could hardly be distinguished from purpose-built coasters.

Although the tried and tested Dutch coaster design motored on until at least the 1970s, post-war changes affected its economy and ubiquity.[53] There was a notable decline in captain-ownership, which fell from over 80 per cent of the fleet in the 1930s to 50 per cent by the 1950s and was to decline further. With growing prosperity in post-war Europe, fewer and fewer Dutch nationals were attracted by a career at sea, with its long hours and prolonged absences from home. As the operation of ships became increasingly complex, it became more important to have a shore-based organisation to handle matters including chartering, brokerage, manning, finance, insurance and compliance with increasing regulations, and hence ownership tended to move from masters themselves to shipping companies.

Vessels very similar to the classic Dutch coaster were built elsewhere in Europe, particularly in Germany well into the 1960s,[54] and even longer in Denmark. Although the Dutch-owned coaster is by no means extinct, during the last quarter of the twentieth century it became less and less distinctive and important, and its story became part of that of other European vessels.

VI

By effectively removing competition from foreign shipyards, especially after the invasion of the Netherlands in 1940, the Second World War and the eventual implementation of a large programme of building for Government account assisted the British shipping industry's embrace of the motor coaster. At the

---

[52]   Fenton, *Coasters: An Illustrated History*, 113.

[53]   Fenton, *Coasters: An Illustrated History*, 115.

[54]   Fenton, *Coasters: An Illustrated History*, 133–42.

same time, a large number of Dutch coasters, escaping from the Netherlands or already at sea during the invasion, became available for requisition, with their management allocated to British companies, giving some their first experience of oil-engined ships.[55] Overall, more motor than steam coasters were built in the United Kingdom during the war, maintaining the pre-war trend for smaller ships to have oil engines, while larger coasters and particularly colliers remained steam driven. An important consideration in wartime was the ready availability of British-mined coal, whereas oil had to be imported.

In terms of design, the wartime programme of coaster building was less focused than that for ocean-going ships.[56] Owners were relatively free to order on their own account, although they were restricted to specifying existing designs to minimise drawing office work. Again to expedite construction, several yards received orders from the Government Ministry to build to existing designs, the Goole yard replicating their 'Proficient' design for the 203-foot *Empire Cliff* and *Empire Foreland*.[57] Table 8.4 enumerates the various types built on Government account, including colliers, diesel and steam coasters.[58] Excluded are those sold before completion for commercial use, shelter-deck vessels built for service in the Far East, and the Clyde puffers known as VICs.

Although most war-built ships were based on pre-war prototypes, notable exceptions were the prefabricated 'Empire Fabric' type.[59] Their origin was in a design of tanker which was foreseen as being needed in considerable numbers to supply fuel and water during the forthcoming Allied landings in France – the CHANTS, short for Channel Tanker. It was originally intended to build 69 of these, but with the satisfactory development of the undersea pipeline PLUTO not all were needed, so 25 hulls were completed as dry cargo vessels. The hulls were flat bottomed to enable them take the ground on beaches, and the hull was doubled to minimise the chances of fuel leaking and causing a major fire hazard. But the major innovation was the use of prefabrication, with sections being built by bridge builders and structural engineering companies. No unit was to weigh more than 13 tons, as they were delivered by lorry to shipyards where the units were welded together. Building was simplified by using only plates that were flat

---

[55]   Some 44 Dutch coasters were available to take part in the evacuation of the British Expeditionary Force from Dunkirk and other French ports in June 1940, with the loss of seven of their number. J. de S. Winser, *BEF Ships: Before, at and after Dunkirk* (Gravesend, 1999), 73–80. Wartime maintenance of Dutch coasters, with their machinery inevitably built in the Netherlands or Germany, was made very difficult by the non-availability of spare parts. As a result, the coasters were progressively consigned to stationary work, including use as barrage balloon vessels, or laid up.

[56]   W.H. Mitchell and L.A. Sawyer, *The Empire Ships*, 2nd ed. (London, 1990), 216–77.

[57]   Mitchell and Sawyer, *Empire Ships*, 231.

[58]   Mitchell and Sawyer, *Empire Ships*, 219–55.

[59]   A. Huckett, 'Empire F Dry Cargo Coasters', Part 1, *Marine News Supplement* (June 2019), S213–S225 and Part 2, *Marine News Supplement* (July 2019), S247–S259.

Table 8.4 Single-deck coasters completed on Government account, 1940–1945

(Where no class name appears to be have been used, that of the first (or only) ship completed is given)

Type		Feet	Builders (numbers built)
Steam colliers	*Empire Bay*	321	Wm. Gray and Co. Ltd (9)
	'Icemaid'[a]	282	Grangemouth Dockyard Co. Ltd (12) Ailsa S.B. Co. Ltd (1)
	Empire Highlander[b]	284	J. Crown & Sons Ltd (1)
Motor colliers	'Severn Collier'[c]	149	Richard Dunston Ltd (4) J. Harker Ltd (2)
Steam coasters	'Tudor Queen'[d]	212	J. Lewis & Sons Ltd (5) Ardrossan Dockyard Ltd (1) G. Brown & Co. Ltd (3)
Motor coasters	*Empire Gat*[e]	211	Harland & Wolff (2) A.J. Inglis (2) Scott & Sons (2)
	Empire Rider	205	Scott & Sons (3)
	Empire Cliff	203	Goole Shipbuilding & Repairing (2)
	Empire Jack[g]	193	Austin & Pickersgill (2) Vickers Armstrong (1)
	Empire Dyke	170	Clelands Ltd (2)
	'Empire Isle'	150	H. Scarr Ltd (2)
	Empire Sloane	149	Shipbuilding Corporation (1)
	'Empire Fabric'	148	Goole Shipbuilding & Repairing (13) H. Scarr Ltd (12)
	Flush deck 'Empire Fabric'[h]	148	Clelands Ltd (2) Shipbuilding Corporation (4)
	Empire Kyle[i]	137	I. Pimblott & Sons Ltd (3) Richards Ironworks Ltd (7) J.S. Watson Ltd (2)
	Empire Creek[j]	136	J. Pollock & Sons Ltd (2)
	Empire Bridge[k]	133	W.J. Yarwood & Sons Ltd (1)

[a] The prototype *Icemaid* was built for the Gas Light and Coke Co. Ltd in 1936 by Austin and Pickersgill Ltd, who were not contracted to build any of the type.

[b] Two of this class were completed in 1946 for collier owners.

[c] The 'Severn Collier' types were built to carry coal from South Wales to the Castlemeads

Table 8.4 *continued*

Power Station at Gloucester. They were notable for having rails rather than bulwarks alongside their hatch. Essentially fairly basic motor coasters, they were put into general trading post-war, with four being eventually converted to sand suckers.

[d] The prototype *Tudor Queen* was built by Burntisland Shipbuilding Co. Ltd for Queenship Navigation Ltd and designed to carry coal from the north-east of England to the Channel Isles. Two more were sold before completion in 1946.

[e] Enlarged versions of the *Yewmount*, built by Scotts in 1939 for John Stewart and Co. Ltd. Four of the five surviving ships were sold to British or Dutch liner companies after the war, the fifth going to Everard as *Angularity*.

[f] These two appear to be repeats of the Goole yard's 'Proficient' design. The yard went on to build two slightly smaller versions for Everards in 1943, with the mainmast moved forward to the fore end of the raised quarterdeck.

[g] Before being acquired by the Government, the first ship of this class had been launched as *River Fisher* for J. Fisher and Sons Ltd of Barrow-in-Furness, who acquired all three in 1946. With particularly wide hatches, they were taken over for their ability to carry heavy items, including gun mountings.

[h] Prefabricated ships: see text below.

[i] A flush-decked version of the 'Empire F' type.

[j] A shallower-drafted version of pair built by Pollock.

[k] Based on the design of *Camroux I* built by Pollock for the Newcastle Coal and Shipping Co. Ltd. Both went into general trading on their sales in 1946.

or curved in just one direction, each one cut using a template. Although with their straight lines and no sheer the ships looked ungainly, their underwater form was refined by tank testing. Even so, with the low-powered engines which were all that were available,[60] only 8 knots could be achieved. Nevertheless, the dry cargo coasters found ready buyers post-war, and at least one survived into the twenty-first century.

With prefabrication enabling 69 hulls to be built very quickly, it seems surprising that it was not employed more widely in coaster construction during wartime. British yards had pioneered its use during the First World War, and experience in the United States showed what was possible. In the event, the only other class of vessel to be prefabricated were the TID dockyard tugs.[61]

With continental European builders unable to compete because of damaged yards or being barred from building, Dutch and German competition was muted in immediate post-war years, and British coaster builders and owners enjoyed exceptionally favourable conditions for almost ten years. The oil

---

[60]   Huckett, 'Empire F Dry Cargo Coasters'. Six builders supplied engines for the 25 Empire Fs: Blackstone and Co. Ltd, Stamford; British Auxiliaries Ltd, Glasgow; Ruston and Hornsby Ltd, Lincoln; Mirrlees, Bickerton and Day Ltd, Stockport; British Polar Engines Ltd, Glasgow; and Petters Ltd, Loughborough.

[61]   W.J. Harvey, *The T.I.D. Tugs of World War Two* (Windsor, 2019).

19: Displaying the angular lines which facilitated prefabrication, the Empire F type yet gave good service to various owners post-war. *Lynn Trader* was built in 1944 as *Empire Fairplay* and eventually passed to Egyptian owners. Her fate is unknown. *Ships in Focus*

engine was by now firmly established as the most economical power plant for a coaster, and all surviving coaster builders produced examples of motor coasters. Design development was gradual, and most ships were similar in layout to pre-war examples although often with styling which updated their appearance. The bridge-aft, raised quarterdeck layout enjoyed a particularly strong following.[62] Lacking the Dutch obsession with achieving a minimal air draught, the superstructure was enlarged so that the wheelhouse was often atop two decks, and generously sized funnels were usually specified to display the owners' colours. The result was a design which was distinctively British even when, in several cases, UK owners ordered them from the Netherlands.[63]

Beauly Firth of 1949 exemplifies the type, although with such muted styling of features such as wheelhouse and funnel that she could easily be mistaken for a vessel built ten years earlier.[64] Responsible for this 168-foot coaster was the Greenock yard which had built extensively for Everards in the 1930s, now

---

[62]   Fenton, *Coasters: An Illustrated History*, 126.

[63]   The Guernsey owner Onesimus Dorey and Sons Ltd took delivery of *Havelet* and *Portelet* to this design from two Groningen yards in the early 1960s. *Lloyd's Register*, 1965.

[64]   Fenton, *Coasters: An Illustrated History*, 126.

20: Typical of post-war, raised quarterdeck coasters with bridge aft, the modest sized Irish-owned *River Avoca* was built at Goole in 1948 as *Stevonia*. She had lost her derricks by the time she was photographed in September 1975. She was broken up 1980. *Author*

known as George Brown (Marine) Ltd. A six-cylinder engine was supplied by the National Gas and Oil Engine Co. Ltd of Ashton-under-Lyne.

Cargo handling arrangements varied in these ships, being at its most primitive in *Beauly Firth*, but becoming progressively more sophisticated over time and as hull length grew. Platforms alongside the masts were installed to carry cargo winches, and a second mast was added immediately ahead of the bridge.[65] Over the typical 20-year life of such ships, however, shoreside gear became so efficient and widespread that derricks were progressively unshipped as being unnecessary and adding both to weight and the need for maintenance. In some cases, masts were also cut down to save topweight.

The desire to place the bridge amidships in larger coasters persisted right into the 1960s and was responsible for some of the most aesthetically satisfying designs of post-war years. Amongst these were 12 ships built from 1949 to 1958 for F.T. Everard and Sons Ltd, exemplified by *Sanguity* of 1956.[66] Each of her three holds was served by 40-foot derricks with a safe working load of 40 tons. Of 230 feet overall, *Sanguity* had a gross tonnage of 1,577, comfortably under the figure of 1,600 gross registered tonnage at which current regulations required a larger crew, including a radio officer and much more sophisticated radio equipment.

---

[65]   For instance, in *Sussexbrook* of 1970. Fenton, *Coasters: An Illustrated History*, 129.
[66]   Fenton, *Coasters: An Illustrated History*, 127.

VII

As steam bulk carrying began with the screw colliers of the 1850s, it is appropriate to look at what were the protracted end days of the dedicated steam collier. As Table 8.4 illustrates, wartime construction concentrated almost exclusively on steam-driven colliers, unsurprising given the ready availability of coal for bunkers. The oil-engined collier had appeared in 1936 with the *Rookwood* and *Lochwood* ordered by France, Fenwick, but these were specifically built for a particular trade, and were quickly sold.[67] Very slowly, other major independent collier owners followed suit, like Stephenson Clarke with their *Seaford* in 1947 – although their largest colliers remained steam driven, albeit with oil firing, culminating in the *Arundel* of 1956.[68] The third big independent owner, William Cory and Son Ltd, made the transition to oil engines only with its *Corbrae* of 1952.[69]

Owners argued, unconvincingly, that moving away from coal-fired steamers would upset the colliery owners they served, but it seems very unlikely that shippers would care about this unless it adversely affected freight rates. In fact the colliers were mostly employed not by the producers of coal but by its consumers, especially the gas and electricity industry. These industries were themselves owners of important collier fleets but shared a reluctance to embrace oil engines.[70] It was the upriver colliers whose length and draught were restricted where oil engines would provide most benefit, helping increase space dedicated to the coal cargo. The colliers of the progressive Wandsworth and District Gas Company had to venture furthest up the Thames to unload, and this company was the first to order an oil-engined collier, delivered as *Mitcham* in 1946.[71] Other gas and electricity undertakings quickly followed suit. But for their larger vessels, working to gas works and power stations below the Thames bridges, steam continued to be specified, with the exception being South Metropolitan Gas Company's *Catford* of 1948, built to serve its large East Greenwich plant.[72] Nationalisation of these utility companies in 1948 for electricity and 1949 for gas had no perceptible effect on engineering policy, and for both industries steam

---

[67]   The anonymous author of a book on France, Fenwick does not reveal details of the charter but notes that it was terminated by mutual agreement after just three years, when the two motor colliers were sold. One problem was the inadequacy of the electricity generation given the auxiliaries, which needed to be powered. Another was the poor quality of the engineers the owners could attract. No further motor ships were ordered by the company until 1955. Anon., *Wm. France, Fenwick & Company Limited* (London, 1954), 66–7.

[68]   Carter, *Stephenson Clarke*, 26.

[69]   Fenton, *Coasters: An Illustrated History*, 76.

[70]   Chesterton and Fenton, *Gas and Electricity Colliers*.

[71]   Chesterton and Fenton, *Gas and Electricity Colliers*, 17–25.

[72]   Chesterton and Fenton, *Gas and Electricity Colliers*, 26–7

power continued to be specified for larger colliers until 1955.[73] These ships did embrace modern technology, with high-pressure water tube boilers, and steel hatch covers, and hopper-sided holds to facilitate grab discharge. At 340 feet overall, with four holds, the last examples built for the electricity industry were impressively large ships. However, their nationalised owners must have had cause to regret the choice of machinery when in the 1960s they were forced to convert them to oil burning. As the last of these ships continued in service for almost 30 years,[74] the east coast coal trade had been served by steam colliers for an unbroken 133 years. Steam powered bulk carrying thus began and effectively ended on the same trade route.

With the advent of natural gas from fields in the North Sea, and the gradual replacement of coal-firing by oil in power stations, the need for colliers began to decline significantly in the 1950s, at which point the nationalised electricity industry had 50 colliers in its fleet and others on charter.[75] Further orders were not needed by this operator until 1984, when inevitably large, diesel-driven bulk carriers were specified, with twice the capacity of the previous steamers.[76] These vessels, with some second-hand acquisitions, saw out the sea-borne delivery of coal to power stations and the ownership of ships by British utilities. They were barely distinguishable from modest-sized ocean-going bulk carriers, which are covered in the next chapter.

VIII

From the 1960s, shipbuilding became increasingly international, with owners willing to, or indeed needing to, look beyond their national shipbuilders when ordering. It is therefore necessary to broaden coverage beyond British, Dutch and German vessel design to look at the numerous trends affecting coaster design and operating efficiency. In 2022, shipbuilding in European countries has fallen to a very low ebb, with coaster building having moved, first to eastern Europe, then to Japan, China and South Korea, with even these being challenged to a greater or lesser extent by yards in Turkey, Malaysia and Vietnam.

---

[73]   For instance, the *Cliff Quay* of 1950. Macrae and Waine, *Steam Collier Fleets*, 202.

[74]   The very last steamer in service was the Central Electricity Generating Board's *James Rowan*, which worked until 1984, when she was the object of a failed preservation attempt. She would have been a fitting memorial to the steam collier and its legacy. Chesterton and Fenton, *Gas and Electricity Colliers*, 107, 117.

[75]   Chesterton and Fenton, *Gas and Electricity Colliers*.

[76]   Given names of prominent individuals in the electricity industry, the British-built and engined *Sir Charles Parsons*, *Lord Hinton* and *Lord Citrine*, completed in 1985 and 1986, were four-hold bulkers of 155 metres overall. After sale in 1999, they spent some years in general trading. The *Lord Citrine* is still trading under the Chinese flag in 2022. https://maritime.ihs.com/ships/detail/8402852.

The last half-century has also seen a decline in the volume of coasting and short-sea shipping,[77] partly due to competition from road and, to a lesser extent, rail transport, but also to a reduction in hitherto important coal shipments.[78] Less relevant to the story of bulk-carrying ships, the purely coastal liner trade has also disappeared thanks to more efficient land transport and containerisation. The latter trend profoundly changed the short-sea element of the liner trade, which overwhelmingly adopted cellular container ships. The overall results have been fewer coastal ships, fewer operators and fewer yards needed to build coastal and short-sea vessels. Trends in construction and design have also become more international as competition intensified to produce vessels which were economical both to build and to operate. However, the key characteristics of a bulk-carrying coaster remain constant: unobstructed holds and hatches, a facility to carry water ballast, and an economical, efficient engine, invariably placed aft.

All holds are essentially boxes to contain cargo, but the term 'box hold' has come to signify one where the frames are eliminated from the walls, so that not just the floor but all four sides are smooth, making it easy to clean between cargoes.[79] Movable hatch covers extend right over the hold. The objectives are to expedite unloading of bulk cargoes, and also to make the vessels container friendly.

Low air draft has been a necessity for coasters habitually using inland waterways where bridges seriously restrict the height of superstructure, funnels and masts. This has been apparent for at least 150 years, as witness the upriver colliers introduced in the 1870s. However, in the 1970s and 1980s there was an explosion in the building of what were dubbed 'sea-river ships', with a low air draft yet providing a clear view ahead for their navigators while at sea.[80] With many owners hoping to participate in sea-river trades, a significant proportion of new coasters had a wheelhouse which could be lowered hydraulically to pass under obstructions but raised to normal height when at sea. Funnels were either very short or eliminated, and masts could be readily folded. Three such ships were built by Cochrane of Selby for ownership or management by Everards in the 1990s.[81] Their length of just under 100 metres is symptomatic of the enlargement of coasters, again in the interests of earning power: doubling the cargo capacity of a ship does not significantly increases its fuel consumption nor does it add to the crew numbers needed. Following their sale after ten years, the company's Marine Superintendent admitted to the author that their trading patterns meant that not one of the three ships had ever needed to lower its

---

[77]   Waine, *British Motor Coasters*, 121.

[78]   This decline was partly compensated by an increase in tanker trades, and a number of owners concentrated on shipment of liquids, both fuel and chemicals. See, for instance, Waine, *British Motor Coasters*, 115–20; A. Huckett, *Rowbotham* (Gravesend, 2002); Garrett, *Everard of Greenhithe*.

[79]   Waine, *British Motor Coasters*, 174, 198.

[80]   Waine, *British Motor Coasters*, 202.

[81]   Garrett, *Everard of Greenhithe*, 52, 250–1.

wheelhouse to negotiate a fixed bridge, so the expense of fitting the equipment was never recouped.[82]

No country has invested more in sea-river ships than the USSR, which had an enormous length of canals and navigable rivers, including the Volga/Don complex. Series construction in a number of yards not only in the USSR and its successors but in both eastern and western Europe saw the fleet multiply, with a variety of sizes to suit different waterways.[83] An overall length of 110 metres (360 feet) was regarded as a maximum at the end of the twentieth century, but there were proposals for vessels of 140 metres (460 feet). Nevertheless, smaller vessels tend to be more flexible, and – perhaps for the first time in the history of coastal shipping – larger vessels have been shortened to increase their versatility.

A significant improvement in operation has been obtained by the replacement of the traditional wood and canvas hatch covers with mechanically operated steel covers.[84] These save both labour and time in port and if properly used and maintained improve seaworthiness. A disadvantage is the space required to stow the folded hatch covers. As the hatch itself needs to be as large as practicable for loading and discharge, this can reduce the size of the accommodation. Although they lessen work for the crew, it is important that mechanical hatch covers are checked to ensure they are seating properly to make certain no water enters the hold. In ships so fitted, the derricks have become largely redundant: one of their major uses having been handling the hatch beams needed with wooden hatch covers.

Other factors meant that the traditional mast, derrick and winch combination has fallen from favour except in the smallest ships.[85] To expedite cargo-handling and hence improve turnround times in port, deck cranes are increasingly fitted, latterly including the travelling cranes which run on tracks incorporated into the hatch coamings.[86] However, this more sophisticated equipment increases weight, initial cost and maintenance requirements, and now with general improvement in onshore craneage (and containerisation) any form of cargo gear is eliminated

---

[82]   Personal communication from K. Garrett.

[83]   See, for instance, C. Cheetham and M. Heinimann, *Modern River Sea Traders* (London, 1996) – a voluminous and useful if rather hastily prepared work, benefiting from the authors' involvement in the operations of these craft and a European working party on inland shipping.

[84]   Cheetham and Heinimann, *Modern River Sea Traders*, 130.

[85]   For instance, small vessels operating to small ports required basic cargo gear as they could not rely on the provision of craneage ashore. These included the diesel-powered successors to Clyde puffers, and also small Norwegian craft, which remote communities depended upon for supplies. For the former, see L. Paterson, *The Light in the Glens: The Rise and Fall of the Puffer Trade* (Colonsay, 1996) and for the latter, D. Bakka, Jr., *Langs kysten i femti år: kystfart og fraktenæring, 1946–1996* (Bergen, 1996).

[86]   For example, in the 1982/83-built *Norbrit Faith* and *Norbritt Hope*. Waine, *British Motor Coasters*, 198.

where possible, with derricks having been progressively removed from older ships. Masts can therefore be less sturdy and are often eliminated or shortened leaving their functions being to display flags, carry steaming lights and support radar equipment and wireless aerials. The trend has been apparent for many years in colliers, especially those on dedicated routes between coal drops and power stations or gas works with mechanised unloading facilities.[87] The exceptions remain ships likely to trade to third-world ports, for instance those in north and west Africa where the ability to self-discharge is vital.

Hull design is an area where much ingenuity has been displayed in improving strength and carrying capacity. The raised quarterdeck design, hallowed in British and Dutch coaster construction, has been abandoned, as it restricted the lengths of both holds and hatches, and also meant there was a point of weakness at the break of the main deck. Sheer is also a thing of the past, with a flush deck, and a raised forecastle and bridge deck being relied upon to provide sufficient buoyancy in a seaway.[88]

Detailed hull construction is governed by rules set by classification societies – most importantly Lloyd's Register of Shipping, Germanischer Lloyd and Norske Veritas – but also by national bodies such as the British Board of Trade and its successors. The measured volume of cargo space contributes to the net registered tonnage of a ship, which in turn is used to calculate dues in harbours and canals and for pilotage, and also has been used by national authorities to set the vessel's geographical trading limits and manning requirements. Hence, owners want the maximum cargo volume they could obtain, but the lowest net registered tonnage. This has led to minute examination of rules and adoption of measures to circumvent them. In this, some national bodies were notoriously prone to favour their own shipowners by minimising measured tonnage. The so-called 'Paragraph' coasters exploited loopholes to keep their tonnage below a certain level, often 500 gross registered tons, below which manning levels were not regulated and certification of officers unnecessary.[89] Characteristics such as the depth of a double bottom or the size of side frames could affect tonnage, although they had no direct bearing on cargo capacity. Perhaps the most widespread, and indeed blatant, example of reducing tonnage has been the concept of the shelter deck. This was an intermediate deck which provided a space between it and the vessel's main deck, which, if open to the atmosphere, was not

---

[87]   The up-river or flatiron colliers employed by London gas companies were some of the earliest coasters to abandon cargo gear. The Wandsworth and Putney Gas Light and Coke Company was the first utility company to build such a collier, but steamers built as early as 1878 by an independent concern, the River Steam Collier Co. Ltd, were probably similar, although no illustrations have yet been found. Chesterton and Fenton, *Gas and Electricity Colliers*, 6.

[88]   Waine, *British Motor Coasters*, 172–81 has general arrangement drawings of typical vessels.

[89]   Waine, *British Motor Coasters*, 199.

counted as a contribution to registered tonnage. So as not to compromise safety, the 'tonnage openings' were kept as small as possible and so unlikely to admit water. Although of most use in liner trade ships, where the intermediate deck was useful for stowing small packages of goods, this was of less interest to bulk carrier owners. However, it was found that fitting 'tweens in ballast tanks, which had no effect whatsoever on cargo capacity, could also reduce the registered net tonnage, and this was adopted by several owners, who fitted lightweight covers over the tanks.[90] In 1982, the International Convention on Tonnage Measurement attempted to end these anomalies by standardising measurement of tonnage: hence gross registered tonnage (grt) and net registered tonnage (nrt) have given way to gross tonnage (GT) and net tonnage (NT).[91]

The ship's intended cargoes has a big influence on hold design. Cargoes vary enormously in density, so for instance the volume of grain or timber which brings a vessel down to its load line is far greater than that of coal or stone. Hence regular carriage of grain is most economical in a voluminous hold. If the hold is not completely filled by a grain or other light cargo, movement of the cargo has to be minimised. Originally this involved laying sacks of grain over the bulk of cargo.[92] To avoid this, movable bulkheads have been specified by ships likely to carry grain or other low-density cargoes.[93] Timber cargoes are somewhat less demanding, being largely waterproof, so a substantial part of the cargo can be carried on deck, provided it is reasonably stabilised and does not adversely affect seaworthiness.[94] This became an important issue when timber exporters introduced packaged cargoes, which were of a set size to reduce handling costs.[95] Hitherto, timbers were loaded loose, and experienced stevedores were skilled at working as much as possible into a given size and shape of hold. Packaged timber does not allow this, hence the quantity of cargo which can be worked into a hold is considerably reduced, and with it the ship's earnings.

Although less frequently loaded on bulk-carrying coasters, cargoes such as fruit and vegetables need good ventilation of the holds, sometimes including fans.[96] An interesting parallel is the carriage of ferrous scrap, which has been found to oxidise in the hold, reducing the oxygen content to a point where crew or others entering the hold could succumb to oxygen deficiency.

The development of oil engines is covered elsewhere in this volume, and the principles discussed apply equally to the less powerful machinery supplied to coastal craft. In particular, turbocharging and intercooling have been applied

---

[90] Waine, *British Motor Coasters*, 174–5 gives examples from the Everard and Stephenson Clarke fleets.

[91] Waine, *British Motor Coasters*, 199.

[92] Waine, *British Motor Coasters*, 125, 179.

[93] Waine, *British Motor Coasters*, 99.

[94] Waine, *British Motor Coasters*, 174.

[95] Waine, *British Motor Coasters*, 125–6, 171, 174, 202.

[96] Waine, *British Motor Coasters*, 169.

in order to generate greater power from modest-sized engines.[97] Unlike modern ocean-going bulk carriers, in the interests of lightness and compactness, coasters are often fitted with medium-speed engines which in turn require reduction gearing to turn the propellor at its most efficient speed.[98] With the desire to minimise crew numbers, unmanned engine rooms with associated alarms and automation are particularly important in coastal vessels.[99] National regulations have on occasion based manning requirements on power output, and this has led owners to specify that engines are rated below a regulation figure. Indeed, downrating of engine power is done in order to prolong the life of engines and reduce maintenance requirements.[100] In contrast to larger bulk carriers, four-stroke cycle machinery has remained popular in coasters.

Manoeuvrability is particularly important in craft using smaller ports and waterways and has been improved by the fitting of electrically driven bow thrusters.[101] Alternatives to bow thrusters are devices such as the Schilling rudder. With an exceptional turning ability owing to its aerofoil shape and horizontal plates at top and bottom, this allows vessels to turn in their own length.[102] The Aquamaster drive offered similar manoeuvrability. It was rather like an outboard motor: it had a vertical drive shaft and propellers which could be turned through 360 degrees, but with a fixed inboard engine.[103]

Auxiliary machinery has grown in importance. From electric winches and capstans, it has expanded to include bow thrusters and equipment for hold ventilation and air conditioning of crew spaces. These developments have seen direct current dynamos give way to lighter alternators in line with greater availability of systems running on alternating current.[104] Hydraulic winches have been increasingly fitted, requiring electricity to power the pumps. These additional requirements, plus the need for consistent power for electronic navigation equipment, have necessitated more powerful and reliable electrical generating capacity.[105]

Improvements in navigating equipment began post-war, with the gradual and rather reluctant fitting of radar to coastal vessels, which – almost invariably frequenting crowded waters – should have been considered more fitting recipients than ocean-going ships. What persuaded some owners was the reduction of insurance premiums that accompanied fitting of radar. More recently, satellite navigation equipment, electronic charts and automatic identification system (A.I.S.) equipment have become almost mandatory.

---

[97]   Waine, *British Motor Coasters*, 125.

[98]   Waine, *British Motor Coasters*, 174 gives examples.

[99]   Waine, *British Motor Coasters*, 181.

[100]   Waine, *British Motor Coasters*, 199.

[101]   Waine, *British Motor Coasters*, 184.

[102]   Waine, *British Motor Coasters*, 199, 202.

[103]   Waine, *British Motor Coasters*, 193–4.

[104]   Waine, *British Motor Coasters*, 169, 175.

[105]   Waine, *British Motor Coasters*, 169.

21: *Centurity* was a larger, oil-engined version of the *Ashfield*, built at Goole in 1956, and somewhat longer at 204 feet. Note her wooden wheelhouse. Her made-up name was bestowed because she was wrongly believed to be the hundredth ship owned by F.T. Everard and Sons Ltd. Photographed in September 1975, she was sold later that year. *Author*

Crew facilities have improved with the adoption of single-berth cabins, easier to provide when the crew of a small vessel can number as few as four. Conversely, life-saving equipment has been reduced to life rafts on such craft, although for vessels over a certain size enclosed, a self-launching lifeboat is required.[106]

Perhaps the biggest change apparent has been the increased size of vessels in the coastal trade. Small ships are still required where ports are restricted in size and shipments small. An example of the size of coaster which is now fully viable in general European coastal trading is the *Scot Isles*, completed in 2021 for one of few remaining British coaster owners, and built by a surviving Dutch builder, Bodewes Shipyard B.V. in Hoogezand.[107] *Scot Isles* measures 90 metres, with a net tonnage of 2,201: a size which would have been respectable in an ocean-going steamer of the 1880s. One characteristic which has not changed greatly is her

---

[106]   Everard's low-air-draft vessels had free-fall lifeboats. Waine, *British Motor Coasters*, 205.

[107]   See https://maritime.ihs.com/ships/detail/9728758.

22: *Holstentor* is a typical, gearless and sheerless motor coaster, built in Spain, owned in Germany, but registered under a flag of convenience in Antigua and Barbuda. Her single hatch with its mechanical cover extends almost the full width of her deck. With a length of 285 feet, and a deadweight of 3,432, she is of a similar size to the average steam tramp of 1890. Photographed in April 2013, she is now under the Latvian ownership as *Salar. Author*

service speed: the output of her German-built oil engine gives 10.5 knots, not significantly higher than the 9 knots an 1880s steam coaster could achieve. As always, increased speed at sea is bought only at a considerable cost in terms of fuel consumption.

With the optimum design for a coaster well established, the focus has continued to be on maximising carrying capacity and hence earnings, and minimising both first cost and running expenses. As in the absence of an autonomous, independent, unmanned ship design, it has so far been impossible to reduce crew below four, although this is governed by national authorities who lay down rules, which also depend on the size of ship and its trading area. Although owners will specify their requirements in terms of speed, capacity for various cargoes, and overall size, competition between builders boils down to who can quickly deliver the most economical but commodious hull, propelled by the most efficient oil engine. This situation is unlikely to change in the foreseeable future.

Chapter Nine

Tramp ship into bulk carrier

I

Although often massively larger than the biggest motor tramp, the modern bulk carrier is not fundamentally different in either use or design. Indeed, it is simply defined as a single-deck ship designed to carry a homogeneous dry cargo. Lloyd's Register of Shipping goes further by insisting it is a general-purpose, single-deck ship of over 10,000 tons deadweight, with machinery aft and water ballast tanks in its hold. Its cargoes are typically those carried by steam and later motor tramps, led by grain, metallic ores, fertilisers, timber and coal. There has been specialisation, most notably in vessels designed for ore or in combination carriers to load either ore or oil, but the majority of bulk carriers offer their operators the same flexibility as to cargoes accepted as did the steam and motor tramp.

This chapter sidesteps the vexed question of which was the first *modern* bulk carrier by tracing the gradual evolution which began, as did the steam tramp, in the British east coast coal trade in the 1850s. There were a number of ocean-going ships with most, and in some cases all, the attributes of a bulk carrier built before the 1960s, when the name was bestowed as building of these ships began to accelerate.[1] The discussion of developments in hull form, fittings and machinery is once again grounded largely in surveys of representative vessels built up until 2020. Leaving aside the insistence by Lloyd's Register of Shipping on it being a general-purpose ship, the bulk carriers designed for specialist cargoes are then reviewed.

II

Although intended solely for coal carrying, the steam collier of the 1850s possessed most attributes of the modern bulk carrier on a much smaller scale: a single deck, generous hatches, an engine placed aft and a capacity to carry

---

[1]   Lloyd's Register of Shipping first used the term bulk carrier in compiling its shipping statistics in 1964. However, it is hardly new, and in the 1954 volume of the annual *Merchant Ships: British Built* (Southampton, 1954) the anonymous compilers use the term freely.

water ballast. From the first such steamers, measuring just 150 feet in length,[2] an optimal size of around 200 feet was reached by the mid-1860s, although as early as 1857 a 250-foot collier was operating.[3] Engines-amidships colliers of this size continued to be built for east coast coal carrying until the Second World War.[4]

An important strand in the development of the bulk carrier is represented by ships built for trading on the Great Lakes of North America, where cargoes of grain, coal and ore have been of particular importance. These were large ships, with engines aft and long clear holds and hatches. Until the opening of the St. Lawrence Seaway, they were confined to inland lakes and interconnecting waterways, and those who built them could make no physical contribution to the production of their ocean-going counterparts. Nevertheless, they had shown what was possible in a practical bulk carrier.

The specialist ore carrier was an important contributor to developing the concept of the bulk carrier, especially those built from 1896 for Rederi A/B Nordstjernan (Axel Johnson) and predecessors of the railway company Trafik A/B Grängesberg-Oxelösund.[5] *Oscar II*, built at Sunderland in 1896, began a sequence of such ships, following Axel Johnson's securing of a contract with William H. Muller to deliver 80,000 tons of iron ore annually from Oxelösund to Rotterdam, from where it was lightered up the Rhine into Germany. Because of the stresses exerted on the hull by a heavy ore cargo, a trunk deck reminiscent of that employed by trunk and turret steamers was chosen to give *Oscar II* and her successors sufficient longitudinal strength. *Oscar II* and her 399-foot successor *Oscar Fredrik*, which became Sweden's largest ship when completed in March 1900, had engines placed amidships. Although smaller, *Lappland* of 1906 and *Polcirkeln* of 1907 conformed to the modern bulk carrier definition with engines aft, both ships having conventional masts and derricks to serve their four holds. *Polcirkeln* survived until 1954.

What had become the world's largest steel plant, that of the Bethlehem Steel Company at Sparrow's Point, Maryland, entered the story in 1917 when its associated shipyard delivered the *Cubore*, 450 feet long with steam turbines placed aft. Sent across the Atlantic, she was unfortunate enough to be torpedoed on her

---

[2]   *John Bowes* was initially measured at 149 feet, but by 1871 had put on a few inches and was now measured as 150 feet. The National Archives, Kew (TNA), Registry of Shipping and Seamen, closed registers for London, CUST 130/61.

[3]   This was the *William Cory*, built by Charles Mitchell at Low Walker for a consortium of coal owners, shipowners and coal merchants, including a William Cory. After having machinery upgraded to two-cylinder compound, she worked for a variety of London owners until broken up in 1900. TNA, Registry of Shipping and Seamen, closed registers for London, CUST 130/57.

[4]   D.R. Chesterton and R.S. Fenton, *Gas and Electricity Colliers* (Kendal, 1984); J.A. Macrae and C.V. Waine, *The Steam Collier Fleets* (Albrighton, 1990).

[5]   R.S. Fenton, 'Swedish Trunks', *Ships in Focus Record*, 5 (1998), 48–53.

return journey to New York in August 1918.[6] She was replaced in 1920 with a similar-sized ship of the same name but driven by an oil engine. Enlargements of these ships to 550 feet gave the *Bethore* and *Steelore*, twin-screw ships propelled on voyages from Chile to Maryland by steam reciprocating and steam turbine machinery respectively.[7]

Swedish interests working in conjunction with the Bethlehem steel plant were then involved in the next development, the commissioning in 1925 of the German-built *Svealand* and *Amerikaland* in 1925. Twin-screw motor ships, at 561 feet they ranked as the world's largest ocean-going cargo ships and were designed to carry Chilean ore on long-term contract to Bethlehem steel.[8] Despite their size they had just three holds, served by a forest of kingposts, and with ample capacity for water ballast. *Amerikaland* was torpedoed and sunk on 3 February 1942, and *Svealand*'s charter expired in 1949, after which she operated in European ore trades until 1969.

Developments were not confined to the ore trade. A significant collier which largely fulfils the definition of a bulk carrier was the *Mercedes* of 1902.[9] Built on the Tyne for Cardiff owners, reportedly for the coal trade from Australia to South America, she was a single-deck ship of 351 feet overall with engines aft and bridge amidships. The British Admiralty recognised her potential, buying her in 1908 and fitting her with Temperley Transporters for transferring South Wales coal to warships, although this seems to have been done mostly in the harbours of Plymouth, Portland and Portsmouth.[10] In 1921, she was sold to Spanish owners and is known to have been in the iron ore trade between Bilbao and Cardiff, foundering on such a voyage in October 1936.[11] A number of other examples of engines-aft dry cargo ships were built in the years prior to the First World War, three British examples being for use in trades from the United States. *August Belmont* of 1902 was given electric cranes to speed discharge.[12] Two were fitted with topside tanks and steel hatch covers which could be raised or lowered in 90 seconds – *Berwindmoor* of 1910 and *Berwindvale* of 1911 – both for carrying coal from US ports to Cuba.[13] All three were converted to tankers during the First World War, *Berwindvale* reverting to dry cargo in 1920.[14]

---

6   T. Starke and W. Schell, *Register of Merchant Ships Completed in 1917* (Gravesend, 1999).

7   *Lloyd's Register*, 1923.

8   N. Tolerton, *Bulk Carriers: The Ocean Cinderellas* (Christchurch, NZ, 2005), 10.

9   P.N. Thomas, *British Ocean Tramps*, vol. 1 (Wolverhampton, 1992), 68.

10   T.A. Adams and J.R. Smith, *The Royal Fleet Auxiliary: A Century of Service* (London, 2005), 27.

11   T. Starke and W. Schell, *Register of Merchant Ships Completed in 1902* (Gravesend, 2011).

12   Thomas, *British Ocean Tramps*, vol. 1, 52.

13   Thomas, *British Ocean Tramps*, vol. 1, 39.

14   N.L. Middlemiss, *The Anglo-Saxon/Shell Tankers* (Newcastle-upon-Tyne, 1990), 32.

In 1920, a French railway, Compagnie des chemins de fer de Paris à Lyon et à la Méditerranée, began to take delivery of a batch of eight large colliers from Middlesbrough.[15] They were intended to carry locomotive coal from British, northern French and Dutch ports to Port de Bouc, near Marseilles. Of 414 feet, they were driven by quadruple-expansion steam engines – unusual choices – but notably were fitted with steel hatch covers. A major component of their 3,000 ton capacity for water ballast comprised topside tanks, an early manifestation of the fittings which characterise modern bulkers. After unloading, *PLM 20* to *PLM 27* would load bauxite in North African ports for northern Europe.

Already referred to, *Silurian* of 1924 deserves to be recorded as the first British general-purpose bulk carrier, with engines placed aft.[16] At 431 feet, with a single deck and a large water ballast capacity just shy of 4,500 tons, she was larger than most contemporary tramps. Unfortunately, the unreliability of her Beardmore oil engines contributed to the demise of her Cardiff owner, and in little more than a year after sale to Furness, Withy she was wrecked in Panama Bay while carrying a timber cargo.

A fleet of relatively large colliers were at work on the east coast of the United States between the wars, moving coal from Hampton Roads to the New England states. Some of these closely resembled modern bulk carriers, for instance a further *Berwindvale*. Built by Bethlehem Steel in 1929, she had engines aft and gear to raise and lower her steel hatch covers.[17] With the need largely to replace the east coast fleet, during the Second World War the US Maritime Commission decided to drastically modify the design of the 'tween deck Liberty type to turn them into colliers.[18] Engines were moved aft and five holds were worked into the hull, beneath which were deep tanks suitable for the water ballast necessary for southbound voyages. Steel hatch covers were fitted – opened and closed by winches on the deck. Topside and wing tanks were fitted in each hold. Although initially fully employed in the east coast US coal trade for which they were designed, towards the end of their lives several were sold and worked in the European bulk trades. With a deadweight of over 11,000 tons, the Liberty colliers met Lloyd's Register of Shipping's definition of the type, and with 24 identical examples completed they rank as the first standard bulk carriers.

Following the Second World War, the two strands in the development of the bulk carrier continued in parallel. As with developments instigated by Bethlehem Steel 30 years earlier, the impetus for development of ore carriers came from the companies refining the ore. In May and June 1950, Hawthorn, Leslie on the Tyne

---

[15]   R.S. Fenton, 'The PLM Colliers 1 to 10', *Ships in Focus Record*, 17 (2001), 10–15 and 'The PLM Colliers 12 to 27', *Ships in Focus Record*, 18 (2001), 68–73.

[16]   D. Jenkins, *Owen and Watkin Williams of Cardiff: The Golden Cross Line* (Kendal, 1991).

[17]   Photograph of *Berwindvale* in the author's possession.

[18]   W.W. Jaffee, *The Liberty Ships from A to Z* (Palo Alto, CA, 2004), 61–5.

completed the 447-foot motor bauxite carriers *Pathfinder* and *Prospector* for the Pan-Ore Steamship Company.[19] This company was a Panamanian subsidiary of the Aluminium Company of America, set up to circumvent Jones Act provisions that meant only US-built ships could trade under the US flag.

A trend to larger crude oil carriers was already under way in the early 1950s, and one of the main protagonists, the US entrepreneur Daniel Ludwig, also enlarged the ore carrier. His 794-foot *Ore Chief*, the first of three turbine-driven, twin-screw sisters, was completed in 1954 at the former naval yard at Kure, which Ludwig had leased.[20]

The largest ore carrier building programme in the 1950s was that instituted by the British Iron and Steel Corporation.[21] A total of 73 ships of three distinct types were built over an 11-year period for long-term charter to the Corporation. Designed to serve its numerous steel works, lengths varied from 427 feet for the smallest class built to access works at Port Talbot and Irlam on the Manchester Ship Canal. Numerically, the largest group, of 44 ships between 505 and 525 feet, was intended to unload at ore berths at Newport, Glasgow, Birkenhead and on Teesside. Five further ships of approximately 600 feet were also built. All had engines aft, some of the smaller sizes having a bridge amidships. Oil engines were fitted except in three cases. *Gleddoch* and *Ormsary* had triple-expansion steam engines while, in complete contrast, the *Morar* was powered by gas turbines. The latter machinery gave considerable trouble and was later replaced with an oil engine. British, Norwegian and French shipowners were involved, and in some cases partnership companies were set up with established shipowners in which the British Iron and Steel Corporation had a 49 per cent financial interest. The ships had the desired effect of reducing transportation costs for the steel industry. Relying entirely on shoreside gear, discharge could be completed in half the time required for a conventional tramp.

For the general-purpose bulk carrier, a clear line of development can be traced from large coastal colliers. In the 1950s, the British company Tate and Lyle was a major importer of cane sugar and to explore carrying this cargo in bulk chartered several large coastal colliers, including the 316-foot *Tempo*[22] and the 292-foot *Hudson Sound*.[23] As a result, in August 1952 the owners of the latter ship, Hudson Steamship Co. Ltd, took delivery of the bulk carrier *Hudson Deep*, which was fixed on a three-year charter to Tate and Lyle. A history of her owners claims she was a development of their raised quarterdeck

---

[19]   A.C. Hardy, *History of Motorshipping* (London, 1955), 181.

[20]   Tolerton, *Bulk Carriers*, 10.

[21]   J. Harrison, 'The Iron Ladies, Part 1', *Ships in Focus Record*, 23 (2003), 154–67 and 'The Iron Ladies, Part 2', *Ships in Focus Record*, 24 (2004), 204–15.

[22]   R.S. Fenton, 'Tate and Lyle Ltd', *Marine News Supplement* (October 2016), S198–S214.

[23]   G. Atkinson, *Hudson Steamship* (Portishead, 2004).

23: Although not built specifically to suit the needs of the British Iron and Steel Corporation, *Weser Ore* was nevertheless on charter to them when seen leaving Birkenhead Docks in October 1975. She had been alongside the gantries in Bidston Dock so that her cargo could be unloaded and railed to the steel works at Queensferry, North Wales. Built in 1959 at Hamburg and owned in Liberia, she was converted to an offshore mining vessel in 1977, as which she survived until 1993. *Author*

coastal colliers, enlarged to 416 foot, with five hatches and a Doxford oil engine. However, builders Readhead of South Shields had a major hand in the design and went on to immediately complete a sister, *Camellia*, for Stag Line and then the steamers *Rookwood* and *Rushwood* for another collier owner, France, Fenwick. The latter pair were also intended for carrying sugar in bulk, but by the time they were delivered, freight rates had fallen, and they were employed in other bulk trades, for which they proved quite suitable.[24] Two British shipping companies primarily interested in the coastal coal trade thus helped to develop the modern bulk carrier.

Tolerton chooses to cite the 1956, Kockums-built *Cassiopeia* as the first modern general-purpose bulk carrier.[25] She had three holds with six wide hatches, plus sloping wing tanks and sloping bulkheads. She was economical to operate, with twice the capacity of a contemporary tramp, and quicker to

---

24   Anon., *Wm. France Fenwick & Company Limited* (London, 1954).
25   Tolerton, *Bulk Carriers*, 12.

24: An early British steam bulk carrier, France, Fenwick's *Rookwood* of 1952 owes its design to builders J. Readhead and Sons Ltd of South Shields, who built similar ships for other British owners. She was sold to Bulgaria in 1961 and survived until 1974. *Author's collection*

load and trim. Swedish owners and builders continued to develop this type of ship, once again in collaboration with US business interests – in the case of *Cassiopeia*, the shipbroker Ole Skaarup.

In the 1960s, a number of owners decided to take middle-aged tankers and convert them as a way of economically entering the dry bulk trades. They were encouraged by a depressed market for tankers as ever-larger crude carriers reduced the cost of carrying oil, resulting in some of the oil majors sending their smaller vessels for scrap when barely ten years old.[26] At times when there was a shortage of dry cargo carriers and a glut of tankers, some of the latter were used for moving grain. The problems of cleaning a hold which had recently held crude petroleum sufficiently well to load grain can be imagined.

---

[26] Some of Shell's L class ships built soon after the Second World War were in service for less than a decade. The last of the class, *Limatula* of 1950, was laid up in April 1959 and did not trade again, going for scrap in August 1960. Her sister *Lyria* of 1946 was more fortunate: sold to a Spanish owner in 1955 and converted to an ore carrier, she gave two full decades of service as *Yebala* before being broken up in 1975. Middlemiss, *The Anglo-Saxon/Shell Tankers*, 167, 141.

III

To examine if and how much the bulk carrier differed from the contemporary motor tramp, Table 9.1 compares data on samples of the two types built in 1960. In all dimensions recorded the bulk carrier was considerably larger than the contemporary motor tramp: gross and net tonnages were both 47 per cent greater, and they were 9 per cent longer, 11 per cent beamier and 11 per cent deeper. However, the ratios of the three linear measurements are quite close, suggesting that the geometry of hull form had not significantly altered. Brake horsepower figures show bulk carrier engines were some 12 per cent more powerful than those of tramps, but average speeds are similar at 14 knots. For oil-engined ships in both categories, two-stroke machinery was overwhelmingly popular. Four of the bulk carriers had steam turbine machinery; almost unknown amongst tramps during any year surveyed. Samples are too small to allow accurate comparisons of the popularity of makes of engine, but Maschinenfabrik Augsburg-Nürnberg, Doxford, Burmeister and Wain and Sulzer were the top four in both categories of ship. All bulk carriers had, by definition, a single deck and engines aft. However, a surprisingly high number of the tramps had 'tween decks or two full-scantling decks.

IV

With numerous examples of bulk carriers completed by shipyards worldwide during the 1950s, Table 9.2 compares those built at ten-year intervals from 1960 to 2020 to track developments in dimensions, power, builders, flags and other major characteristics.

The most striking aspect of Table 9.2 is the massive growth in average size of bulk carriers over 60 years, which has been commented on by others.[27] Average net tonnages grew by 422 per cent and lengths by 42 per cent. However, this growth was not quite linear, the sample for the year 2000 showing declines in size since 1990. This was almost certainly due to 1990 seeing the completion of some particularly large vessels intended for ore carrying, coming mainly from two of the big three South Korean builders, Hyundai and Samsung. Over the next two decades growth resumed and in 2020 average sizes had surpassed the year 2000 figures.

Currently (2022), the largest dry bulk carriers in service are used to carry iron ore from mines in Brazil to China or Europe. It remains to be seen whether, as happened with ultra large crude carriers, a maximum practical size has been reached with these giants which measure 362 metres and can each carry 400,000 tons of ore.

---

27   Tolerton, *Bulk Carriers*.

Table 9.1 Comparison of motor tramps and bulk carriers built in 1960

Characteristic	Motor tramp (1960)	Bulk carrier (1960)	Comparison
Sample size	*35*	*25*	
Gross tonnage (average)	7,876	11,612	Bulk carrier >> Tramp
Gross tonnage (range)	3,369–11,612	4,368–20,206	Bulk carrier >> Tramp
Net tonnage (average)	4,463	6,554	Bulk carrier >> Tramp
Net tonnage (range)	1,787–7,960	2,252–13,719	Bulk carrier >> Tramp
Length feet (average)	480	523	Bulk carrier > Tramp
Length feet (range)	416–518	383–681	Bulk carrier > Tramp
Beam feet (average)	62	69	Bulk carrier > Tramp
Beam feet (range)	53–70	51–90	Bulk carrier > Tramp
Depth feet (average)	27	30	Bulk carrier > Tramp
Depth feet (range)	20–32	22–35	Bulk carrier > Tramp
Length/beam ratio	7.74	7.57	Tramp > Bulk carrier
Beam/depth ratio	2.3	2.3	Bulk carrier = Tramp
Length/depth ratio	17.8	17.4	Bulk carrier = Tramp
Single deck	1/33	25	–
Two decks	17/33	0	Tramp >> Bulk carrier
1 + shelter decks	15/33	0	
Engines aft	10/33	25/25	Bulk carrier >> Tramp
2SCSA	34/35	18/19	Bulk carrier >> Tramp
Speed knots	14	14	Tramp = Bulk carrier
BHP	5,483	6,115	Bulk carrier > 12%
MAN engine	6/35 (17%)	7/21 (33%)	
Doxford engine	6/35 (17%)	6/21 (28%)	
B&W engine	7.35 (20%)	7/21 (33%)	
Sulzer engine	7/35 (20%)	2/21 (10%)	

Sources are *Lloyd's Register*, 1961 and *Merchant Ships: World Built*, vol. 9 (Southampton, 1961). Samples are random, except that where there was more than one sister ship only one was included; ships with insufficient data were excluded.

Table 9.2 Characteristics of bulk carriers built 1960–2020

Characteristic	1960	1970	1980
Sample size	*25*	*25*	*40*
Gross tonnage (average)	11,612	17,577	21,138
Gross tonnage (range)	4,368–20,206	10,688–68,010	7,884–56,480
Net tonnage (average)	6,554	11,141	14,219
Net tonnage (range)	2,252–13,719	6,254–12,695	6,326–41,839
Length metres (average)*	159.5	175	183
Length metres (range)*	117–207.5	145–197	133–265
Beam metres (average)*	21	24.5	27.5
Beam metres (range)*	15.5–27.5	20.5–28.5	21–40
Depth metres (average)*	9	10.5	11
Depth metres (range)*	6.5–10.5	9.5–11.5	8.6–10.4
Length/beam ratio	7.57	7.14	6.7
Beam/depth ratio	2.3	2.3	2.5
Length/depth ratio	17.4	16.6	16.6
Single deck	25	25	37/38
Two decks	0	0	1/38
2SCSA	18/19	20	37/40
4SCSA		5	3/40
Speed knots	14	16	15
BHP	6,115	10,738	12,145
Holds			5.6 (4–9)
Cargo gear (cranes)	12/16	22/24	21/31
MAN engine/MAN B&W	7/21 (33%)	1	4
Doxford engine	6/21 (28%)	1	0
B&W engine	7/21 (33%)	8	7
Sulzer engine	2/21 (10%)	11	19
Mitsubishi		1	5
Wartsila			
Other engines		3	5
Cylinders (number)	6 (3–9)	6.8 (6–12)	7 (5–10)

* *Lloyd's Register* for 1960 and 1970 uses feet: these have been converted to metres.

1990	2000	2010	2020
40	*40*	*40*	*40*
52,393	37,014	53,645	58,881
8,897–131,479	9,878–90,876	17,986–53,645	22,350–173,271
31,215	22,526	30,446	34,184
4,212–77,096	5,489–57,695	10,380–60,504	12,020–82,506
232	205	228	234
143–332	137–290	170. 7–327	180–339
36.5	32.7	36.3	37.6
19.4–54	23–47	27–55	30–62
14	12.6	20	20.41
8.2–20	8.3–18	13.7–29.25	14.6–29.5
6.4	6.2		6.2
2.6	2.6		1.8
16.6	16.2		11.4
40	40	40	40
0	0	0	0
40	40	40	40
0	0	0	0
13.9	14	14.14	14.35
13,860	11,709	16,513	14,387
7 (4–11)	6 (4–9)	6.4 (4–9)	6.5 (5–9)
10/38	24/40	18/40	17/40
	0	37	37
			0
27	25		See MAN
10	5		0
3	10	1	1
		2/	3
0	0	0	0
5.85 (5–7)	6 (5–8)	6 (5)	6 × 37.3 × 7

V

The wide ranges of tonnages and lengths apparent in Table 9.2 reinforces the conclusion drawn in chapters on steam and motor tramps, that bulk carriers were built to meet the requirements of many individual trades, and to operate between a large variety of terminal ports. Given the size range, the industry has coined a number of terms for bulk carriers, largely reflecting their stratification by size and hence the waterways they are capable of using.

For the general-purpose bulk carrier – the second most numerous type – Handysize indicates a length of up to 180 metres, with a deadweight up to 46,000 tons. Four or five holds are served by cargo gear typically comprising cranes positioned between each hold, each with a safe working load up to 35 tonnes. Handysize ships are suited for ports with length and draught restrictions, or without the necessary shoreside equipment for loading or discharging ships of this size. More recently, the term Handymax has been used for those up to 55,000 tons deadweight.

Supramax or Ultramax is applied to the next largest size, up to 190 metres, with a deadweight of between 50,000 and 60,000 tons. Again, five holds are served by four cranes.

Largest numerically are the Panamax vessels, whose size is constrained by the dimensions of locks on the Panama Canal to a length of 229 metres and a beam of 32 metres. It is apparent from the survey how designers and shipbuilders have been able to achieve ever larger tonnages while keeping within these dimensions, such ships having reached almost 80,000 deadweight tons. Vessels of Panamax size in the survey have up to seven holds. The term Post-Panamax is used for vessels whose length or beam just exceeds the limits for Panamax vessels.

Kansarmax takes its name from a port in Equatorial Guinea whose major export is bauxite. Length is limited to 229 metres, and *Lloyd's Register* tends to lump these vessels in with the Panamax type.

Suezmax usually refers mostly to crude oil carriers. There are no locks on the Suez Canal, but the draught of ships is currently constrained to 22 metres by the dimensions of the channel.

Capesize indicates that the ship is too large to navigate the Suez Canal. For these craft the only physical limitations on size are those imposed by their loading or discharge berths. For *Lloyd's Register*, the term Capesize is applied to bulk carriers over 250 metres and 100,000 tons deadweight. These have seven to nine holds and are invariably gearless.

Valemax describes the largest size of bulk carrier, with an overall length up to 362 metres and deadweights up to 400,000 tons, making them the largest dry cargo ships afloat. The class currently comprises almost 70 ore carriers built in China, South Korea and Japan, and are designed to trade between the quarries of Vale S.A. in Brazil and China or Europe.[28]

---

[28]   See https://en.wikipedia.org/wiki/valemax.

25: A modern black freighter: the bulk carrier *CMB Virginie* is anchored off Gibraltar waiting for bunkers in October 2011. She is described as 'large, handy size'. Built at Zhenjiang, China in 2011 for the Belgian company Bocimar, she is still in existence in 2022 as *Racoon*, Greek-owned and Panama-flagged. *Author*

Other designations refer to individual canals, waterways and ports: Seawaymax indicating up to 226 metres as the limit for using the St. Lawrence Seaway, Dunkirkmax for a length restriction of 289 metres for ore carriers discharging at this French port, Malaccamax for the 330 metres limiting transit of the Malacca Strait and Newcastlemax for the beam of 47 metres, which is the maximum for entering the coal port in New South Wales.

VI

One of the most striking features of the 60 years of bulk carrier building is how the design of engines has been regularised. Up to 1980, the four-stroke oil engine was specified for some craft, but since then the two-stroke has remained supreme. Not only that, but just one manufacturer's design has triumphed. The Burmeister and Wain engine grew in popularity up to 1990, and since its manufacturer was taken over by Maschinenfabrik Augsburg-Nürnberg, what is now known as the MAN B&W type engine has consistently enjoyed over 90 per cent of the bulk carrier market. Sulzer, the market leader in 1980, has either dropped out or been driven out of this market, while two relative newcomers, Mitsubishi and Wartsila, are the only other players, with a very small market share. It should be stressed that these figures refer to the engine *designs*, as the great majority are now built under licence, invariably in the Far East.

Brake horsepower (BHP) figures have increased along with size, the average figure for 2010 being 170 per cent larger than that for 1960. The figure fell slightly in 2020, despite the size of vessels continuing to increase. As a crude comparison of power and size, the ratio of net tonnage to BHP in 1960 was 0.93, in 2010 it was 0.48, so that one BHP was driving forward at 14 knots twice the net tonnage. With no leaps forward in oil engine technology, this improvement results from marine engine builders coaxing ever more power from the two-stroke, direct-drive machinery. Also important are changes in hull form, propellor and rudder design based on tank testing, and computer simulation intended to improve water flow around the hull.

Average speed peaked at 16 knots in 1970 but has since fallen back to just over 14 knots. A significant factor has been concerns about fuel consumption, with fuel prices rising, and especially with more expensive low-sulphur fuels being obligatory in western European waters. Although this speed is more than the 9 to 10 knots considered adequate for steam tramps of 1900, it reflects a continuing need for economy in operation in a highly competitive market.

A development apparent in motor tramps is an increase in power output, which usually involved incorporating extra cylinders in the machinery, with a widespread view amongst engineers that there was an optimum size to individual cylinders. However, despite the brake horsepower of bulk carrier oil engines having more than doubled since 1960, from 1980 the norm has become just six cylinders, with only three of the largest, most powerful engines built in 2020 warranting an increase to seven cylinders.

Figures for ballast capacity are available only for the diminishing number of bulk carriers that are surveyed by Lloyd's Register of Shipping. From these, it is apparent that total water ballast capacity has grown in parallel with the size of the ship – from 9,000 tons in 1960, 11,000 in 1970 and a leap to 36,000 in 1980, although the last figure drew on data from only a small number of ships. Typically, water ballast is carried in double bottoms, in wing tanks low in the sides of the holds, and topside tanks that are hopper-shaped and fitted in the upper part of the hold. Topside tanks are widespread features of bulk carriers. Carrying a heavy cargo such as iron ore in the bottom of a hold makes a vessel very 'stiff' in a seaway. By acting like the weight on the end of a pendulum, the heavy cargo gives an abrupt, unpleasant, and potentially dangerous rolling motion. By adding weight higher up in the hold, topside tanks filled with ballast water help to smooth this motion.

Bulk carriers are increasingly being built with double hulls, which enhances their safety and can reduce internal damage. Frames, brackets and other scantlings are enclosed in the void space between the outer and inner shells, leaving the insides of the hold smooth. This facilitates cleaning the holds of traces of a previous cargo and reduces the danger of damage from grabs or other cargo-moving gear such as bulldozers.[29]

---

[29]   See www.bulkshippingguide.com (2010).

Along with size increases, the survey highlights the significant shift in shipbuilding from European yards to the Far East. In 1960, British yards held top position in the league table, notable orders in that decade being those for more than 30 examples of the Cardiff class vessels delivered by Upper Clyde Shipbuilders, orders initiated by the long-established South Wales owners, Reardon Smith.[30] Despite such relative successes, however, Britain was overtaken by Japan by 1970. Ten years later, Japan was building half the world's bulk carriers, but by 1990 a challenge from South Korea became apparent. Between 2000 and 2010, Chinese shipbuilding staged a huge leap forward, and displaced Japan as bulk carrier builder of choice. However, Japanese yards proved resilient, and maintained their second place to China in 2020. It would seem that the other colossus of Far East shipbuilding, South Korea, had lost interest in building bulk carriers, preferring to accept orders for more valuable and sophisticated work, including gas tankers.

In terms of the flags under which bulk carriers initially operate, the situation has become more and more opaque, with the actual nationality of the owners or operators effectively hidden by the now almost universal practice of adopting flags of convenience. Whilst from 1960 to 1990 the 40 ships in each survey carried 13 to 14 different national flags, 2000 saw Panama taking the lead, which it maintained through to 2020, with Liberia and Hong Kong in secondary places.

VII

Although most of the bulk carriers up to Panamax size are suitable for many of the commodities carried in bulk, there are also a number of specialist types.

The most venerable specialised vessels are ore carriers, whose origins can be traced back at least to the 1890s. Constructional considerations ensure that these ships have sufficient longitudinal strength and that the tank tops are robust anough to take a particularly heavy and dense cargo. In some instances, only alternate holds are filled with ore, and the stresses this puts on the hull require special strengthening. Ore carriers are almost invariably gearless, as terminals usually have efficient shoreside gear which minimises time spent loading and discharging. Long-term charters to ore exporters or steel works are usual and, given that routes such as Brazil to China or Australia to western Europe are fixed, ore carriers can be exceptionally large.

Ore/bulk/oil vessels (OBOs) are equipped to carry either ore or crude petroleum. The Swedish Trafik A/B Grängesberg-Oxelösund began building this type in 1945 with the *Rautas* and *Raunala* ordered from Gotaverken.[31] In 1955, the 789-foot self-unloader *Sinclair Petrolore*, built at the Kure naval yard, showed this approach was practicable for much larger combination carriers. More typical in size were Grängesberg-Oxelösund's *Malgomaj* and *Mertainen*, ordered

---

[30]   Tolerton, *Bulk Carriers*, 39–40.

[31]   Tolerton, *Bulk Carriers*, 63.

26: *Stolt Vista* was built in 1955 at Malmo for Trafik A/B Grängesberg-Oxelösund as the combination ore-oil carrier *Vistasvagge*. When this photograph was taken in May 1974 she was probably carrying chemicals. She was broken up in 1979. *Author*

from Gotaverken in 1959, which at around 200 metres when delivered were still larger than most contemporary bulk carriers. They had two centre holds for ore, with 26 tanks below them for oil.

The advantage claimed for combination carriers was that their ability to carry two types of cargo reduced the number of voyages they would have to make in ballast. This might have held true for ships carrying ore southwards from Swedish or Norwegian ports, but until the recent opening of steel works in oil-exporting countries, other two-way flows were few, and ballast voyages were still inevitable. A more likely reason for their popularity was that they gave owners the opportunity to take part in either the ore or petroleum trades, depending on whichever was seen to have greater earning potential. A major disadvantage was their considerably higher cost, as extra hull strengthening was needed for ore carrying, while extensive pipe runs, pumps, hold cleaning and gas-freeing equipment had to be fitted for petroleum cargoes. Holds taking both petroleum and ore needed gas-tight hatches, and water ballast capacity was also essential. These features also made OBOs heavy on maintenance, and following a number of high-profile disasters they have largely fallen out of favour with owners.[32] *Lloyd's*

---

[32]   These included the *Berge Istra* in 1976 and *Berg Vanga* and *Derbyshire* in 1960, although the circumstances of their losses cannot all be attributed to their construction. Tollerton, *Bulk Carriers*, 169–77.

Register's figures indicate that the popularity of OBOs peaked around 1980, with 424 in service, but this had declined to 205 ships by 2000.[33]

Self-unloading bulk carriers have enjoyed some popularity, initially on the Great Lakes of North America, but more recently in oceanic and coastal trades. The most common method of discharge involves a conveyor belt in a tunnel at the bottom of the hold, fed with cargo by gravity through gates in the bottoms of the holds.[34] The conveyor feeds an unloading boom at the bow or stern which discharges the cargo ashore. Some large self-unloaders, designed to supply a Japanese coal terminal, employ a computer-controlled system incorporating gantry cranes with a grab and a conveyor belt system.[35] In addition to being able to unload cargoes at ports lacking shoreside equipment, discharge takes place without the holds being opened, so problems with dust are largely avoided, and cargoes are minimally exposed to the elements. The considerable additional cost of self-unloaders means that they are usually built on the basis of long-term charters.

Wood chip carriers are self-unloaders designed to carry shredded soft wood for paper making. Wood chips expand significantly if they get wet, and the expansion can be powerful enough to damage the ship's structure, so hatches must be watertight rather than just weathertight.[36] The chips have a very low density, hence the high-sided appearance of these ships. They typically have large hoppers situated on deck between the hatches. High-speed deck cranes with grabs discharge the wood chips into these hoppers, which feed them on to a conveyor belt, which discharges them from doors in the bow.

A number of bulkers have been built with equipment to load and discharge bulk cement. They work on the principle that when air is blown through a cement cargo it behaves like a liquid. The cement is pumped out to silos through a flexible pipe carried on a boom.[37]

Conbulkers – able to carry bulk cargoes or containers – were a short-lived and commercially rather unsuccessful type. The Canadian Cast company mounted a serious challenge to established container operators on the North Atlantic in the 1980s, carrying containers westbound and returning to Europe with ore from ports on the St. Lawrence River. Eventually these ships were outclassed by pure container ships, which grew immensely in size and offered shippers much higher speeds.[38] However, recent shortages of container ships in the wake of disruptions to supply chains during the Covid pandemic and the temporary blocking of the Suez Canal have seen bulk carriers being employed to carry empty containers eastbound from Europe.

---

[33] Tolerton, *Bulk Carriers.*

[34] See www.bulkshippingguide.com (2010).

[35] Tolerton, *Bulk Carriers*, 73–4.

[36] See www.bulkshippingguide.com (2010).

[37] S. Cox and D. Georgandis, *Brief Introduction to Cement Carriers.* www.howerobinson.com/wp-content/uploads/2017/11/Intro-to-Cement-Carriers-2017.pdf.

[38] Tolerton, *Bulk Carriers*, 59–60.

Not to be confused with open-hold ships used for container carrying, open-hatch bulk carriers have holds which are effectively large, regular-sided boxes, stretching almost to the full width of the ship. The pioneers were built in 1963 – the Norwegian *Bessegen* and *Rondeggen* – in order to carry rolls of newsprint on the North American coast.[39] A major innovation was the fitting of three Munckloaders – large gantry cranes travelling on a track alongside the holds. Instead of loading the easily damaged rolls of newsprint individually, they were hoisted aboard on spreaders capable of lifting eight rolls at a time. The open-hatch designation is somewhat misleading, as holds are covered by hydraulically operated folding steel hatch covers. Open-hatch ships have proved capable of efficiently carrying other cargoes that can be unitised, including packaged timber, wood pulp, steel coils, metal ingots and even 20-foot containers. Older vessels are fitted with gantry cranes, but many have conventional deck cranes.

Timber carriers do not load down to their marks when their holds are full because wood is much less dense than other types of bulk cargo. Hence these ships are designed to carry large deck cargoes. The logs, which can often weigh 20 tonnes, are held in place by fixed or collapsible stanchions (or a mixture of the two) at the edge of the weather deck and secured with lashings.

VIII

Over the last six decades, the bulk carrier has replaced the tramp ship. Although the largest ships dwarf the tramps of the 1960s, their characteristics remain similar, with large hatches, capacious holds and economical and reliable machinery directly driving a single screw. A two-stroke oil engine is invariably placed aft, and all are by definition single-deck ships. Ships up to 190 metres (Ultramax type) almost always have cargo gear in the form of electric deck cranes, with a safe working load of around 35 tonnes. Larger ships are generally gearless. The majority are suitable for most types of bulk cargo, but there is some specialisation, for instance for carrying ore, timber or wood chips. There is huge variation in size, from 10,000 gross tons up to 200,000 for the biggest ore carriers. Building these ships has become restricted to yards in China, Japan and South Korea. Owners can choose from a number of 'off the peg' designs from these yards, minimising cost by reducing design time and streamlining production. Ownership in far eastern countries is also common but is often difficult to trace because of the widespread adoption of flags of convenience. Like its predecessors, steam and later motor tramps, bulk carriers play an enormously significant role in world shipping and trade, as the subsequent two chapters will explore.

---

[39]   Tolerton, *Bulk Carriers*, 69–70.

Chapter Ten

The shipping industries and powered bulk carrying

I

The shipping industry had to adapt to the advent and continued importance of powered bulk carriers, as the types, size and efficiency of these vessels profoundly changed the finance, management, operation, brokerage, chartering, insurance and – not least – manning of the ships. The impact on shipbuilding and the nascent marine engineering business was even more far-reaching. This chapter reviews how changes affected those who owned, managed or were otherwise associated with the running of bulk carriers, those who built their hulls and engines, those who crewed them and the ports around the world where they were loaded and discharged.

II

With an iron or steel hull and engine costing many times more than the contemporary wooden sailing vessel, potential owners needed novel methods to finance bulk carriers. Although early iron steam colliers were funded by the traditional method of offering 64th shares to investors, a steamer costing over £8,000 put each share at a price few but the wealthy could afford.[1] Once legislation allowed joint stock companies to be readily formed, shares at much more moderate prices could be offered; for instance, in the 1850s, the General Iron Screw Collier Co. Ltd attempted to raise £400,000 in shares priced at £5.[2] This immediately posed the problem of promoting the company to sufficient potential investors. Networks of agents sprang up, whose employment involved in some cases

---

[1]   For instance, the General Iron Screw Collier Co. Ltd put the cost of a new screw collier at around £8,150. The National Archives, Kew (TNA), company registration papers, class BT 31/172/519.

[2]   General Iron Screw Collier Co. Ltd, TNA, company registration papers, class BT 31/172/519.

going from door to door offering to sell shares.[3] Capital was also raised through existing business networks, for instance early screw colliers were financed through the charterers, builders, brokers, factors and colliery owners involved in the east coast coal trades. Banks and other institutions financed ships through mortgages and other financial instruments. Those running powered vessels thus needed to attract investors on a much larger scale than was the case with sailing vessels. They also had to sustain this investment base with regular reports to shareholders and occasional encouragement to increase existing investments. Clerical effort had to be directed to keep up-to-date statutory registers of investors, a time-consuming process but which facilitated paying dividends and soliciting further subscriptions. As the cost of ships rose in the twentieth and twenty-first centuries, relations with the financial institutions who had the resources to finance them had to be maintained.

With its rapid turnround and ability to make more voyages in a given period than a sailing vessel, the steamer required more intense management, which had to look further than one voyage ahead. Finding employment for a steam ship, either on a voyage basis or through time chartering, was another call on the time and energies of the manager, and this necessitated increases in office staff and the emergence of the steamship manager as a distinct profession.[4] The operation of a steamer also involved supervision of the maintenance and survey of its hull and machinery, leading to the appointment of marine and engineering superintendents.

Aided by the introduction of telegraphic communication, tramping companies relied on a network of brokers in loading ports to fix cargoes and in turn their work had to adapt to meet the intensive employment which steamship owners required. Agents in both loading and discharging ports were needed to conduct ship's business with harbour and other authorities and to liaise between them and the vessel's master. These networks were vital to the success of a tramping business and had to be set up and monitored.

Not least amongst the clusters of shore-based businesses serving the shipping industry, marine insurance also had to evolve with the increase in the number

---

[3]   By such means some Cardiff owners achieved excellent reputations in, and hence further investment from, certain geographical areas, for instance Reardon Smith in west Yorkshire, no doubt helped by giving his companies and his ships local names such as *Leeds City* and *Bradford City*. D. Jenkins, *From Ship's Cook to Baronet: Sir William Reardon Smith's Life in Shipping, 1856–1935* (Cardiff, 2011), 71–3. When floating the Graig Shipping Company in 1919, Idwal Williams sold a large number of shares around Wigan through one share salesman. D. Jenkins, *Graig: One Hundred Years in Shipping* (Preston, 2019), 7.

[4]   Such managers, joining as juniors and gradually acquiring experience and confidence with existing tramp operators, were themselves instrumental in floating new tramp shipping ventures. There are a number of examples in J.G. Jenkins and D. Jenkins, *Cardiff Shipowners* (Cardiff, 1986).

and value of steamers. This meant partly at least supplementing the mutual clubs which had sufficed for many sailing vessels. Under this system a group of local shipowners agreed that if one of their members had a ship lost or damaged his costs would be met by 'calls' on other members of the association. This system could not cope with the increased values of steamers, and insurance companies expanded their activities in shipping, and syndicates of investors were set up to underwrite ships.[5]

Another ancillary profession to be affected by the growth in steam ships of all kinds was ship surveying. This was carried out partly by government-appointed bodies such as the British Board of Trade and its successors who inspected ships to ensure that statutory regulations on construction, maintenance, operation and crewing were observed. Surveys of both hulls and machinery were also carried out by independent classification societies who acted in the interests of insurers and charterers.[6] Surveyors were usually drawn from experienced seagoing staff or more recently from those who took degree courses in naval architecture or engineering.

III

The steam bulk carrier and other types of iron ship put an end to the era when shipbuilding was almost a cottage industry, with a shipwright able to turn out a wooden hull with simple facilities and a handful of employees on a beach or a river bank. Demanding as it did new finance, machinery and skills, the transition to building in iron proved impossible for all but the largest and most firmly established shipbuilders. Those that made the change needed to grow considerably in size and structure, with consequent demands on finance, machinery, manpower and management.[7] Finance began with raising the capital or organising the credit needed to equip an iron or steel shipbuilding operation. Success here very much depended on the ambition, financial circumstances and particularly the contacts of the individuals establishing, re-equipping or taking

---

[5]   The best-known syndicates are the 'names' who are 'members' of Lloyd's of London, who still underwrite shipping and offshore industrial activity.

[6]   See, for instance, N. Watson, *Lloyd's Register: 250 Years of Service* (London, 2010).

[7]   There is extensive literature on British shipbuilding, and in particular the reasons why an industry which had achieved world domination in building iron and steel ships declined so dismally in the twentieth century. See, for instance, S. Pollard and P. Robertson, *The British Shipbuilding Industry, 1870–1914* (Cambridge, MA, 1979); J.R. Parkinson, *The Economics of Shipbuilding in the United Kingdom* (Cambridge, 1960); S. Ville, *Shipbuilding in the United Kingdom in the Nineteenth Century: A Regional Approach* (St. John's, Newfoundland, 1993); and L. Johnman and H. Murphy, *British Shipbuilding and the State since 1918: A Political Economy of Decline* (Liverpool, 2002).

over the yard. If and when this was successfully accomplished and an order won (two significant but not necessarily simple steps), money was raised from stage payments from the customer. For instance, a proportion of the contract price would be paid at keel laying, another sum after shell plating of the hull was completed, one following launch and a final payment after delivery. Financial incentives were often required to secure orders, for instance offering to fund or organise a mortgage on the intended ship or to take over an older vessel, a form of the part-exchange familiar in the motor industry. The shipbuilder hoped and aimed for a reasonable profit after the costs of labour, materials, equipment and establishment charges had been paid.

The cyclical nature of the shipping industry inevitably gave the shipbuilder financial problems. According to Tinbergen, this cycle usually occupied eight years.[8] It is generally accepted that the shipping cycle begins with freight rates rising and owners anxious to secure new tonnage, a period accompanied by rising building costs as builders reacted to a growing demand. Freight rates then peaked, and demand plummeted, although the builder was still expecting to deliver vessels already on the stocks at prices ruling when ordered. As orders dwindled, building prices fell, but the owners who appreciated the nature of the financial cycle, and had deep pockets, took the opportunity to build ships at a minimum price, if only to sell at a profit when market conditions improved.[9] As freight rates recovered, the cycle began over again.

As the Scottish shipbuilder A. Murray Stephen stated in 1944, 'No other industry has had such a record of booms and slumps in the past as British shipbuilding'.[10] Using a biblical analogy, Stephen further questioned 'how any industry could function satisfactorily when it is alternately subjected to famine and feast, when the feasts attract speculators, who in turn make the famines worse?' The generally accepted length of the trade cycle in British shipbuilding was seven years. Thus, the shipbuilder had to make sufficient profits in the good year to survive the six succeeding bad ones. However, he had other options. The major one was to remove his major unit cost, labour, by laying off a proportion of his workforce. In a casualised industry such as shipbuilding, labour was therefore a variable rather than a fixed cost of production. The wider social and economic costs of such actions could be catastrophic, especially in regions where shipbuilding was the major industry, such as Clydeside, Belfast,

---

[8]   J. Tinbergen, 'Ein Schiffbauzyklus?' *Weltwirtschaftliches Archiv*, 34, no. 2 (1931), 152. For a critical discussion of Tinbergen's theories, in English, see J.R. Parkinson, *Economics of Shipbuilding*, 78–9.

[9]   Perhaps the best exponent of this approach was the Burrell family of Glasgow, who read the market correctly over three separate cycles. N.L. Middlemiss, *Travels of the Tramps: Twenty Tramp Fleets* (Newcastle-upon-Tyne, 1989), 82–90.

[10]   'Full Employment in British Shipyards, Presidential Address by A. Murray Stephen, M.C., B.A.', Institution of Engineers and Shipbuilders in Scotland (Glasgow, 1944), 2.

Barrow-in-Furness and Tyne and Wear.[11] The yards on the Wear and elsewhere which specialised in tramp ship production often suffered the most in depressions, as this sector of shipping was subjected to deeper troughs and peaks in earnings than the liner sector.

Neither did layoffs encourage any degree of loyalty amongst employees, and this affected working practices in a strictly demarcated workforce and their willingness to make changes, subjects which have been well documented in works about the British shipbuilding industry.[12] Similar considerations applied in the related industries of marine engineering and in iron and steel ship repairing, although the latter activity was less subject to fluctuations in work, as damaged ships usually had to be repaired at the expense of the insurer no matter what was the state of the market. Marine engineering was of course the father of the steam ship and developed as a distinct and important branch of engineering solely as a consequence of the invention of the powered vessel.

The equipment of early yards building in iron was fairly rudimentary, with probably little beyond a forge for crafting iron work. Initially, much of the work was of necessity done by hand, including drilling and riveting, with assembly of the iron work being assisted by pole derricks to hoist heavy items. Machinery for drilling, plate bending and casting, plus enhanced craneage would be installed as and when finance was available, and particularly when management was convinced that it would increase output. The pace of its introduction was also dictated by the availability of such machinery and its cost. The industry for producing such machinery and machine tools developed alongside shipbuilding and was subject to the same fluctuations in demand.

A shipyard which was building in iron needed skills largely removed from those of shipwrights shaping timber with an adze, and top and bottom sawyers labouring in their sawpits. Perhaps the only skill which could be imported in early years was that of the blacksmith, as fabricating the structure of an iron ship required cutting and drilling plates, frames, ribs and other scantlings, drilling rivet holes, joining the pieces by riveting, and caulking the seams between plates.[13] All these skills needed to be learned by new recruits, and a system evolved whereby a seven-year apprenticeship (later reduced to five years) had to be served before they were considered qualified as 'tradesmen'. Nevertheless, a

---

[11]   This was especially so in the interwar period; see L. Johnman and H. Murphy, 'An Overview of the Economic and Social Effects of the Interwar Depression on Clydeside Shipbuilding Communities', *International Journal of Maritime History*, 18, no. 1 (2006), 227–54.

[12]   This is a recurring theme in, for instance, Pollard and Robertson, *British Shipbuilding Industry*, and is also recorded starkly, in the words of those involved, in A. Slaven and H. Murphy (eds), *Crossing the Bar: An Oral History of the British Shipbuilding, Ship Repairing and Marine Engine-Building Industries in the Age of Decline, 1956–1990* (St. John's, Newfoundland, 2013).

[13]   G.C. O'Hara, *Ironfighters, Outfitters and Bowler Hatters* (Prestwick, 1997), 11–12.

large number of other workers – regarded (often inappropriately) as unskilled – were needed, including labourers to move frequently very heavy items, and the so-called 'helpers' who were an essential part of riveting and plating squads. For example, riveting required holders-on, catchers and rivet heaters, while tradesmen (riveters, left- and right-handed) hammered the rivet into shape first by hand and later with hydraulic and pneumatic power. In addition to the iron or steel workers, who largely belonged to the Boilermakers Society, a growing number of outfit trades were required, their number and variety increasing as ships grew more sophisticated, including joiners, caulkers, painters, riggers, carpenters, plumbers and electricians. To some extent, the skills of outfitters were transferable from and to other industries, and as their work grew more technical, electricians and some others served apprenticeships which included a school-learning component.

The practice of demarcation, with various tradesmen insisting that only they could carry out certain work, had its origins in lengthy apprenticeships to acquire skills, the insecurity of work in shipyards, and the practice of yard management in devolving much of their work to the squads of tradesmen. This practice, along with the involvement of a number of well-organised trade unions representing different groups, was a reason for conflict with yard management, whose shortcomings were often apparent to the workforce.[14]

Management of shipyards has come in for heavy criticism, especially for its perceived failure in Britain to modernise yard equipment and working practices.[15] There is truth in that training in management skills and even in practices of engineering and naval architecture were often considered unnecessary. Recruitment of managers was often from the underqualified sons of the yard owners or their peers.

IV

The effect of the introduction of steam on seafarers and their working lives was profound. Work on a steamship became somewhat safer and less arduous for deck crews, while new employment opportunities presented themselves, particularly in the engine room.

However, the adoption of steam did not immediately abolish the need for setting, furling and caring for sails. Until late in the nineteenth century, most steamers were equipped with masts, rigging and yards, with sails provided at least when the ship was new. It became apparent that the assistance given by sails

---

[14]   For labour, see H. Murphy, 'Labour in the British Shipbuilding and Ship Repairing Industries in the Twentieth Century: An Overview', in R. Varela, H. Murphy and M. van der Linden (eds), *Shipbuilding and Ship Repair Workers around the World: Case Studies, 1950–2010* (Amsterdam, 2017), 47–116.

[15]   Slaven and Murphy, *Crossing the Bar.*

was of only marginal benefit in terms of speed yet involved expensive canvas and rigging. Of particular concern amongst owners of tramp ships, reduction in the use of sails could cut manning requirements, already diminished by the introduction of steam-driven capstans and winches. The need to go aloft was thus reduced, but not eliminated, as standing rigging and items of cargo gear still needed to be maintained. Other activities for seamen remained largely unchanged, including handling mooring ropes, steering, painting, cooking and serving food. To these were added the drudgery of chipping iron and steel plates prior to painting.

Steam engines needed tending and firing, requiring engineers for supervising and overhauling machinery, donkeymen and greasers for routine maintenance, and firemen for the arduous toil of keeping boilers stoked and removing ash from furnaces. Marine engineering gradually emerged as a profession, with shipowners rather grudgingly accepting that technical training was useful alongside hard-won practical experience for those tending steam engines. Firemen were recruited from the young and often the poor, with occasional opportunities for promotion to greaser or donkeyman. One effect of introducing steam was that, at least in British ships, social distinctions arose between those working as seamen, largely on deck or on the bridge, and those in the engine room. This extended to segregation of seamen and firemen, often housed in opposite sides of a forecastle, while accommodation for engineers was often physically separated from that of the master and his officers. There are suggestions that such distinctions might have been less rigid in a tramp ship, where crews were smaller, and it was recognised that deck and engineering departments were mutually dependent.

By making voyage durations more predictable, steam made employment at sea more attractive, as did the increased professionalisation of deck and engineering officers. Adoption of steam also had an effect on accident rates. With its iron or steel hull and an engine, the steam vessel was less likely to become a casualty during a voyage than a sailing ship. However, through making far more voyages in a given period, this advantage was largely eroded over a steamer's career, and this is apparent in statistics that indicate that the active life of a steamer was, on average, no longer than that of a sailing vessel in the same trade.[16]

V

Ports and harbours and their associated industries, including stevedoring and storage activities, had to adapt to the needs of steam bulk vessels to achieve a short turnround and to the increasing size of vessels. Since the introduction of steam, at least, authorities responsible for dock facilities were under commercial

---

[16]   For a comparative study in the coastal bulk trades, see R.S. Fenton, 'Did Steam Make Shipping Safer?' *Mariners Mirror*, 108, no. 2 (May 2022), 177–89.

pressure to improve and enlarge their facilities or risk losing to rival ports the financially valuable steam trade.

Almost the first requisite of the steam ship was a fast turnround. Costing much more to build and run than a sailing vessel, it could only be made to pay if it was worked more intensively, and prolonged time spent in harbour was anathema to its owners. Thus, access to quays, docks and piers had to be easy, working practices sharpened, and where possible mechanical devices installed to improve loading and unloading, including cranes, elevators and tips for bulk commodities. The development of hydraulic power was an important development, the first hydraulic cranes developed by William Armstrong being manufactured in 1846.[17]

Good transport connections to inland towns, especially railways, were also desirable to move raw materials and finished goods. Installing railways within a dock system was often difficult given the narrowness of quays and the angularity of the docks themselves. One answer was to build goods sheds and sidings as close as possible to docks and move goods between them by road.

As steam ships grew in length, breadth and depth, port entrances and particularly locks into closed docks had to be enlarged, often an almost unending process at ports such as Liverpool over the last 200 years. As Jackson points out, dock building was not always the answer – as at Aberdeen, where the steamers providing an intensive coastwise service benefited from being able to move on and off berths quickly.[18] This was not the case for ports on the west coast of Britain where the tidal range was amongst the largest in the world – explaining why Liverpool was always ahead of its rival London in building its closed dock estate.[19] However, the same problem of rapid turnround of passenger vessels – estuarial, coastal and ocean-going – was only solved by building a floating landing stage at Liverpool, the first installed in 1848.[20] Jetties in the Mersey for tanker traffic also appeared in the twentieth century.[21] A further problem presented by the growing size of steamers was the length of quay they occupied, as it was not possible to crowd them into docks as was done with sailing vessels. In 1840, evidence was presented to the House of Commons that a dock built to cater for 140 sailing ships could accommodate only 35 foreign-going steamers.[22]

With the increasing size of steam ships, dredging was often needed to provide sufficient depth in approach channels, again an almost unending task carried out at the expense of the harbour authority and necessitating a fleet of steam-powered dredgers. Jarvis provides an indication of how intensive this work

---

17   W.W. Tomlinson, *The North-Eastern Railway* (1915), 437, cited by G. Jackson, *The History and Archaeology of Ports* (Tadworth, 1983), 99.

18   Jackson, *History and Archaeology of Ports*, 74–5.

19   Jackson, *History and Archaeology of Ports*, 77–83.

20   Jackson, *History and Archaeology of Ports*, 78.

21   A. Jarvis, *Liverpool: A History of 'The Great Port'* (Liverpool, 2014), 161.

22   Evidence of James Walker to a House of Commons Committee in 1840, quoted by Jackson, *History and Archaeology of Ports*, 75.

had to be at Liverpool: in the 1855 to 1856 financial year, Mersey Docks and Harbour Board's hopper barges serving the dredgers made a total of 3,242 trips.[23]

Particularly in the age of the bulk carrier, loading and unloading installations had to be significantly enlarged, often requiring them to be situated in deep water, outside conventional harbours. Typically, facilities moved downriver, such as the developments at Tilbury opening in 1886,[24] the initial opening of Gladstone Dock in 1913,[25] Seaforth Docks at Liverpool in 1972,[26] and the great expansion which gave rise to Europort in the Netherlands (this was not just downriver but took place on land created in what had been the North Sea).[27] Where ports could not enlarge, or their owning bodies could not afford to do so, closure was often the inevitable result. A large number of ports around the British Isles suffered this fate, particularly in the latter half of the twentieth century. Running a port, just like operating a shipping company or a shipyard, was a competitive activity, and inability to compete spelt failure and closure, or, even sadder, turning a place of once industrial-scale activity into a marina for the yachts of the well-heeled.

---

[23]   Jarvis, *Liverpool*, 75.

[24]   W. Paul Clegg, *Docks and Ports 2: London* (Shepperton, 1987), 30.

[25]   Jackson, *History and Archaeology of Ports*, 122.

[26]   Jarvis, *Liverpool*, 236.

[27]   Hans Meyer, 'Port of Rotterdam', in S.K. Al Naib, *European Docklands: Past, Present and Future* (London, 1991), 25–36.

Chapter Eleven

The consequences of the bulk carrier
for industry and society

I

The economic significance of the powered bulk carrier is the effect it has had on industrial development through increases in the size of ships and the economy and the regularity with which cargoes can be delivered. This in turn has had effects on society as a whole. The impact went beyond those millions whose livelihoods depended on industries exporting or importing bulk cargoes, extending to all consumers of these industries' products. Although shipping of cargoes in bulk was well established before propulsion by steam was applied to this sector from the 1850s, mechanical propulsion plus the introduction of iron and later steel hulls has made delivery of bulk commodities more efficient, cheaper and – important to many industries – timelier.

The term 'globalisation' has been coined fairly recently to describe the growing interdependence of the world's economies. Along with industrialisation and mass production, an important factor has been facilitation of cross-border trades by the steamship. Amongst various theories as to when globalisation began, the early nineteenth century is suggested with the growing ability of railways and ships to carry goods at ever reducing costs,[1] so that freight charges became a diminishing factor in determining the price of the goods. Bulk carriers have played a major part in this process. For instance, Kaukiainen, citing several indexes, has concluded that since 1870 – when the first ocean steam tramps

---

[1]   O'Rourke and Williams date the beginning of globalisation to the years 1820 to 1850, concomitant with the spread of railways and the introduction of steam ships. This may put a disproportionate emphasis on railways. The half-century did see developments in shipping, with operators on important routes aiming to timetable sailings, greatly facilitated by early steam ships. However, these services catered essentially for passengers and high-value or perishable cargoes. The present work has argued that only after the 1850s, with the introduction of steam colliers and steam tramps, were significant economies achieved in the transport of the bulk commodities that accounted for the preponderance of cargoes shipped internationally. K.H. O'Rourke and S.G. Williams, 'When Did Globalisation Begin?' *European Review of Economic History*, 6, no. 1 (2002), 23–50.

appeared – and the outbreak of the First World War tramp freight rates fell by between 33 per cent and 45 per cent.[2] Much more recently, container ships have had a similar effect as agents of globalisation.[3]

Only recently have the environmental effects of shipping come into sharp focus with concerns about carbon dioxide emissions and their part in climate change. A further environmental issue concerns biosecurity, which is especially relevant to the bulk carrier with its requirement to take in and discharge ballast water and the potential to introduce alien species to marine environments.

II

The first industries to feel the effects of improvements from the adoption of steam bulk carrying were coal mining, gas generation and iron production, being joined in the twentieth century by electricity generation. All came to rely on the carriage of coal or iron ore in large consignments and particularly their timely delivery. Iron and steel production grew significantly with the use of larger vessels carrying iron ore, coal and limestone, plus distribution of both iron itself and a by-product of its production, the basic slag used as a phosphate-rich fertiliser. Mining of coal, metallic ores and stone quarrying developed as sea transportation reduced costs, making it possible to exploit rich deposits remote from areas where the material was processed, or the stone utilised. Flour milling expanded with bulk deliveries of grain, and cheaper distribution by coastal steamers. Civil engineering, and in particular port and harbour construction, benefited from more efficient delivery of stone, gravel, sand and cement.

It is testimony to the economy of water transport that many industries found it worthwhile to relocate their production facilities to coastal locations or those adjacent to major waterways. The classic examples were the principal gas producers of London, which, in the 1870s and 1880s, built Thames-side works, for instance, at Beckton and at East Greenwich, so that they could be supplied directly by sea.[4] In the case of the Beckton works, the development took place less than two decades after steam carriage of Northumberland and Durham coal

---

[2]   Y. Kaukiainen, 'Growth, Diversification and Globalization: Main Trends in International Shipping Since 1850', in L.R. Fischer and E. Lange, *International Merchant Shipping in the Nineteenth and Twentieth Centuries: The Comparative Dimension* (St. John's, Newfoundland, 2008), 37. Kaukiainen cautions that this cannot be attributed solely to improvements in ships, as port facilities were also improved.

[3]   F. Broeze, *The Globalization of the Oceans: Containerisation from the 1950s to the Present* (Liverpool, 2002) and M. Levinson, *The Box: How the Shipping Container Made the World Smaller and the World Economy Bigger* (Princeton, NJ, 2008).

[4]   D.R. Chesterton and R.S. Fenton, *Gas and Electricity Colliers* (Kendal, 1984), 40, 26.

had begun. Later, but even more impressive, was the building of a chain of power stations along the Thames, from Tilbury inland as far as Kingston, all served by steam and later diesel colliers.[5]

For mining, quarrying and other extractive industries, a coastal or riverside location was often essential for economical operation. This was not often possible for coal, but the importance of sea carriage to collieries can be judged from the plateways and railways which were built, the canals dug, or river navigations improved to move coal to tidewater. British examples include the coalfields in Durham, Northumberland, South Wales, Yorkshire and the Lanarkshire, Ayrshire and Fife coalfields of Scotland. Much extraction of slate and china clay was also remote from the coast, but railways were laid to the nearest ports, which themselves were often built specially to export these products.[6] Stone quarrying in coastal locations include those at Portland, around Cornwall, Mid and North Wales and the west of Scotland.[7]

Many large iron and steel works had waterside locations to facilitate the import of ore by bulk carriers, and in the United Kingdom these locations included Birkenhead, Irlam on the Manchester Ship Canal, Newport, Port Talbot, Teesside and Workington.[8] European examples include Ijmuiden, Dunkirk, Ghent and – connected by river – those in the Rhine and Ruhr valleys.

Size is an important determinant of the economy of operation of a bulk carrier. There are two aspects to the economy of cargo-carrying, identified as hauling capacity and handling capacity.[9] Building a bigger ship contributes to increasing its efficiency as a hauler of a commodity but tends to reduce the efficiency of loading or unloading the cargo. The latter is constrained by the cargo-handling facilities of the terminal ports. As the surveys in this work have repeatedly shown, to reflect these constraints, bulk carriers have always been built in a wide variety of sizes to suit the available cargoes and with cargo gear, or lack of it, which reflects the facilities of the ports they are expected to use.

---

[5]   B. Pedroche, *London's Lost Power Stations and Gasworks* (Stroud, 2013).

[6]   Port Penrhyn and Port Dinorwic on the Menai Straits owe their existence to inland slate quarries, connected by narrow gauge railways. J. Lindsay, *A History of the North Wales Slate Industry* (Newton Abbot, 1974), 170–84; R.S. Fenton, *Cambrian Coasters* (Kendal, 1989), 92–103, 136–51. Harbours at Charlestown, Pentewan, Par and Fowey were developed or grew in importance thanks to extensive inland china clay pits. J. Armstrong, 'The Coastal Trade in China Clay', in P. Payton, A. Kennerley and H. Doe, *The Maritime History of Cornwall* (Exeter, 2014), 284–95.

[7]   P. Stanier, *Quarries of England and Wales: An Historic Photographic Record* (Truro, 1995) includes photographs taken by those carrying out the Geological Survey of Great Britain, which recorded the size and complexity of many quarries and their production methods.

[8]   J. Hill, 'The Iron Ladies', *Ships in Focus Record*, 3 (2003), 154–67.

[9]   J.O. Jansson and D. Shneerson, 'Economies of Scale in General Cargo Ships', *Review of Economics and Statistics*, 60 (1987), 287–93.

III

A wide range of other industries have also benefited from cheaper and more reliable delivery of their raw or processed materials. This effect could be highly significant. For instance, in 1900 shipbuilding in Britain consumed 50 per cent of the nation's output of steel, and because of the necessary waterside locations of the industry much of it could be delivered by water.[10]

Many similar situations can be identified internationally. For instance, more efficient sea transportation opened up immense areas to agriculture, as seen in the expansion of wheat production in the Ukraine, in both South and North America and in Australia. Most of this wheat was surplus to local requirements and was exported, mainly to Europe. This was of equal importance to the consuming nations: taking figures from Britain as the first nation comprehensively to industrialise, population almost doubled from 1861 to 1911, with over 80 per cent of it now concentrated in urban areas. This expansion was possible because of the improved efficiency of moving grain and other agricultural products by sea. Export of livestock, especially from North America, benefited particularly from the arrival of steam, reducing voyage times to Europe and making delivery times predictable. Movement of meat to Europe from distant producing countries, for instance Argentina, Uruguay, Australia and New Zealand, was feasible only when steam ships made it possible to employ refrigeration machinery. The effect on the producing countries was profound, as previously the only products from livestock production they were able to export were wool, treated hides and bone.

More efficient sea transport opened up quarrying of coal and metallic ores remote from industrialised countries where it was processed. Chapter 9 of the current work refers to the development of iron ore carriers, working, for instance, between the west coast of South America and steel works on the eastern seaboard of the United States, and from Norway and Sweden to Germany, the Netherlands and the United Kingdom. Iron ore from Spain was a staple of tramp ships, and the increasing efficiency of these ships led to an inexorable decline in British ore production.[11] A more recent example is the

---

[10]   In practice, shipbuilding tended to be concentrated close to iron and steel works, for instance on the Tyne, Wear and Clyde and at Barrow-in-Furness. The remoteness of the Thames from sources of iron and coal has been cited as one reason for the drastic decline in the late nineteenth century of local shipbuilding, which was once a world leader in producing sophisticated iron steam ships. See, for instance, A.J. Arnold, *Iron Shipbuilding on the Thames, 1832–1915: An Economic and Business History* (Aldershot, 2000), 151. The British yards most remote from centres of iron production were those of Workman, Clark and Harland and Wolff in Belfast, but these survived through cheap sea carriage of iron and steel from the west of Scotland, the Tyne and Tees. M. Moss and J.R. Hume, *Shipbuilders to the World: 125 Years of Harland and Wolff, Belfast, 1861–1986* (Belfast, 1986).

[11]   Once exploiting one of the richest deposits of haematite in the United Kingdom, the mines of what is now Cumbria declined slowly as a result of competition from imported

employment of the world's largest dry bulk carriers, the 'Valemax' type, which can each carry 400,000 tons of Brazilian iron ore to the steel mills of China or Europe.

IV

The development of steam bulk carrying was a major factor in facilitating industrialisation, particularly during the last quarter of the long nineteenth century, and this had far-reaching effects on society. Most notably, in the United Kingdom it helped drive the move from rural-based, agrarian and local industries to largely factory-based employment, and the associated urbanisation as labour moved to growing industrial towns. The increasing reach and efficiency of sea transportation of raw materials and manufactured goods was a factor in continuing this trend. The twentieth century saw the spread of the industrialisation pioneered in Europe and the United States, most dramatically to Japan, the USSR, India, South Korea and China.

Although the term globalisation is of recent coinage, the trend it refers to can be traced at least as far back as the industrial revolution. Factory-based production, with increasing mechanisation through the harnessing of water and later steam power, achieved such economies that manufacturing became concentrated on a small number of regions. At first these were predominantly within the United Kingdom, but they spread, first to the United States and later to Germany.[12] Exporting a large range of products, from textiles and crockery to railway locomotives and ships themselves, had a deleterious and sometimes disastrous effect on relatively primitive local industries in the receiving countries. Is it cynical to suggest that globalisation only became an issue in western countries during the latter quarter of the twentieth century when a massive reversal saw manufacturing undergoing a shift to the Far East, and especially to Japan, South Korea and mainland China? Shipping played its part in this, with containerisation lowering transportation costs for manufactured items, while the growing size of bulk carriers had a similar effect on raw materials for the eastern industries and foodstuffs for their growing populations.

Spanish ore. See, for instance, A. Harris, *Cumberland Iron: The Story of Hodbarrow Mine, 1855–1968* (Truro, 1970), 82.

[12] Mathias suggests the concept of an industrial revolution 'implies the onset of a fundamental change in the structure of an economy, a fundamental redeployment of resources away from agriculture'. P. Mathias, *The First Industrial Nation: An Economic History of Britain, 1700–1914*, 2nd ed. (London, 1983), 2. Although Mathias's subtitle suggests that the industrial revolution started in Great Britain in 1700, he points to earlier examples, such as the urbanisation of brewing in London during the seventeenth century.

V

Until recently, the environmental effects of sea transportation have caused little concern outside organisations which campaign on environmental issues. The focus on climate change and other 'green' issues has altered this, and the shipping industry has, belatedly, been forced to respond, or perhaps more accurately to begin to think about responding.

Oil fuels used in ships have typically had a relatively high sulphur content, which result in the exhaust containing significant levels of sulphur oxides, which are harmful to human populations and have other environmental effects such as causing acid rain. A first and rather limited step has been to insist that ships burn fuel with a low sulphur content, although this applies only to certain Emission Control Areas, including the coasts of western Europe. The International Maritime Organization has published a protocol on the subject, but like all of its initiatives this requires adoption by individual member states, which is often a slow process.[13] As low-sulphur marine gas oils are considerably more expensive to produce than high-sulphur heavy fuel oils, scrubbing systems have been developed to allow the use of the latter to continue. The systems use a water stream to dissolve the sulphur oxides in exhaust emissions, which are either discharged into the sea or stored for on-shore disposal.

Although shipping is statistically the least damaging form of transport in terms of carbon dioxide produced when the value of the products carried are considered, the sheer volume of world shipping means that its total output is significant. If targets to reduce global warming are to be met, shipping has to cut its carbon output by half before 2050. The shipping industry may well answer that the figure for carbon dioxide output would be even higher without the larger ships which have been developed since the Second World War, with the economies in fuel consumption they offer, plus the efforts of marine engineers and naval architects to increase the efficiency of their machinery and hull forms. However, the options for further responses, including replacement of the marine oil engine, are few.

Nuclear power for commercial cargo-carrying ships has not achieved commercial success as the power plants present problems of maintenance, refuelling and disposal of radioactive waste. Moreover, any potential growth in this type of ship has been unwelcome or barred in many ports because of the catastrophic effect of a malfunction in their power plants. The US-built cargo/passenger *Savannah* of 1962 was essentially experimental and proved too small for commercial viability. It became a museum ship after its reactor had been

---

[13]   International Maritime Organization's MARPOL Protocol, Annex VI defines high sulphur content fuels are those containing more than 3.5 per cent sulphur and requires these to be replaced by fuels containing less than 0.5 per cent sulphur. https://imo.org/en/ourwork/environment/pages/air-pollution.aspx.

removed.[14] The German ore carrier *Otto Hahn* of 1968 operated successfully until 1983, when its nuclear reactor was replaced by an oil engine. It was scrapped in 2009.[15] The Japanese *Mutsu* built in 1972 sailed for just 83,000 miles on trials and encountered technical and politico-legal problems. Its reactor was removed in 1992.[16] The only nuclear cargo ship operating commercially in 2022 is the Russian lighter carrier *Sevmorput* of 1988, used on the northern sea route between Russian ports in Europe and Asia.[17] Although nuclear power has been used in naval vessels, especially submarines and aircraft carriers, in civilian ships its main use has been in Russian icebreakers, largely built in Finland.

Use of liquefied natural gas (LNG) in place of oil fuel is a means of partially reducing carbon emissions. LNG is largely methane, CH_4, whereas other hydrocarbon fuels consist of a mixture of heavier hydrocarbons, containing more carbon atoms per molecule. Energy is released when the bonds between the atoms are broken, and because methane has just one carbon to four hydrogen atoms, less carbon dioxide is emitted than when higher hydrocarbons are burnt. Carbon capture is also a possibility for reducing carbon dioxide emissions, and although the technology is being energetically developed, practical applications are currently lacking. Reduction in the carbon dioxide emissions of shipping is likely to come not from some significant breakthrough but by small but incremental gains.

A further environmental concern about shipping is the carriage of non-endemic plants or animal species in ballast tanks. Bulk carriers, and to a lesser extent other classes of ship, carry large amounts of water ballast on up to half their voyages. Taking on ballast in one part of the world and discharging it in another has been blamed for introducing damaging organisms to new environments. Under protocols of the International Maritime Organization, ballast water management systems are being made mandatory. These require ballast water to be exchanged in mid-ocean, or active management of the water to kill any organisms present.[18]

VI

Shipping has had far-reaching effects on industry, agriculture and society itself. It helped propel industrialisation and urbanisation and has encouraged crop cultivation in areas well removed from consumers. By radically reducing transportation costs it has been a significant factor in globalisation, for good

---

[14]   See https://maritime.dot.gov/ships/nssavannah.

[15]   See https://maritime.ihs.com/ships/details/index/6416770.

[16]   See https://jaif.or.jp/en/nuclear-power-ship-designated-as-special-ship-heritage.

[17]   See https://maritime.ihs.com/ships/details/index/8729810.

[18]   See, for instance, https://classnu.com/server/w/?classnu35.

and for ill. Bulk and container shipping in particular have become so vital to the world economy that it is almost impossible to envisage their importance shrinking, let alone them ceasing altogether.[19] To achieve the desired 50 per cent reduction in shipping's carbon emissions, enormous advances will have to be made in harnessing wind, tidal or solar power to drive ships, or in overcoming the powerful objections on safety and environmental grounds to using nuclear energy.

---

[19]   Noting that from 1880 to 2000 the average size of a ship grew from 500 gross tons to 11,400 tons, Kaukiainen remarks that 'it is difficult to conceive how modern commodity flows could be handled by relying on nineteenth-century shipping technology'. Kaukiainen, 'Growth, Diversification and Globalization', 50, 54.

Chapter Twelve

Black freighters: Lines of development

Drawing on the evidence presented in the foregoing chapters, it is possible to chart a line which over 170 years directly connects the *John Bowes* of 1852 with the giant Valemax ore carriers of today. A closely parallel line can also be drawn between the small steam coasters which emerged from the Clyde in the 1870s and today's coastal bulk carriers.

The concept of an economical, steam-powered coal carrier germinated in Great Britain in the 1840s. It was after several inconclusive experiments that it flowered, although not quite fully, in the screw collier *John Bowes*. With its steam engine, iron hull, wide hatches and clear holds, it required only refinement of its water ballast arrangements – specifically the fitting of tanks into a double bottom – to become the prototype of the powered bulk carrier. The screw collier's ability to fulfil the demanding delivery requirements of coal for the London gas industry, while enabling the collieries to secure large contracts, meant it was developed and multiplied so quickly that in under a decade 75 had been built.

External events demonstrated that the screw collier had potential well beyond the British east coast coal trade. The War Office's logistical inabilities were demonstrated in the Crimea, and screw colliers were amongst a fleet of steamers urgently requisitioned to carry supplies. That these craft were quite capable of steaming to the Black Sea was not lost on their owners and others. The screw colliers themselves began to be employed on longer routes, especially to the Baltic and Mediterranean. Joint stock companies were set up to own and run them, the General Iron Screw Collier Co. Ltd and various iterations of the London Steam Navigation Co. Ltd. However, despite the ambition of these companies and their impressive ability to raise capital, the most successful operators of bulk-carrying steamers proved to be individual investors. Mostly based in London or north-east England, many had themselves some interest or experience in the coal trade, as colliery owners, merchants, coal factors or ship brokers, and had the necessary ship management skills. Some of the better-known and long-lived British tramp shipping companies began in this way in the 1860s.

The transition of the screw collier into the ocean-going steam tramp was helped significantly by technological developments which increased a steamer's range and economy. Most significant were those which made the steam engine more efficient and reliable. Improvements in boiler design and construction methods were fundamental and succeeded in producing steam at considerably higher pressures. To employ this steam efficiently, compound engines were developed which allowed the steam to expand in two stages. Advances in practices and equipment in shipbuilding and in naval architecture also facilitated the growth and multiplication of both screw collier and steam tramp. The earliest examples of the latter were slightly larger than contemporary colliers (this was more apparent in tonnage than in overall dimensions), but hull forms were quite similar, with the engines-amidships configuration being overwhelmingly adopted for tramps and larger colliers. The logical development of compounding, three-stage expansion of steam, together with a doubling of cargo capacity, produced by 1890 a steam tramp, which, largely built and owned in Great Britain, captured much of the bulk-carrying trades from sailing vessels. The triple-expansion engine with its Scotch boilers would serve the collier and tramp for the next half-century.

The development of the steam coaster owes much to the pioneering work on screw colliers, but its evolvement was less direct. For two decades after the *John Bowes* was built, steam penetration of coastal and short-sea bulk trades other than carrying coal from the Tyne and Wear to London was not significant. Both the cargoes and the ports used tended to be small, and trades continued to be served by sailing coasters which were numerous and cheap. Vessels similar to the screw colliers of the 1850s and 1860s were unnecessarily large and expensive, but the potential of steam power was recognised. With progressive developments in the technology and construction of boilers and machinery, a smaller version of the screw collier emerged in the 1870s, appropriate in size for the cargoes offering, but with a compact and economical steam engine. Most of these steam coasters were originally the products of small western Scottish shipyards, notably those around Paisley, building for shipowners already experienced in the coastal trades. Little if any direct part in this development was owed to the builders and owners of screw colliers, but the obvious success of the latter, which was well covered in the technical press, stimulated the adoption of the same technological solutions, including the capacity for carrying water ballast. Scottish yards continued to supply most steam coasters, just as yards in the north-east of England which pioneered screw colliers moved on to become the major builders of steam tramps. The steam coaster underwent improvements in efficiency and economy, parallel to those of larger steamers, and by 1890 it was being built in considerable numbers and a variety of sizes which enabled it to dominate most coastal and short-sea bulk trades.

Until the end of the nineteenth century, steam colliers, tramps and coasters alike were very much the province of British builders and owners. The former had become suppliers of these steamers to the world, the latter were active in almost every bulk trade worldwide. Slowly, this dominance faded. It was not British but continental European engineers who largely developed and applied the marine oil engine. Oil-engined tramps appeared gradually, the First World War both inhibiting the adoption of oil engine in merchant ships, while also stimulating refinements in this machinery for naval vessels that enabled it to challenge the steam engine in the 1920s. British owners were still the major players in tramp shipping, ocean and coastal, but the impetus for developing the marine oil engines passed to Danish, Dutch, German and Swiss engineers. In Britain, only Doxford produced an oil engine that made an impact internationally, the many other British marine engineering companies contenting themselves with licensing and perhaps tweaking overseas designs.

Outside of the engine room, the motor tramp of 1926 did not differ greatly from its steam contemporary: they were comparable in overall size both dimensionally and in tonnage. But increasingly the economic advantage lay with the motor tramp, in terms of more thermally efficient machinery and the additional cargo space made available as coal bunkers no longer needed to occupy the most useful hull space for cargo. The elimination of firemen helped reduce crew size, although recruitment of suitably skilled engineers continued to be an issue, cited by less innovative owners as one reason for clinging to steam.

The depression of the late 1920s and 1930s hit tramp shipping hard but had the effect of stimulating the shipbuilding and marine engineering industries to refine their products and fight to remain competitive. Developments like the opposed-piston oil engine and the 'reheater' steam engine maintained some balance between the attractions of the steam and the motor tramp. However, as the price of oil fuel dropped compared with that of coal, the economic advantages of the motor tramp became undeniable. The Second World War helped to postpone the change: the urgent requirement of the Allies to replace lost tonnage outweighed technical and economic considerations, so that building of steam tonnage greatly predominated. However, it proved the swansong of the steam bulk carrier, and the 1950s saw the last of them built for coastal and ocean trading.

The motor tramp did not remain unchallenged for long. The decade which saw it reach dominance also witnessed the emergence of the bulk carrier as a competitor. In technical terms, the bulk carrier differed essentially only in size. The features which had proved so successful in the screw collier – large holds and hatches, and a capacity for water ballast – were perpetuated, although both underwent refinement and growth. The term 'bulk carrier' was defined to mean a single-deck vessel, with engines aft. Many tramps had been built with a single deck, and aft had been a convenient place to put engines since the earliest screw colliers. Some specialisation ensued, seeing the multiplication and growth in size of the ore carrier, a type which had been built in small numbers for at least half a century. There was a relatively short-lived fashion for building combination carriers suitable for both oil and ore cargoes, but their additional costs proved a major disadvantage. Timber, wood chip, cement carriers and self-unloaders have been built in small numbers, but the majority of bulk carriers share with their steam and motor tramp predecessors the ability to carry almost any dry bulk cargo. The main differentiating factor is size, and the range of dimensions and capacities amongst bulk carriers is far larger than it was with tramps. Indeed, they are labelled with an indicator of size, from Handysize, through Panamax and Capesize to Valemax, defining the trades, ports or waterways to which they are suited. Up in size to Panamax, cargo gear is usually fitted, as it was in tramps, although deck cranes have replaced derricks. For the larger vessels, cargo gear is omitted, as these vessels – mainly ore carriers – tend to be built for long-term employment between terminals with shoreside loading and unloading facilities. Although engines are more powerful, even more economical in fuel consumption, and do not need continuous manning, in fundamental principle they have not changed since the demise of the motor tramp. The slow speed oil engine which directly turns the propellor, invariably turbocharged, is still typically a two-stroke with solid fuel injection.

The line of development of the coastal bulk carrier has proceeded in parallel with that of larger craft. The steam coaster gave way to the motor coaster during the 1920s and 1930s, grew in size, and usually shed its cargo gear. Mechanical hatch covers were fitted, radar grudgingly funded by its owner, and holds became more capacious and easier to clean between cargoes. Most notably, crew size was drastically cut. The modern motor coaster is now simply the small brother of the ocean-going bulk carrier.

The significance of steam and motor tramps and their successor the bulk carrier cannot be overstated. The introduction of steam changed shipping profoundly, from the owner's office to the bridge and engine room, new skills were needed, new specialities and new professions conceived. Shipbuilding underwent fundamental changes and marine engineering was born. The effects spread wider, with the size, cost and timeliness of deliveries allowing industry and agriculture to expand. Industrialisation gained momentum, and agriculture became more mechanised and dependent on man-made fertilisers. Changes in the structure of employment followed, and with it the consequent shift of populations to industrial areas. Bulk shipping, along with the parallel development of containerisation, has been a major driver of globalisation, with the cost of transporting a commodity or product no longer a significant factor in where it is mined, quarried, manufactured or grown.

All this, for good or ill, was facilitated by the development of the powered bulk carrier, from its beginnings with the screw colliers built on the Tyne and elsewhere, through the steam and motor tramp which for the best part of a century efficiently moved coal, grain, ores, fertilisers and timber round the world, through to the efficient bulk carriers of today. Black freighters have undoubtedly contributed to changing the world.

Select Bibliography

Books

Adams, T.A. and Smith, J.R. *The Royal Fleet Auxiliary: A Century of Service* (London, 2005).

Anon. *Merchant Ships: British Built* (Southampton, 1954).

Anon. *Merchant Ships: World Built*, vol. 9 (Southampton, 1961).

Anon. *Two Hundred and Fifty Years of Shipbuilding by the Scotts at Greenock* (Glasgow, 1961).

Anon. *Wm. France, Fenwick and Company Limited* (London, 1954).

Appleyard, H.S. *Bank Line, 1885–1985* (Kendal, 1985).

Armstrong, J. 'Climax and Climacteric: The British Coastal Trade, 1870–1930', in D.J. Starkey and A.G. Jamieson (eds), *Exploiting the Sea: Aspects of Britain's Maritime Economy since 1870* (Exeter, 1998).

———. 'British Coastal Shipping: A Research Agenda for the European Perspective', in J. Armstrong and A. Kunz, *Coastal Shipping and the European Economy, 1750–1980* (Mainz, 2002).

Armstrong, J. and Bagwell, P.S. 'Coastal Shipping', in D.H. Aldcroft and M.J. Freeman (eds), *Transport in the Industrial Revolution* (Manchester, 1983).

Arnold, A.J. *Iron Shipbuilding on the Thames, 1832–1915: An Economic and Business History* (Aldershot, 2000).

Atkinson, G. *J. and A. Gardner and Co. Ltd: Shipowners and Quarrymen* (Portishead, 2002).

———. *Hudson Steamship* (Portishead, 2004).

Bakka, Jr., D. *Langs kysten i femti år: kystfart og fraktenæring, 1946–1996* (Bergen, 1996).

Bowman, A.J. *Kirkintilloch Shipbuilding* (Kirkintilloch, 1983).

Broeze, F. *The Globalization of the Oceans: Containerisation from the 1950s to the Present* (Liverpool, 2002).

Burrows, G.W. *Puffer Ahoy!* (Glasgow, 1981).

Capper, C. *The Port and Trade of London* (London, 1862).

Carter, C.J.M. *Stephenson Clarke* (Kendal, 1981).

Cheetham, C. and Heinimann, M. *Modern River Sea Traders* (London, 1996).

Chesterton, D.R. and Fenton, R.S. *Gas and Electricity Colliers* (Kendal, 1984).

Clarke, J.F. *Building Ships on the North East Coast: Part 1, c.1640–1914* (Whitley Bay, 1997).

——. *Building Ships on the North East Coast: Part 2, c.1914–c.1980* (Whitley Bay, 1997).

Cooper, M. *J. and C. Harrison: The History of a Family Shipping Venture* (Preston, 2012).

——. *The Ocean Class of the Second World War* (Barnsley, 2022).

Corlett, E.C.B. *The Iron Ship* (London, 1990).

——. 'The Screw Propeller and Merchant Shipping, 1840–1865', in B. Greenhill (ed.), *The Advent of Steam: The Merchant Steamship before 1900* (London, 1993).

Cox, S. and Georgandis, D. *Brief Introduction to Cement Carriers*. www.how erobinson.com/wp-content/uploads/2017/11/Intro-to-Cement-Carriers-2017.pdf.

Craig, R. 'Aspects of Tramp Shipping and Ownership', in K. Matthews and G. Panting (eds), *Ships and Shipbuilding in the North Atlantic Region* (St. John's, Newfoundland, 1978).

——. *The Ship: Steam Tramps and Cargo Liners, 1850–1950* (London, 1980).

——. *British Tramp Shipping, 1750–1914* (St. John's, Newfoundland, 2003).

Dear, I. *The Ropner Story* (London, 1986).

Elphick, P. *Liberty: The Ships That Won the War* (London, 2001).

Emmerson, G.T. *John Scott Russell: A Great Victorian Engineer and Naval Architect* (London, 1977).

Everard, S. *The History of the Gas Light and Coke Company, 1812–1949* (London, 1949).

Falkus, M. *The Blue Funnel Legend* (London, 1990).

Farr, G. *Shipbuilding in Devon* (NMM Monograph No. 22) (Greenwich, 1976).

Fayle, C.E. *Seaborne Trade*, 3 vols. (London, 1921–3).

Fenton, R.S. *Monroe Brothers, Shipowners* (Kendal, 1982).

——. *Cambrian Coasters*: *The Steam and Motor Coasters of Mid and North Wales* (Kendal, 1989).

——. 'Coastal and Short-Sea Shipping', in R. Gardiner, *The Golden Age of Shipping: The Classic Merchant Ship, 1900–1960* (London, 1994), 81–96.

——. *Mersey Rovers* (Gravesend, 1997).

——. *Coasters: An Illustrated History* (Barnsley, 2011).

——. *Tramp Ships: An Illustrated History* (Barnsley, 2013).

Fenton, R.S. and Patterson, S. 'Joseph Fisher and Sons', in R.S. Fenton and J. Clarkson, *British Shipping Fleets* (Preston, 2000).

Fenton, R.S. and Robertson, P. *William Robertson and the Gem Line* (Preston, 2009).

Finch, R. *Coals from Newcastle* (Lavenham, 1973).

Garrett, K.S. *Everards of Greenhithe*, 2nd ed. (Windsor, 2017).

Gray, L. *The Ropner Fleet, 1874–1974* (Kendal, 1975).

Gray, L. and Lingwood, J. *The Doxford Turret Ships* (Kendal, 1975).

Greenhill, B. (ed.) *The Advent of Steam: The Merchant Steamship before 1900* (London, 1993).

——. 'Steam before the Screw', in B. Greenhill (ed.), *The Advent of Steam: The Merchant Steamship before 1900* (London, 1993), 11–27.

Greenlaw, J. *The Swansea Copper Barques and Cape Horners* (Swansea, 1999).

Griffiths, D. *Steam at Sea: Two Centuries of Steam-Powered Ships* (London, 1997).

——. 'Triple Expansion and the First Shipping Revolution', in B. Greenhill (ed.), *The Advent of Steam: The Merchant Steamship before 1900* (London, 1993), 106–26.

Griffiths, D., Lambert, A. and Walker, F. *Brunel's Ships* (London, 1999).

Hardy, A.C. *History of Motorshipping* (London, 1955).

Harley, C.K. 'The Shift from Sailing Ships to Steamships, 1850–1890: A Study in Technological Change and Its Diffusion', in D.N. McCloskey, *Essays on a Mature Economy: Britain after 1840* (London, 1971).

Harris, A. *Cumberland Iron: The Story of Hodbarrow Mine, 1855–1968* (Truro, 1970).

Harvey, W.J. *The T.I.D. Tugs of World War Two* (Windsor, 2019).

Haws, D. *Merchant Fleets 6: Blue Funnel Line* (London, 1984).

Heaton, P.M. *The Reardon Smith Line: The History of a South Wales Shipping Venture* (Newport, 1984).

Hogg, P. and Appleyard, A. *The Pyman Story* (Hartlepool, 2000).

Hope, R. *A New History of British Shipping* (London, 1990).

Huckett, A. *Rowbotham* (Gravesend, 2002).

Jackson, G. *The History and Archaeology of Ports* (Tadworth, 1983).

Jaffee, W.W. *The Liberty Ships from A to Z* (Palo Alto, CA, 2004).

Jarvis, A. 'Alfred Holt and the Compound Engine', in B. Greenhill (ed.), *The Advent of Steam: The Merchant Steamship before 1900* (London, 1993).

Jenkins, D. *Owen and Watkin Williams of Cardiff: The Golden Cross Line* (Kendal, 1991).

——. *From Ship's Cook to Baronet: Sir William Reardon Smith's Life in Shipping, 1856–1935* (Cardiff, 2011).

——. *Graig: One Hundred Years in Shipping* (Preston, 2019).

Jenkins, J.G. and Jenkins, D. *Cardiff Shipowners* (Cardiff, 1986).

Johnman, L. and Murphy, H. *British Shipbuilding and the State since 1918: A Political Economy of Decline* (Exeter, 2002).

Kaukiainen, Y. 'Growth, Diversification and Globalization: Main Trends in International Shipping since 1850', in L.R. Fischer and E. Lange, *International Merchant Shipping in the Nineteenth and Twentieth Centuries: The Comparative Dimension* (St. John's, Newfoundland, 2008).

Kennedy, J. *The History of Steam Navigation* (Liverpool, 1904).

Kennedy, N.W. *Records of Early British Steamships* (Liverpool, 1933).

Kirkcaldy, A.W. *British Shipping: Its History, Organisation and Importance* (London, 1914).

Lane, T. (ed.) *Grey Dawn Breaking: British Merchant Seafarers in the Late Twentieth Century* (Manchester, 1986).

Levinson, M. *The Box: How the Shipping Container Made the World Smaller and the World Economy Bigger* (Princeton, NJ, 2008).

Lindsay, J. *A History of the North Wales Slate Industry* (Newton Abbot, 1974).

Lingwood, J. *Chapman of Newcastle* (Kendal, 1985).

——. *SD14: The Full Story* (Preston, 2004).

McAlister, A.A. and Gray, L. *H. Hogarth and Sons Limited* (Kendal, 1976).

McDonald, D. *The Clyde Puffer* (Newton Abbott, 1977).

Macrae, J.A. and Waine, C.V. *The Steam Collier Fleets* (Albrighton, 1990).

Mallett, A.S. *Idyll of the Kings: The History of King Line, 1889–1978* (Kendal, 1980).

Mathias, P. *The First Industrial Nation: An Economic History of Britain, 1700–1914*, 2nd ed. (London, 1983).

Metaxas, B.N. *The Economics of Tramp Shipping* (London, 1971).

Middlemiss, N.L. *Travels of the Tramps: Twenty Tramp Fleets* (Newcastle-upon-Tyne, 1989).

———. *The Anglo-Saxon/Shell Tankers* (Newcastle-upon-Tyne, 1990).

———. *British Shipbuilding Yards*, vol. 1, *North East Coast* (Newcastle-upon-Tyne, 1993).

———. *Black Diamond Fleets* (Gateshead, 2000).

Minchinton, W.E. *Industrial South Wales, 1750–1940: Essays in Welsh Economic History* (London, 1969).

Mitchell, W.H. and Sawyer, L.A. *The Oceans, the Forts and the Parks* (Liverpool, 1966).

———. *British Standard Ships of World War 1* (Liverpool, 1968).

———. *The Liberty Ships*, 2nd ed. (London, 1985).

———. *The Empire Ships*, 2nd ed. (London, 1990).

Murphy, H. 'Labour in the British Shipbuilding and Ship Repairing Industries in the Twentieth Century: An Overview', in R. Varela, H. Murphy and M. van der Linden, *Shipbuilding and Ship Repair Workers around the World: Case Studies, 1950–2010* (Amsterdam, 2017), 47–116.

Newman, B. *Plate and Section Working Machinery in British Shipbuilding, 1850–1945* (Glasgow, 1993).

———. *Materials Handling in British Shipbuilding, 1850–1945* (Glasgow, 1996).

O'Donoghue, K.J. and Appleyard, H.S. *Hain of St Ives* (Kendall, 1986).

O'Hara, G.C. *Ironfighters, Outfitters and Bowler Hatters* (Prestwick, 1997).

Orbell, J. *From Cape to Cape: The History of Lyle Shipping* (Edinburgh, 1978).

Palmer, C.M. 'On the Construction of Iron Ships and the Progress of Iron Shipbuilding on the Tyne, Wear and Tees', *Report of the Thirty-Third Meeting of the British Association for the Advancement of Science 1863* (London, 1864), 694–701.

Palmer, S. 'Experience, Experiment and Economics: Factors in the Construction of Early Merchant Steamships', in K. Matthews and G. Panting (eds), *Ships and Shipbuilding in the North Atlantic Region* (St. John's, Newfoundland, 1978).

———. 'British Shipping from the Late Nineteenth Century to the Present', in L.R. Fischer and E. Lange, *International Merchant Shipping in the Nineteenth and Twentieth Centuries: The Comparative Dimension* (St. John's, Newfoundland, 2008), 133–4.

Parkinson, J.R. *The Economics of Shipbuilding in the United Kingdom* (Cambridge, 1960).

Paterson, L., *The Light in the Glens: The Rise and Fall of the Puffer Trade* (Colonsay, 1996).

Pedroche, B. *London's Lost Power Stations and Gasworks* (Stroud, 2013).

Pollard, S. and Robertson, P. *The British Shipbuilding Industry, 1870–1914* (Cambridge, MA, 1979).

Pope, R. *Atlas of British Social and Economic History since c.1700* (London, 1989).

Quartermaine, P.N. *Metcalf Motor Coasters Limited* (Kendal, 1965).

Robins, N. *Birds of the Sea: 150 Years of the General Steam Navigation Company* (Portishead, 2007).

Rowland, K.T. *Steam at Sea: A History of Steam Navigation* (Newton Abbot, 1970).

Salmon, A. *A Sideways Launch* (Rainham, 1992).

Scott, J.R. *An Epitome of the Progress of the Trade in Coal to London since 1755* (London, 1869).

Slaven, A. 'The Shipbuilding Industry', in R. Church, *The Dynamics of Victorian Business* (London, 1980).

Slaven, A. and Murphy, H. (eds) *Crossing the Bar: An Oral History of the British Shipbuilding, Ship Repairing and Marine Engine-Building Industries in the Age of Decline, 1956–1990* (St. John's, Newfoundland, 2013).

Smith, R. *Sea-coal for London: History of the Coal Factors in the London Market* (London, 1961).

Sothern, J.W.M. *Marine Diesel Oil Engines*, vol. 1, 7th ed. (Glasgow, 1944).

Stanier, P. *Quarries of England and Wales: An Historic Photographic Record* (Truro, 1995).

Starke, T. and Schell, W. *Register of Merchant Ships* (Gravesend, 2011). (Individual volumes cover completions in every year from 1870 to 1970.)

Starkey, D.J. 'Industrial Background to the Development of the Steamship', in B. Greenhill (ed.), *The Advent of Steam: The Merchant Steamship before 1900* (London, 1993).

Sturmey, S.G. *British Shipping and World Competition* (St. John's, Newfoundland, 2010).

Tenold, S. 'Norwegian Shipping in the Twentieth Century', in L.R. Fischer and E. Lange, *International Merchant Shipping in the Nineteenth and Twentieth Centuries: The Comparative Dimension* (St. John's, Newfoundland, 2008).

Thomas, P.N. *British Ocean Tramps*, vol. 1, *Builders and Cargoes* (Wolverhampton, 1992).

——. *British Ocean Tramps*, vol. 2, *Owners and Their Ships* (Albrighton, 1992).

Tolerton, N. *Bulk Carriers: The Ocean Cinderellas* (Christchurch, NZ, 2005).

Ville, S. ed. *Shipbuilding in the United Kingdom in the Nineteenth Century: A Regional Approach* (St. John's, Newfoundland, 1993).

Waine, C.V. *British Motor Coasters* (Lydney, 2018).

Waine, C.V. and Fenton, R.S., *Steam Coasters and Short Sea Traders*, 3rd ed. (Albrighton, 1994).

Walker, F.M. *Song of the Clyde: A History of Clyde Shipbuilding* (Cambridge, 1984).

Watson, N. *The Bibby Line, 1807–1990* (London, 1990).

——. *Lloyd's Register: 250 Years of Service* (London, 2010).

Winser, J. de S. *BEF Ships: Before, at and after Dunkirk* (Gravesend, 1999).

Annual publications, various years

Lloyd's Confidential Index (London).
Lloyd's Register (London).
Mercantile Navy List (London).

Journals

Mitchell's Steam-Shipping Journal (August 1859–69).

Journal articles

Anon. 'The Clearpool', *Shipbuilding and Shipping Record* (30 January 1936), 124–8.

Allen, E.E. 'On the Comparative Cost of Transit by Steam and Sailing Colliers, and on the Different Methods of Ballasting', *Proceedings of the Institute of Civil Engineers*, 14 (1854–5), 318–73.

Appleyard, H.S. 'Ropner Trunk Deck Steamers, Part 1', *Ships in Focus Record*, 2 (1997), 82–91.

——. 'Ropner Trunk Deck Steamers, Part 2', *Ships in Focus Record*, 3 (1997), 154–9.

Bowen, F.C. (writing as FCB), 'Ships That Made History 5, the *John Bowes*', *Shipbuilding and Shipping Record* (30 September 1937), 421–2.

Bruce, J.G. 'The Contribution of Cross-Channel and Coastal Vessels to Developments in Marine Practice', *Journal of Transport History*, 4, no. 2 (1959), 65–80.

Coates, J. and Waymouth, B. 'The Change from Wood to Steel Ships', *Transactions of the Newcomen Society*, 71 (1999–2000), 257–68.

Dyer, H. 'The First Century of the Marine Engine', *Transactions of the Institute of Naval Architects*, 30 (1889), 87.

Fenton, R.S. 'Swedish Trunks', *Ships in Focus Record*, 5 (1998), 48–53.

——. 'The Clyde Puffer', *Archive*, 30 (2001), 49–64.

——. 'The PLM Colliers 1 to 10', *Ships in Focus Record*, 17 (2001), 10–15.

——. 'The PLM Colliers 12 to 27', *Ships in Focus Record*, 18 (2001), 68–73.

——. 'The Innis Boats: A Reappraisal', *Ships in Focus Record*, 26 (2003), 86–98.

——. 'Doxford and the Economies', *Ships Monthly* (June 2012), 28–31.

——. 'Tate and Lyle Ltd', *Marine News Supplement* (October 2016), S198–S214.

——. 'Ard Coasters', *Ships in Focus Record*, 64 (2018), 2–14.

Fenton, R.S. and Guegan, M. 'Hansen Shipbuilding, Bideford', *Ships in Focus Record*, 14 (2000), 75–81.

——. 'Hansen Shipbuilding, Bideford', *Ships in Focus Record*, 15 (2001), 158–63.

Fenton, R.S. and Harvey, W. 'Rea Colliers', *Ships in Focus Record*, 63 (2016), 138–46.

Fenton, R.S. and others, 'The Arch Deck Steamers', *Ships in Focus Record*, 29 (2004), 28–33.

——. 'The Arch Deck Steamers', *Ships in Focus Record*, 30 (2005), 92–104.

Harlaftis, G. and Thompson, J. 'European Family Firms in International Business: British and Greek Tramp Shipping Firms', *Business History*, 46, no. 2 (2004), 220–7.

Harrison, J. 'The Iron Ladies, Part 1', *Ships in Focus Record*, 23 (2003).

——. 'The Iron Ladies, Part 2', *Ships in Focus Record*, 24 (2004).

Hodgson, G.B. 'The Genesis of the Screw Collier', *Nautical Magazine*, 70 (1901), 176.

Huckett, A. 'Empire F Dry Cargo Coasters, Part 1', *Marine News Supplement* (June 2019), S213–S225.

——. 'Empire F Dry Cargo Coasters, Part 2', *Marine News Supplement* (July 2019), S247–S259.

Jansson, J.O. and Shneerson, D. 'Economies of Scale in General Cargo Ships', *Review of Economics and Statistics*, 60 (1987), 287–93.

Johnman, L. and Murphy, H. 'An Overview of the Economic and Social Effects of the Interwar Depression on Clydeside Shipbuilding Communities', *International Journal of Maritime History*, 18, no. 1 (2006), 227–54.

Knauerhaus, R. 'The Compound Steam Engine and Productivity Changes in the German Merchant Fleet, 1871–1887', *Journal of Economic History*, 27 (1968).

Martin, S.B. and McCord, N. 'The Steamship Bedlington, 1841–54', *Maritime History*, 1, no. 1 (1971), 46–72.

Maywald, K. 'The Construction Costs and the Value of the British Merchant Fleet, 1850–1938', *Scottish Journal of Political Economy*, 3 (February 1956).

Nance, C.T. (writing as 'The Commodore'). 'The Future of Sail', *Sea Breezes*, 50, no. 365 (1975), 296–301.

O'Conalláin, T. 'Dublin Gas Boats', *Ships in Focus Record*, 7 (1998), 146–54.

Robertson, J.C. and Hagan, H.H. 'A Century of Coaster Design and Operation', *Transactions of the Institution of Engineers*, 97 (1954), 204–56.

Seaton, A.E. 'Progress in Marine Engineering in the Mercantile Marine', *Transactions of the Institute of Naval Architects*, 33 (1892), 74–80.

Tinbergen, J. 'Ein Schiffbauzyklus', *Weltwirtschaftliches Archiv*, 34, no. 2 (1931), 152.

Websites

https://classnu.com/server/w/?classnu35.

https://en.wikipedia.org/wiki/valemax.

https://imo.org/en/ourwork/environment/pages/air-pollution.aspx.

https://jaif.or.jp/en/nuclear-power-ship-designated-as-special-ship-heritage.

https://maritime.dot.gov/ships/nssavannah.

https://maritime.ihs.com/ships/details/index.

https://theicct.org/publications/hydrogen-and-propulsion-systems-jan22.

www.bulkshippingguide.com.

www.southampton.ac.uk/~assets/doc/The%20Future%20of%20Batteries%20in%20the%20Marine%20Sector.pdf.

Archives

Guildhall Library, London
Parliamentary Papers
Report of the Select Committee on Thames Conservancy, 1863, Q.4687–954, 3102,
    2127–31; Q.2959
Returns of Registered Steam Vessels of UK
    Jan. 1851, 1851 (196) (310) L.II229, 235
    Jan. 1852, 1852 (219) XLIX.35
    Jan. 1852–4, 1854 (141) LX.219
    Jan. 1855, 1854–5 (473) XLVI.293
    Jan. 1857, 1857 Session 2 (87) XXXIX.61
    Jan. 1858, 1857–8 (488) L.II.83
    Jan. 1859, 1859 Session 2 (26) XXVII.493
Return Relating to the Ships Engaged as Regular Transports, between the 1st of
    January 1855 and the 1st of April 1856, 1856 (345) XLI.341

London Metropolitan Archives
Minutes of the Court of the Chartered Gas Light and Coke Company, B/GLCC 23/1,
    23/2, 24/1, 24/2, 25/1, 25/2, 26/1 26/2, 27/1, 27/2, 28/1, 28/2, 29/1, 29/2, 30/1 and
    30/2 and covering the period 1852–70
Minutes of the Board of the Equitable Gas Light and Coke Company, B/EGLC/8,
    covering the period 1852–8
Minutes of the Imperial Gas Light and Coke Company, B/IMPGLC/20, B/IMPGLC/21
    and B/IMPGLC/30, covering the period 1853–74
Minutes of the Board of the South Metropolitan Gas Light and Coke Company,
    SMET/III/4/1 and 4/2, covering the period 1850–1857
Minutes of the Board of the Wandsworth and Putney Gas Light and Coke Company,
    B/WPGC/III/1, covering the 1850s
Minutes of the Board of the Commercial Gas Company, B/CGC/3, 11/1851 to 3/1855

Mitchell Library, Glasgow
Registry of Shipping and Seamen, closed registers for Glasgow

The National Archives, Kew (TNA)
Closed registers for London, CUST 130
Crew agreements, class BT 98.
Records of Dissolved Companies, class BT 31
Registry of Shipping and Seamen, transcripts and transactions, series IV, closed
    registers
Transactions for the period 1855–89, class BT 109
Transcripts and transactions for the period 1890–1955, class BT 110
Transcripts and transactions received between 1786 and 1854, class BT 107
Transcripts for the period 1855–89, class BT 108

National Archives of Scotland, Edinburgh
Registry of Shipping and Seamen, closed registers for Scottish ports

Science Museum Library, London
John Scott Russell's notebooks, MS 516/1–7

Tyne and Wear Archives, Newcastle-upon-Tyne
Palmer's Letter Book, 1357/7
Registry of Shipping and Seamen, closed registers for Newcastle

World Ship Society, Archive and Library, Chatham Historic Dockyard
Yard Lists compiled by World Ship Society members

Conference papers

Fenton, R.S. 'Was the Steam Coaster a Scottish Invention?' Annual Scottish Maritime History Conference, Glasgow, 2013.
Snaith, G.R. and Buxton, I. 'The Development of the Bulk Carrier', Proceedings of the Conference on Tanker and Bulk Carrier Terminals Held at the Institution of Civil Engineers, 13 November 1969, London.

Theses

Fenton, R.S. 'Transition in the UK Coastal Bulk Trades: 1840 to 1914', PhD thesis, Thames Valley University, 2005.
Harley, C.K. 'Shipbuilding and Shipping in the Late 19th Century: A Study of Technological Change, Its Nature, Diffusion and Impact', PhD thesis, Harvard University, 1972 (copy in Caird Library and Archive, National Maritime Museum, Greenwich).

General Index

Ackroy-Stewart, Herbert (oil engine
    designer) 156n51
Admiralty 122
aft peak tank 78, 92, 95–6, 98, 100,
    109–10, 116, 148, 172–3
air injection 158
Arcform hull 124–5
arch deck steamers 121–2
auxiliary engines 163, 171, 181, 189, 199
auxiliary equipment 150, 152, 196
awning decks 78–9, 113
Ayre, Wilfred (shipbuilder) 122

Ballard, Maxwell (ship designer) 122
ballast *see* water ballast
Bauer-Wach exhaust turbine 128
Bell, William (coal owner) 28
Bessemer converter 83
blast injection 158
Board of Trade 117
Boiler, Scotch 42, 51 126
Boilermakers Society 222
boilers (*see also* steam pressure) 38–54,
    56, 58–60, 75, 78, 94, 108, 111–12,
    120, 126–7, 130–1, 135, 147, 150,
    152, 156, 161–2, 164, 166, 174, 191,
    223, 235
boilers-on-deck steamer 131
bow thrusters 196
Bowes, John and Partners (coal owners)
    30, 34
box holds 192
bridge control of engine 173
British Corporation 112n3

British vs overseas-built steam tramps
    132
Brock, Walter (Denny engineer) 51
Brunel, Isambard K. 42, 43, 57
bulk carrier definition 199, 237
bulk shipping definition 1
bulk trades, introduction of steam xvi
bulkheads 116, 195, 204
Burntisland Economy design 124–5
business cycle in shipping 220

Campbell, G.T.R. (naval architect) 154
Capesize bulk carriers 210
carbon emissions 232–4
Cardiff class bulk carriers 213
cargo gear 21, 51, 105, 110, 115, 138,
    152, 168, 170, 173–4, 178, 189, 193,
    211–12, 216, 219, 226, 228, 233–4,
    241–2, 247, 256
cargo liners 2, 5
cement carriers 215
CHANTS (Channel Tanker) 185
china clay ports 229n6
Christiansen and Meyer engine 131
classification societies 194
Clyde puffers 88, 108–0, 164, 185,
    193n85
Coal Turn Act 24
Coal Whippers' Act 33
coaster, definition xvii
colliers vs tramps 74
combination carriers 213–15
conbulkers 215
concrete hulls 170

condensers 49
containerisation 1–3, 5, 192–3, 215–16, 228, 231, 234
convoys 122
crew facilities 197
Crimean War 22, 25, 32, 63–4, 66, 84, 235
Crinan Canal 108
cylinder numbers 212

deck cranes 193
deep tanks 116
demurrage 24, 28, 31, 33
Diesel, Dr Rudolf (engineer) 136n4, 163
distribution of steam coaster builders 106–7
double bottoms 13, 75, 78, 83–4, 92, 95–6, 98–100, 106, 109–10, 116, 147–8, 173, 194, 212, 235
double hulls 212
double-acting oil engine 158–9
Doxford Economy type 150, 159
Dublin, Ringsend Basin 93, 101n28
Dunkirkmax bulk carriers 211
Dutch coaster designs 171, 180–5

Eastern Counties Railway 25n62
economics of bulk carrying 229
electricity industry (nationalised) 191
Empire Fabric type 185, 188
environmental effects of shipping 232
exhaust turbines 124, 128, 131

finance 217
First World War standards 122–3
flags of convenience 213, 216
forepeak tanks 78, 92, 98–9, 116, 172
Fort and Park type 125
Forth and Clyde Canal 108
Fortune type 155
four-stroke oil engines 157–8, 206, 211, 216
Fox, Samson (and corrugated furnace) 43
Freedom type 154–6

Freedom II type 155
freight rates 24, 26–9, 32–3, 131, 171, 174, 181, 183, 190, 204, 220, 228
Friendship type 155
furnace, corrugated 43, 46

gas industry (nationalised) 191
gas turbines 203
Gebbie, J. Ramsay (Doxford chairman) 150
Gideon-type coaster 182
globalisation 227, 231, 233–4
Goole Proficient type 173, 185
grain 2n4, 4–5, 12, 64, 83–4, 87n3, 101, 117, 118n6, 121, 153, 195, 199–200, 205, 228, 230, 238
Grand Surrey Canal 31
Great Lakes of North America 200
Great Northern Railway 19, 28
Greek shipping 7

Hall, Samuel (and surface condenser) 49
Handymax bulk carriers 210
Handysize bulk carriers 210–11
harbour deck 118, 120
Havers, Arthur (Doxford draughtsman) 118
Hispania type 156
hold ventilation 195
horsepower 149
hot-bulb engine 163–4
Howden, James (and Scotch boiler) 42, 43

Institution of Engineers and Shipbuilders in Scotland 39, 108
Institution of Naval Architects 39
intercooling 195
International Convention on Tonnage Measurement 195
iron hulls xv, 11, 13, 15, 48n49, 57–9, 149, 206, 235
iron ore 14, 64, 83–4, 89, 139, 153, 200–1, 206, 212, 228, 230–1
iron plate manufacture 38, 55

iron shipbuilding 219–22
iron to steel transition 53–4, 80
Isherwood, Sir Joseph (ship designer)
121, 123
Isherwood system 121

joint stock companies 217

Kansarmax bulk carriers 210
King, William (engine builders) 110
Kirk, A.C. (engineer) 51
Koster-ship 182

Lancefield Engine Works, Glasgow
137n10
Liberty colliers 202
Liberty replacements 154–6, 160, 172,
174, 178
Liberty type 3–4, 21–2, 125, 143–4,
172, 220, 258–60
liner shipping, definition 1–2
liner trades, number of ships 5–6
liquefied natural gas as fuel 233
liquid bulk cargoes 4
Lloyd's Register (register book) 45, 48,
73, 92, 98, 131, 147
Lloyd's Register of Shipping (classi-
fication society) 48n49, 57, 59,
112n2, 149, 174, 181, 194, 202, 210,
212
London gas companies hiring screw
colliers
Commercial Gas Light and Coke
Company 23, 32
East Greenwich Gas Works 32
Equitable Gas Light Company 30,
32
Gas Light and Coke Company
21–9, 32
Imperial Gas Light Company 22–3,
28–9
Independent Gas Light Company
23
London Gas Light and Coke
Company 23, 30, 32
Phoenix Gaslight and Coal
Company 32
South Metropolitan Gas Light and
Coke Company 31, 32, 190
Wandsworth and District Gas
Company 190
longitudinal framing 121
low air draft 192

Malaccamax bulk carriers 21
marine engineering profession 223
marine insurance 218
masts 115, 170–2, 194, 200, 207, 210,
218, 240
McDougall, Alexander (whaleback
designer) 117
McIntyre, John (ballast tank designer)
16
McIntyre tanks 15, 16, 97
mechanical hatch covers 192–3, 198
Meldahl, K.G. (ship designer) 131
Merchant Shipping Act (1854) 43
Miers, Thomas (Commercial Gas
Company) 66
monitor type 121
motor vs steam tramps 145
Munckloaders 216

navigating equipment 196
New Koster type 182
Newcastlemax bulk carriers 211
Newry Ship Canal 94, 101n28
newsprint carriers 153
North Eastern Marine Engineering Co.
Ltd. 125, 127
North Sands type 125
nuclear power 233–4

OBOs (ore/bulk/oil vessels) 213–15
Ocean type (Second World War) 125
oil engine makers 156, 163–4, 195–6
Allen, Sons and Co. Ltd. W.H. 176
Atlas-Diesel M.V. 173–9
Beardmore and Co. Ltd., William
142–3, 165, 167–8

Bolinder, J.C. and G. 142, 163,
     165–9, 180
British Auxiliaries Ltd. 175–8, 180
British Polar Engines Ltd. 179
Brons Motorenfabriek 171
Burmeister and Wain 137, 142,
     143n22, 149, 157, 159, 173,
     206, 211
Cantieri Navale Tosi 141
Clyde Shipbuilding and
     Engineering Co. Ltd. 140
Crossley Brothers Ltd. 174
Diesel Motorer, A.B. 137
Doxford and Sons Ltd., William
     141, 149, 157, 206, 237
Fiat 138, 141, 157, 159
Gardner and Son, L. 176
Gotaverken, Akt 142
Harland and Wolff Ltd. (B&W)
     137n12, 143, 149, 157, 159, 178
Humboldt-Deutzmotoren 171,
     175–9, 182
Kincaid and Co. J.G. (B&W) 149,
     175, 177, 178
Klöckner-Humboldt-Deutz 180
Kromhout Motorenfabriek 163, 165,
     167, 171
Lysekil A.B. 168
Maschinenfabrik Augsburg-
     Nürnberg (MAN) 149, 156–7,
     159, 206, 211
McIntosh and Seymour 142
Mirrlees, Bickerton and Day Ltd.
     137, 140, 177
Mitsubishi H.I. Ltd. 208
National Gas and Oil Engine Co.
     Ltd. 189
Neptune (Swan, Hunter) 137
Newbury Diesel Co. Ltd. 175–9
Nydqvist and Holm A.B. 177
Petters Ltd. 176, 180
Plenty and Sons 169, 171
Plenty-Still Co. Ltd. 175
Polar, Atlas A.B. 137–8, 140–1
Richardson, Westgarth and Co.
     Ltd. 140

Ruston and Hornsby Ltd. 177, 179
Stork Werspoor B.V. 171
Sulzer Brothers 136, 140, 149, 157,
     206
Swan, Hunter and Wigham
     Richardson Ltd. 141
Tuxham A.S. 165, 167
Vickers-Peters 168–9
Wallsend Slipway Co. Ltd. 141
Wärtsilä O/Y 211
Werkspoor N.V. 132
Wichmann Motorfabrikk 180
oil firing of boilers 127
oil vs steam engines 135, 162
open-hatch bulk carriers 216
open-hearth furnace 46
opposed piston engines 123, 150, 157,
     159
ore carriers 154, 200–3, 213
ore/bulk/oil carriers 213–15

paddle propulsion 12
Palmer, Charles (coal owner and
     shipbuilder) 15n21, 16, 19, 21, 30,
     34, 57, 66
Panama Canal 210
paragraph ships 194
Parson's exhaust turbine 129
plating 38
Plimsoll, Samuel (load line advocate) 21
port adaptations for steam ships 223–5
Post-Panamax 210
prefabricated ships 123, 126, 185, 187
Primasa-121 type 156
Prinsep, William (London Gas
     Company) 66
professionalisation of engineering 39

quarterdeck, raised 75, 79–80, 94–100,
     110, 172, 182, 187–9, 194, 203

rail delivery of coal to London 19–21
Rankine, Professor MacQuorn (thermo-
     dynamics principles) 38, 57
Regents Canal Dock 29
reheater engine 127, 133, 237

reverse sheer 122
rigging 92, 96
riveting 38, 56, 129

sailing vessels xv, xvi, 12–14, 16, 19,
    24, 26–7, 29, 32–3, 37, 57, 59,
    69–71, 107, 111, 127n35, 163, 171,
    173, 180–1, 217–19, 223–4, 230
Samuel, Marcus (Shell Oil) 138, 156
Santa Fe type 156
Scheepshypotheekbanken (Dutch
    mortgage provider) 183
Schilling rudder 196
Schneider, Henry W. (iron master)14
Scrap and Build scheme 150
screw collier xv, xvi, 8–8, 11–35, 37, 39,
    42, 45–9, 51, 59–61, 66–5, 69–70,
    73–3, 80–5, 87–91, 95, 100, 102,
    10–17, 109–10, 124, 133, 161, 164,
    170–1, 180, 186, 190–1, 217–18,
    235–8
SD14 type 154–5
sea-coal to London 16
seafarers and steam 222
sea-river ships 192–3
Seawaymax bulk carriers 211
self-trimmer 118
self-unloaders 216
shade deck 78–9
shelter-decker 78–9, 113–16, 125,
    129n41, 131, 134, 143, 147–8, 150,
    154, 182, 185, 194
shipbuilders
    Abdela and Mitchell Ltd.,
        Queensferry 167–9
    Ailsa Shipbuilding Co. Ltd., Ayr
        and Troon 133, 173, 176
    Ansaldo San Giorgio, Spezia 141
    Ardrossan Dockyard Ltd. 167,
        174–9
    Armstrong, Whitworth and Co.
        Ltd., Newcastle 141
    Astilleros Españoles S.A., Bilbao
        156
    Austin, S.P. and Son Ltd.,
        Sunderland 81, 100, 176

Austin and Pickersgill, Sunderland
    154–5
Bainbridge, Willington
    Quay-on-Tyne 102
Barclay, Curle and Co. Ltd.,
    Glasgow 102, 137
Bartram and Sons Ltd., Sunderland
    151
Beardmore and Co. Ltd., William,
    Dalmuir and Govan 167
Bethlehem Steel Company,
    Maryland 200–2
Blumer, John, Sunderland 82
Blythswood Shipbuilding Co. Ltd.,
    Glasgow 143
Bodewes Shipyard B.V., Hoogezand
    197
Bowdler, Chaffer and Co.,
    Seacombe 83, 102, 106
Brown and Co. Ltd., George,
    Greenock 172, 175–9, 188
Burgerhout, Rotterdam 142
Burmeister and Wain, Copenhagen
    137, 147, 151, 153
Burntisland Shipbuilding Co. Ltd.
    123–4, 176–8
Caledon Shipbuilding and
    Engineering Co. Ltd., Dundee
    150, 174, 176–9
Cammell, Laird and Co.
    (Shipbuilders and Engineers)
    Ltd., Birkenhead 168
Candlish, Fox and Co.,
    Middlesbrough 192
Cantieri Navali Riuniti, Ancona
    140
Cantieri Navali Tosi, Taranto 141
Chalmers and Co. Ltd., William,
    Rutherglen 165, 167–8
Clayton, J., Liverpool 18, 102
Clyde Shipping and Engineering
    Co. Ltd., Port Glasgow 137,
    139
Cochrane and Sons Ltd., Selby
    192
Coutts, John, Walker-on-Tyne 102

Craggs and Sons Ltd., Robert,
    Middlesbrough and Stockton
    81–2
Cramm, George, Chester 18, 102
Cran, Leith 165, 167
Crichton and Co. Ltd., Connah's
    Quay 168–9
De Gideon, Scheepsbouwerf,
    Groningen 172
Denny, Alexander, Dumbarton 102
Denny and Brothers Ltd., William
    17, 51, 54, 89, 102
Denton, Gray, West Hartlepool 81
Doxford and Sons Ltd., William,
    Sunderland 81, 141, 150–1
Duncan and Co., Robert, Port
    Glasgow 82
Eltringham and Co. Ltd., J.T.,
    South Shields 81
Euskalduna, Bilboa 142
Federal, Kearney, New Jersey 142
Fellows and Co. Ltd., Yarmouth
    169, 172–3, 175–6
Fullerton and Co., John, Paisley 96,
    106, 110
Gill, Sunderland 102
Goole Shipbuilding and Repairing
    Co. Ltd. 172, 175–9
Gotaverken, Akt, Gothenburg 142,
    153, 213–14
Gray and Co. Ltd., William, West
    Hartlepool 131
Hanna, Donald and Wilson, Paisley
    106
Hansen Shipbuilding and Repairing
    Co. Ltd., Bideford 106n33
Harland and Wolff Ltd., Belfast
    137n10, 143, 178
Harvey and Co., Hayle 89, 102,
    106
Haswell, Sunderland 102
Hawthorn, Leslie (Ship Builders)
    Ltd., R. and W., Newcastle
    152, 176, 178, 202
Hay, J., and J., Kirkintilloch 108–9
Henderson, Renfrew 192

Hepple and Co. Ltd., South Shields
    167, 169
Hill and Sons Ltd., Charles, Bristol
    142, 177, 179
Hoby, J.W. and Co, Renfrew 102
Hodgson and Gardner, Sunderland
    81
Hyundai H.I. Co. Ltd., Ulsan
    206
Inglis Ltd., A. and J., Glasgow 174,
    178
Irvine, Robert and Co., West
    Hartlepool 102
Ishikawajima-Harima Heavy
    Industries, Japan 154–5
Jeffrey and Co. Ltd., A. Alloa 165,
    167–8
Kockums, Malmo 204
Koster Hzn Scheepsbouwerf de
    Gideon, J., Groningen 181–2
Kure Naval Yard, Japan 203, 213
Laing and Co. Ltd., Sir James,
    Sunderland 17–19, 81–2, 91,
    102, 105
Livingstone and Cooper Ltd.,
    Hessle 168
London and Glasgow Engineering
    and Iron Shipbuilding Co. Ltd.
    103
Lübecker Flenderwerke, Lübeck
    148
Lungley, Charles, London 17, 103
Lytham Shipbuilding and Engineer
    Co. Ltd. 94, 169
Mare and Co., C.J., Blackwall 17
Marshall, Thomas D., South
    Shields 103
Maudslay, Son and Field, East
    Greenwich 103
McGregor and Sons, Peter,
    Kirkintilloch 108, 165, 167
McIntyre and Co., H., Paisley 106
McNab and Co., Greenock 103
Migliardi, Filli, Savona 141
Millwall Iron Works, Thames 193
Mitchell and Co., Charles, Low

Walker 17–19, 81–2, 89, 193, 200
Odense Staalsskips, Odense 142
Osbourne, Graham, Sunderland 121
Oswald, T.R. and Co., Sunderland 81, 193
Palmer Brothers and Co., Newcastle 14, 16–19, 27, 81–2, 84, 89, 103
Pearse and Co., M. Stockton 89
Pile, John, West Hartlepool 104
Pile, Spence and Co. Ltd., West Hartlepool 19, 81, 194
Pile, W., Sunderland 104
Pollock and Co. Ltd., James, Faversham 168–70, 176, 179
Price, J.T., Neath Abbey 89, 104
Price and Company 31
Priestman, John and Co., Sunderland 120
Ray, J., Sunderland 104
Raylton, Dixon and Co. Ltd., Middlesbrough 138, 140
Readhead and Sons Ltd., John, South Shields 204–5
Reid and Co. Ltd., John, Greenock 104
Rennie Forrest Shipbuilding Co. Ltd., Wivenhoe 168
Richardson, Newcastle 82, 103
Richardson Brothers, Hartlepool 104
Richardson, Duck, and Co. Ltd., Stockton 18, 82, 104–5
Robb Ltd., Henry, Leith 174–9
Ropner Shipbuilding and Engineering Co. Ltd., Stockton 120
Samsung H.I. Co. Ltd., Geoje 206
Samuda Brothers, Poplar 18, 104
Samuelsson, and Co. M., Hull 105
Schlesinger, Davies and Co., Wallsend 81–2, 105
Scott, J.E., Greenock 18
Scott and Sons (Bowling) Ltd. 94, 180

Scott Russell, John, Millwall 17, 24, 25, 34, 39, 42, 57
Seath and Co., T.B., Rutherglen 105
Short Brothers Ltd., Sunderland 82
Simons and Co., William, Renfrew 18, 105
Smith, T. and W., North Shields 81–2, 105
Smith's Dock Co. Ltd., Middlesbrough 140–1, 176–8
Sodra Varv A/B, Stockholm 141
Stephen, A.M., Glasgow 220
Stothert and Co., J.K., Bristol 89, 105
Strand Slipway, Sunderland 81
Sturge, Swansea 89, 105
Swan, Hunter and Wigham Richardson Ltd., Newcastle 82, 122, 136–7, 140–1
Swan, Maryhill and Dumbarton 105, 108
Thompson and Sons Ltd., Joseph L., Sunderland 82, 125
Thompson and Sons Ltd., Robert, Sunderland 81
Toward and Co., T., Newcastle 89
Tyne Iron Shipbuilding Co., Willington Quay 82
Union Shipbuilding Co., Kelvinhaugh 105
Upper Clyde Shipbuilders Ltd., Glasgow 213
Vernon, Thomas and Co., Liverpool 17, 89, 105, 106
Walpole, Webb and Co., Dublin 105
Watson, J., Sunderland 81
Werf De Noord, Alblasserdam 181
White and Co. Ltd., J. Samuel, Cowes 169
Williamson and Son Ltd., Richard, Workington 179
Wills and Packham, Sittingbourne 168–9
Wingate and Co., Thomas, Glasgow 6, 105

Withy, Alexander and Co., West
    Hartlepool 81, 91–2
Wood and Reid, Clyde 89
Wood, Skinner and Co. Ltd., Bill
    Quay 81, 99n27
Yarwood and Co. Ltd., W.J.,
    Northwich 168
shipbuilding labour 55, 220–1
shipbuilding materials handling 54–5
shipbuilding mechanisation 56
shipbuilding productivity 57–8
shipowners
    Ald Shipping Co. Ltd. 177, 179
    Allsup and Sons Ltd., Samuel 168
    Anchor Line 152
    Atkinson and Prickett Ltd. 179
    Australind Steam Shipping Co.
        Ltd. 155
    Bank Line 7, 143, 147
    Bevis, Frank 164, 167
    Blue Funnel Line 43
    Bocimar International B.V. 211
    Booker Brothers and Co. 179
    British India S.N. Co. Ltd. 6
    British Iron and Steel Corporation
        203–4
    Brocklebank, T. and J. 168
    Burns and Laird Lines Ltd. 178
    Burrell, Henry 120
    Cast Shipping Ltd. 215
    Cayzer, Irvine and Co. Ltd. 119
    Central Electricity Authority 161n3
    Central Electricity Generating
        Board 191n74
    Chambers and Co., James 129
    Chellew, R.B., 119n41
    Christopherson, H.W. 168
    Clan Line Steamers Ltd. 7, 119
    Coast Lines Ltd. 175–8
    Coasting Motor Shipping Co. Ltd.
        164–8, 173
    Commercial Steamship Co. Ltd. 70
    Compagnie des Chemins de
        Fer de Paris à Lyon et à la
        Méditerranée 202
    Cory, John 6
    Cory, Lohden 70
    Cory and Co. Ltd., William 27, 30,
        34, 66, 100, 190, 200
    Danish East Asiatic Company 137,
        147
    Darwen and Mostyn Iron Co. Ltd.
        179
    Dickinson, William 70
    Dixon and Harris 70
    Duke, James 26, 29
    Dunbar, Duncan 31
    Dundee, Perth and London
        Shipping Co. Ltd. 176–7, 179
    Elliot Lowrey and Dunford 70
    Empresa Lineas Maritimos
        Argentinas 156
    Evans, John Frederick 23
    Evans and Co. Ltd., T.E. 176–7, 179
    Everard and Sons Ltd., F.T. 171,
        173, 175–9, 189, 192
    Fenwick, John 68
    Fenwick and Reay 70
    Fenwick and Stobart 70
    Fisher, Newry 179
    Flower Motor Ship Co. Ltd. 138
    Ford and Jackson 22, 24, 25
    France, Fenwick and Co. Ltd. 177,
        190, 204–5
    Furness, Withy 202
    Gardner, J. and A. 174, 176–8
    Gas Light and Coke Company 99
    General Iron Screw Collier Co.
        Ltd. 16, 21–4, 28, 30, 31, 37,
        65, 69, 83, 217, 235
    General Steam Navigation
        Company 6, 12, 176, 178, 182
    Gillie and Blair 169
    Glenlight Shipping Co. Ltd. 108n35
    Gooch, J.V. 25n62
    Gordon and Co. 6, 70
    Gossage, W. 168
    Gourlay, E.T. 70
    Gourley, Edward 71
    Great Yarmouth Shipping Co. Ltd.
        175, 177
    Hain Steamship Co. Ltd. 7

HAPAG 7
Harris and Dixon Ltd. 24, 25
Harrison Ltd., J. and C. 70
Harrison (Shipping) Ltd., H. 176,
    178
Hay family, Kirkintilloch 109–10
Headlam and Sons 113
Hill, J.L. 68
Hogarth and Sons, H. 112n3
Holt, Alfred 25, 43
Horlock, F.W. 176–7
Hudson Steamship Co. Ltd. 203
Hull Gates Shipping Co. Ltd. 178–9
Hunt, R.H. 176
Isherwood Arcform Ships Ltd. 124
Jackson, Ralph 16
Jenkins, S.J. 176
Johnson, Axel 200
Joicey, James 27
Jonassohn and Elliott 28
Kindiesel Shipping Co. Ltd. 173, 77
King Line Ltd. 7
Kish, T. 71
Laing, James 71
Lambert Brothers Ltd. 68, 70, 72
Lamport and Holt Line Ltd. 6
Lawes and Surtees 70
London and Rochester Trading Co.
    Ltd. 177
London Steam Navigation Co Ltd.
    67–8, 83, 235
London Steam Shipping Co. Ltd.
    68–9
London Steam Steamship Co. Ltd.
    69
London, Brighton and South Coast
    Railway Company 14
Ludwig, Daniel 203
MacCallum and Sons Ltd. 173
Mann, Macneal and Co. 166–7
Mercantile Steamship Co. Ltd. 70
Mersey Docks and Harbour Board
    225
Metcalf, T.J. 176, 178
Metcalf Motor Coasters Ltd. 170,
    172

Monroe Brothers 101n29
Morel Brothers 6
Mories, Munro and Nicol 31
Morrison, John and Son 70
Mostyn Coal and Iron Co. 169
Muller, William H. 200
Newcastle Coal and Shipping Co.
    Ltd. 176
Norddeutscher Lloyd 7
Nordstjernan Rederi A.B. 200
Ocean Steamship Co. Ltd. 6, 25, 43
Oppenheimer 168
Pan-Ore Steamship Company 203
Paton, J.M. and Hendry, P.D. 164
Peninsular and Oriental Steam
    Navigation Co. (P&O) 6, 7
Petersen, Tate and Co. 118
Phillips, John Orwell 23
Pollock and Co. Ltd., James 168,
    170
Prior, Alfred 30
Pyman Brothers Ltd. 6, 70
R. and J.H. Rea 101n29
Rees, Perry and Harris 168
Ridley, Son and Tulley. Jno., 71
Road Maintenance and Supply Co.
    Ltd. 169
Robertson, William 96, 107–8, 110,
    173, 176, 178–9
Ropner and Co Ltd., Sir Robert 34,
    112n3, 120
Ross and Marshall Ltd., Greenock
    109
Runciman Shipping Co. Ltd.,
    Walter 71, 151–2
Skaarup, Ole 205
Smith and Sons Ltd., Sir William
    Reardon 7, 112n3, 218n3
Stephenson Clarke and Co. Ltd. 23,
    30, 31, 45, 161n3, 190
Stewart, John 179
Stobart, William 22, 28
Straightback Steamship Co. Ltd.
    120
Summers and Sons, John 167–70
Sutherland and Co. Ltd., B.J. 150

Tate and Lyle Ltd. 203
Trafik A.B. Grängesberg-
    Oxelösund 139, 213–14
Transatlantic, Rederi A.B. 139
Truman, Hanbury and Buxton 168
Tyne-Tees Steam Shipping Co. Ltd.
    176, 178
Vale S.A. 310
Vernon, John H. 168–9
Watson Shipping Ltd., Thomas 176,
    179
Watts, Milburn and Co. 70
Watts, Ward and Co. 70
Watts, Watts and Co. Ltd. 70, 151
Westoll Ltd., James 71
Wharton, J. 178–9
Williams, Idwal 218n1
Williams, Owen 145
Williamson Ltd., David 173, 175
Wilson, H. 178
Young, Ehlers and Co. 70
Zillah Shipping and Carrying Co.
    Ltd. 94
Shipping Controller 112n2
slate ports 229n6
solid injection 158
spar decks 78–9, 113
St Lawrence Seaway 131, 200, 211
steam collier *see* screw collier
steam engine 11–12, 33, 133, 137–8,
    146, 151, 173, 253–5
    beam 47
    compound 50, 74–5, 93, 131, 137
    efficiency 40, 52–3, 56, 58, 68, 112,
        133, 136, 145, 235, 254
    geared 47
    horizontal 47
    inverted 47–8
    oscillating 47–8
    quadruple expansion 46, 51
    reheat 237
    side-lever 31
    triple expansion 46, 51, 78, 94,
        111–12, 131, 143, 169
steam pressures 11, 57–64, 67–9, 71,

    78, 92, 94, 96, 129–30, 132, 144–6,
        150, 175–8, 181–2, 209, 236, 247
steam ships, proportion of British fleet
    12
steam to motor coaster conversions 180
steam tramp vs motor tramp 145
steam vs motor tramps 145
steam vs oil engines 135, 162
steam vs sail tonnage (1870–90) 111
steamship manager as a profession 218
steel hatch covers 124, 201–4
straightback steamers 120
Straker (coal factor) 68
Suez Canal 85, 210
Suezmax bulk carriers 210
supercharging 158
superheating of steam 51–2, 124
Supramax bulk carriers 210
surveying of ships 219

tanker to bulk carrier conversions 205
tankers 163
Temperley Transporters 201
Thompson Economy design 125
three-island hull 79, 116
timber cargoes 16, 22, 30, 34, 83, 98,
    105, 119, 149, 153, 171, 195, 200,
    213, 216–17, 220, 234, 256
tonnage, deadweight xvii
tonnage, gross xvii, 73n20
tonnage, net xvii, 73n20
tonnage minimisation 194
tonnage openings 79, 113, 195
topside tanks 201–2, 212, 219–20, 230
tower deck ships 120
tramp trades, numbers of ship in 5–6
trunk 200
trunk deck ships 116, 120
turbocharging 158, 195
turret deck ships 116, 118–19, 121,
    200
twin screws 13
two- vs four-stroke oil engines 157–8
two-cylinder compound engines 131
two-stroke oil engines 206, 211, 216

Ultramax bulk carriers 210, 216
unmanned engine rooms 196
up-river colliers 162–3, 190, 194n87
US coal trade 201–2

Valemax bulk carriers 210, 231
VICs (Clyde puffers) 185

War Office 25, 29, 235
water ballast xvi-xvii, 2, 3, 13–16, 29,
    31, 48n48, 63, 73, 75, 78, 83n27, 84,
    86, 92, 93, 95–6, 98, 100, 109–12,
    116, 130n43, 131, 138–9, 145, 148,
    164, 172–3, 192, 195, 199–202, 212,
    214, 228, 233, 235–7

Waymouth, Bernard (surveyor) 57
welding 56, 126
Weser type 156
whaleback steamer 117
wing tanks 116, 134, 166, 202, 204, 212,
    222
wood chip carriers 215

X-lighters 166, 171

Ship Index

Aaron Manby (1822) 11
Abelia (1915) 138, 141
Aberdeen (1881) 51
Ability (1928) 169, 171–2
Ability (1943) 173
Acclivity (1931) 175
Accruity (1935) 176
Acrity (1934) 172, 175
Activity (1931) 175
Actuality (1933) 175
Actuosity (1933) 175
Ada (1880) 91
Adaptity (1935) 176
Adelfotis (1908) 119
Admiral Cator (1858) 70
Admiral Kanaris (1858) 70
Admiral Vernon (1921) 169
Adria (1864) 68
Affaric (1934) 173, 175
Agamemnon (1865) 43
Agate (1878) 44, 91, 93
Agnes Jack (1865) 102
Alita (1921) 169
Allerton (1913) 95
Alma (1855) 89
Alnwick (1936) 178
Alouette (1938) 182
Amenity (1928) 169, 171–2
Amenity (1943) 173
Amerikaland (1925) 158, 160n62, 201
Amethyst (1870) 44
Amy (1870) 51n64
Andoni (1) (1935) 176
Andoni (1937) 179
Anglian Coast (1935) 176

Angularity (1934) 175
Angularity (1941) 187
Annie Vernon (1856) 89, 105–6
Anonity (1936) 177
Ansaldo San Giorgio I (1918) 138, 141
Ansaldo San Giorgio II (1918) 138, 141
Ansaldo San Giorgio III (1918) 138, 141
Antilope (1939) 183
Antiquity (1933) 175
Antrim Coast (1937) 178
Apricity (1933) 175
Aqueity (1934) 175
Arabis (1915) 138, 141
Arantza-Mendi (1923) 142
Arawai (1939) 179
Arbroath (1935) 176
Arbutus (1854) 89
Archimedes (1840) 47
Ardclinis (1870) 44
Ardito (1921) 139
Arduity (1935) 176
Aridity (1931) 175
Arran Firth (1921) 169
Arrino (1974) 155
Arrivaine (1934) 173, 175
Arthur Gordon (1854) 14
Arum (1914) 138, 141
Arundel (1956) 161n3, 190
Aseity (1935) 176
Ashanti (1936) 177
Ashfield (1914) 93–4, 197
Assiduity (1930) 172, 175
Assurity (1917) 171
Aston (1867) 105
Atlantic Coast (1934) 175

August Belmont (1902) 201
Augusta (1849) 14, 89, 105
Aurora (1863) 68
Aurora (1932) 153

Balsa (1947) 161n2, 180n39
Basingstoke (1865) 102
Bass Rock (1892) 95
Beal (1936) 178
Beauly Firth (1949) 188–9
Bebside (1864) 104
Beckton (1869) 104
Bedlington (1842) 13, 17, 103
Beechdene (1890) 127
Begerin (1937) 178
Belmont (1865) 102
Ben Earn (1909) 120
Ben Truman (1921) 168
Benguela (1936) 177
Benmore (1874) 70
Berge Istra (1972) 214n32
Berge Vanga (1973) 214n32
Berrington (1865) 44, 104
Berwick (1855) 17, 105
Berwindmoor (1910) 201
Berwindvale (1911) 201–2
Bessegen (1963) 216
Bessie (1865) 102
Bethore (1922) 201
Biddick (1864) 44, 102
Black Boy (1854) 17, 103
Black Diamond (1855) 17, 22–3, 26, 29, 64, 70
Black Duck (1863) 105
Black Prince (1854) 17, 64, 67, 97, 105
Black Sea (1855) 17, 104
Black Swan (1864) 65, 105
Blonde (1863) 67, 103
Blue Cross (1869) 44, 105
Boston (1866) 104
Boston Trader (1936) 177
Bradley (1867) 105
Brandon (1854) 50, 85
Brendonia (1937) 178
Bride (1864) 102
Brier Rose (1892) 95

Britannia (1926) 128
British Coast (1934) 175
British Empire (1902) 95
Briton (1854) 17, 104
Briton Ferry (1852) 89
Brockley Combe (1938) 179
Broomhill (1878) 99
Brunette (1861) 67, 104
Burham (1865) 98

C.S. Butler (1865) 23, 104
Cabenda (1936) 177
Calatum (1908) 91
Calgary (1912) 137, 140
Cambridgeshire (1865) 102
Camellia (1953) 204
Cameo (1937) 178
Camroux I (1934) 176, 187
Camroux II (1935) 176
Camroux III (1935) 176
Captain McClure (1876) 44
Carbon (1855) 17, 22, 25, 64, 102
Carita (1913) 167, 170
Carmenita (1921) 169
Caroline (1853) 17, 21–2, 24–6, 29–31n81, 33, 42–3, 48, 64, 97, 105
Carrick Coast (1934) 175
Cassiopeia (1956) 204–5
Castle Combe (1936) 177
Catford (1948) 190
Century (1956) 197
Chagford (1937) 178
Chanticleer (1853) 17, 64, 10
Charles M (1935) 176
Charles W. Wetmore (1891) 117–18
Charlotte Dundas (1801) 40
Chastine Maersk (1923) 142
Cheshire (1904) 95
Chester (1855) 17, 64, 10
Clarissa Radcliffe (1904) 120n10
Clearpool (1935) 116n3, 128
Cleator (1854) 25n63, 43
Cliff Quay (1950) 191n73
CMB Virginie (2011) 211
Cochrane (1854) 17, 103
Collier (1849) 14, 89, 104

Collin (1915) 91
Comet (1812) 11
Conida (1936) 177
Conservator (1865) 104
Conside (1847) 14, 17, 103
Contest (1857) 17, 105
Contest (1880) 44
Corbrae (1948) 190
Cordene (1924) 99n25
Cornish Coast (1937) 178
Countess of Durham (1855) 17, 104
Countess of Strathmore (1853) 17, 67, 103
Coxwold (1938) 179
Crescence (1936) 177
Cristo (1916) 168
Cromwell (1865) 67, 103
Cubore (1917) 200
Cuirassier (1860) 104–5

Dane (1855) 17, 103
Daniel M (1936) 178
Deptford (1860) 102
Derbyshire (1976) 214n32
Derwent (1855) 17, 67, 102
Derwent (1866) 103
Despatch (1864) 27, 104
Deva (1857) 89
Devon Coast (1936) 177–8
Devonshire (1894) 95
Dieppe (1854) 42
Dordrecht (1922) 142
Dorington Court (1939) 3n7, 125
Doris Thomas (1920) 93
Dorita (1921) 169
Dorset (1866) 100
Dorset Coast (1936) 178
Drake (1938) 182
Dromedary (1869) 67, 105
Dublin (1866) 105
Dudley (1865) 105
Dudley (1885) 71
Dumbarton Youth (1847) 89, 102
Durham (1853) 17, 30, 67, 103

Eagle (1853) 17, 25, 42–3, 48, 97, 105
Earl of Durham (1854) 17, 103
Earl of Elgin (1861) 102
Earsdon (1855) 17, 25, 64, 104
Eastwood (1870) 97
Eavestone (1912) 138, 140, 157
Ebony (1947) 161n2, 180
Edenor (1911) 121
Edith (1861) 103
Edith (1900) 91, 94
Eglinton (1877) 44
Eilian (1918) 163
El Ray James II (1954) 42
Elagh Castle (1879) 44
Eldorita (1921) 169
Ellen M (1830) 172
Ellen Sinclair (1863) 23, 27
Elmdene (1939) 131
Embassage (1935) 125
Emerald (1879) 44
Empire Bay (1940) 186
Empire Bridge (1941) 186
Empire Canning (1944) 151
Empire Cliff (1940) 185–6
Empire Creek (1941) 186
Empire Dyke (1942) 186
Empire Fairplay (1944) 188
Empire Favour (1945) 151
Empire Foreland (1941) 185
Empire Gat (1941) 186
Empire Highlander (1945) 186
Empire Kyle (1941) 186
Empire Rider (1943) 186
Empire Sloane (1946) 186
Empire Wave (1941) 125
Enfield (1897) 120
Erasmus Wilson (1876) 44
Eucadia (1961) 152
Eupatoria (1856) 17, 67, 103
Europa (1862) 68–9
Experiment (1788) 11
Experiment (1845) 14–15, 17, 104
Express (1847) 89

Fairfax (1865) 67, 103
Falcon (1853) 17, 25n62, 48, 97, 105
Falcon (1861) 105
Fanny Lambert (1863) 104
Fatfield (1865) 103
Fauvette (1935) 176
Felita (1914) 170
Fenella (1870) 44
Fenham (1868) 65, 98–9
Fer (1921) 169
Fernmoor (1934) 151
Fife Coast (1932) 175
Finchale (1869) 103
Firefly (1854) 17, 67, 97, 105
Fleswick (1899) 95
Fleurita (1913) 168
Florence Nightingale (1856) 17, 42, 104
Fordonian (1912) 137n9, 140
Frankland (1869) 103
Fulgens (1912) 99
Fullagar (1920) 168

Galgorm Castle (1879) 44–5
Gazelle (1869) 70
General Codrington (1855) 17, 104
General Codrington (1868) 103
General Havelock (1861) 102
Generton (1935) 116n4
George Elliot (1863) 102
George Hawkins (1855) 17, 104
Georgita (1920) 168
Gideona (1924) 181
Gladonia (1939) 179
Glamis (1936) 177
Gleddoch (1953) 203
Glen (1935) 176
Goosebridge (1879) 80
Gosforth (1856) 70
Gracie (1879) 44–5
Grangesberg (1903) 118
Great Britain (1843) 43, 47
Great Eastern (1854) 29, 42, 47
Great Northern (1854) 17, 26, 102
Great Western (1838) 41

Grit (1934) 175

H.P. Stephenson (1872) 67, 70
Haggerston (1852) 17, 23, 48, 85, 97,
    105–6
Hamen (1949) 180
Hampshire (1866) 103
Harparees (1921) 168
Harraton (1867) 102
Hartlepool (1865) 102
Hastings (1864) 70, 105
Haswell (1861) 102
Havelet (1965) 188n63
Hawk (1854) 17, 21–2, 25–6, 48, 97, 105
Hawthorns (1861) 104
Hayle (1867) 102
Hazelfield (1948) 174
Heather Pet (1921) 169
Helmsman (1903) 93
Henry Morton (1860) 97, 104
Hercules (1857) 17
Hermiston (1939) 116n4
Hetton (1854) 17, 103
Holstentor (1989) 198
Houghton (1866) 103
Hove (1913) 174
Hudson Deep (1952) 203
Hudson Sound (1950) 203
Hugh Taylor (1869) 98–9
Hullgate (1937) 178
Hunwick (1852) 16–17, 105
Hurstwood (1906) 100
Hutton Chaytor (1855) 17, 66–7, 104

Ibis (1860) 104
Icemaid (1936) 186n8
Iduna (1868) 70
Imperial (1854) 17, 23, 29, 97, 105
Inchbrayock (1909) 93
Indorita (1921) 169
Innisagra (1912) 165, 167
Innisbeg (1912) 165, 167
Inniscroone (1912) 165, 167
Innisdhu (1912) 165, 167

Inniseanne (1913) 165, 167
Innisfree (1913) 165–7
Innisglora (1913) 165, 167
Innishowen (1913) 165, 167
Innisinver (1913) 165, 167
Innisjura (1913) 165, 167
Inniskea (1912) 165, 167
Innislargie (1913) 165, 167
Innismurray (1912) 165, 167
Innisnee (1912) 165, 67
Innisshannon (1913) 165–7
Innistrahull (1913) 165, 167
Innisulva (1914) 165, 168
Innisvera (1914) 165, 168
Iron Age (1854) 14, 89, 100
Isabella Croll (1854) 89
Isleford (1913) 166, 180
Italia (1860) 68

J.E. McConnell (1867) 67, 104
J.M. Strachan (1865) 104
J.R. Hinde (1864) 96–8
Jacinth (1937) 179
James Dixon (1859) 17, 104
James Joicey (1863) 23, 26–7, 33, 104
James Kennedy (1857) 89, 105
James Rowan (1955) 133, 161n3, 191n74
James Southern (1865) 105
James Southern (1887) 70
James Tennant (1893) 91
Jane Bacon (1865) 102
Jarrow (1853) 30, 64, 67, 103
Jessie Brown (1861) 102
John (1849) 89, 104
John Bowes (1852) 14–16, 17, 30, 34, 48,
    51, 60, 66, 75n22, 81, 85, 92, 97,
    103, 106, 235–6
John Fenwick (1861) 104
John Johnasson (1863) 103
John Liddell (1863) 103
John Mcintyre (1863) 104
John R. Hinde (1864) 104
Jolly Days (1935) 176, 180
Jolly Girls (1936) 177
Jolly Nights (1935) 176, 180

Jonita (1921) 169
Joseph Rickett (1879) 99
Joseph Straker (1863) 65
Justitia (1862) 68
Jutlandia (1912) 137

Karri (1938) 179
Kattegat (1936) 153
Kelloe (1866) 102
Kenley (1879) 70
Kent (1881) 98–9
Kestor (1936) 177
Kielder Castle (1868) 70
Killingworth (1855) 17, 103
Kindiesel (1936) 173–4, 177
King James (1925) 121
Kingswood (1931) 128
Kirkless (1865) 102

Lady Alice Hill (1866) 104–5
Lady Alice Kenlis (1867) 105
Lady Alice Lambton (1853) 17, 26, 41,
    97, 103
Lady Beatrix (1863) 102
Lady Berriedale (1853) 1–3, 17, 32, 41,
    48, 85, 96, 105
Lady Derby (1865) 67, 103
Lady Havelock (1861) 102
Lady Sheila (1935) 176
Lady Sophia (1938) 179
Lady Stella (1936) 176
Laffitte (1877) 44
Lairdsbank (1936) 178
Lairdscrest (1936) 178
Lairdswood (1936) 178
Lambton (1857) 17, 97–9, 103
Lancashire (1892) 93
Lancaster (1867) 102
Langdon (1882) 99
Langley (1868) 103
Laponia (1922) 139, 142
Lappland (1906) 200
Larry Bane (1875) 91
Latchford (1897) 93
Latona (1863) 68

Lee Lee (1917) 168, 171
Limatula (1950) 205n26
Linda (1873) 71
Lindisfarne (1870) 65
Linkmoor (1961) 152
Lise (1931) 150
Llandaff (1865) 75
Loanda (1936) 177
Lochee (1937) 179
Lockwood (1936) 177
Londonderry (1857) 17, 104
Lord Alfred Paget (1870) 97
Lord Citrine (1985) 191n76
Lord Hinton (1985) 191n76
Lowestoft Trader (1934) 175
Lowther Castle (1937) 129
Lucena (1913) 91
Ludworth (1866)
Lulea (1922) 139, 142
Lumley (1865) 102
Lutona (1917) 168
Lynn Trader (1944) 188
Lyon (1857) 17, 103
Lyria (1946) 205n26

M.E. Clark (1865) 104
Magna Carta (1865) 27
Malgomaj (1959) 213
Mallard (1936) 178
Marcita (1920) 168
Margam Abbey (1865) 104
Margretian (1923) 142–3
Marley Hill (1854) 17, 64, 67, 103
Marmora (1856) 17, 104
Mary Nixon (1865) 104
May Queen (1864) 67, 103
Medora (1864) 68
Medusa (1862) 102
Medway (1879) 70–1, 80, 98–9
Mercedes (1902) 201
Mersey (1891) 95
Mertainen (1959) 213
Merthyr (1866) 104
Minerva (1861) 68
Miranda (1865) 68–9

Miriam (1862) 104
Mitcham (1946) 190
Molliette (1919) 168, 170
Monitoria (1905) 121
Monksville (1947) 180
Morehampton (1873) 71
Morfa (1862) 104–5
Moss Rose (1890) 93
Mutsu (1972) 233
Mytongate (1938) 179

Natalian (1865) 102
Nerissa (1877) 44
Neva (1864) 70
New Pelton (1855) 17, 22, 26, 29, 105
New Pelton (1865) 97, 104
Newburn (1861) 102
Newton Colville (1864) 103
Nicholas Wood (1854) 17, 22, 28–9, 64,
    67, 103
Nile (1864) 70
Nonsuco (1938) 150
Norbrit Faith (1982) 193n86
Norbrit Hope (1983) 193n86
Nordnes (1932) 153n40
Norfolk Coast (1937) 179
Norman (1854) 17, 103
Normanby (1855) 17, 104
Norseman (1864) 105
Northman (1846) 47
Northumberland (1853) 17, 67, 103
Northumbria (1869) 97, 104

Ocean Coast (1935) 176
Ocland (1907) 120
Ogarita (1911) 164, 167, 170
Ogmore (1866) 10
Orangemoor (1911) 119
Ore Chief (1954) 203
Oriana (1867) 68
Ormsary (1953) 203
Orwell (1864) 104
Oscar II (1896) 200
Oscar Fredrik (1900) 200
Ottercap (1868) 102

Otto Hahn (1968) 233

Pacific Coast (1935) 176
Palmyra (1866) 68
Pathfinder (1950) 203
Pelaw (1869) 70
Pelton (1876) 70
Pembroke Coast (1936) 177
Penrose (1908) 119
Pioneer (1854) 17
PLM20 (1920) 202
PLM27 (1922) 202
Plover (1936) 178
Polcirkeln (1907) 200
Polita (1921) 169
Pompey Power (1949) 180
Portelet (1961) 188n63
Preston (1853) 89
Primrose (1885) 93
Primrose (1910) 95
Primula (1921) 141
Primus (1865) 102
Progress (1848) 31
Propontis (1874) 46, 51, 86
Prospector (1950) 203
Pyrope (1935) 173

Q.E.D. (1844) 13, 15n29, 17, 102
Queen's Channel (1894) 93

Racoon (2011) 211
Rajah (1853) 17, 103
Raunala (1945) 213
Rautas (1945) 213
Rechid (1855) 17, 104
Red Hand (1914) 168
Resolute (1857) 15n29, 17
Resolute (1869) 10
Rio Diamante (1928) 121
River Avoca (1948) 189
River Fisher (1941) 187
River Trent (1935) 176
Romagna (1910) 136, 140
Rondeggen (1963) 216
Rookwood (1936) 177, 190

Rookwood (1952) 204–5
Ross D. Mangles (1854) 17, 22, 28–9, 67, 103
Rouen (1857) 17, 97, 104
Roxana (1868) 68–9
Runswick (1930) 113
Rushwood (1953) 204
Ryhope (1869) 103

Sabrina (1865) 68
Sagacity (1936) 177
Sagamore (1893) 118n6
Saint Angus (1936) 174, 177
Saint Bedan (1937) 74, 178
Saint Kentigern (1937) 174
Saint Modan (1910) 91
Saint Ronaig (1937) 174
Salar (1989) 198
Salisbury (1866) 103
Samson (1860) 71, 102
Samson (1874) 70
Samuel Laing (1854) 16–17, 103
Sanguity (1956) 189
Sapphire (1881) 94, 96
Sapphire (1935) 173, 176
Sardinian (1855) 17, 64, 104
Savannah (1962) 232
Saxon (1854) 17, 104
Saxon (1879) 44
Scot Isles (2021) 197
Seaford (1947) 190
Seaton (1857) 17, 104
Sedulity (1936) 177
Selandia (1912) 137
Sentinel (1860) 104
Sequacity (1937) 173, 179
Serenity (1937) 178
Sevmorput (1988) 233
Sexta (1874) 46
Sherburn (1866) 99, 102
Shoreham (1872) 44
Signality (1937) 179
Silurian (1924) 142–3, 202
Silverburn (1952) 131
Sincerity (1936) 177

Sinclair Petrolore (1955) 213
Sir Charles Parsons (1985) 191n76
Sir James Duke (1861) 23, 104
Sir John Easthope (1853) 17, 64, 67, 103
Sir William (1914) 168, 170
Skagerak (1936) 153n
Sodality (1938) 179
Sodium (1887) 91
South Tyne (1871) 70
Southampton (1865) 102
Spinel (1937) 179
Spinway C (1899) 136n2
Spirality (1939) 179
St. George (1856) 103
Statira (1865) 68
Steelmotor (1923) 142
Steelore (1922) 201
Stevonia (1948) 189
Stolt Vista (1955) 214
Stoneboat (1921) 169
Strassa (1921) 139, 142
Stratum (1921) 168
Suavity (1937) 178
Summity (1939) 179
Sunderland (1866) 102
Sutherland Endeavour (1975) 155n49
Supremity (1939) 179
Sussexbrook (1970) 189n65
Sutherland (1935) 150
Svealand (1917) 138, 141
Svealand (1925) 158, 160n62, 201
Swastika (1915) 168
Sybil (1879) 80
Sylfaen (1883) 93

Tanfield (1865) 97, 104
Tempo (1945) 203
The Lady Mostyn (1938) 179
Thomas Lea (1864) 104
Thomas Powell (1856) 89, 10
Thornley (1866) 105
Toiler (1911) 136, 140
Tolfaen (1877) 44
Tom John Taylor (1861) 105
Trevethick (1866) 23, 97–9, 104

Trunkby (1896) 120
Tudor Queen (1941) 187
Tureby (1936) 153
Turret (1892) 118–19, 121
Tyne (1853) 17
Tyne (1856) 17
Tyne (1863) 65
Tynedale (1868) 103
Tynemount (1913) 137, 140, 160

Union (1854) 17, 103
Upton (1865) 51, 98
Uskbridge (1959) 133

Vanderbyl (1864) 105
Vedra (1855) 15n29, 17, 64, 102
Velinheli (1892) 91
Velocity (1857) 105
Venetia (1864) 68
Venoge (1904) 136n3
Violette (1919) 168, 170
Virginia Bolten (1958) 148n28
Viscount Lambton (1856) 17
Vistasvagge (1955) 214
Volunteer (1862 or 8) 71, 103
Vulcanus (1910) 136
Vulture (1856) 17, 25–6, 102

War Sword (1917) 123
Warita (1920) 168
Warkworth (1869) 99
Wear (1865) 103
Weardale (1867) 102
Wearmouth (1855) 17, 22–3, 29, 102
Welsh Coast (1938) 179
Wentworth (1865) 105
Weser Ore (1959) 204
Wheatfield (1909) 95
Whitley Park (1854) 17, 103
Wilita (1920) 168
Will o'th Wisp (1854) 89
William Cory (1857) 17, 75, 97, 103, 200n3
William Coulman (1866) 103
William France (1856) 17

William Hunter (1865) 104
William Hutt (1853) 17, 64, 67, 103
Windermere (1857) 89, 105
Wisbeach (1865) 104
Wooler (1936) 178

Yebala (1946) 205n26
Yewmount (1939) 179, 187
Yngaren (1921) 139, 141

Zeearend (1913) 181
Zeemeeuw (1911) 181